Wissenschaftliche Untersuchungen
zum Neuen Testament · 2. Reihe

Begründet von Joachim Jeremias und Otto Michel
Herausgegeben von
Martin Hengel und Otfried Hofius

46

Love without Pretense

Romans 12.9-21 and Hellenistic-Jewish
Wisdom Literature

by

Walter T. Wilson

J. C. B. Mohr (Paul Siebeck) Tübingen

Die Deutsche Bibliothek – CIP-Einheitsaufnahme

Wilson, Walter T.:
Love without pretense: Romans 12,9–21 and Hellenistic-Jewish wisdom literature /
by Walter T. Wilson.
– Tübingen: Mohr 1991
  (Wissenschaftliche Untersuchungen zum Neuen Testament: Reihe 2; 46)
  ISBN 3-16-145756-0
NE: Wissenschaftliche Untersuchungen zum Neuen Testament / 02

© 1991 by J. C. B. Mohr (Paul Siebeck), P.O. Box 2040, D-7400 Tübingen.

This book may not be reproduced, in whole or in part, in any form (beyound that permitted by copyright law) without the publisher's written permission. This applies particularly to reproductions, translations, microfilms and storage and processing in electronic systems.

The book was printed by Gulde-Druck in Tübingen on acid-free paper from Papierfabrik Niefern and bound by Heinr. Koch in Tübingen.

Printed in Germany.

ISSN 0340-9570

In Memory of
George Bernard Walsh
1946-1989

Associate Professor and Chairman
Department of Classical Languages and Literatures
University of Chicago
1971-1989

εὕδουσι δ' ὀρέων κορυφαί τε καὶ φάραγγες
πρώονές τε καὶ χαράδραι
φῦλά τ' ἑρπέτ' ὅσα τρέφει μέλαινα γαῖα
θῆρές τ' ὀρεσκῷοι καὶ γένος μελισσᾶν
καὶ κνώδαλ' ἐν βένθεσσι πορφυρέας ἁλός·
εὕδουσι δ' οἰωνῶν φῦλα τανυπτερύγων.

Now sleep both the mountain peaks and ravines,
the headlands and the valleys,
and all the creeping things that the black earth feeds,
the mountain-bred beasts and the family of bees,
and the monsters in the depths of the dark-gleaming sea--
asleep too are all the birds, their wings outstretched.

Alcman, fragment 89

Acknowledgements

The following investigation of Romans 12.9-21 is the slightly revised version of a University of Chicago dissertation accepted by the Department of New Testament and Early Christian Literature in June, 1990. It is a pleasure to acknowledge here the assistance of those committee members who supervised its preparation--without their sage counsel the study certainly would not have been possible. I am especially indebted to my advisor and thesis director, Professor Hans Dieter Betz, whose insight and support proved invaluable at every stage of the project. Many thanks also go to the readers, Professors Arthur W. H. Adkins and Wendy R. Olmsted, for their advice and encouragement. I am also grateful to Professor Martin Hengel for his decision to include the thesis in the *Wissenschafliche Untersuchungen zum Neuen Testament* series. Professor Philip E. Devenish was also kind enough to assist in proofreading and made a number of useful suggestions.

The book is dedicated to the memory of Professor George B. Walsh, former chairman of the Department of Classical Languages and Literatures at the University of Chicago, who died of cancer on February 7, 1989.

Table of Contents

Acknowledgements V

Abbreviations XI

Introduction 1

Chapter One: The Gnomic Saying in Antiquity 9

    The Gnomic Saying: Definition and Description 11

    The Structure of the Gnomic Saying 24

Chapter Two: The Contexts and Genres of Gnomic Wisdom 40

    The Contextualization of Gnomic Sayings 41

    The Genres of Gnomic Wisdom 51

        Gnomic Poetry 56
        Gnomologia 68
        Wisdom Instruction 81

    Concluding Remarks 88

Contents

Chapter Three: The Literary Composition of Romans 12.1-21 91

    General Description of the Sources 92

    Analysis of the Discourses 95

        LXX Proverbs 3.11-35 96
        Ben Sira 6.18-37 105
        Pseudo-Phocylides 70-96 112
        The Testament of Naphtali 2.2-3.5 119

    Analysis of Romans 12.1-21 126

    Concluding Remarks 147

Chapter Four: Analysis of Romans 12.9-21 149

    12.9: The Thematic Statement and Protreptic Maxim 150

    12.10-13 and the Use of Imperatival Participles 156

    12.14 and its Relationship with the Synoptic Gospels 165

    The Theme(s) and Structure of 12.14-21 172

    12.15 177

    12.16 179

    12.17-19 186

    12.20-21 195

    Concluding Remarks 198

Conclusion 200

Bibliography 213

    Primary Sources 213

    Secondary Sources 219

Index of Passages 241

Index of Modern Authors 256

Index of Subjects 261

Index of Greek Words 262

Abbreviations

The abbreviations used for this study are from the "Instructions for Contributors," *Journal of Biblical Literature* 107 (1988) 579-596, with the following additions:

BLS	Bible and Literature Series
BT	Bibliotheca Teubneriana
CQ	*Classical Quarterly*
DSp	*Dictionnaire de spiritualité ascétique et mystique*
FF	Forum Fascicles
GBSNTS	Guides to Biblical Scholarship, New Testament Series
HB	Herders Bibelkommentar
KP	*Der Kleine Pauly: Lexikon der Antike*
LÄ	*Lexikon der Ägyptologie*
LEC	Library of Early Christianity
OCT	Bibliotheca Oxoniensis (Oxford Classical Texts)
SNTW	Studies of the New Testament and its World
WF	Wege der Forschung

A more complete list of abbreviations for secondary literature may be found in Siegfried Schwertner, *IATG: Internationales Abkürzungsverzeichnis für Theologie und Grenzgebiete* (Berlin, New York: de Gruyter, 1974).

Introduction

In coming to terms with the role played by Judaism in the development of early Christianity, the various ideas and methods associated with wisdom--however this concept is to be defined--merit serious consideration. It appears that the sapiential traditions conditioned the thought of the early Christians in numerous and diverse ways, and that these traditions have some bearing on our understanding not only of the theological and ethical aspects of the New Testament writings but of their literary and rhetorical characteristics as well. The growing number of critical studies concerned with such issues bears witness to this fact and serves as an indication of the significance of such phenomena for modern interpretation.[1] It does not occasion any surprise, therefore, that in the New Testament the impact of sapiential forms and themes is evident in a number of texts, both gospels and epistles. Recent investigations of the synoptic sayings source Q, for instance, have emphasized its literary affinities with ancient wisdom genres.[2] Among the letters of the New

---

[1] In addition to the works cited below see Robert L. Wilken, ed., *Aspects of Wisdom in Judaism and Early Christianity* (University of Notre Dame Center for the Study of Judaism and Christianity in Antiquity 1; Notre Dame, London: University of Notre Dame Press, 1975); Max Küchler, *Frühjüdische Weisheitstraditionen: Zum Fortgang weisheitlichen Denkens im Bereich des frühjüdischen Jahweglaubens* (OBO 26; Freiburg: Universitätsverlag; Göttingen: Vandenhoeck & Ruprecht, 1979) esp. 553-592; John D. Crossan, ed., *Semeia 17: Gnomic Wisdom* (Chico, CA: Scholars Press, 1980); Klaus Berger, "Hellenistische Gattungen im Neuen Testament," *ANRW* II.25.2 (1984) 1049-1074; idem, *Formgeschichte des Neuen Testaments* (Heidelberg: Quelle & Meyer, 1984) 62-67; Hermann von Lips, *Weisheitliche Traditionen im Neuen Testament* (WMANT 64; Neukirchen-Vluyn: Neukirchener Verlag, 1990).

[2] See John S. Kloppenborg, *The Formation of Q: Trajectories in Ancient Wisdom Collections* (Studies in Antiquity and Christianity; Philadelphia: Fortress, 1987) esp. 171-245, 263-316. Numerous other studies have focused on the gnomic features of the synoptic tradition, for example Rudolf Bultmann, *The History of the Synoptic Tradition* (trans. John Marsh; Oxford: Blackwell, 1968[2]) 69-108; James M. Robinson, "LOGOI SOPHON: On the Gattung of Q," *Trajectories through Early Christianty* (ed. idem and Helmut Koester; Philadelphia: Fortress, 1971) 71-113 [= *The Future of Our Religious Past: Essays in Honor of Rudolf Bultmann* (ed. idem; New York, Evanston, San Francisco: Harper & Row, 1971) 84-130]; Dieter Zeller, *Die weisheitlichen Mahnsprüche bei den Synoptikern* (FB 17; Würzburg: Echter Verlag, 1983[2]); Charles E. Carlston, "Proverbs, Maxims, and the

Testament, James has generated the most interest on account of the sapiential nature of its structure and message.³ Of course, such discussions of wisdom influence in early Christianity are hardly restricted to the canonical texts; the Gospel of Thomas, for example, has attracted a fair amount of attention in this regard.⁴

Like any other field of comparative study, the investigation of how the wisdom traditions influenced early Christianity carries with it a host of basic interpretive problems. First of all, the terms 'wisdom,' 'sapiential,' and so forth are notoriously difficult to define with any precision. For this study, we will take as a starting point the corpus of 'wisdom' texts in the Hebrew Bible and Apocrypha, especially Proverbs, Qohelet, the Wisdom of Solomon, Ben Sira, and the 'wisdom psalms'. The definition of wisdom may then be extended secondarily to describe materials of different dates and provenances that possess theological, ethical, or literary qualities comparable to these sources. Thus many texts that are not primarily sapiential in character may be understood to take advantage of sapiential themes or conventions. In practice,

---

Historical Jesus," *JBL* 99 (1980) 87-105; idem, "Wisdom and Eschatology in Q," *Les Paroles de Jésus--The Sayings of Jesus: Mémorial Joseph Coppens* (ed. Joël Delobel; BETL 59; Leuven: Leuven University Press, 1982) 101-119; John D. Crossan, *In Fragments: The Aphorisms of Jesus* (San Francisco: Harper & Row, 1983); Leo G. Perdue, "The Wisdom Sayings of Jesus," *Forum* 2 (1986) 1-34; Ronald A. Piper, *Wisdom in the Q-Tradition: The Aphoristic Teaching of Jesus* (SNTSMS 61; Cambridge: Cambridge University Press, 1989); Alan P. Winton, *The Proverbs of Jesus: Issues of History and Rhetoric* (JSNTSup 35; Sheffield: JSOT, 1990); cf. von Lips, *Weisheitliche Traditionen*, 197-227.

[3] For instance, Ulrich Luck, "'Weisheit' und Leiden: Zum Problem Paulus und Jakobus," *TLZ* 92 (1967) 253-258; idem, "Der Jakobusbrief und die Theologie des Paulus," *TGl* 61 (1971) 161-179; idem, "Die Theologie des Jakobusbriefes," *ZTK* 81 (1984) 1-30; J. A. Kirk, "The Meaning of Wisdom in James: Examination of a Hypothesis," *NTS* 16 (1969-70) 24-38; Martin Dibelius, *James: A Commentary on the Epistle of James* (rev. Heinrich Greeven; Hermeneia; Philadelphia: Fortress, 1975) s.v. wisdom, wisdom literature; Franz Mußner, *Der Jakobusbrief* (HTKNT 13.1; Freiburg, Basel, Wien: Herder, 1975³) esp. 168-175; Rudolf Hoppe, *Der theologische Hintergrund des Jakobusbriefes* (FB 28; Würzburg: Echter Verlag, 1977) 39-71, 146-148; Ernst Baasland, "Der Jakobusbrief als neutestamentliche Weisheitsschrift," *ST* 36 (1982) 119-139; idem, "Literarische Form, Thematik und geschichtliche Einordnung des Jakobusbriefes," *ANRW* II.25.5 (1988) 3646-3684; Peter H. Davids, *The Epistle of James: A Commentary on the Greek Text* (NIGTC; Grand Rapids: Eerdmans, 1982) 51-56 and s.v. wisdom; idem, "The Epistle of James in Modern Discussion," *ANRW* II.25.5 (1988) 3621-3645; Ralph P. Martin, *James* (WBC 48; Waco, TX: Word Books, 1988) s.v. wisdom; von Lips, *Weisheitliche Traditionen*, 409-437.

[4] See, for instance, William A. Beardslee, "Proverbs in the Gospel of Thomas," *Studies in the New Testament and Early Christian Literature: Essays for A. P. Wikgren* (ed. David E. Aune; NovTSup 33; Leiden: Brill, 1972) 92-103; Stevan L. Davies, *The Gospel of Thomas and Christian Wisdom* (New York: Seabury, 1983); F. T. Fallon and Ron Cameron, "The Gospel of Thomas: A *Forschungsbericht* and Analysis," *ANRW* II.25.6 (1988) 4195-4251 with further bibliography.

of course, such descriptions can be problematic; as we will see below, not the least difficulty is posed by the fact that the Jewish wisdom texts themselves exhibit considerable diversity. Second, as these comments suggest, the extent to which ancient Jewish wisdom may be fairly designated a 'tradition,' as if it constituted some coherent and uninterrupted religious movement, is suspect. It seems rather more accurate to speak of the distinct sapiential qualities of individual texts and then to explore in what ways and to what degree these materials are related to one another. This raises a third question, explaining precisely how one wisdom text or corpus of texts 'influenced' the thoughts of a particular author, especially a non-sapiential author. In many instances there is no evidence of direct borrowing, and so attention must be paid to more subtle matters of shared theological perspectives and themes as well as common literary and rhetorical practices. Finally, it should be emphasized that none of these questions can be correctly addressed by treating Jewish and Christian wisdom in isolation. As a means of comprehending and describing human experience wisdom in its various modalities exercised considerable influence throughout the ancient world, and it became a prevalent aspect of life not only--or even especially--in Judaism and Christianity, but in Near Eastern and Greco-Roman civilizations as well. Thus wisdom represented a nearly universal phenomenon, and numerous parallels in content, form, and function may be detected among the different texts and traditions.

As these observations indicate, there were indeed many facets to the ancient sapiential traditions. One of the most common practices, and the focus for this study, was the composition and collection of sententious sayings, or maxims (Greek γνῶμαι, Latin *sententiae*). Ancient people valued such gnomic sayings not only because they were artistic and memorable, but also because they were useful for making practical decisions about day-to-day life and functioned as a means of preserving the insights of other cultures and previous generations. On account of their succinct form and universal utility, gnomic sayings were also characterized by a relatively high degree of cross-cultural influence and borrowing. In addition, the style of communication associated with gnomic wisdom exhibited considerable flexibility with respect to content, setting, and purpose, and its impact on the literature of the time was hardly restricted to any particular group of texts or genres.

That the apostle Paul and his congregations also participated in the sapiential traditions of their time seems clear, and an array of modern analyses has been devoted to the topic of wisdom in the Pauline corpus, particularly as it is

4   *Introduction*

discussed in 1 Corinthians 1.18-3.23.[5] Like many of his contemporaries, Paul also formulated gnomic sentences in his writings; these precepts often figure prominently in the ethical sections of his letters, though they are on occasion employed elsewhere as well.[6] Commenting on a sequence of such *sententiae* in Galatians 5.25-6.10, Hans Dieter Betz noted that the investigation of Paul's wisdom sentences "remains a *desideratum* of New Testament scholarship."[7] Indeed, outside of Betz's occasional though insightful observations, the form, function, and background of Paul's gnomic wisdom has prompted only scant interest.[8] The purpose of the present study is to meet, in part, this need by conducting a critical investigation of the sort Betz has called for in his *Galatians*

---

[5] For a survey of recent literature see E. Elizabeth Johnson, *The Function of Apocalyptic and Wisdom Traditions in Romans 9-11* (SBLDS 109; Atlanta: Scholars Press, 1989) 23-49. Among the numerous noteworthy studies are Ulrich Wilckens, *Weisheit und Torheit: Eine exegetisch-religionsgeschichtliche Untersuchung zu 1 Kor. 1 und 2* (BHT 26; Tübingen: Mohr-Siebeck, 1959); Hans Conzelmann, "Paulus und die Weisheit," *NTS* 12 (1965-66) 231-244; idem, *1 Corinthians: A Commentary on the First Epistle to the Corinthians* (trans. James W. Leitch; Hermeneia; Philadelphia: Fortress, 1975); Birger A. Pearson, "Hellenistic-Jewish Wisdom Speculation and Paul," in Wilken, *Aspects of Wisdom*, 43-66; Richard A. Horsley, "Wisdom of Word and Words of Wisdom in Corinth," *CBQ* 39 (1977) 224-239; James A. Davis, *Wisdom and Spirit: An Investigation of 1 Corinthians 1.18-3.20 against the Background of Jewish Sapiential Traditions in the Greco-Roman Period* (Lanham, MD: University Press of America, 1984); Eckhard J. Schnabel, *Law and Wisdom from Ben Sira to Paul: A Tradition Historical Enquiry into the Relation of Law, Wisdom, and Ethics* (WUNT 2.16; Tübingen: Mohr-Siebeck, 1985); Hans Dieter Betz, "The Problem of Rhetoric and Theology according to the Apostle Paul," *L'Apôtre Paul: Personnalité, Style et Conception du Ministère* (ed. Albert Vanhoye; BETL 73; Leuven: Leuven University Press, 1986) 16-48; von Lips, *Weisheitliche Traditionen*, 318-350.

[6] In addition to Romans 12.9-21 and Galatians 5.25-6.10, Paul's gnomic formulations include Romans 12.3, 13.7, 14.7, 22b; 1 Corinthians 1.25, 3.18b, 19a, 8.1b, 2, 13.13, 16.13-14; 2 Corinthians 6.14b, 8.12, 9.6, 10.18, 14b, 13.5a; Galatians 4.18a, 5.9; Philippians 2.4, 14, 3.16, 4.5a; 1 Thessalonians 5.13b-22. Cf. Romans 1.22, 2.11, 3.4a, 8b, 5.3-4, 13.8; 1 Corinthians 1.29, 14.38, 15.32-33; 2 Corinthians 8.21, 9.7, 12.9b; Galatians 4.12; Philippians 2.1-3, 4.8. Further see the references in note 8.

[7] Hans Dieter Betz, *Galatians: A Commentary on Paul's Letter to the Churches in Galatia* (Hermeneia; Philadelphia: Fortress, 1979) 291 n. 5.

[8] Hans Dieter Betz, "De laude ipsius (Moralia 539A-547F)," *Plutarch's Ethical Writings and Early Christian Literature* (ed. idem; SCHNT 4; Leiden: Brill, 1978) 378-381; idem, *Galatians*, 291-311; idem, *2 Corinthians 8 and 9: A Commentary on Two Administrative Letters of the Apostle Paul* (Hermeneia; Philadelphia: Fortress, 1985) s.v. sententia. Regarding Paul's gnomic sentences, Betz (*Galatians*, 291 n. 5) also refers to Johannes Weiss, "Beiträge zur Paulinischen Rhetorik," *Theologische Studien: Herrn Professor D. Bernhard Weiss zu seinem 70. Geburtstag dargebracht* (ed. C. R. Gregory et al.; Göttingen: Vandenhoeck & Ruprecht, 1897) 165-247; Rudolf Bultmann, *Der Stil der paulinischen Predigt und die kynisch-stoische Diatribe* (FRLANT 13; Göttingen: Huth, 1910) [reprint, Göttingen: Vandenhoeck & Ruprecht, 1984]; Norbert Schneider, *Die rhetorische Eigenart der paulinischen Antithese* (HUT 11; Tübingen: Mohr-Siebeck, 1970).

commentary. As he demonstrated there, a careful reading of Paul's gnomic sayings in terms of their historical context can be of use not only in the exegetical task, but also in clarifying the nature of the apostle's relationship with contemporary literary practices and in better understanding the presuppositions and methods of his ethical teaching. In the course of addressing these more specific interpretive problems, it is hoped that the analysis below can also contribute to some of the broader issues regarding gnomic wisdom in the ancient world and the significance of such wisdom for early Christianity.

While Paul has recourse to gnomic sentences on a number of occasions, this investigation will focus on a passage where a fairly high concentration of such sayings occurs, Romans 12, and in particular Romans 12.9-21. To be sure, this represents only a sample of the apostle's gnomic wisdom, and so its investigation here may be considered a kind of test-case for the study of this literary form in the Pauline corpus. Yet, having stated this caveat, the significance of the chapter for the interpretation of Pauline theology and ethics ought to be emphasized. As most commentators acknowledge, this chapter forms an integral part of the most careful and thorough exposition of Paul's theology that we possess, his epistle to the Romans. In many respects, Romans 12 represents the nearest thing we have to a general statement of Paul's program for Christian ethical thought and behavior. It serves as both an essential corollary to the theological discussions that precede in chapters 1-11 as well as an introduction to the explicit treatment of ethical questions in chapters 12-15. In this chapter the apostle presents a number of his most crucial ethical concepts: the cultic self-sacrifice of Christian life, the discernment of God's will, the church as the body of Christ, and ἀγάπη ("love") as the basic perspective and motivation of Christian ethical conduct.

As an examination of any recent commentary on Romans will show, the exegesis of chapter 12 poses a range of serious and intriguing challenges to modern scholars.[9] While a familiarity with the basic exegetical issues

---

[9] The most significant contributions to the modern interpretation of Romans 12.9-21 have come from the various commentaries on Romans; those consulted most often for this study are Hans Lietzmann, *An die Römer* (HNT 8; Tübingen: Mohr-Siebeck, 1933[4], 1971[5]); C. E. B. Cranfield, *A Critical and Exegetical Commentary on the Epistle to the Romans* (ICC; 2 vols.; Edinburgh: T. & T. Clark, 1975, 1979); Heinrich Schlier, *Der Römerbrief* (HTKNT 6; Freiburg, Basel, Vienna: Herder, 1977); Otto Michel, *Der Brief an die Römer (*MeyerK 4; Göttingen: Vandenhoeck & Ruprecht, 1955[10], 1978[14]); Ulrich Wilckens, *Der Brief an die Römer* (EKKNT 6; 3 vols.; Zürich, Einsiedeln, Cologne: Benziger Verlag; Neukirchen-Vluyn: Neukirchener Verlag, 1978, 1980, 1982); Ernst Käsemann, *Commentary on Romans* (trans. and ed. Geoffrey W. Bromiley; Grand Rapids: Eerdmans, 1980); Franz-Josef Ortkemper, *Leben aus dem Glauben: Christliche Grundhaltungen nach Römer 12-13* (NTAbh 14; Münster: Aschendorff, 1980); Dieter Zeller, *Der Brief an die Römer* (RNT; Regensburg:

connected with the chapter will have a bearing on our study, the objective here is to investigate Romans 12 against the background of relevant ancient texts that make use of gnomic wisdom and to explore what implications this has for the interpretation of the literary composition and rhetorical function of the chapter as well as for our understanding of the importance of the gnomic style for Paul's ethics. Because the bulk of gnomic forms and themes is concentrated in 12.9-21, this section will constitute the center of attention for the discussion. As we will see below, the structuring of the material and the presentation of the exhortation in this passage conforms in numerous ways to the conventions observed in composing ancient gnomic wisdom.

At the same time, it appears that Paul has also carefully integrated this passage into its immediate literary environment, Romans 12.1-21, and that the ethical appeal made in vv. 9-21 is effective and meaningful only when interpreted within this larger context. Consequently, the investigation of 12.9-21 must also take into account the fundamental literary and rhetorical characteristics of chapter 12 as a whole as well as the unity and development of its material argument. The analysis will show that the sapiential features of Romans 12 are not restricted to vv. 9-21, but rather the character of the literary composition and mode of argumentation in the entire chapter is intelligible in terms of the ancient wisdom materials. Thus it appears that the literary setting that Paul provides for the material in 12.9-21 and the manner in which these verses have been integrated into their context are intelligible in terms of gnomic wisdom.

In addition to these considerations, it is also important to bear in mind that Romans 12 comprises part of the larger body of the epistle and contributes in a number of ways to Paul's overall intention in addressing the Roman Christians. Thus the material and functional relationship between chapter 12 and Paul's letter to the Romans in its entirety will also be a topic for consideration.

In order to come to grips with the problems of the composition and purpose of Romans 12 most effectively, it is necessary to analyze in some detail how the passage corresponds with existing literary parallels. Because they constitute the most immediate background for interpreting Paul's epistles, Hellenistic-Jewish and early Christian gnomic texts play a prominent role in this regard. However, on account of the typically cosmopolitan scope of the content and appeal of gnomic wisdom, the relevant comparative materials must extend beyond these texts to include Near Eastern and Greco-Roman sources as well. This is also necessary because it is plain that Paul himself has been influenced to

---

Pustet, 1985); James D. G. Dunn, *Romans* (WBC 38; 2 vols.; Dallas: Word Books, 1988); Walter Schmithals, *Der Römerbrief: Ein Kommentar* (Gütersloh: Mohn, 1988).

a significant degree by Hellenistic as well as Jewish and Christian literary conventions and ethical ideas.

Because of the importance of these ancient comparative materials for our analysis, as well as the complicated nature of gnomic wisdom in general, it will be useful to consider these sources at some length before proceeding to the text at hand. This involves, first of all, investigating the basic features and distinctions to be found within the corpus of gnomic texts, paying attention to both basic sayings as well as more complex structures and genres. Beyond this we will also consider in what ways gnomic forms may interact with non-gnomic genres and be utilized by authors to develop more sophisticated arguments and exhortations. Thus our inquiries will not be limited strictly to gnomic forms and genres, but will also take into account related and complementary forms of communication.

In clarifying the relationship of Romans 12 with these comparative materials, it is plain that Paul did not rely on any specific model or special source, either from the body of wisdom texts or elsewhere. Rather it appears that he has to some degree inculcated the fundamental ethos of the sapiential traditions familiar to us from these texts and takes advantage of a number of their basic conventions here, creating a new composition that suits his own ethical and literary needs in writing to the Roman Christians. So while the degree to which the chapter resembles the ancient gnomic texts is a central consideration, there is also a pressing need to remain sensitive to any ways in which Paul has adapted or modified the forms and concepts typical of the sapiential idiom. Hence it is crucial to look for innovations as well as conventions in the composition of Romans 12, especially when dealing with an author as creative and versatile as Paul.

Significantly, the similarities that Romans 12 exhibits with ancient gnomic sources are not restricted to a particular section of the chapter or to a certain sort of feature. Rather, its sapiential qualities are manifest on a number of levels, and each of these will have some bearing on the conclusions to be reached concerning its design and meaning. Most important are the following:

1) the overall literary organization of the chapter and the structure of its larger formal units, vv. 1-2, 3-8, and 9-21,
2) the chapter's mode of argumentation, the rhetorical objectives and strategies which it exhibits,
3) the nature of the constituent literary forms employed within the chapter, for example, maxims and proverbs, and
4) the substance of the chapter's message and appeal, such things as its themes, concepts, and terminology.

With respect to each of these features Romans 12 demonstrates important similarities with other ancient literary materials that employ gnomic forms and take advantage of the gnomic style. Furthermore, and as we will see below, analyzing Romans 12 in terms of gnomic literature also underscores the unified and sophisticated character of the chapter's composition and message, and is of use in understanding the role that gnomic wisdom plays in Paul's ethical thought.

Chapter One

The Gnomic Saying in Antiquity

A practice that seems to be shared by virtually every culture is the coining, use, and preservation of wise or sententious sayings. While this is particularly true with respect to pre-modern societies, even in modern times the study and employment of such sayings continues, and the variety of terms used to denote these sayings--maxim, proverb, epigram, aphorism, precept, and so on--are an indication of both their currency and their complexity. Perhaps the most remarkable quality of gnomic wisdom is its multi-dimensional character; gnomic utterances may exhibit features and applications that fall under the auspices of such diverse fields as poetry, rhetoric, ethics, philosophy, religion, and law. This diversity, in combination with the memorable formulation and practical insight that these sayings typically possess, often ensures them of longevity as well as wide circulation. On account of these qualities, gnomic wisdom as a whole is not a strictly literary phenomenon, and to a greater extent than many other forms gnomic sayings operate within the unsettled territory that separates written and oral communication.

In light of these characteristics, it comes as no surprise that the identification, description, and classification of the varieties of gnomic wisdom have proven to be notoriously difficult tasks.[1] Different attempts, both ancient and modern, to impose clear distinctions on the gnomic saying and its literary neighbors are often too vague or arbitrary to be of use in categorizing given

---

[1] For some broader and more recent treatments of the issues involved in the investigation of gnomic communication see Heinz Krüger, *Studien über den Aphorismus als philosophische Form* (Frankfurt am Main: Nest, 1957); Joseph P. Stern, *Lichtenberg: A Doctrine of Scattered Occasions* (Bloomington, IN: Indiana University Press, 1959); Archer Taylor, *The Proverb and an Index to the Proverb* (Hatboro, PA: Folklore Associates; Copenhagen: Rosenkilde and Bagger, 1962^2); Gerhard Neumann, ed., *Der Aphorismus: Zur Geschichte, zu den Formen und Möglichkeiten einer literarischen Gattung* (WF 356; Darmstadt: Wissenschaftliche Buchgesellschaft, 1976); Lutz Röhrich and Wolfgang Mieder, *Sprichwort* (Realien zur Literatur; Stuttgart: Metzler, 1977). While such studies possess a decidedly modern vantage-point they are still of use in comprehending the functions of ancient gnomic wisdom and will be cited on occasion in the discussion that follows.

forms or in understanding precisely what an author may have intended by a saying. Generally speaking, any investigation of gnomic wisdom must take into account a host of ambiguities associated with creating and applying precise generic or functional definitions. Frequently it is impossible to render a firm decision regarding the form and purpose of a particular saying, and careful analysis must allow for qualifications and complexities in its descriptions as well as a certain degree of indefiniteness.

Such interpretive complications arise in part from the fact that sententious sayings participate in a wide arena of literary and cultural conventions, and these must be examined in order to grasp the complexities of the gnomic style. An additional problem is the great flexibility gnomic sayings demonstrate rhetorically. On account of the utility and compactness of gnomic sayings, generally they are free to roam from their original or intended context and enjoy the potential to operate in new and varying literary and social settings. More than other forms, for the gnomic saying context is determinative for meaning. Thus we must be sensitive to the functional and hermeneutical flexibility that gnomic communication exhibits; determinations regarding identity and purpose for a certain saying in one rhetorical situation do not necessarily hold true when it is incorporated into a different one. And so as a guideline for the study of gnomic texts it seems more constructive to concentrate on the sorts of exegetical methods and critical questions that must be brought to bear in a particular investigation rather than to insist on rigorously-defined genres or hard-and-fast functional distinctions.

In this chapter and the next we will examine some of these critical questions, particularly as they apply to the sapiential literature of the Hellenistic era, in order to understand better the ideas and methods that accompanied the formulation of gnomic wisdom in Hellenistic Judaism and early Christianity. While it is important to take into account the width and breadth of wisdom literature in the ancient world and the broader background against which Paul and other early Christians wrote, the focus is on those aspects of gnomic wisdom that will best inform the investigation of Romans 12, as well as of the expectations that Paul's audience in Rome may have brought to their reading of the chapter. Qualifications of this sort are crucial since the form and function of gnomic sayings are to a large extent based upon material assumptions peculiar to the cultural and moral environment within which they are created and used. Every instance of gnomic wisdom presupposes both certain shared ethical concepts and experiences, as well as certain principles regarding the appropriate content, circumstances, and goals of the gnomic style. As critics, we must be aware of these presuppositions as they apply to a specific document, author, group, culture, language, or time. Consequently, the discussions that follow will be brief and restricted in scope, as well as somewhat tentative, since they are not intended to stand on their own as a compendium of ancient gnomic forms and texts (much less gnomic discourse as a whole), but rather are meant to provide a practical introduction to the study of Paul as a gnomic author and of Romans 12 as gnomic literature.

The study of ancient gnomic wisdom falls conveniently into two areas of investigation, one pertaining to the gnomic saying itself and the other to the larger literary settings or genres in which it is characteristically utilized. The first of these will occupy the attention of this chapter. To begin with, it is necessary to introduce and describe the salient characteristics of the literary structure most basic to the study, namely the γνώμη, or "maxim." Since this form does not constitute a strictly limited literary category, many of its basic features are best understood in relation with similar forms such as the proverb, chreia, epigram, and so forth, and these comparisons will form the heart of the description. In the remainder of the chapter, borrowing from the linguistic model of the English folklorist Alan Dundes, the structure of the maxim will be outlined. The purpose of Dundes' method is to isolate and relate some of the "patterns of thought" that gnomic sayings typically exhibit, and his approach may be effectively applied to Hellenistic sayings as a means of depicting their independent structure and purpose.

The Gnomic Saying: Definition and Description

While the terminology is often imprecise, the most common Greek word for a sententious saying is γνώμη (Latin *sententia*), which will be translated here as maxim, gnomic saying, or wisdom saying.[2] Before describing it in greater detail, we might begin by offering a very basic definition. A maxim is a complete saying that is short and striking, sometimes poetic. It is the individually-inspired composition of a single writer and not the product of tradition or the masses, though it may subsequently achieve wide circulation and popularity. While maxims do not constitute folklore, and are not traditional in a technical sense, their content and composition are often predicated upon the same customary ideas and means of expression, as well as the cultural conventions and social norms, that may be found in traditional sources. With respect to purpose, maxims convey assertions derived from

---

[2] On the wider meanings of the term see Konstantin Horna, "Gnome, Gnomendichtung, Gnomologien," *PWSup* 6 (1935) 74-76; S. Mouraviev, "Gnome," *Glotta* 51 (1973) 69-78.

human experience regarding ethical choice and behavior; they strive to establish generalized rules or paradigms that will be of use in making practical ethical decisions or in influencing the actions of others. Though they often represent themselves as authoritative conclusions, maxims in fact convey insights that are subjective and contingent. Their validity and relevance, therefore, depend upon the special features of the rhetorical situations in which they are utilized.

The most important, and often most difficult, distinction to be made regarding gnomic sayings is between the maxim and the proverb, or παροιμία.[3] Both forms are gnomic; but while a maxim represents the creation of a particular, usually identifiable, author, a proverb is derived from popular or folk culture. Within modern biblical studies the debate over the relationship between the *Volkssprichwort* and the *Weisheitsspruch* is long, complex, and largely unresolved.[4] For the most part, critics describe the former as a linear, prose saying originating with the (variously defined) 'folk' in a largely oral setting.[5] Proverbs convey common--often rural or domestic--images and easily recognizable ideas; simple comparisons and metaphorical language are regular features. These folk sayings normally project themselves as empirical conclusions, and so are more observational and retrospective than didactic. The wisdom saying, or maxim, on the other hand, is the bilinear creation of a wise sage originating in some scholarly or scholastic setting. As a whole maxims are more poetic and literary (making use of the *parallelismus membrorum*), more didactic, and less metaphorical than proverbs.

To be sure, such descriptions are difficult to apply in practice. For instance, Proverbs 10.1ff., which constitutes a collection of literary, bilinear maxims, possesses a fair amount of observational material, metaphorical language, and rural images, and a number of its sayings bear some resemblance to Hebrew proverbs. A further complication is that some of the maxims in this collection

---

[3] Cf. Karl Rupprecht, "Παροιμία," *PW* 18.4 (1949) 1707-1735.

[4] Carol R. Fontaine (*Traditional Sayings in the Old Testament: A Contextual Study* [BLS 5; Sheffield: Almond, 1982] 2-27) provides a useful survey of the literature; of special interest are Otto Eißfeldt, *Der Maschal im Alten Testament* (BZAW 24; Gießen: Töpelmann, 1913) 45-52; André Jolles, *Einfache Formen* (Tübingen: Niemeyer, 1965[3]) 150-170; Hans-Jürgen Hermisson, *Studien zur israelitischen Spruchweisheit* (WMANT 28; Neukirchen-Vlyun: Neukirchener Verlag, 1968) 27-64; Claus Westermann, "Weisheit im Sprichwort," *Schalom: Studien zu Glaube und Geschichte Israels, Festschrift Alfred Jepsen zum 70. Geburtstag* (ed. Karl-Heinz Bernhardt; Arbeiten zur Theologie 1.46; Stuttgart: Calwer, 1971) 73-85; James L. Crenshaw, "Wisdom," *Old Testament Form Criticism* (ed. John H. Hayes; Trinity University Monograph Series in Religion; San Antonio: Trinity University Press, 1974) 229-236; cf. idem, *Old Testament Wisdom: An Introduction* (Atlanta: John Knox, 1981) 66-91.

[5] On the concept of "folk" see Fontaine, *Traditional Sayings*, 30-32.

incorporate or reformulate proverbs, and others may be patterned after popular sayings.[6] On the other hand, those sayings from ancient Judaism that have been identified as proverbs are preserved only in literary sources, such as the narrative and prophetic books of the Hebrew Bible. Consequently, we must take into account the theological, historical, and literary motives of these sources, and allowances must be made for the possibility of the modification or 'contamination' of the form, context, or use of folk sayings by subsequent writers and editors.[7]

Observations such as these are symptomatic of the underlying fact that both the maxims and proverbs of a particular culture are predicated upon more-or-less the same pool of social conventions, moral values, and ethical perspectives, including even the specific terms, phrases, or formulae employed to articulate these concepts. If we move beyond the Hebrew Bible to consider the larger corpus of gnomic sayings in antiquity, determinations of what constitutes a proverb or a maxim appear to be even more difficult to make since there is no consistent formal difference between the two forms comparable to the linear-bilinear distinction made in Jewish literature.[8] At least in theory, all proverbs were at one time maxims, and all maxims are potential proverbs. As James G. Williams observes, the decisive factor in distinguishing the proverb from the maxim (which he calls aphorism) is "the difference in principle between a *collective* voice and an *individual* voice":

> Both are non-narrative forms that reveal and conceal a tension between the general (truth, principle, concept) and the particular (case, experience of subject), each seems to provide and evoke insight, and both may be

---

[6] Eißfeldt, *Der Maschal*, 45-47; Taylor, *The Proverb*, 16-22; R. B. Y. Scott, "Folk Proverbs of the Ancient Near East," *Transactions of the Royal Society of Canada* 55 (1961) 47-56 [reprint, *Studies in Ancient Israelite Wisdom* (ed. James L. Crenshaw; Library of Biblical Studies; New York: KTAV, 1976) 417-426]; idem, *The Way of Wisdom in the Old Testament* (New York: Macmillan, 1971) 12-18, 63-70; Roland E. Murphy, "The Interpretation of Old Testament Wisdom Literature," *Int* 23 (1969) 289-301; idem, "Form Criticism and Wisdom Literature," *CBQ* 31 (1969) 475-483; Fontaine, *Traditional Sayings*, 12-14; James G. Williams, "The Power of Form: A Study of Biblical Proverbs," *Semeia* 17 (1980) 48-52.

[7] On these problems see Fontaine, *Traditional Sayings*, 72-76 and passim.

[8] Regarding some of the wider problems involved in this distinction see James G. Williams, *Those Who Ponder Proverbs: Aphoristic Thinking and Biblical Literature* (BLS 2; Sheffield: Almond, 1981) 78-80; cf. Bartlett J. Whiting, "The Nature of the Proverb," *Harvard Studies and Notes in Philology and Literature* 14 (1930) 273-307; Alexander H. Krappe, *The Science of Folklore* (London: Methuen, 1930) 143-148; Nigel Barley, "A Structural Approach to the Proverb and Maxim with Special Reference to the Anglo-Saxon Corpus," *Proverbium* 20 (1972) 737-750; Crossan, *In Fragments*, 12-25, 79-81.

paradoxical, although aphorism in modern western history is more associated with paradox and irony. What really distinguishes the two, if and when the distinction is valid, is their function, a function that does not always show itself in formal literary signs. The proverb expresses the voice of the human subject as ancient, collective wisdom, whereas aphorism (certainly the modern literary aphorism) brings the subjectivity of the individual more to the fore. But both accord a significant role to the human origin of the word spoken, whatever the ultimate grounding of authority of the utterance.[9]

The crucial factor in differentiating the two forms is not necessarily morphology, but rather the perspective of an author, as well as the audience, toward the purpose and history of a given saying. While determining this perspective proves to be in many cases simply impossible, an ongoing concern in the analysis of any gnomic writing must be the ultimate origin and literary history of its sayings, as well as their level of literary sophistication, use of metaphorical language, rhetorical context(s), and so forth.

As Williams' comments imply, another feature common to both the proverb and maxim is their self-presentation as bits of tried-and-true traditional wisdom, a quality that contributes to their value and persuasiveness. In many ancient societies gnomic wisdom served a preservational function, making the practical knowledge of the past available for future use. No doubt this was due in part to the fact that the impersonal and uncompromising posture of gnomic discourse lays claim to an absoluteness and objectivity that stands outside the immediacies of specific situations or historical occurrences.[10] At the same time, however, maxims and proverbs typically draw from and contribute to the particular social and cultural environment in which they are employed. On account of this characteristic, the study of a given society's gnomic formulations is frequently of use in understanding its history, culture, and folklore.[11] It follows, then, that the outlook of ancient gnomic wisdom was characteristically conservative, positive, and optimistic, and that it was well-

---

[9] Williams, *Those Who Ponder Proverbs*, 80.

[10] Westermann, "Weisheit im Sprichwort," 73-85; Gerhard von Rad, *Wisdom in Israel* (trans. James D. Martin; London: SCM, 1972), 31-34, cf. 53-73; Heinrich Lausberg, *Handbuch der literarischen Rhetorik* (Munich: Hueber, 1973[2]) §§ 872-873; John Mark Thompson, *The Form and Function of Proverbs in Ancient Israel* (The Hague: Mouton, 1974) 27-31; Williams, *Those Who Ponder Proverbs*, 26-28, 40-42; Crossan, *In Fragments*, 25-28; Berger, "Hellenistische Gattungen," 1051-1059.

[11] Fontaine (*Traditional Sayings*, 43-63) provides a survey of modern folklore studies which have a bearing on the interpretation of gnomic sayings.

suited to creating an impression of order out of an otherwise puzzling world.[12]

In some of these respects, however, the maxim differs from the proverb. Since the composition of a maxim is connected with a certain individual, its force depends less on the weight of shared cultural norms or traditional values and more on the strength of the author's own reputation and skill. Thus many otherwise anonymous maxims are ascribed to authoritative figures--Solomon, Solon, Menander, and so forth--in order to lend them legitimacy. It is important to bear in mind, however, that whether a writer makes use of a proverb, cites the maxim of another author, or formulates a new maxim, the effectiveness of the formulation is contingent largely upon the author's own ethos vis-à-vis the audience and the skill evident in applying the saying in an appropriate manner.[13]

Attribution to a named authority is also a constant feature of the chreia, which is a brief, self-contained narrative of an instructional nature. A chreia typically relates some edifying episode from the life of a noteworthy historical figure, whose climactic saying or action normally concludes the story.[14] Some

---

[12] See Klaus Koch, "Gibt es ein Vergeltungsdogma im Alten Testament?" *Um das Prinzip der Vergeltung in Religion und Recht des Alten Testaments* (WF 125; Darmstadt: Wissenschaftliche Buchgesellschaft, 1972) 130-180 [originally in *ZTK* 52 (1955) 1-42]; von Rad, *Wisdom in Israel*, 74-96, 113-143; Crenshaw, "Wisdom," 231-236; Thompson, *Form and Function*, 28-31, 68-73; Walther Zimmerli, "Concerning the Structure of Old Testament Wisdom," in Crenshaw, *Studies*, 175-207 [originally, "Zur Struktur der alttestamentlichen Weisheit," *ZAW* 51 (1933) 177-204]; Roland E. Murphy, "Wisdom--Theses and Hypotheses," *Israelite Wisdom: Theological and Literary Essays in Honor of Samuel Terrien* (ed. John G. Gammie, Walter A. Brueggemann, W. Lee Humphreys, and James M. Ward; New York: Union Theological Seminary; Missoula, MT: Scholars Press, 1978) 35-42; Williams, *Those Who Ponder Proverbs*, 35-46; Fontaine, *Traditional Sayings*, 32-43; Philip J. Nel, *The Structure and Ethos of Wisdom Admonitions in Proverbs* (BZAW 158; Berlin, New York: de Gruyter, 1982) 83-88, 101-115.

[13] Cf. James L. Crenshaw, "Wisdom and Authority: Sapiential Rhetoric and its Warrants," *Congress Volume: Vienna 1980* (ed. J. A. Emerton; VTSup 32; Leiden: Brill, 1981) 10-29.

[14] On the chreia and its relationship with the maxim see Horna, "Gnome," 75-76 [with additional notes by Kurt von Fritz, 87-89]; Lausberg, *Handbuch*, §§ 1117-1120; Crossan, *In Fragments*, 227-312; Berger, "Hellenistische Gattungen," 1074, 1092-1110; Robert C. Tannehill, "Types and Functions of Apophthegms in the Synoptic Gospels," *ANRW* II.25.2 (1984) 1792-1829; Ronald F. Hock and Edward N. O'Neil, *The Chreia in Ancient Rhetoric; Volume I: The Progymnasmata* (SBLTT 27, Graeco-Roman Religion Series 9; Atlanta: Scholars Press, 1986) 3-60; Kloppenborg, *The Formation of Q*, 290-292, 306-316, 340-341; cf. the series of essays in Daniel Patte, ed., *Semeia 29. Kingdom and Children: Aphorism, Chreia, Structure* (Chico, CA: Scholars Press, 1983). Many authors note the imprecision of the terminology in ancient texts. For instance, the Τῶν ἑπτὰ σοφῶν ἀποφθέγματα (text: Hermann Diels and Walter Kranz, eds., *Die Fragmente der Vorsokratiker* [3 vols.; Berlin: Weidmann, 1952[6]] 1.62-66) are clearly maxims by the definition of the term given here.

of these climactic sayings may also be designated maxims, yet these differ from conventional maxims because they are accompanied by a narrative description that provides a logical and rhetorical environment for the utterance. Thus the chreia betrays a biographical interest alongside the didactic one. Further, the narrative setting is determinative for the maxim's meaning: the saying in a chreia is given in response to some definite set of circumstances and so has a fixed context that focuses or restricts its interpretation. Wisdom sayings that are not incorporated into a chreia carry with them no such relevance restrictions and their formulation is not bound to a specific individual or a concrete social or historical situation. Thus their potential meanings and contexts are more open-ended and flexible.[15]

Perhaps the most obvious characteristic of a maxim is its succinct, arresting, and memorable composition. Because gnomic discourse generally has recourse to heightened language and common poetic devices, a maxim will often evoke an emotional and aesthetic response that accompanies its moment of intellectual or ethical insight.[16] An invariable characteristic of all aphoristic discourse is a profound connection between content and form, and a certain sensitivity to the means by which language structures and conditions its subject matter. Of the phenomenon of "gnomic apperception" Gerhard von Rad writes:

> A decisive factor in the understanding of it is the close connection, even unity, between content and form. It is not the case that the perception lay ready somewhere and needed only its appropriate form of expression. Rather, it exists only in this form, or else it does not exist at all. The process of becoming aware of the perception and of giving linguistic expression to it

---

[15] The comments in Nicolaus of Myra's *Progymnasmata* (text: Hock and O'Neil, *The Chreia*, 262-265) are representative; he observes that the maxim differs from the chreia in that 1) it has only a saying and never an action, 2) it is never attributed to someone, 3) it is general advice and not composed on the basis of some set circumstances, 4) it is always ethical, while the chreia is also employed for the sake of wit. For further references to the progymnasmata, see Benjamin Fiore, *The Function of Personal Example in the Socratic and Pastoral Epistles* (AnBib 105; Rome: Biblical Institute Press, 1986) 42.

[16] On the artistic qualities of gnomic wisdom see von Rad, *Wisdom in Israel*, 25-34; Taylor, *The Proverb*, 135-183; Ivo Braak, *Poetik in Stichworten: Literaturwissenschaftliche Grundbegriffe* (Kiel: Hirt, 1969³) 28-95; Bengt Holbeck, "Proverb Style," *Proverbium* 15 (1970) 470-472; Williams, "The Power of Form," 35-58; idem, *Those Who Ponder Proverbs*, 24-26, 65-90; Robert Alter, *The Art of Biblical Poetry* (New York: Basic Books, 1985) 163-184; Neal R. Norrick, *How Proverbs Mean: Semantic Studies in English Proverbs* (Trends in Linguistics, Studies and Monographs 27; Berlin, New York, Amsterdam: Mouton, 1985) 46-51. Also see Charles H. Kahn, *The Art and Thought of Heraclitus: An Edition of the Fragments with Translation and Commentary* (Cambridge, New York: Cambridge University Press, 1979) 87-95.

in word and form are one and the same act. Thus, in this manner of formation, the main concern is not with a useful didactic means to easier retention and remembering. The constitutive meaning possessed by the word, the linguistic form, here points back to much more rudimentary noetic processes. The frequency of paronomasia in these proverbs, of assonance and alliteration, still shows us something of the magical, incantatory function possessed by the resonance of the word.[17]

The wise sage exploits the resources of poetic expression in order to achieve a fuller appreciation of his topic and to transform his moral concepts into aesthetic objects with a greater aura of truth. The artistic features employed by gnomic authors also contribute to the compactness and memorability of maxims, as well as to their marked oral qualities.[18] On account of their poetic nature, it is impossible to translate or rationalize gnomic sayings without doing damage to the impact they have in their original formulation.[19] So as a rule, both the effective transmission and reception of gnomic wisdom relies on aesthetic discrimination and an adeptness at the literary craft.

In these respects the maxim resembles the epigram, a brief, witty poem whose best representatives may be found in the *Anthologia Graeca*.[20] Indeed, some epigrammatists formulate maxims and integrate them into their poems, while others avail themselves of ethical themes familiar from gnomic texts.[21] On the other hand, many of the same literary features that characterize epigrammatic writing also inform the composition of even the most serious maxims; among these are meter and metrical effects, parallelism, antithesis, chiasmus, paronomasia, asyndeton, anaphora, and rhyme. There are,

---

[17] Von Rad, *Wisdom in Israel*, 30.

[18] On the oral qualities of maxims see Thompson, *Form and Function*, 25-27; Crossan, *In Fragments*, 37-42; Kevin Robb, "Preliterate Ages and the Linguistic Art of Heraclitus," *Language and Thought in Early Greek Philosophy* (ed. idem; La Salle, IL: Hegeler Institute, 1983) 153-206; Robert J. Connors, "Greek Rhetoric and the Transition from Orality," *Philosophy and Rhetoric* 19 (1986) 38-64, esp. 45, 56; Norrick, *How Proverbs Mean*, 43-46; cf. Walter J. Ong, *Orality and Literacy: The Technologizing of the Word* (New Accents; London, New York: Methuen, 1982) 26-27, 31-77.

[19] Jolles, *Einfache Formen*, 160-170; William McKane, *Proverbs: A New Approach* (OTL; Philadelphia: Westminster, 1970) 22-26; Williams, *Those Who Ponder Proverbs*, 69-78.

[20] Text, translation, and commentary: Andrew S. F. Gow and Denys L. Page, eds., *The Greek Anthology: Hellenistic Epigrams* (2 vols.; Cambridge: Cambridge University Press, 1965); idem, eds., *The Greek Anthology: The Garland of Philip and Some Contemporary Epigrams* (2 vols.; Cambridge: Cambridge University Press, 1968); Denys L. Page, ed., *Further Greek Epigrams* (Cambridge: Cambridge University Press, 1981).

[21] Jules Labarbe, "Aspects gnomiques de l'épigramme grecque," *Foundation Hardt pour L'Etude de L'Antiquité Classique, Entretiens* 14 (1967) 349-383.

nevertheless, distinctions to be made between the two forms, especially with respect to length and function. While epigrams are by definition concise, on average they consist of two or more sentences and are frequently several lines long. Hence epigrams represent more developed and complex compositions than maxims. In addition, the epigrammatists write chiefly to delight and amuse their readers; the classifications applied to certain epigrams--funerary, dedicatory, erotic, and so forth--suggest some of the possible secondary functions that may be attached to them as well. Although the authors of gnomic sayings are also sensitive to the artistic impact of their compositions, concerns of this sort are clearly subordinate to ethical and instructional ones.[22]

Wisdom sayings do not record observations about peculiar or singular occurrences, nor are they statements of technical or necessary facts, which is often the case with the ἀφορισμός (aphorism). This term, though it may refer to a maxim, includes any sort of pithy, summarizing sentence, particularly those of a scientific nature, such as Hippocrates' ΑΦΟΡΙΣΜΟΙ.[23] Maxims, on the other hand, represent subjective assertions regarding ethical purpose, choice, or action derived from what most people agree is likely or possible.[24]

---

[22] Cf. Küchler, *Weisheitstraditionen*, 237-240; Kloppenborg, *The Formation of Q*, 290.

[23] Text and translation: W. H. S. Jones, trans., *Hippocrates* (LCL; 4 vols.; Cambridge: Harvard University Press; London: Heinemann, 1923-1931) 4.98-221; cf. Jonathan Barnes, "Aphorism and Argument," in Robb, *Language and Thought*, 92-94; further see Gilles Maloney, Paul Potter, and Winnie Frohn-Villeneuve, *Répartition des oeuvres hippocratiques pars genres littéraires* (Québec: Université Laval, 1979). Quintilian's use of the technical term *sententia* is also very broad, referring to virtually any sort of short saying, including the chreia, see *Institutio Oratoria* 1.9.3-5, 8.5.1-35; cf. M. L. Clarke, *Rhetoric at Rome: A Historical Survey* (New York: Barnes and Noble, 1953) 127-128; Jean Cousin, *Etudes sur Quintilian* (2 vols.; Paris: Boivin, 1935-1936) [reprint, Amsterdam: Schippers, 1967] 1.432-436; Lewis A. Sussman, *The Elder Seneca* (Mnemosyne Sup 51; Leiden: Brill, 1978) 35-38, also s.v. sententiae; Crossan, *In Fragments*, 230-232; Kloppenborg, *The Formation of Q*, 291 n. 91.

[24] On the ethical aspects of maxims see Aristotle *Rhetorica* 2.21; Seneca *Epistulae Morales* 95; Horna, "Gnome," 74-75; Demetrios K. Karathanasis, *Sprichwörter und sprichwörtliche Redensarten des Altertums in den rhetorischen Schriften* (Speyer am Rhein: Pilger, 1936) 60-91; Karl Bielohlawek, *Hypotheke und Gnome: Untersuchungen über die Griechische Weisheitsdichtung der vorhellenistischen Zeit* (Philologus Sup 32.3; Leipzig: Dieterich'sche Verlagsbuchhandlung, 1940) 59-73; Hans Margolius, "On the Uses of Aphorisms in Ethics," *The Educational Forum* 28 (1963) 79-85 [reprinted as "Aphorismen und Ethik," in Neumann, *Der Aphorismus*, 293-304]; Jolles, *Einfache Formen*, 150-156; Lausberg, *Handbuch*, §§ 872-873; Hermisson, *Studien zur israelitischen Spruchweisheit*, 64-96; von Rad, *Wisdom in Israel*, 74-96, 113-137; Antje Hellwig, *Untersuchungen zur Theorie der Rhetorik bei Platon und Aristoteles* (Hypomnemata 38; Göttingen: Vandenhoeck & Ruprecht, 1973) 264-267; Thompson, *Form and Function*, 28-38, 67-80; John J. Collins, "Proverbial Wisdom and the Yahwist Vision," *Semeia* 17 (1980) 1-17; Berger, "Hellenistische Gattungen," 1051-72; Norrick, *How Proverbs Mean*, 41-43; Abraham J. Malherbe, *Moral Exhortation: A Greco-Roman Sourcebook* (LEC 4; Philadelphia: Westminster, 1986) 109-111; cf. Roger D.

Definition and Description

In formulating a gnomic saying an author seizes upon some widely recognized principle regarding the conduct of daily life and then applies it to a practical situation of universal concern. Because they strive to create generalized statements based upon representative experiences and insight, maxims are "infinite" and timeless, though their subject matter is frequently quite concrete and specific.[25] Maxims normally purport to embody the forever and universally valid findings of common human experience; they are ethical conclusions which, through their literary formulation, become available for future edification and manipulation. As a practical conclusion, a gnomic saying is "self-confirming, commending itself to empirical validation or to disconfirmation" in various ethical situations.[26] In this way it may operate as a principle of ethical decision-making, or as a means of categorizing human actions and their consequences. Generally, gnomic utterances endeavor to create models of thought and behavior that will guide and correct the lives of those who use and adhere to them.[27]

While maxims furnish insights of broad validity, they are not accompanied by instructions on how and when they may be appropriately utilized. By virtue of its concreteness of language and imagery and specificity of subject matter, the relevance of a maxim is not confined to a singular event, but rather the saying reveals a recurring pattern of ethical phenomena and then recommends itself as a means of depicting or controlling these phenomena. Yet it is this very concreteness and openness that ensures that a maxim falls short of a mandatory rule or natural law. Because the suitability of gnomic sayings in particular situations rests on limited generalizations and partial similarities, they are more appropriately described as ethical paradigms than laws. Maxims do not 'fit' every comparable situation in the same way or to the same degree, and so an amount of tentativeness and subjectivity comes into play when considering their composition, application, and interpretation.[28] These qualities are manifest in

---

Abrahams, "Introductory Remarks to a Rhetorical Theory of Folklore," *Journal of American Folklore* 81 (1968) 143-158; Kenneth J. Dover, *Greek Popular Morality in the Time of Plato and Aristotle* (Berkeley: University of California Press, 1974) 50-51.

[25] Lausberg, *Handbuch*, §§ 872-873.

[26] Crenshaw, "Wisdom," 231, cf. 235.

[27] See further Arland D. Jacobson, "Proverbs and Social Control: A New Paradigm for Wisdom Studies," *Gnosticism and the Early Christian World: In Honor of James M. Robinson* (ed. James E. Goehring, Charles W. Hedrick, Jack T. Sanders, with Hans Dieter Betz; FF 2; Sonoma, CA: Polebridge, 1990) 75-88 and the sources cited there.

[28] On the comments made in this paragraph see Abrahams, "Introductory Remarks," 143-158; McKane, *Proverbs*, 25-33; Heda Jason, "Proverbs in Society: The Problem of Meaning and Function," *Proverbium* 17 (1971) 617-623; Barley, "Structural Approach," 739-741; von Rad, *Wisdom in Israel*, 33-34, 97-110, 115-124, 138-143; Röhrich and Mieder, *Sprichwort*,

a gnomic collection, where there is seldom any attempt to establish a consistent ethos or viewpoint. Sayings are simply juxtaposed without regard to their mutual implications. It is left to the reader to resolve the ambiguities and inconsistencies and to construe a comprehensive meaning for the text.[29]

These features of gnomic discourse are brought into relief when the maxim is compared with certain related forms. The *praeceptum* (precept), especially as it is described by Seneca in *Epistulae Morales* 94 and 95, resembles the maxim in form and function.[30] Precepts are practical rules that counsel proper behavior in typical ethical situations. They are often linked with what the Stoics identified as "appropriate acts" (καθήκοντα or *officia*) and are derived from the "preferred" goals of relative value (προηγμένα).[31] Precepts are not philosophical teaching *per se* but rather operate as advice and reminders, rousing the audience and focusing their attention. Seneca argues that precepts are beneficial because they refresh the memory, help prioritize confusing matters, and articulate a suitable ethical course. A fairly large number of Seneca's precepts may also be designated maxims, and he provides some examples in *Epistulae Morales* 94.27-28. However, by *praecepta* Seneca

---

78-82; Collins, "Proverbial Wisdom," 1-17; Barbara Kirshenblatt-Gimblett, "Toward a Theory of Proverb Meaning," *The Wisdom of Many: Essays on the Proverb* (ed. Alan Dundes and Wolfgang Mieder; Garland Folklore Classics 1; New York, London: Garland, 1981) 111-121 [originally in *Proverbium* 22 (1973) 821-827]; Peter Seitel, "Proverbs: A Social Use of Metaphor," in Dundes and Mieder, *The Wisdom of Many*, 122-139 [originally in *Genre* 2 (1969) 143-161]; Williams, *Those Who Ponder Proverbs*, 35-46; Fontaine, *Traditional Sayings*, 43-71; cf. Arvo Krikmann, "On Denotative Indefiniteness of Proverbs," *Proverbium: Yearbook of International Proverb Scholarship* 1 (1984) 47-91; idem, "Some Additional Aspects of the Semantic Indefiniteness of Proverbs," *Proverbium: Yearbook of International Proverb Scholarship* 2 (1985) 58-85.

[29] See the comments in Chapter Two on gnomologia.

[30] I. G. Kidd, "The Relation of Stoic Intermediates to the *Summum Bonum*, With Reference to Change in the Stoa," *CQ* 5 (1955) 181-194 [reprinted as "Stoic Intermediates and the End for Man," *Problems in Stoicism* (ed. A. A. Long; London: University of London, Athlone, 1971) 150-172]; idem, "Moral Actions and Rules in Stoic Ethics," *The Stoics* (ed. John M. Rist; Berkeley, Los Angeles: University of California Press, 1978) 247-258; Hildegard Cancik, *Untersuchungen zu Senecas Epistulae morales* (Spudasmata 18; Hildesheim: Olms, 1967) 42-45; A. Dihle, "Posidonius' System of Moral Philosophy," *JHS* 93 (1973) 50-57; cf. Winfried Trillitzsch, *Senecas Beweisführung* (Berlin: Akademie-Verlag, 1962) 67-68. For a more comprehensive view of Seneca's letters see Robert Coleman, "The Artful Moralist: A Study of Seneca's Epistolary Style," *CQ* 24 (1974) 276-289; D. A. Russell, "Letters to Lucilius," in *Seneca* (ed. C. D. N. Costa; Greek and Latin Studies, Classical Literature and its Influence; London, Boston: Routledge & Kegan Paul, 1974) 70-95.

[31] Dihle ("Posidonius' System," 51, 54) refers to Cicero *De Officiis* 3.5, Epictetus *Encheiridion* 30, Clement of Alexandria *Paedagogus* 1.107; cf. A. D. Leeman, "Posidonius the Dialectician in Seneca's Letters," *Mnemosyne* 7 (1954) 233-240; Kidd, "Moral Actions," 251.

implies paraenesis in a far wider sense than just gnomic sayings, and so the term seems to encompass virtually any sort of advice, admonition, or exhortation. Subsequently, many of Seneca's precepts are not gnomic at all, but specific injunctions to perform particular actions. The recipient of such precepts is not expected so much to interpret and apply the commands rationally as merely to obey.

The corollary or reference point of these precepts is what Seneca calls *decreta*, the dogmatic or categorical doctrines of an ethical system.[32] As he argues in *Epistulae Morales* 95, such doctrinal statements are necessary for acquiring virtue since they explain how and why the sorts of actions indicated by precepts should be carried out. Because these axioms are understood as binding truths, they may not be ignored or controverted by adherents of the philosophical system from which they derive. The abstract and theoretical quality of *decreta* differentiates them from maxims, which characteristically display more concrete and pragmatic concerns. In addition, gnomic wisdom does not command the same degree of irrefutability and absoluteness as *decreta*, but admits of limitations and contingencies in its regimen of thought.

The qualities that distinguish the wisdom saying from the *praeceptum* and *decretum* also differentiate it from other forms such as legal statements and oracular utterances, though here again the borders are not always sharply drawn. That the coining of maxims was somehow connected with legal practice in ancient Israel seems clear, and a number of wisdom sayings resemble legal statements in both form and content.[33] Among the Greeks, several gnomic collections, particularly the *Praecepta Delphica*,[34] functioned in a legal, even cultic, capacity in their respective communities.[35] In addition, some of the

---

[32] Kidd, "Moral Actions," 252-253.

[33] Erhard Gerstenberger, *Wesen und Herkunft des apodiktischen Rechts* (WMANT 20; Neukirchen-Vluyn: Neukirchener Verlag, 1965); Wolfgang Richter, *Recht und Ethos: Versuch einer Ortung des weisheitlichen Mahnspruches* (SANT 15; München: Kösel, 1966) 68-146; C. M. Carmichael, "Deuteronomic Laws, Wisdom, and Historical Traditions," *JSS* 12 (1967) 198-206; Thompson, *Form and Function*, 33-34, 76-79; Küchler, *Weisheitstraditionen*, 52-54; Nel, *Structure and Ethos*, 92-97; Phillip R. Callaway, "Deuteronomy 21.18-21: Proverbial Wisdom and Law," *JBL* 103 (1984) 341-353; von Lips, *Weisheitliche Traditionen*, 51-69; cf. Joseph Blenkinsopp, *Wisdom and Law in the Old Testament: The Ordering of Life in Israel and Early Judaism* (Oxford Bible Series; London, New York: Oxford University Press, 1983).

[34] Text: Wilhelm Dittenberger, *Sylloge Inscriptionum Graecarum* (4 vols.; Leipzig: Hirzel, 1920³) [reprint, Hildesheim: Olms, 1960] 3.392-397 (no. 1268); Friedrich Hiller von Gaertringen, *Inscriptiones Graecae* 12.3 (Berlin: Reimer, 1920³) no. 188; cf. F. W. Hasluck, "Inscriptions from the Cyzicus District," *JHS* 27 (1907) 62-63.

[35] Küchler, *Weisheitstraditionen*, 241-243, 258-259; Berger, "Hellenistische Gattungen," 1053-1054, 1069-1073; Kloppenborg, *The Formation of Q*, 337.

figures to whom gnomic anthologies are attributed, Solomon for instance, were also noteworthy political or legal figures.[36]

Despite these connections, there are crucial differences with respect to the nature of the authority and the type of interpretation appropriate for these forms. By and large, gnomic wisdom does not demand the same obligatory or compulsory acceptance as the law. Maxims are not binding in all applicable situations at all times for all people. They are not enforced by any absolute or impartial authority. Instead, the prevalence of a maxim depends upon individual evaluations of its charm or utility. Further, maxims are rarely subsumed under any highly coordinated or integrated system of thought comparable to that of a legal document. While their stance is apparently impartial and uncompromising, maxims have meanings that are often restricted, sometimes contradictory; they encapsulate a series of largely unconnected glimpses of the concrete manifestations of order rather than articulate an abstract or theoretical scheme. As a result, the reasoning connected with gnomic wisdom presents a paradox, for while its ostensible purpose is to establish order and maintain continuity, the progression of thought in many gnomic texts seems fractured and unsystematic--they have the effect of jolting the reader from one judgement or view to the next. Therefore aphoristic thinking is broad and universal, but individuals are permitted to stand alone in their particularity in so far as they are not bound to some contrived set of rules or abstractions.[37]

---

[36] Walter Brueggeman (*In Man We Trust: The Neglected Side of Biblical Faith* [Atlanta: Knox, 1972]) concentrates on the monarchy as the locus of Israelite wisdom; cf. Albrecht Alt, "Solomonic Wisdom," in Crenshaw, *Studies*, 102-112 [originally, "Die Weisheit Salomos," *TLZ* 76 (1951) 139-144]; R. B. Y. Scott, "Solomon and the Beginnings of Wisdom in Israel," *Wisdom in Israel and in the Ancient Near East: Presented to Professor Harold Henry Rowley* (ed. Martin Noth and D. Winton Thomas; VTSup 3; Leiden: Brill, 1955) 262-279 [reprint, Crenshaw, *Studies*, 84-101]; Glendon E. Bryce, *A Legacy of Wisdom: The Egyptian Contribution to the Wisdom of Israel* (Lewisburg: Bucknell University Press; London: Associated University Presses, 1979) 163-210. Heraclitus and some of the Seven Sages were known as lawgivers and political leaders, see Heinrich Dörrie, "Herakleitos," *KP* 2 (1967) 1045-1048; Hans Gärtner, "Die Sieben Weisen," *KP* 5 (1975) 177-178 and the references provided there. On legal proverbs see Taylor, *The Proverb*, 86-97; Röhrich and Mieder, *Sprichwort*, 72-77.

[37] Jolles, *Einfache Formen*, 150-159; Philip E. Lewis, "The Discourse of the Maxim," *Diacritics* 2 (1972) 41-48; Hans Margolius, "System und Aphorismus," in Neumann, *Der Aphorismus*, 280-292 [originally in *Schopenhauer-Jahrbuch* 41 (1960) 117-124]; Franz H. Mautner, "Der Aphorismus als literarische Gattung," in Neumann, *Der Aphorismus*, 19-74, esp. 51-52 [originally in *Zeitschrift für Aesthetik und Allgemeine Kunstwissenschaft* 27 (1933) 132-175]; Zimmerli, "The Structure of Old Testament Wisdom," 175-207; Küchler, *Weisheitstraditionen*, 163-164; Williams, *Those Who Ponder Proverbs*, 26-34, 47-63; Nel, *Structure and Ethos*, 89-97; Collins, "Proverbial Wisdom," 1-17; Kloppenborg, *The*

Maxims also display certain material and formal similarities with oracular utterances. Some of the responses known to have originated from the Delphic oracle, for instance, appear in whole or in part in the gnomic anthologies of the *Corpus Paroemiographorum Graecorum*. The editors of these proverb collections would also on occasion attribute an oracular origin to some of their proverbs.[38] A number of utterances described by ancient writers as oracles may be categorized as gnomic sayings as well, especially γνῶθι σαυτόν ("know thyself"), inscribed at the entrance to the Delphic oracle and ascribed to numerous wise sages.[39] On a more basic level, maxims share some topical and morphological characteristics with oracles, though the latter admit of a far wider range of forms and subject matter and, initially at least, are designed in response to specific inquiries. In meaning, both maxims and oracles are often in need of subsequent clarification and, as it were, decoding; their interpretation is open-ended and seldom plain or complete upon first hearing.[40]

By the same token, while some gnomic collections may associate their sayings with an oracle, they do not normally represent themselves as divine in origin or authority.[41] Instead they are ascribed to wise and gifted individuals, whose inspired insight enables them to perceive and express the complexities of human life and experience, whether it be divinely instituted or not. So maxims do not, like oracles, reveal inevitable predictions or unalterable judgements. In addition, while an oracle may be initially obscure or opaque, it is intended to have only one meaning and one application; any other understandings are misunderstandings. With gnomic wisdom, however, there are no such limitations. New meanings and applications for a wisdom saying are not only

---

Formation of Q, 302-303; cf. Paul Requadt, "Das Aphoristische Denken," in Neumann, *Der Aphorismus*, 331-377 [originally in idem, *Lichtenberg: zum Problem der deutschen Aphoristik* (Stuttgart: Kohlhammer, 1964²) 133-165].

[38] Joseph Frontenrose, *The Delphic Oracle: Its Responses and Operations* (Berkeley: University of California Press, 1978) 24-35, 43-53, 83-87, 440; cf. Seneca *Epistulae Morales* 94.27-28.

[39] See below p. 180 n. 97.

[40] Frontenrose, *Delphic Oracle*, 58-87; cf. Michael Fishbane, *Biblical Interpretation in Ancient Israel* (Oxford: Clarendon, 1985) 443-446, 458-524. Some useful ancient discussions of the oracle may be found in Plutarch *Moralia* 384c-438e; text and translation: Frank Cole Babbitt, et al., trans., *Plutarch's Moralia* (LCL; 15 vols.; Cambridge: Harvard University Press; London: Heinemann, 1927-69) 5.194-501.

[41] Kloppenborg, *The Formation of Q*, 301-302. There is, of course, a strong theological background for the Jewish wisdom collections, but their source is still represented as human; see, for instance, von Rad, *Wisdom in Israel*, 32-33, 53-73; James L. Crenshaw, "Prolegomenon," in Crenshaw, *Studies*, 22-35; Berend Gemser, "The Spiritual Structure of Biblical Aphoristic Wisdom," in Crenshaw, *Studies*, 208-219 [originally in *Adhuc Loquitur: Collected Essays of Dr. Berend Gemser* (ed. A. van Selms and A. S. van der Woude; Leiden: Brill, 1968) 138-149].

anticipated but desirable. Because a maxim is concrete, paradigmatic, and subjective, its effectiveness in a given context, as well as its aptness in future surroundings, depend upon the hearer's ability to discern the limitations of the gnome itself and to perceive correctly the situations in which it is to be utilized. The interpretation of any maxim, therefore, invites rational inquiry and reappraisal as the limited nature of its perspective and application manifests itself under scrutiny. Consequently the communication associated with gnomic wisdom is not only keenly rhetorical but also decidedly heuristic. The gnomic style self-consciously promotes intellectual reflection, ethical criticism, and personal creativity, and so it conveys a relatively high degree of individualization, to the extent that an individual may accept, reject, modify, and invent maxims. Because of these paradoxical qualities, gnomic wisdom may not only transmit and reaffirm traditional order, but also undermine and transcend order with a vision of counter-order.[42]

The Structure of the Gnomic Saying

Now that the basic characteristics and functions of gnomic wisdom have been discussed, we may move on to its morphology. To begin with, a maxim may be categorized according to the tense of its main verb. A maxim governed by an indicative verb is a *wisdom sentence*, and by an imperative verb a *wisdom admonition*. The difference in the hermeneutic that these two categories recommend for themselves should be emphasized but not overstated.[43] The wisdom admonition, on one hand, directly addresses the reader, demanding acceptance and the desired response. Gnomic wisdom's instructional function,

---

[42] For more on the comments in this paragraph see Stern, *Lichtenberg*, passim; William A. Beardslee, "Uses of the Proverb in the Synoptic Gospels," *Int* 24 (1970) 61-73; Lewis, "The Discourse of the Maxim," 41-48; Hermann U. Asemisson, "Notizen über Aphorismus," in Neumann, *Der Aphorismus*, 159-176, esp. 161-169 [originally in *Trivium* 7 (1949) 144-161]; Wilhelm Grenzmann, "Probleme des Aphorismus," in Neumann, *Der Aphorismus*, 177-208, esp. 187-197 [originally in *Jahrbuch für Aesthetik und Allgemeine Kunstwissenschaft* (Stuttgart, 1951) 122-144]; Requadt, "Das Aphoristische Denken," passim; Gerald T. Sheppard, *Wisdom as a Hermeneutical Construct* (BZAW 151; Berlin, New York: de Gruyter, 1980) 100-119; Williams, *Those Who Ponder Proverbs*, 47-63 and passim; Crossan, *In Fragments*, 3-18; Winton, *The Proverbs of Jesus*, 71-83.

[43] On the relationship between indicative and imperative in gnomic wisdom, see Zimmerli, "The Structure of Old Testament Wisdom," 178-184; Hermisson, *Studien zur israelitischen Spruchweisheit*, 160-162; von Rad, *Wisdom in Israel*, 31; Crenshaw, "Wisdom," 231-236; Küchler, *Weisheitstraditionen*, 162-163; Nel, *Structure and Ethos*, 16-17; Zeller, *Mahnsprüche*, 15-32.

somewhat concealed in the sentence, is overt in the admonition, where the ethical appeal and educative goal is made explicit. However, though it conveys a forceful or didactic tone, the admonition often betrays descriptive or observational features as well, and, like all gnomic sayings, it remains open to a certain degree of qualification and re-interpretation. Thus it possesses the same categorical tone and individual alignment as the sentence. On the other hand, within most every wisdom sentence it is possible to detect an implied imperative. Maxims of this sort often exhibit an epideictic function in so far as they posit a model of behavior to be accepted or rejected by the audience, thus heightening their level of ethical awareness. Furthermore, wisdom sentences are often employed in contexts that are clearly didactic or hortatory, and so are transformed from mere empirical observations into rules applied to ethical decision-making. For the interpretation of a maxim, therefore, what seems at least as important as the tense of the main verb is the maxim's rhetorical environment, which involves such matters as the nature of the writer's authority, the motivations and purposes in writing, his relationship with the audience, and the literary context provided for the saying.[44]

While linguistic distinctions such as wisdom admonition and wisdom sentence have their place in the interpretive task, they are hardly an adequate means of depicting the design and logic of a literary form as complex and fluid as the maxim. In his investigation of English proverbs, folklorist Alan Dundes attempted to go beyond the linguistic or surface structure of gnomic sayings in order to analyze their underlying patterns of thought.[45] His goal was not to describe the content or images of these sayings, nor to isolate their grammatical or architectural formulae. His structural method, rather, suggests some of the characteristic ways in which gnomic forms organize and relate their concepts. Subsequent scholars have adopted modified versions of Dundes' method in the study of other bodies of texts, including the wisdom literature of the Hebrew Bible, and it may be effectively employed in our introduction of Hellenistic maxims.[46]

---

[44] "[E]ven when the sentence appears to have no didactic intent, one must recognize the effect of the didactic context into which it has ultimately been placed. Hence the sentence is seldom morally neutral." Crenshaw, "Prolegomenon," 15; cf. Fontaine, *Traditional Sayings*, 139-170; Norrick, *How Proverbs Mean*, 41-43.

[45] Alan Dundes, "On the Structure of the Proverb," in Dundes and Mieder, *The Wisdom of Many*, 43-64 [originally in *Proverbium* 25 (1975) 961-973; also reprinted in *Analytic Essays in Folklore* (ed. Alan Dundes; Studies in Folklore 2; The Hague, Paris: Mouton, 1975) 103-118].

[46] Fontaine, *Traditional Sayings*, 34-36, 63-67; Raymond C. van Leeuwen, *Context and Meaning in Proverbs 25-27* (SBLDS 96; Atlanta: Scholars Press, 1988) 47-54; Winton, *The*

Dundes' analysis starts with the assumption that all maxims depend to some extent upon "topic-comment" constructions. The topic is the apparent referent, the thing described or qualified, while the comment is the assertion made regarding the topic. The topic and comment may be identical with the maxim's grammatical subject and predicate, though this is not necessary in each case. According to Dundes, every maxim consists of at least a single "descriptive element," that is, a unit with one topic and one comment, for example μηδὲν ἄγαν ("nothing overmuch" [Solon 1]).[47]

Within the topic-comment system a very wide range of material relationships is possible. Dundes attempts to make sense of these possibilities by situating topic-comment constructions on a semantic axis, which serves to coordinate and relate typical patterns of thought. Towards one end of the axis are those sayings which are termed "identificational," and towards the other those that are considered "oppositional." Some maxims are primarily identificational, others primarily oppositional, but most are to varying degrees combinations or composites of identificational and oppositional features. In his investigation, Dundes described in what ways maxims are identificational or oppositional and what sorts of identifications and oppositions are characteristically found in these sayings. The important categories may be represented on the axis as follows:

```
        identificational    ▲
                            │    equation
                            │    non-opposition
                            │    similarity
                            │    cause-and-effect
                            │    comparison
                            │
                            │    contrast
                            │    causal contradiction
                            │    antithesis
                            │    negation
        oppositional        ▼
```

Below, each of these categories will be described in turn, drawing from the Hellenistic sources of both Jewish-Christian and Greek maxims for illustrations.

Proverbs of Jesus, 36-52; cf. Röhrich and Mieder, *Sprichwort*, 60-64; Norrick, *How Proverbs Mean*, 55-57.

[47] Text: Diels and Kranz, *Die Fragmente der Vorsokratiker*, 1.63.14; my translation.

Beginning at the identificational end of the axis and moving towards the center, we encounter first those maxims exhibiting an "equational structure." This structure may take on various transformations. If the saying consists of an explicit identity then there are virtually no oppositional features. Other equational maxims may suggest a definition, or an equivalence of topic and comment, or an invariable association of the two. These are functions for which maxims are well-suited, and in fact an entire gnomic anthology, the collection of sayings in the ΒΙΟΣ ΣΕΚΟΥΝΔΟΥ ΦΙΛΟΣΟΦΟΥ, is devoted to this task.[48] In the equational type of maxim the verb εἰμί occurs regularly, as well as the omission of the copula altogether. Some examples:

μέτρον ἄριστον
Due measure is best. [Cleobulus 1][49]

καλὸν ἡσυχία
Silence is good. [Periander 2][50]

ὁ μὴ ἰώμενος ἑαυτὸν ἐν τοῖς ἔργοις αὐτοῦ,
ἀδελφός ἐστι τοῦ λυμαινομένου ἑαυτόν.
A man who does not help himself by his labor,
is brother of him that ruins himself. [LXX Proverbs 18.9]

Wisdom admonitions of the equational type frequently call upon the readers to identify or associate themselves with a certain ideal or model, for instance:

ὁποῖος θέλεις εὐχόμενος εἶναι, ἀεὶ ἔσο.
Whatever sort of person you desire to be when praying, be such always.
[Sextus *Sententiae* 80][51]

Related to this are maxims characterized by Dundes as merely "nonoppositional." In Greek literature the best representatives of this type are simple, terse commands such as μὴ θρασύνου (Solon 13) or γνῶθι σαυτόν (Chilon 1).[52] In these admonitions we might consider the addressee to be the

---

[48] For text and translation see Ben E. Perry, ed., *Secundus the Silent Philosopher* (APA Philological Monographs 22; Ithaca: Cornell University Press, 1964) 78-91. The sayings collection consists of twenty questions followed by a series of two-word responses, e.g. τί ἄνθρωπος; τύχης παίγνιον, φυγὰς βίου, etc.

[49] Text: Diels and Kranz, *Die Fragmente der Vorsokratiker*, 1.63.2; my translation.

[50] Text: Ibidem, 1.65.15; my translation.

[51] Text and translation: Richard A. Edwards and Robert A. Wild, eds., *The Sentences of Sextus* (SBLTT 22; Chico, CA: Scholars Press, 1981) 24-25.

[52] Text: Diels and Kranz, *Die Fragmente der Vorsokratiker*, 1.63.20, 25.

topic, while the comment is the command itself. Such maxims are, in a way, equational, since they require correspondence between topic and comment.

Another variety of identificational maxim aims at classification of the topic. A saying of this type may describe its topic by stating of what sort it is or what category it belongs to:

ὁ πλοῦτος οὐ τῶν ἀγαθῶν,
ἡ πολυτέλεια τῶν κακῶν,
ἡ σωφροσύνη τῶν ἀγαθῶν.
Wealth is not one of the good things,
extravagance is one of the bad,
discretion is one of the good. [*Gnomologium Epictetum* 10a][53]

Some maxims classify their topic by depicting an attribute that is considered most characteristic of it. Others may group the topic with persons, actions, or situations that share similar features; in some cases the saying may suggest that the same label applies to different activities, for example:

τὸν φίλον κακῶς μὴ λέγε μηδ' εὖ τὸν ἐχθρόν·
ἀσυλλόγιστον γὰρ τὸ τοιοῦτον.
Don't speak evil of a friend nor well of an enemy,
for things of this sort are unreasonable. [Pittacus 8][54]

Many so-called numerical sayings may also be included under this heading. R. B. Y. Scott observed in Proverbs 30.15-31 several examples of "the numerical proverb of classification." He also specified other sayings that make use of "progressive classification," such as Proverbs 27.3.[55] Classificatory sayings represent generalizations that draw from observations about a number of specific instances to a conclusion about the larger class to which the instances belong; the conclusions argue that what holds true of the class will also apply to its individual members. These maxims serve to organize and situate phenomena and so aid in establishing criteria for evaluating specific ethical actions and ideas.

Another sort of identification present in maxims is similarity, resemblance, or analogy between the topic and the comment. Many of these sayings employ

---

[53] Text: Heinrich Schenkl, ed., *Epicteti Dissertationes ab Arriano Digestae* (BT; Stuttgart: Teubner, 1916²) [reprint 1965] 479-480; my translation.

[54] Text: Diels and Kranz, *Die Fragmente der Vorsokratiker*, 1.64.15-16; my translation.

[55] R. B. Y. Scott, *Proverbs. Ecclesiastes* (AB 18; Garden City, New York: Doubleday, 1965) 7.

metaphors or similes. The *Gnomica Homoeomata*, edited by Anton Elter, is an anthology of "gnomic similitudes" of this type;[56] number 47 is representative:

τῆς ἀλαζονείας καθάπερ τῶν κεχρυσωμένων ὅπλων,
οὐχ ὅμοιά ἐστι τὰ ἐντὸς τοῖς ἐκτός.
With false pretension, as with a gold-plated shield,
the inside is not the same as the outside.[57]

Often these maxims will use comparison to make abstract or difficult concepts more accessible; they may also imply the true implications or more profound meaning of an action:

οὐρανὸς ὑψηλός, γῆ δὲ βαθεῖα,
καρδία δὲ βασιλέως ἀνεξέλεγκτος.
Heaven is high and earth is deep,
and a king's heart impenetrable. [LXX Proverbs 25.3]

μὴ διαμάχου μετὰ ἀνθρώπου γλωσσώδους,
καὶ μὴ ἐπιστοιβάσῃς ἐπὶ τὸ πῦρ αὐτοῦ ξύλα.
Don't argue with a chatter-box of a man,
and (so) don't heap wood upon his fire. [Ben Sira 8.3]

Such vivid images clarify ethical actions and attitudes by making them more concrete and memorable. The parallels that these sayings draw are legitimate and useful because of their ability to assign the topic and comment to the same class or category on a specific level. By identifying a particular similarity, the author focuses attention on those qualities or characteristics of the phenomenon in question that are deemed to be especially important or applicable.

The next category of wisdom sayings deals with cause and effect, and with the consequences and implications of ethical decisions. Many maxims of this type show how the presence of one quality or condition invariably produces another:[58]

---

[56] Anton Elter, *Gnomica Homoeomata* (5 parts; Bonn: C. George, 1900-1904). Cf. the similar collections in ΕΚ ΤΩΝ ΠΑΡΑ ΠΥΘΑΓΟΡΕΙΟΙΣ ΑΛΛΟΙΣ ΤΕ ΟΜΟΙΩΜΑΤΩΝ in *Fragmenta philosophorum graecorum* (ed. Friedrich W. A. Mullach; 3 vols.; Paris: Didot, 1881, 1883) 1.485-509.

[57] Text: Elter, *Gnomica Homoeomata*, 5.10; my translation.

[58] Similar in function are many of the so-called gnomic *concatenations* examined by, among others, Dibelius, *James*, 94-99.

ἰσότης φιλότητα ἀπεργάζεται
Equality produces amity. [Plato *Leges* 757A][59]

ὁ μὲν φθονούμενος πάντοτε ἀνθεῖ,
ὁ δὲ φθονῶν μαραίνεται.
Whenever the one who is envied flourishes,
the envious one wastes away. [Testament of Simeon 3.3][60]

Wisdom admonitions of this type often supply motives for their commands by specifying the final result or goal, or by suggesting possible outcomes, either positive or negative:

μὴ πίστευε τύχῃ καὶ πιστεύσεις θεῷ.
Don't believe in luck and you will believe in God.
[Moschion ΥΠΟΘΗΚΑΙ 10][61]

τίμα τὸ ἄριστον, ἵνα καὶ ἄρχῃ ὑπὸ τοῦ ἀρίστου.
Honor what is best that you may be governed by what is best.
[Sextus *Sententiae* 42][62]

μὴ διαμάχου μετὰ ἀνθρώπου δυνάστου,
μήποτε ἐμπέσῃς εἰς τὰς χεῖρας αὐτοῦ.
Don't contend with a strong man,
lest you fall into his hands. [Ben Sira 8.1]

By drawing a definite causal link between topic and comment, these sayings show how one phenomenon may stand for or represent another. The emphasis on regularly recurring connections in cause-and-effect maxims aids in giving human experience a sense of predictability and a semblance of order.

The final category of sayings found on the identificational half of the axis is that group that compares the topic with the comment. Like the maxims that address similarity or resemblance in the topic-comment relation, these sayings focus on a particular feature or characteristic common to both elements. Comparative sayings, however, concentrate on how the topic possesses a

---

[59] Text and translation: R. G. Bury, trans., *Plato: Laws* (LCL; 2 vols.; London: Heinemann; Cambridge: Harvard University Press, 1926) 1.412-413.

[60] Text: Marinus de Jonge, ed. (with Harm W. Hollander, H. J. de Jonge, Th. Korteweg), *The Testaments of the Twelve Patriarchs: A Critical Edition of the Greek Text* (PVTG 1.2; Leiden: Brill, 1978) 17; my translation.

[61] Text: Schenkl, *Epicteti Dissertationes*, 496; my translation.

[62] Text and translation: Edwards and Wild, *The Sentences of Sextus*, 20-21.

greater or lesser degree or proportion of this feature than the comment. Thus these sayings raise questions of priority or relative value. For instance:

οἶνος καὶ μουσικὰ εὐφραίνουσι καρδίαν,
καὶ ὑπὲρ ἀμφότερα ἀγάπησις σοφίας.
Wine and music rejoice the heart,
but above them both is love of wisdom. [Ben Sira 40.20]

By means of the concrete comparison, this maxim, like others in the category, emphasizes some aspect of the topic that is easily understood and felt but not immediately apparent, and so points out in exactly what way it is superior. Other sayings may use comparison to indicate some more profound or edifying characteristic of an ethical action or idea:

οὐχ οὕτως χρείαν ἔχομεν τῆς χρείας παρὰ τῶν φίλων
ὡς τῆς πίστεως τῆς περὶ τῆς χρείας.
It is not so much our friends' help that helps us
as the confidence of their help. [*Gnomologium Vaticanum* 34][63]

μὴ μόνον ἐπαινεῖτε τοὺς ἀγαθοὺς ἀλλὰ καὶ μιμεῖσθε.
Do not only praise good people but imitate them as well.
[Isocrates *Nicocles* 61][64]

Some maxims evaluate a series of items by ranking them:

εὐδαίμων πρῶτον μὲν ὁ μηδενὶ μηδὲν ὀφείλων,
εἶτα δ' ὁ μὴ γήμας, τὸ τρίτον, ὅστις ἄπαις.
Happy is he, first, who owes no man anything;
next he who has not married; third, he who is childless.
[*Anthologia Graeca* 11.50.1-2][65]

Some numerical proverbs are also comparative. These sayings do not only group a number of items under the same heading, but they also highlight the relative importance of the final, climactic member of the list, for example Ben

---

[63] Text: Graziano Arrighetti, ed., *Epicuro: Opere* (Biblioteca di cultura filosofica 41; Torino: Einaudi, 1983[2]) 147; translation: Cyril Bailey, ed., *Epicurus: The Extant Remains* (Oxford: Clarendon, 1926) [reprint, Westport, CT: Hyperion, 1979] 111.

[64] Text: George Norlin, trans., *Isocrates* (LCL; 2 vols.; Cambridge: Harvard University Press; London: Heinemann, 1928, 1929) 1.112; my translation. Isocrates uses the same formula (μὴ μόνον ... ἀλλὰ καὶ ...) for his maxims in *Nicocles* 41, 54, 57.

[65] Text and translation: Gow and Page, *Garland of Philip*, 1.170-171.

Sira 26.28.[66]

Now we may consider the topic-comment categories that fall at the oppositional end of the semantic axis. These types of maxims may be thought of as the counterparts of those described above; they negate or deny what identificational maxims would assert. Of the oppositional structures identified by Dundes, four in particular occur frequently in the Hellenistic corpus: negation, antithesis, causal contradiction, and contrast.

First among the oppositional types are those concerned with the negation of identity or equivalence between topic and comment. The opposition may be produced through overt negation (topic ≠ comment) or either the topic or the comment may be negative. Some examples:

οὔθ' ὁ τὴν χρείαν ἐπιζητῶν διὰ παντὸς φίλος,
οὔθ' ὁ μηδέποτε συνάπτων·
He is no friend who is continually asking for help,
nor he who never associates help with friendship.
[*Gnomologium Vaticanum* 39a][67]

καὶ οὐκ ἔστιν σοφία πονηρίας ἐπιστήμη,
καὶ οὐκ ἔστιν ὅπου βουλὴ ἁμαρτωλῶν φρόνησις.
The knowledge of wickedness is not wisdom,
neither at any time the counsel of sinners prudence. [Ben Sira 19.22]

νόμιζε μηδὲν εἶναι τῶν ἀνθρωπίνων βέβαιον.
Consider that nothing in human life is stable.
[Pseudo-Isocrates *Ad Demonicum* 42][68]

These sayings may be thought of as definitions that warn against false appearances, deception, or potential fallacies in ethical reasoning and judgement. They indicate the true nature of phenomena by denying the association of the topic with special qualities or ideas articulated in the comment.

Another sort of opposition is present when the topic is the antithetical contradiction of the comment, or the two are mutually exclusive. In the first example, the contradiction is brought into relief through analogy:

---

[66] Cf. Ben Sira 23.16-18, 25.7-8, 26.5-6. Some "better" sayings are also comparative, e.g. Proverbs 24.5, 27.10b; Ben Sira 20.25, 40.19a, 20.

[67] Text: Arrighetti, *Epicuro*, 147; translation: Bailey, *Epicurus*, 111.

[68] Text and translation: Norlin, *Isocrates*, 1.28-29. Norlin also refers to Pseudo-Isocrates *Ad Demonicum* 29 and Theognis 585.

ὥσπερ δρόσος ἐν ἀμήτῳ καὶ ὥσπερ ὑετὸς ἐν θέρει,
οὕτως οὐκ ἔστιν ἄφρονι τιμή.
As dew in harvest and as rain in summer
so there is no honor in a fool. [LXX Proverbs 26.1]

τὸ γὰρ τοῖς ἄλλοις φεύγειν τὰ κακὰ παρακαλευόμενον
οὐκ ἂν αἴτιόν ποτέ τινι κακίας γένοιτο.
For that which orders others to flee evil
would never cause evil to someone.
[Pseudo-Libanius ΕΠΙΣΤΟΛΙΜΑΙΟΙ ΧΑΡΑΚΤΗΡΕΣ 78][69]

Some maxims suggest two extremes of behavior and then exhort the reader to pursue a middle course, for instance:

μήτ' εὐήθης ἴσθι μήτε κακοήθης
Be neither guileless nor malicious. [Bias 5][70]

Other sayings may highlight the benefit of the desired response by contrasting it with its opposite:

κακοῖσι δὲ μὴ προσομίλει
ἀνδράσιν, ἀλλ' αἰεὶ τῶν ἀγαθῶν ἔχεο.
Do not associate with bad men,
but always hold fast to the good. [Theognis 31b-32][71]

Sayings like this have a particularly sharp didactic and rhetorical intent since the options they present are so final and clear-cut and the oppositions admit of no grey areas.

In sayings that make use of causal opposition, either the cause or the consequences of the topic is denied or deemed impossible. Thus these maxims essentially represent the counterpart of the category of sayings discussed above that deal with cause and effect. The oppositions that these maxims assert frequently result from the contrast of what can and cannot be done. Causal opposition sayings often try to save the reader from faulty inferences based upon only obvious or accidental connections between phenomena.

---

[69] Text: Abraham J. Malherbe, trans., *Ancient Epistolary Theorists* (SBLSBS 19; Atlanta: Scholars Press, 1988) [originally in *Ohio Journal of Religious Studies* 5 (1977) 3-77] 78; my translation.

[70] Text: Diels and Kranz, *Die Fragmente der Vorsokratiker*, 1.65.5-6; my translation.

[71] Text: Martin L. West, ed., *Iambi et Elegi Graeci ante Alexandrum Cantati* (OCT; 2 vols.; Oxford: Clarendon, 1971-72) 175; my translation.

βουλὴ πονηρὰ χρηστὸν οὐκ ἔχει τέλος.
Bad counsel can't have a good result. [Menander *Sententiae* 134][72]

ἀπὸ ἀκαθάρτου τί καθαρισθήσεται;
καὶ ἀπὸ ψευδοῦς τί ἀληθεύσει;
From an unclean thing what can be cleansed?
and from that which is false what truth can come? [Ben Sira 34.4]

διὰ γὰρ τοῦ μὴ πονεῖν οὐ φεύγεται πόνος.
For by not toiling toil is not avoided. [Pseudo-Crates *Epistle* 4.3][73]

οὐ γενήσῃ σοφὸς οἰόμενος εἶναι πρὸ τοῦ εἶναι.
You will never be wise thinking to be so before you are.
[Sextus *Sententiae* 199][74]

By identifying inappropriate or unacceptable relationships between means and ends, these sayings suggest ethical limits or boundaries, and exemplify valid logic in making practical judgements.

The final sort of opposition to be considered is contrast. As the chart of the semantic axis given above indicates, contrast and comparison are relatively close in function, and Dundes observes that all gnomic sayings are potentially propositions that compare and/or contrast.[75] The important distinction is that while comparison refers to discovering identificational features that the topic and comment have in common, contrast refers to delineating the differences or oppositional features. So in a comparative maxim the author's evaluation of the topic and comment differs only in degree (e.g. x is good but y is better), while in a contrastive maxim it differs in kind (e.g. x is good but y is bad). Some illustrations:

βέλτερον ὑφ' ἑτέρου ἢ ὑφ' ἑαυτοῦ ἐπαινέεσθαι.
Better to be praised by another than by yourself.
[*Gnomologium Democrateum* 114][76]

---

[72] Text: Siegfried Jaekel, ed., *Menandri Sententiae* (BT; Leipzig: Teubner, 1964) 40; my translation.

[73] Text and translation: Abraham J. Malherbe, et al., trans., *The Cynic Epistles: A Study Edition* (SBLSBS 12; Missoula: Scholars Press, 1977) 56-57.

[74] Text: Edwards and Wild, *The Sentences of Sextus*, 38; my translation.

[75] Dundes, "On the Structure of the Proverb," 54.

[76] Text: Diels and Kranz, *Die Fragmente der Vorsokratiker*, 2.165.3-4; my translation.

ἃ ψέγεις, μηδὲ ποίει.
Whatever you criticize do not do. [Sextus *Sententiae* 90][77]

τὰ ἀφανῆ τοῖς φανεροῖς τεκμαίρου.
Determine what is unseen from what is seen. [Solon 20][78]

These maxims frequently point out the importance of proper behavior by contrasting it with reciprocal or opposite behavior, or behavior that is considered absurd. Some typical contrasts are word vs. deed, intention vs. action, and appearance vs. reality.[79]

According to Dundes' model, all gnomic sayings contain at least one topic-comment unit. The majority of maxims, however, including many of those already cited, include more than one descriptive element and these elements may overlap and interrelate in a number of ways. Many of these more complex sayings may be broken down into smaller descriptive elements, and so it is possible to speak of a hierarchy of topics and comments within them. Proverbs 10.1 provides a simple example:

υἱὸς σοφὸς εὐφραίνει πατέρα,
υἱὸς δὲ ἄφρων λύπη τῇ μητρί.
T: A wise son (t_1) makes his father glad (c_1),
C: but a foolish son (t_2) is a grief to his mother (c_2).

The primary topic (T) is the first cola, which contrasts with the second cola, the primary comment (C); also within each cola there is a complete descriptive element with topic and comment (t_1, c_1, and t_2, c_2). Thus a thorough analysis of the maxim's structure would have to take into account the characteristics of these subordinate descriptive elements as well as the primary one. Another consideration is the relationship that exists between the subordinate topics (t_1 and t_2) the subordinate comments (c_1 and c_2). With regard to these structures, the possible interrelationships may be classified into three broad categories.

In the first category, both the topics and the comments are identical, parallel, or comparable; in other words, both the relationships between t_1 and t_2 and between c_1 and c_2 fall on the identificational end of Dundes' semantic axis. For example:

---

[77] Text and translation: Edwards and Wild, *The Sentences of Sextus*, 26-27.
[78] Text: Diels and Kranz, *Die Fragmente der Vorsokratiker*, 1.63.22-23; my translation.
[79] Dundes ("On the Structure of the Proverb," 58) provides a list of "traditional semantic contrastive pairs."

ὥσπερ τὸ εὐθὺ εὐθέος οὐ δεῖται,
οὕτως οὐδὲ τὸ δίκαιον δικαίου.

As what is straight is not in need of something straight,
so what is just is not in need of something just.

[*Gnomologium Epictetum* 49][80]

Repetition of one or more words is common:

τίς θεὸς γνῶθι· γνῶθι δὲ τί τὸ νοοῦν ἐν σοί.

Know who God is; know the understanding that is within you.

[Sextus *Sententiae* 394][81]

As well as analogies:

ὥσπερ ὄρνεα πέταται καὶ στρουθοί,
οὕτως ἀρὰ ματαία οὐκ ἐπελεύσεται οὐδενί.

As birds and sparrows fly,
so a curse shall not come upon anyone without a cause.

[LXX Proverbs 26.2]

In most cases, the T-C relationship is also identificational, and so the subordinate descriptive elements reinforce the overall sense of equivalence and parallelism.

In the second category, both the topics and the comments are oppositional or contrasted. The t_1 to t_2 and c_1 to c_2 relations fall on the oppositional end of the semantic axis. Sometimes the oppositions may be nearly antithetical, but more often they contrast actions or ideas considered appropriate in different circumstances or that are dependent upon particular perceptions or contingencies. Here are some illustrations:

προσποιεῖσθε μὲν πάντα, γινώσκετε δὲ οὐδέν.

You pretend to everything, but know nothing.

[Pseudo-Diogenes *Epistle* 28.5][82]

ὁ ἀτιμάζων πένητας ἁμαρτάνει,
ἐλεῶν δὲ πτωχοὺς μακαριστός.

He that dishonors the needy sins,
but he that has pity on the poor is most blessed. [LXX Proverbs 14.21]

---

[80] Text: Schenkl, *Epicteti Dissertationes*, 489; my translation.
[81] Text and translation: Edwards and Wild, *The Sentences of Sextus*, 64-65.
[82] Text and translation: Malherbe, *Cynic Epistles*, 120-121.

ἐπὶ τὰ δεῖπνα τῶν φίλων βραδέως πορεύου,
ἐπὶ δὲ τὰς ἀτυχίας ταχέως.
To the dinners of friends go slowly,
but to their misfortunes quickly. [Chilon 5][83]

οὐκ ἐκδικηθήσεται ἐν ἀγαθοῖς ὁ φίλος,
καὶ οὐ κρυβήσεται ἐν κακοῖς ὁ ἐχθρός.
A friend can't be avenged in prosperity,
and an enemy can't be hidden in adversity. [Ben Sira 12.8]

These types of maxims are effective because their compressed form forces the oppositional elements into close proximity, creating tension and heightening the intensity of the antithesis.

In the third category, either the topics or the comments are parallel or comparative, while the other set of elements are oppositional or contrasted. Authors frequently utilize maxims with this structure to contrast two aspects of the same quality or issue, for instance:

ἔστι γὰρ αἰσχύνη ἐπάγουσα ἁμαρτίαν,
καὶ ἔστιν αἰσχύνη δόξα καὶ χάρις.
For there is a shame that brings sin,
and there is a shame that is glory and grace. [Ben Sira 4.21]

These sorts of statements serve to dramatize the complexity of the topic and indicate the contingencies involved in describing and evaluating certain occurences. Often the assertions appear somehow contrary to normal logic or conventional expectations:

φίλοι οὐ πάντες οἱ ξυγγενέες,
ἀλλ' οἱ ξυμφωνέοντες περὶ τοῦ ξυμφέροντες.
Friends are not all those born to one's family,
but those who agree regarding what is expedient.
[*Gnomologium Democrateum* 107][84]

πάντα ὁ ἄνθρωπος καὶ οὐδὲν ὁ ἄνθρωπος.
Man is everything and man is nothing. [Aesop *Proverbia* 142][85]

---

[83] Text: Diels and Kranz, *Die Fragmente der Vorsokratiker*, 1.63.27-28; my translation.
[84] Text: Ibidem, 2.164.1-2; my translation.
[85] Text: Ben E. Perry, ed., *Aesopica* (Urbana: University of Illinois Press, 1952) 1.286; my translation.

Other sayings in this category concentrate on the reciprocity of human deeds or the correlation of opposing ethical phenomenon:

ἄρχεσθαι μαθὼν ἄρχειν ἐπιστήσῃ.
Learning to be ruled you shall understand how to rule. [Solon 10][86]

οἵ τ' αὐτῷ κακὰ τεύχει ἀνὴρ ἄλλῳ κακὰ τεύχων.
A man makes trouble for himself when he makes trouble for an other.
[Hesiod *Opera et Dies* 265][87]

As the examples show, patterns of this sort may furnish authors with a striking means of expressing their ironic or paradoxical understanding of human behavior and experience. Sayings of this type are particularly well-suited to provoking the reader to reflection and re-evaluation since they tend to undermine customary thinking and logic.

In concluding this section, we should note that Dundes' model is not the only one available to the student of ancient gnomic wisdom, nor has it gone without some subsequent criticism.[88] However, as an introduction to this type of communication his approach does offer several advantages. First of all, it is an effective and easily-grasped means of explaining how gnomic sayings 'work', that is, how they regularly manipulate and juxtapose their ideas and concepts. Thus it demonstrates in concrete terms what gnomic wisdom accomplishes in general. In this way his model offers some insights into the characteristic perspective and ethos of this mode of literary expression. The system is also useful on account of its flexibility and scope; it is able to depict both basic and more complex sayings, as well as forms related to maxims, such as proverbs and precepts.

Dundes' work is also important because it facilitates an understanding of maxims without depending on an analysis of their grammar, syntax, or style; thus it represents an initial step towards a description of this literary form that is valid in cross-cultural terms. In line with this, the application of the model to wisdom sayings of the Hellenistic era has highlighted the numerous literary and structural similarities that exist among the fairly diverse sources of gnomic wisdom in antiquity, including Jewish and Christian wisdom. At the same time,

---

[86] Text: Diels and Kranz, *Die Fragmente der Vorsokratiker*, 1.63.18-19; my translation.

[87] Text: Martin L. West, *Hesiod: Works and Days* (Oxford: Clarendon, 1978) 108, cf. 222-223; my translation.

[88] Fontaine, *Traditional Sayings*, 63-65; Norrick, *How Proverbs Mean*, 51-79; cf. Asemisson, "Notizen über Aphorismus," 169-175; Grenzmann, "Probleme des Aphorismus," 197-208; Röhrich and Mieder, *Sprichwort*, 60-64; Berger, "Hellenistische Gattungen," 1058-1068.

Dundes' identificational-oppositional axis allows us to describe and compare a wide variety of sayings without forcing them into rigid categories, and so takes account of the various and often nuanced patterns of thought present in gnomic formulations.

Chapter Two

The Contexts and Genres of Gnomic Wisdom

It has already been suggested that an important area of investigation for the study of ancient gnomic wisdom is the various sorts of literary contexts within which authors generally employ wisdom sayings. While the description of the independent content and structure of a maxim represents an obvious starting-point in determining its meaning, very often the literary, rhetorical, and historical settings provided for the maxim play an equally vital role in its interpretation. Therefore an appreciation for the qualities of the larger texts where gnomic wisdom was customarily employed in antiquity constitutes a fundamental corollary to the study of the sayings themselves. In this regard a number of issues may figure into the analysis of a given maxim and the text in which it is situated. Questions will arise, for instance, with regard to how the maxim functions in supporting or developing the argument of the text, or the manner in which two or more maxims may be joined to create more sophisticated units. Other issues will concern the text itself, its literary genre and style, the rhetorical stance and objectives of its author, the cultural and historical circumstances accompanying its composition, and so forth.

In order to understand better the background against which Romans 12.9-21 was composed it is necessary to address some of these contextual and generic issues, which may be divided into two general areas of inquiry. The first pertains to the kinds of methods commonly employed by ancient authors to incorporate or 'contextualize' maxims into larger literary frameworks. The examination of these methods provides some insight into how gnomic sayings were typically utilized in ancient literature and how these sayings may interact with their literary and rhetorical environments. The second involves distinguishing and describing the basic features of the ancient genres that were characterized by the gnomic style, taking into account their morphology, purpose, and setting. The investigation of these genres will begin with certain conventional means of communication that often made use of gnomic wisdom in antiquity, such as speeches, diatribes, and letters. Such forms are important to our discussion since Paul's correspondence generally demonstrates clear literary and rhetorical similarities with them. Prominent position, however, will be given to three somewhat more specific and restricted genres. These genres, all of which are strictly sapiential in nature, appear to form the most pertinent background for the analysis of Romans 12; they are gnomic poetry, gnomologia, and wisdom instruction.

The Contextualization of Gnomic Sayings

Aside from the sterile environments provided for them by collections and anthologies, maxims are meant to be integrated into particular literary contexts and applied to particular rhetorical situations. In addition to the description of the maxim itself, a key consideration for both ancient and modern authors has been how maxims are best contextualized, that is, how they may be effectively used to develop and support discussions, arguments, exhortations, and so forth. The focus here is not the typical social settings, such as those examined by contemporary folklorists and paroemiologists,[1] but with the immediate literary context within which maxims function, and with the literary structures that may accompany their use. While it would be possible to name a great many contexts or patterns, five in particular occur frequently in the ancient sources and these are representative of how gnomic sayings were commonly utilized by authors of various sorts of literature: 1) maxims may be 'personalized'; 2) they may be supported by reasons or epilogues; 3) they may be supplemented with examples or illustrations; 4) they may be employed as evidence or proof; and 5) they may operate at the beginning or conclusion of a distinct section of text.

One way that an author could accommodate gnomic sayings to a particular setting or audience was to somehow personalize their communication. This technique frequently aided in establishing or reinforcing the relationship (either real or projected) that existed between the speaker and the audience. An author could make the intended message seem more immediate and familiar by representing the sayings as being spoken by or addressed to specific figures. The sharp contrast between the universal concepts that gnomic wisdom generally conveys and any particular or private references enabled the writer to quickly shift plains of reference, underscoring the authoritative application of the ideas expressed in timeless terms to the special circumstances of the case at hand.

---

[1] For a discussion of these studies see Fontaine, *Traditional Sayings*, 28-71, cf. 139-170.

The personalizing of gnomic wisdom could be accomplished in several ways. One technique, common in the Near Eastern wisdom instructions discussed below, involved the interjection of a form of personal address such as "my son" in the midst of the gnomic discourse. In addition to lending a measure of authority to the instruction, this personal address may also play a formal role, marking off the beginning of a discrete textual unit. The author of the Letter of James makes use of the address ἀδελφοί μου ("my brothers") or ἀδελφοί μου ἀγαπητοί ("my beloved brothers") in a similar manner.[2] Another, more sophisticated, strategy was to express gnomic sayings in the first or second person, or in the form of a rhetorical question, or to employ terms within the sayings that refer to either the speaker or the reader.[3] Illustrations of such devices may be found in the series of maxims in Qohelet 10.1-20; here are vv. 3-6:

καί γε ἐν ὁδῷ ὅταν ἄφρων πορεύηται,
    καρδία αὐτοῦ ὑστερήσει,
    καὶ ἃ λογιεῖται πάντα ἀφροσύνη ἐστίν.
ἐὰν πνεῦμα τοῦ ἐξουσιάζοντος ἀναβῇ ἐπὶ σέ,
    τόπον σου μὴ ἀφῇς,
    ὅτι ἴαμα καταπαύσει ἁμαρτίας μεγάλας.
ἔστιν πονηρία, ἣν εἶδον ὑπὸ τὸν ἥλιον,
    ὡς ἀκούσιον, ὃ ἐξῆλθεν ἀπὸ προσώπου τοῦ ἐξουσιάζοντος·
ἐδόθη ὁ ἄφρων ἐν ὕψεσι μεγάλοις,
    καὶ πλούσιοι ἐν ταπεινῷ καθήσονται·

Even when a fool walks along the road,
    his heart is in want, and he reckons everyone else a fool.
If the spirit of the one in authority rises up *against you*,
    do not relinquish *your place*;
    for it is a remedy that will bring an end to great mistakes.
There is an evil that *I have observed* under the sun,
    it comes unwillingly from before the one in authority;
The fool is given high office,
    but the rich are given humble posts.

The first and last sayings in this passage (vv. 3 and 6), like most of the rest in the chapter, are cast in impersonal, third-person declarations. By contrast, verses 4-5, as well as 7, 14, and 20, either indicate the direct application of the sayings

---

[2] James 1.2, 16, 19, 2.1, 5, 14, 3.1, 10, 12, 4.11, 5.7, 12, 19.
[3] Cf. Quintilian *Institutio Oratoria* 8.5.6-7; Lausberg, *Handbuch*, §§ 872-874.

to the readers' circumstances or imply the process by which the speaker came to these gnomic judgements. The verses accomplish this by means of second-person imperatives (vv. 4, 20), first-person indicatives (vv. 5, 7), and rhetorical question (v. 14), as well as personal references (e.g. "against you," v. 4). In addition to the variety of expression they add, these sayings strengthen the author-audience relationship, encourage self-reflection, and demand a more immediate response from the reader.

As noted above, the meaning of a gnomic saying is seldom restricted, but usually remains open-ended, even ambiguous. In order to clarify their motivations and focus interpretation, gnomic authors sometimes supplement their maxims with reasons, epilogues, or brief explanations.[4] The rhetorical handbooks favor this practice since it transforms a gnomic saying from a raw assertion or opinion into an enthymeme, a type of deductive proof.[5] The handbooks recommend that epilogues be attached especially when a maxim is unclear, controversial, or paradoxical.[6] Since these are not qualities inherent in maxims themselves, the decision to add an epilogue depended to some extent upon the rhetorical circumstances accompanying the maxim's use, viz., the author's perception of how the audience will receive the formulation.

The epilogues exhibit great range in form and purpose. They are often employed simply as a means of material support. Occasionally, they will amplify some special aspect of the wisdom saying, or apply it to the personal or immediate needs of the audience, perhaps encouraging a specific course of action that the saying generally recommends. The explanation may limit the maxim's application by suggesting a meaning that is not immediately apparent or by implying interpretations contingent upon particular circumstances. Many times the epilogue is contrastive, placing two possible interpretations or outcomes of the saying in opposition. Here are some examples:

---

[4] Aristotle *Rhetorica* 2.21.2-7; Quintilian *Institutio Oratoria* 8.5.4, 9-10; Pseudo-Cicero *Rhetorica ad Herennium* 4.17.24-25, 4.44.56-57; Seneca *Epistulae Morales* 95.61-64; Hermogenes *Progymnasmata* 4; Horna, "Gnome," 74-75; Lausberg, *Handbuch*, § 875; W. Spoerri, "Gnome," *KP* 2 (1967) 823; Josef Martin, *Antike Rhetorik: Technik und Methode* (Handbuch der Altertumswissenschaft 2.3; Munich: Beck, 1974) 123; Sigrid Schweinfurth-Walla, *Studien zu den rhetorischen Überzeugungsmitteln bei Cicero und Aristoteles* (Mannheimer Beiträge zur Sprach- und Literaturwissenschaft 9; Tübingen: Gunter Narr, 1986) 63-65.

[5] Cf. Aristotle *Rhetorica* 1.2; Pseudo-Aristotle *Rhetorica ad Alexandrum* 30^{a}23-39, 31^{a}35-40; Quintilian *Institutio Oratoria* 5.14; Lausberg, *Handbuch*, §§ 371, 875, 879; Martin, *Rhetorik*, 102-106.

[6] Aristotle *Rhetorica* 2.21.7; Pseudo-Aristotle *Rhetorica ad Alexandrum* 30^{b}1-7; cf. Seneca *Epistulae Morales* 94.10-11, 27; Sextus Empiricus *Adversus Mathematicos* 1.279-281.

οὐκ ἔστιν ἀνδρῶν ὅς τις ἔστ' ἐλεύθερος
ἢ χρημάτων γὰρ δοῦλός ἐστιν ἢ τύχης.
There is no man who is really free,
for he is the slave of either wealth or fortune. [Aristotle *Rhetorica* 2.21.2][7]

οὐκ ἔστιν μαθητὴς ὑπὲρ τὸν διδάσκαλον·
κατηρτισμένος δὲ πᾶς ἔσται ὡς ὁ διδάσκαλος αὐτοῦ.
A pupil is not superior to the teacher;
but everyone who has finished (his training) will be like his teacher.
[Luke 6.40][8]

καλὸν νόμος, ἀλλ' οὐ κρείττων φιλοσοφίας·
ὃ μὲν γὰρ βιάζεται μὴ ἀδικεῖν, ἡ δὲ διδάσκει.
Law is good, but not better than philosophy;
for while the former compels one not to act unjustly,
the latter instructs one not to do so. [Pseudo-Crates *Epistle* 5.6-7][9]

ἡγοῦ τῶν ἀκουσμάτων πολλὰ πολλῶν εἶναι χρημάτων κρείττω·
τὰ μὲν γὰρ ταχέως ἀπολείπει, τὰ δὲ πάντα τὸν χρόνον παραμένει·
σοφία γὰρ μόνον τῶν κτημάτων ἀθάνατον.
Believe that many precepts are better than much wealth;
for wealth quickly fails us, but precepts abide through all time;
for wisdom alone of all possessions is imperishable.
[Pseudo-Isocrates *Ad Demonicum* 19][10]

As these samples indicate, the epilogue is frequently introduced by γάρ and authors on occasion may attach two or more epilogues to the same maxim. In addition, the epilogue is sometimes yet another maxim, serving to buttress and explain the initial gnome. In this case the maxims serve as mutual support for one another.

Authors may also expand upon or clarify their gnomic sayings through the addition of an example or illustration.[11] Sometimes the illustration can take the form of a complementary or auxiliary maxim, for instance Ben Sira 11.2-3:

---

[7] Text and translation: John H. Freese, trans., *Aristotle: The "Art" of Rhetoric* (LCL; Cambridge: Harvard University Press; London: Heinemann, 1984) 280-281.

[8] Cf. Matthew 10.24-25; John 13.16, 15.20; Dialogue of the Saviour 53.

[9] Text: Malherbe, *Cynic Epistles*, 56; my translation.

[10] Text and translation: Norlin, *Isocrates*, 1.14-15.

[11] Pseudo-Aristotle *Rhetorica ad Alexandrum* 38^{b}29-39^{a}38; Pseudo-Cicero *Rhetorica ad Herennium* 4.44.56-58; Hermogenes *Progymnasmata* 4; Donald L. Clark, *Rhetoric in Greco-Roman Education* (New York: Columbia University Press, 1959) 188-190; Alva W. Bennett, "Sententia and Catalogue in Propertius (3,9,1-20)," *Hermes* 95 (1967) 222-243; Cancik,

μὴ αἰνέσῃς ἄνδρα ἐν κάλλει αὐτοῦ
καὶ μὴ βδελύξῃ ἄνθρωπον ἐν ὁράσει αὐτοῦ.
μικρὰ ἐν πετεινοῖς μέλισσα,
καὶ ἀρχὴ γλυκασμάτων ὁ καρπὸς αὐτῆς.
Do not commend a man for his beauty,
nor loathe a person for his appearance.
Least among winged things is the bee
but of sweet things her fruit is the best.

More often authors will clarify a maxim with an expanded illustration, frequently drawing from episodes of everyday life, for example James 1.22-24:

Γίνεσθε δὲ ποιηταὶ λόγου καὶ μὴ μόνον ἀκροαταὶ παραλογιζόμενοι ἑαυτούς. ὅτι εἴ τις ἀκροατὴς λόγου ἐστὶν καὶ οὐ ποιητής, οὗτος ἔοικεν ἀνδρὶ κατανοοῦντι τὸ πρόσωπον τῆς γενέσεως αὐτοῦ ἐν ἐσόπτρῳ· κατενόησεν γὰρ ἑαυτὸν καὶ ἀπελήλυθεν καὶ εὐθέως ἐπελάθετο ὁποῖος ἦν.
Be doers of the word, not merely hearers, deceiving yourselves. Because if someone is (only) a hearer of the word and not a doer, he is like the person who looks at his natural appearance in a mirror; for he looks at himself and goes away, and immediately he forgets what he looked like.[12]

The simile, following the wisdom admonition in v. 22, functions as an illustration, extending the meaning of the maxim by dramatizing the implications of disobedience. The imagery continues in v. 25, where the author offers a positive example. In this way the illustration also serves as a transitional device, carrying the argument of the epistle forward.[13]

Epictetus *Dissertationes* 1.2.1-2 provides another sample of this sort of usage. In an exhortation characterized by the diatribe style, Epictetus discusses how one may maintain discipline and preserve a proper countenance at all times, even in difficult circumstances:

Τῷ λογικῷ ζῴῳ μόνον ἀφόρητόν ἐστι τὸ ἄλογον, τὸ δ' εὔλογον φορητόν. πληγαὶ οὐκ εἰσὶν ἀφόρητοι τῇ φύσει. --Τίνα τρόπον;-- Ὅρα πῶς· Λακεδαιμόνιοι μαστιγοῦνται μαθόντες ὅτι εὔλογόν ἐστιν.
To the rational being only the irrational is unendurable, but the rational is endurable. Blows are not by nature unendurable. --How so?-- Observe how:

Untersuchungen, 26-27; Lausberg, *Handbuch*, § 875; Fiore, *Personal Example*, 65-66, 73. On occasion the examples or illustrations are quite long, e.g. Pseudo-Phocylides 162-174.
[12] Translation: Dibelius, *James*, 108.
[13] Cf. Ibidem 112-116.

Lacedaemonians take a scourging once they have learned that it is rational.[14]

Epictetus opens this discourse with a maxim (1.1) followed by an assertion regarding its application (1.2a). In response to an objection raised by his imaginary interlocutor, Epictetus then invokes an example from a Spartan religious practice (1.2b) in order to buttress the assertion. This reference verifies the maxim in 1.1 and clarifies Epictetus' understanding of the key terms "rational" and "irrational" by submitting a vivid and convincing image which was no doubt familiar to his intended readers.

In antiquity gnomic wisdom represented a convenient source of evidence or proof, and authors frequently composed maxims in support of their arguments.[15] The striking formulation and uncompromising posture of gnomic sayings made them useful as rules of behavior or grounds for action. By means of gnomic discourse a speaker could apply a judgement that commended itself as universally true to a specific decision, establishing an ethical presupposition. In Pseudo-Isocrates *Ad Demonicum* 2, for instance, the author explains his reasons for writing the ethical treatise, referring to Demonicus' father, Hipponicus:

ἡγούμενος οὖν πρέπειν τοὺς δόξης ὀρεγομένους καὶ παιδείας ἀντιποιουμένους τῶν σπουδαίων ἀλλὰ μὴ τῶν φαύλων εἶναι μιμητάς, ἀπέσταλκά σοι τόνδε τὸν λόγον δῶρον, τεκμήριον μὲν τῆς πρὸς ὑμᾶς εὐνοίας, σημεῖον δὲ τῆς πρὸς Ἱππόνικον συνηθείας· πρέπει γὰρ τοὺς παῖδας, ὥσπερ τῆς οὐσίας, οὕτω καὶ τῆς φιλίας τῆς πατρικῆς κληρονομεῖν.

So then, since I deem it fitting that those who strive for distinction and are ambitious for education should emulate the good and not the bad, I have dispatched to you this discourse as a gift, in proof of my good will toward you and in token of my friendship for Hipponicus; for *it is fitting that a son should inherit his father's friendships even as he inherits his estate.*[16]

This maxim effectively equates behavior that is taken for granted (inheriting a father's property) with behavior that is not nearly so obvious but which is clearly in the author's interests (inheriting a father's friends). Casting the assertion in a gnomic form makes it appear as a self-evident rule of order and

---

[14] Text and translation: W. A. Oldfather, trans., *Epictetus* (LCL; 2 vols.; New York: Putnam's Sons; London: Heinemann, 1926, 1928) 1.14-15.

[15] Aristotle *Rhetorica* 3.17.9; Pseudo-Aristotle *Rhetorica ad Alexandrum* 28^{a}16-24, 38^{b}29-39^{a}38, 42^{b}34-43^{a}6; Hermogenes *Progymnasmata* 4; Horna, "Gnome," 79; Lausberg, *Handbuch*, §§ 872-873, 876; Martin, *Rhetorik*, 122-124, 257-258.

[16] Text and translation: Norlin, *Isocrates*, 1.4-5.

tradition, and so the maxim not only advocates the author's actions but also serves as a reminder of what is basically expected of Demonicus. By depicting the relationship between the author and reader in terms of an ongoing obligation, the saying establishes a more receptive mood in Demonicus and so it plays a programmatic role in the treatise's introduction.

A more argumentative and plainly rhetorical use of a maxim is found in Philo *De Virtutibus* 196; here "Nobility" (εὐγένεια) addresses her rebellious and unrighteous descendants:

τί δὴ μελετήσαντες ἀλλοτρίωσιν τὴν δι' ἔργων τὴν ἐν λόγῳ συγγένειαν εὐπρεπὲς ὄνομα ὑποδυόμενοι καθυποκρίνεσθε; παραγωγὰς γὰρ καὶ κεκομψευμένας ἀπάτας οὐκ ἀνέχομαι, διότι ῥᾴδιον μὲν καὶ τῷ τυχόντι εὐπροσώπους λόγους εὑρεῖν, ἤθη δ' ὑπαλλάξασθαι πονηρὰ χρηστοῖς οὐ ῥᾴδιον.

You have done your best by your actions to make yourselves strangers, why do you hypocritically assume a specious name and call yourselves kinsmen? So I cannot overlook (your) seductive arts and clever wiles, because *it is easy for anybody to devise good-sounding words, but not easy to change bad morals to good.*[17]

As both Aristotle and Quintilian recognize, maxims are best suited to those speakers whose character or experience lends authority to their ethical observations and judgements.[18] By assigning his comments to a figure who may appropriately speak in such terms, Philo delivers his argument here more forcefully because he obviates the necessity of speaking to the audience in such a moralizing manner. In formulating this gnomic saying, "Nobility" both justifies her decision and condemns the audience's behavior. The maxim identifies the ethical character of the rebellious descendants by categorizing their actions in sweeping terms and so indicates their true nature and the ultimate meaning of their hypocrisy.[19]

A third example comes from the letter of Paul preserved in 2 Corinthians 8,

---

[17] Text and translation: Francis H. Colson, George H. Whitaker, and Ralph Marcus, trans., *Philo* (LCL; 12 vols.; New York: Putnam's Sons; London: Heinemann, 1929-1962) 8.284-285.

[18] "For who would tolerate a boy, or a youth, or even a man of low birth who presumed to speak with all the authority of a judge and to thrust his precepts down our throats?" Quintilian *Institutio Oratoria* 8.5.8; text and translation: H. E. Butler, trans., *Quintilian*, (LCL; 4 vols.; Cambridge: Harvard University Press; London: Heinemann, 1920-1922) 3.286-287; cf. Aristotle *Rhetorica* 2.21.9; Seneca *Epistulae Morales* 94.1-15.

[19] For more on wisdom in Philo's writings see Jean Laporte, "Philo in the Tradition of Biblical Wisdom Literature," in Wilkin, *Aspects of Wisdom*, 103-141.

where he exhorts the congregations in Corinth to contribute to the Jerusalem collection. As Hans Dieter Betz has demonstrated, the chapter is a letter fragment of the so-called mixed type, possessing both advisory (vv. 1-15) and administrative (vv. 16-23) components.[20] The composition of the former section in particular appears to be informed by the conventions of Greco-Roman deliberative rhetoric and is organized as follows: *exordium* (vv. 1-5), *narratio* (v. 6), *propositio* (vv. 7-8), *probatio* (vv. 9-15).[21] The second 'proof' of the *probatio* is vv. 10-12:

καὶ γνώμην ἐν τούτῳ δίδωμι· τοῦτο γὰρ ὑμῖν συμφέρει, οἵτινες οὐ μόνον τὸ ποιῆσαι ἀλλὰ καὶ τὸ θέλειν προενήρξασθε ἀπὸ πέρυσι· νυνὶ δὲ καὶ τὸ ποιῆσαι ἐπιτελέσατε, ὅπως καθάπερ ἡ προθυμία τοῦ θέλειν, οὕτως καὶ τὸ ἐπιτελέσαι ἐκ τοῦ ἔχειν. εἰ γὰρ ἡ προθυμία πρόκειται, καθὸ ἐὰν ἔχῃ εὐπρόσδεκτος, οὐ καθὸ οὐκ ἔχει.

On this point I am giving you my advice: This is the expedient (thing to do) for you who a year ago began (the collection) ahead (of others) in regard not only to action but also to determination. Now then, complete the action, so that as there was your eager determination there may also be its completion--in proportion to what you possess. For *if the the willingness is present, (the gift is) acceptable (when it is) in proportion to what one possesses, not what one does not possess.*[22]

The gnomic saying in 8.12, like a number of others from antiquity, addresses a potential disparity between willing and doing an action. Here Paul articulates an essential rule on gift-giving, in particular on sacrificial gifts to God, which serves as a proof-text in support of his deliberative argument. The gnomic formulation posits a model for behavior that the Corinthians are expected to accept and emulate; consequently it carries with it a clear admonitory force. Specifically, the maxim represents Paul's determination of what constitutes an acceptable gift, and so elucidates what is important about the Corinthians' prospective actions and the way in which they are to be carried out.

Gnomic sayings may also operate at the beginning or conclusion of a distinct section of text. A saying in this position may serve as a basic heading for what follows, or as a sort of transition device from one topic to the next. Take, for example, Pseudo-Phocylides 42-47:

---

[20] Betz, *2 Corinthians 8 and 9*, 131-139.
[21] Ibidem, 38-40.
[22] Ibidem, translation: 37; commentary: 63-67.

ἡ φιλοχρημοσύνη μήτηρ κακότητος ἁπάσης.
χρυσὸς ἀεὶ δόλος ἐστὶ καὶ ἄργυρος ἀνθρώποισιν.
Χρυσέ, κακῶν ἀρχηγέ, βιοφθόρε, πάντα χαλέπτων,
εἴθε σε μὴ θνητοῖσι γενέσθαι πῆμα ποθεινόν·
σεῦ γὰρ ἕκητι μάχαι τε λεηλασίαι τε φόνοι τε,
ἐχθρὰ δὲ τέκνα γονεῦσιν ἀδελφειοί τε συναίμοις.
Love of money is the mother of all evil.
Gold and silver are always a lure for men.
Gold, originator of evil, destroyer of life, crushing all things;
would that you were not a desirable calamity to mortals!
For your sake there are battles and plunderings and murders,
and children become the enemies of their parents and brothers
(the enemies) of their kinsmen.[23]

Here the first maxim, perhaps a reformulated proverb, stands a sort of general 'text' for which what follows on lines 43-47 is a more specific commentary or elucidation. In this way the initial maxim generates further examples and motives, as well as additional, subordinate maxims, in order to create a cluster or paragraph of sayings.[24]

On the other hand, a maxim may also conclude a section of text. In this position, it summarizes what precedes and drives it home in a memorable way. The rhetorical handbooks refer to such sayings as ἐπιφώνημα or *clausula*.[25] Quintilian's remarks concerning the *clausula* reflect both the popularity and the abuse of *sententiae* in first-century Rome. After commenting upon the traditional meaning and use of the *clausula*, he writes:

---

[23] Text and translation: Pieter W. van der Horst, *The Sentences of Pseudo-Phocylides* (SVTP 4; Leiden: Brill, 1978) 90-91; cf. 142-146.

[24] Patrick W. Skehan and Alexander A. DiLella (*The Wisdom of Ben Sira: A New Translation with Notes* [AB 39; Garden City, New York: Doubleday, 1987] 24-25) observe that in Ben Sira a single maxim may introduce a series of other sayings that develop a particular topic or theme from several points of view, for example 15.11-20, 21.1-10, 23.16-21, 26.1-4; they also note that a maxim may serve as a topic sentence at the beginning of an extended exhortation which includes other gnomic sayings, for example 2.1-6, 16.1-4, 18.30-19.3, 28.12-16.

[25] According to Quintilian (*Institutio Oratoria* 8.5.10-13) the *epiphonema* is an exclamation attached to the close of a statement or proof by way of climax while the *clausula* is merely a conclusion; cf. Clarke, *Rhetoric at Rome*, 94-97, 134; Spoerri, "Gnome," 823; Lausberg, *Handbuch*, §§ 875, 879; Martin, *Rhetorik*, 257. Kloppenborg (*The Formation of Q*, 196-197, 221-223, 342-345) identifies Q 10.16 and 12.34 as summarizing maxims; cf. Winton, *The Proverbs of Jesus*, 128.

> Sed nunc aliud volunt, ut omnis locus, omnis sensus in fine sermonis feriat aurem. Turpe autem ac prope nefas ducunt, respirare ullo loco, qui acclamationem non petierit. Inde minuti corruptique sensiculi et extra rem petiti; neque enim possunt tam multae bonae sententiae esse, quam necesse est multae sint clausulae.
> But today something more is meant, for our rhetoricians want every passage, every sentence to strike the ear by an impressive close. In fact, they think it a disgrace, nay, almost a crime, to pause to breathe except at the end of a passage that is designed to call forth applause. The result is a number of tiny epigrams, affected, irrelevant and disjointed. For there are not enough striking *sententiae* in the world to provide a close to every period.[26]

A less stylized and more philosophical illustration of this practice may be found in another diatribal passage from Epictetus *Dissertationes*. In 1.4, Epictetus begins by arguing that true moral progress is not measured by apparent evidence such as memorization of difficult books, but by a virtuous character and sound ethical judgement (1.4.1-12). He then turns to the audience, issuing an ethical challenge: "So show me, then, your progress in matters like the following ... " (13). Two illustrations of progress follow, one from athletics (13-14), the other from study and scholarship (14-16); both demonstrate that the means of accomplishing a goal are of less significance than what they contribute towards the goal itself. He then closes the section with a maxim (17):

μηδέποτε οὖν ἀλλαχοῦ τὸ ἔργον ζητεῖτε, ἀλλαχοῦ τὴν προκοπήν.
So never look for (your) work in one place and (your) progress in another.[27]

The admonition summarizes the argument, drawing a broad and rather indefinite insight from the specific illustrations in 13-16 and applying it to the readers. In this way Epictetus clarifies what he expects of his students and provides them with a paradigmatic rule which they in turn may employ in various new situations.

This concludes the discussion of contextualization. As with the treatment of gnomic forms, it would be impossible to canvass all the potential applications and contexts for maxims in Hellenistic literature. However, the survey does represent some of the more widespread and significant methods, and these contextual techniques indicate how maxims were typically intended by their authors and understood by their readers. It is clear from the examples provided

---

[26] Quintilian *Institutio Oratoria* 8.5.13-14; text and translation: Butler, *Quintilian*, 3.288-289.
[27] Text and translation: Oldfather, *Epictetus*, 1.32-33.

that maxims were in fact regularly employed in a purposeful way to further the strategic interactional aims of those who utilized them. The discussion above has also indicated some of the ways in which an author could combine two or more gnomic sayings in the formation of an argument or exhortation. We should bear in mind, too, that for the most part the different functions identified here are not mutually exclusive; maxims often operate in several different capacities within the same text. All things considered, the question of contextualization is of special concern in the study of gnomic sayings, since to a greater extent than many other literary forms their context often appears to be determinative for their intended meaning and hermeneutic.

The Genres of Gnomic Wisdom

Before beginning the examination of the different genres that typically utilized gnomic wisdom in antiquity, a preliminary distinction should be made regarding the two types of materials involved. The first group of texts to be considered are designated *non-sapiential genres*, which include such forms as speeches and letters. These materials are not characterized by the presence of wisdom sayings, though their authors often take advantage of gnomic forms since they are of use in achieving their broader objectives. The second category is that much smaller corpus for which the employment of gnomic wisdom constitutes an essential generic characteristic; these are gnomic poetry, gnomologia, and wisdom instruction. Of course, these *sapiential genres*, as they will be designated here, hardly exhaust the modes of communication employed by wisdom writers (including those categorized here as non-sapiential), and a number of wisdom texts, Job for instance, make only haphazard use of maxims. For the sake of convenience, in the discussions that follow the contents of both the non-sapiential and sapiential genres will be referred to as 'gnomic', though we should remain aware that this applies in a thorough-going sense only to the latter group.

Gnomic sayings were a popular and adaptable form, valuable in virtually any sort of literary genre and appropriate for almost any type of style. Of interest to our investigation is their use in Greco-Roman rhetoric, exhortation, and epistolography, since it is clear that Paul's writings are indebted to these well-established fields of study. With respect to the practice of rhetoric, the handbooks indicate that the maxim was an essential component of the ancient orator's repertoire, and even a cursory reading of any Greek or Latin oration will confirm this fact. While the speakers of all sorts of speeches could profit by them, maxims were associated particularly with the deliberative branch of rhetoric, the art of persuasion and dissuasion.[28] Generally speaking, maxims became invaluable as tools of oratory; this was not only because they seemed vivid, memorable, and convincing, but also because they helped to clarify the moral purpose, προαίρεσις, of a speech and the moral character of the speaker.[29] Maxims are often an indication of where an orator stands in regard to the audience and they may serve as an expression of the values he hopes to demonstrate that he shares with them. As Aristotle observes, maxims are persuasive because they appeal to the emotions of the audience in so far as they are pleased to hear the orator express their specific views in general terms: "Wherefore the speaker should endeavor to guess how his hearers formed their preconceived opinions and what they are, and then to express himself in regard to them."[30] As Aristotle's comments suggest, there is a process of experimentation and discovery that accompanies the speaker's formulation of maxims as he endeavors to discern the ethical views of his listeners and then to advantageously convey his own position and arguments in these terms. The author of the *Rhetorica Ad Herennium* takes note of the impact this practice may have on the audience: " ... the hearer, when he perceives that an indisputable principle drawn from practical life is being applied to a cause, must give it his tacit approval."[31] By and large, maxims profit the orator most when he perceives that the audience possesses some vague notion or feeling, but has yet to articulate it in a definite manner. The maxims formulated in response to such a situation are of use in prioritizing confusing issues and establishing an agenda, and so may help galvanize opinion or serve as a rallying-point for the audience's identity and purpose. These functions, in turn, contribute to the

---

[28] Hermogenes *Progymnasmata* 4 defines the maxim as follows: Γνώμη ἐστὶ λόγος κεφαλαιώδης ἐν ἀποφάσει καθολικῇ, ἀποτρέπων τι, ἢ προτρέπων ἐπί τι, ἢ ὁποῖόν ἐστιν ἕκαστον δηλῶν. ("A maxim is a summary saying, in a statement of general application, dissuading from something, persuading toward something, or showing what is the nature of each."); text: Christian Walz, ed. *Rhetores Graeci* (9 vols.; Stuttgart, Tübingen: J. G. Cotta, 1835) 1.24; my translation. Significantly, the apotreptic and protreptic functions assigned to the maxim here are precisely those used to describe the deliberate kind of rhetoric by Aristotle *Rhetorica* 1.3.3-5. Cf. Lausberg, *Handbuch*, §§ 224-238; George A. Kennedy, *The Art of Persuasion in Greece* (Princeton: Princeton University Press, 1963) 203-206. For an example of gnomic wisdom in New Testament deliberative rhetoric see idem, *New Testament Interpretation through Rhetorical Criticism* (Studies in Religion; Chapel Hill, London: University of North Carolina Press, 1984) 60.

[29] Aristotle *Rhetorica* 2.21.16; cf. Hellwig, *Untersuchungen*, 264-267.

[30] Aristotle *Rhetorica* 2.21.15; text and translation: Freese, *Rhetoric*, 286-287.

[31] Pseudo-Cicero *Rhetorica ad Herennium* 4.17.25; text and translation: Harry Caplan, trans., *[Cicero] Rhetorica ad Herennium* (LCL; Cambridge: Harvard University Press; London: Heinemann, 1954) 290-293.

speaker's ethos and stature vis-à-vis the audience and assist him in defining and asserting his role as a competent, trustworthy, and authoritative figure.

These qualities of gnomic discourse made it attractive to the authors of exhortation as well. The hortatory literature is related in style and substance to both the deliberative and epideictic branches of rhetoric, though it in fact transcends the conventional rhetorical distinctions and belongs more under the auspices of moral philosophy than oratory.[32] While the literary forms and topics of gnomic wisdom may play a role in any sort of exhortation, they belong especially to what is commonly called paraenesis, or *praeceptio*.[33] These terms refer to exhortation, broad in application and traditional in content, that calls upon the hearer to continue on a previously chosen ethical course. In contrast with protreptic speech, paraenesis does not introduce a significant quantity of new information or call upon the audience to pursue a different or unaccustomed way of life. Nor does it address a specific or occasional decision, like advice.[34] Most often, paraenetic texts contain a host of materials and ideas

---

[32] Theodore Burgess, "Epideictic Literature," *University of Chicago Studies in Classical Philology* 3 (1902) 214-248; Paul Wendland, *Anaximenes von Lampsakos: Studien zur ältesten Geschichte der Rhetorik* (Berlin: Weidmann, 1905) 81-101; Berger, "Hellenistische Gattungen," 1075; Stanley K. Stowers, *Letter-Writing in Greco-Roman Antiquity* (LEC 5; Philadelphia: Westminster, 1986) 51-52.

[33] "By paraenesis we mean a text which strings together admonitions of general ethical content"; Dibelius, *James*, 3. Dibelius notes on pp. 5-11 that paraenesis is seldom homogeneous or entirely original; among its important features are eclecticism, a lack of continuity of thought, the repetition of motifs, and the absence of application to a single audience or set of circumstances. For more on the formal and material qualities of paraenesis see Burgess, "Epideictic Literature," 228-234; Wendland, *Anaximenes*, 81-101; Rudolf Vetschera, *Zur griechischen Paränese* (Programm des Staatsgymnasiums zu Smichow; Smichow: Rohlicek & Sievers, 1912); Konrad Gaiser, *Protreptik und Paränese bei Platon: Untersuchungen zur Form des Platonischen Dialogs* (Tübinger Beiträge zur Altertumswissenschaft 40; Stuttgart: Kohlhammer, 1959) 148-196; Cancik, *Untersuchungen*, 16-35; James I. H. McDonald, *Kerygma and Didache: The Articulation and Structure of the Earliest Christian Message* (SNTSMS 37; Cambridge: Cambridge Unversity Press, 1980) 69-100; Leo G. Perdue, "Paraenesis and the Epistle of James," *ZNW* 72 (1981) 242-256; Abraham J. Malherbe, "Exhortation in I Thessalonians," *NovT* 25 (1983) 238-256 [reprint, idem, *Paul and the Popular Philosophers* (Minneapolis: Fortress, 1989) 49-66]; idem, *Paul and the Thessalonians: The Philosophic Tradition of Pastoral Care* (Philadelphia: Fortress, 1987) 70-78; Berger, "Hellenistische Gattungen," 1075-1077; Leo G. Perdue and John G. Gammie, eds., *Semeia 50. Paraenesis: Act and Form* (Atlanta: Scholars Press, 1990); von Lips, *Weisheitliche Traditionen*, 356-438; cf. Karl-Wilhelm Niebuhr, *Gesetz und Paränese: Katechismusartige Weisungsreihen in der frühjüdischen Literatur* (WUNT 2.28; Tübingen: Mohr-Siebeck, 1987).

[34] This nomenclature hardly accounts for the vagaries of ancient and modern usage, or for the host of ancient exhortatory texts that do not fit neatly into any one category. Burgess ("Epideictic Literature," 230, cf. 228-234) summarizes protrepsis and paraenesis as follows: "Technically the προτρεπτικὸς λόγος is an exhortation to some general course--philosophy,

already familiar to the audience, but present them in such a way that they serve the text's special aims, which are typically encouragement, admonition, or consolation. Given their traditional and familiar as well as ethical qualities, it follows that maxims and proverbs, occasionally employed in a loosely-organized series, constitute regular features of paraenesis. Other typical components include prescriptions and prohibitions, examples offered for imitation, catalogues of virtues and vices, and reminders of what the listeners already know or have already accomplished.

A distinct type of exhortation is the diatribe, which frequently exhibits both protreptic and paraenetic aims.[35] While the diatribe has been associated chiefly with Cynic and Stoic philosophers, it was a fairly prevalent literary phenomenon in the Hellenistic world. Recent studies have also shown how the diatribe style influenced the writings of Hellenistic Jews and early Christians, including those of Paul, particularly his letter to the Romans.[36] The hortatory mode of address associated with the diatribe dealt with practical ethical topics in a popular, lively, and often satirical manner. It was employed in different sorts of communication, including school instruction, public discourse, and letters. In tone and content the diatribe also differed somewhat from author to author, though some features, especially dialogue with an imaginary interlocutor, remain constant. In addition to the regular store of paraenetic materials, the authors of diatribes, including Paul, regularly quoted or formulated gnomic

---

rhetoric, virtue. It gives a comprehensive view, setting forth the advantages and removing the objections. ... παραίνεσις presents a series of precepts which will serve as a guide of conduct under fixed conditions." For more see Vetschera, *Paränese*, 3-9; Fiore, *Personal Example*, 39-42; Malherbe, *Moral Exhortation*, 121-129; Stowers, *Letter-Writing*, 91-125. On protreptic literature see Ingemar Düring, *Aristotle's Protrepticus: An Attempt at Reconstruction* (Studia Graeca et Latina Gothoburgensia 12; Göteborg: Elanders Boktryckeri Aktiebolag, 1961); Mark D. Jordan, "Ancient Philosophic Protreptic and the Problem of Persuasive Genres," *Rhetorica* 4 (1986) 309-333.

[35] In addition to the references in the following note, see Burgess, "Epideictic Literature," 225, 234-244; André Oltramare, *Les Origines de la Diatribe Romaine* (Lausanne, Geneva, Neuchâtel: Payot, 1920) passim; Wilhelm Capelle and Henri-Irenée Marrou, "Diatribe," *RAC* 3 (1957) 990-1009.

[36] On the influence of the diatribe in Jewish and Christian wisdom texts, see, for example, James M. Reese, *Hellenistic Influence in the Book of Wisdom and its Consequences* (AnBib 41; Rome: Biblical Institute Press, 1970) 110ff.; Dibelius, *James*, 1-3 and s.v. diatribe; William R. Schoedel, "Jewish Wisdom and the Formation of the Christian Ascetic," in Wilken, *Aspects of Wisdom*, 183-190; Davids, "The Epistle of James," 3630-3631. On the diatribe and Paul see Bultmann, *Der Stil der paulinischen Predigt*, passim; Betz, *Galatians*, s.v. diatribe; Stanley K. Stowers, *The Diatribe and Paul's Letter to the Romans* (SBLDS 57; Chico, CA: Scholars Press, 1981); Thomas Schmeller, *Paulus und die Diatribe: Eine vergleichende Stilinterpretation* (NTAbh 19; Münster: Aschendorff, 1987).

sayings.[37] Besides the advantages they offered to exhortation generally, maxims were compatible with the simple, terse sentences and sharp, pointed style characteristic of many diatribes. They also provided suitable ammunition for the diatribe writers on account of their memorable formulation and accessible subject matter. They represented a succinct and convenient argument that took advantage of traditional values and the deep-seated regard most people had for them.

An important medium of exhortation was the letter, and both paraenetic and diatribal materials were incorporated within epistolary frameworks.[38] Exhortatory letters do not ordinarily concentrate on teaching dogma or on the exchange of information *per se*, but rather strive to influence the behavior and disposition of the recipient in a positive way. In connection with this, it was also considered desirable that letters be brief and direct, as well as friendly and conversational. In all these respects maxims were recognized as effective means of expression. So, for instance, in Pseudo-Libanius' handbook, ΕΠΙΣΤΟΛΙΜΑΙΟΙ ΧΑΡΑΚΤΗΡΕΣ, which provides forty-one examples of typical epistolary styles, the following model letters contain maxims: the paraenetic letter (52), the didactic letter (78), the letter of encouragement (83), and the letter of consultation (84).[39] The model advisory type of letter in Pseudo-Demetrius ΤΥΠΟΙ ΕΠΙΣΤΟΛΙΚΟΙ also makes use of a maxim.[40] Thus both authors seem to recommend a gnomic style, or at least the use of gnomic sayings, for these sorts of letters. Other writers also suggest the discreet and

---

[37] Schmeller, *Paulus und die Diatribe*, 115, 145, 185, 208, 264, 310, 365, 392, 432; Stowers, *The Diatribe*, 132, cf. 137; Malherbe (*Moral Exhortation*, 130) cites the following as sententious sayings connected with the Pauline diatribe: Romans 14.7; 1 Corinthians 5.6, 15.33; cf. idem, "The Beasts at Ephesus," *JBL* 87 (1968) 71-80 [reprint, idem, *Paul and the Popular Philosophers*, 79-90]. Betz (*Galatians*, 22-23, 291-311, cf. 264-270) connects Paul's maxims in Galatians 5.25-6.10 with the diatribe style.

[38] On exhortation in letters see Hermann W. G. Peter, *Der Brief in der römischen Literatur: Literargeschichtliche Untersuchungen und Zusammenfassungen* (Abhandlungen der philologisch-historischen Classe der königl. sächsischen Gesellschaft der Wissenschaften 20.3; Leipzig: Teubner, 1901) 3-28, 225-242; Anne Marie Guillemin, *Pline et la vie littéraire de son temps* (Collection d'études latines 4; Paris: Société d'édition "Les Belles Lettres," 1929) 32-40, 67-73, 127-150; Cancik, *Untersuchungen*, 46-61, 71-75; William G. Doty, *Letters in Primitive Christianity* (GBSNTS; Philadelphia: Fortress, 1973) 37-39, 57-60; Stowers, *The Diatribe*, 69-75; idem, *Letter-Writing*, 36-40, 91-152; Fiore, *Personal Example*, 42-44, 84-100, 193-195; Malherbe, *Moral Exhortation*, 79-85; Franz Schnider and Werner Stenger, *Studien zum neutestamentlichen Briefformular* (NTTS 11; Leiden: Brill, 1987) 76-107. Further see Betz, *Galatians*, 23 n. 114; idem, *2 Corinthians 8 and 9*, 129-140.

[39] Text and translation: Malherbe, *Epistolary Theorists*, 66-81; cf. Stowers, *Letter-Writing*, 51-57, 94-96.

[40] Text and translation: Malherbe, *Epistolary Theorists*, 30-41; cf. Stowers, *Letter-Writing*, 51-57, 107-108.

non-argumentative employment of proverbs and maxims in letters, exhortatory and otherwise.[41] Of course, the epistolary corpus itself bears witness to these recommendations: the 'Cynic Epistles', the *Epistulae Morales* of Seneca, Porphyry's *Ad Marcellam*, and the Letter of James are a small sample of the epistles that regularly address their readers with gnomic sayings.[42]

While the composition of maxims in the speeches, exhortations, and letters of antiquity has an indisputable bearing on our understanding of the presence and function of gnomic formulations in the Pauline epistles, their study hardly provides a thorough survey of all the modalities available for collecting and presenting sententious sayings in Hellenistic Judaism and early Christianity. Further, none of these genres can adequately account for the complex material and compositional qualities of Romans 12.9-21. For this, we must turn to the three prominent sapiential genres of the ancient world that are characterized by the gnomic style: gnomic poetry, gnomic anthologies, and wisdom instruction.

Gnomic Poetry

To begin with, we should take note of the features that distinguish this genre. First, as its name suggests, a vital formal component of gnomic poetry is the gnomic saying. Accordingly, a second characteristic is that the ethical themes and instructional stance of the genre are the same as those typically connected with wisdom sayings. Thus the issues raised in gnomic poems include proper ethical behavior, familial and civic responsibilities, moral questions and problems, moderation and self-control, and so forth. Third, the representatives of the genre are poetic or hymnic in composition. In Greek gnomic poems the dactylic hexameter and the elegiac couplet were apparently the standard rhythms, though gnomic poets also had recourse to iambic, choliambic, trochaic, anapaestic, and other meters as well.[43] Finally, gnomic poems are for the most part short--a paragraph or so in length--and their contents are united by a common theme and outlook, though a fair number of them deviate in these regards.

Within the Hebrew Bible and the literature of Hellenistic Judaism modern

---

[41] Malherbe, *Epistolary Theorists*, 14, 18-19, 60-61, 64-65; cf. Berger, "Hellenistische Gattungen," 1362.

[42] Cf. Fiore, *Personal Example*, 18, 133.

[43] Gustav A. Gerhard, *Phoinix von Kolophon: Texte und Untersuchungen* (Leipzig: Teubner, 1909) 253-255; Horna, "Gnome," 76-78.

scholars have identified a number of gnomic poems; these are frequently referred to as 'didactic poems' and 'wisdom hymns'.[44] Compositions of this sort, most of which are located in wisdom books, do not themselves constitute a separate genre but rather are to be compared with similar texts from non-wisdom literature, especially the Psalms. Their morphology, therefore, is familiar from Hebrew hymns, thanksgivings, prayers, and laments, though their themes are sapiential and their tone is exhortatory. Accordingly, most of these wisdom texts take advantage of hymnic features such as the participial style and the praise of God as creator and redeemer, even while including sapiential components such as maxims, rhetorical questions, and concluding warnings. Ben Sira 10.14-18, for example, has been described by W. Baumgartner as hymnic:[45]

The thrones of the arrogant God overturns
   and enthrones the humble in their stead;
The roots of the proud God plucks up,
   to plant the lowly in their place.
The last traces of the proud God sweeps away
   and digs out their roots from the subsoil.

---

[44] W. Baumgartner, "Die literarischen Gattungen in der Weisheit des Jesus Sirach," *ZAW* 34 (1914) 161-198; H. Ludin Jansen, *Die spätjüdische Psalmendichtung. Ihr Entstehungskreis und ihr "Sitz im Leben": Eine literaturgeschichtlich-soziologische Untersuchung* (Skrifter utgitt av Det Norske Videnskaps-Akademi i Oslo II.3; Oslo: Jacob Dybwad, 1937) 55-94; H. Gese, "Weisheitsdichtung," *RGG* 3 (1959) 305-306; Frank Crüsemann, *Studien zur Formgeschichte von Hymnus und Danklied in Israel* (WMANT 32; Neukirchen-Vlyun: Neukirchener Verlag, 1969) 115-121; Patrick W. Skehan, *Studies in Israelite Wisdom and Poetry* (CBQMS 1; Washington D.C.: Catholic Biblical Association, 1971); von Rad, *Wisdom in Israel*, 38-40, 206-226; Crenshaw, "Wisdom," 247-248; cf. Eduard Norden, *Agnostos Theos: Untersuchungen zur Formengeschichte religiöser Rede* (Leipzig, Berlin: Teubner, 1913) [reprint, Darmstadt: Wissenschaftliche Buchgesellschaft, 1956] 177-207; J. Kenneth Kuntz, "The Canonical Wisdom Psalms of Ancient Israel: Their Rhetorical, Thematic, and Formal Dimensions," *Rhetorical Criticism: Essays in Honor of James Muilenburg* (ed. Jared J. Jackson and Martin Kessler; Pittsburgh: Pickwick, 1974) 186-222; Al Wolters, "Proverbs XXXI.10-31 as Heroic Hymn: A Form-Critical Analysis," *VT* 38 (1988) 446-457. Regarding Hellenistic-Jewish texts, James H. Charlesworth ("Jewish Hymns, Odes, and Prayers [ca. 167 BCE--135 CE]," *Early Judaism and its Modern Interpreters* [ed. Robert A. Kraft and George W. E. Nickelsburg; SBLBMI 2; Philadelphia: Fortress; Atlanta: Scholars Press, 1986] 422, cf. 411-436) observes that wisdom motifs are dominant in late hymns and prayers (e.g. Baruch 3.9-4.4), though modern scholars have failed to clarify why and to what extent; cf. Carey A. Moore, *Daniel, Esther, and Jeremiah: The Additions. A New Translation with Introduction and Commentary* (AB 44; Garden City, New York: Doubleday, 1977) 295-304. On the relationship between *The Teachings of Silvanus* and Hellenistic hymns see Schoedel, "Jewish Wisdom," 190-193.

[45] Baumgartner, "Gattungen," 175.

He plucks them from the face of the earth and roots them out,
    and effaces the memory of them from among men.
Insolence is not allotted to a human,
    nor impudent anger to one born of woman.[46]

With regard to length, topic, and its rather rudimentary progression of thought, this hymn is typical of Jewish gnomic poems. The passage consists of a series of parallel statements with a number of participles that dramatize the mighty acts of God; it concludes with a summarizing maxim that formulates a fundamental rule of conduct. The hymn addresses a prominent sapiential subject, depicting divine punishment of the powerful and arrogant while exhorting the faithful to shun pride and unjust violence. Since "the beginning of wisdom is fear of the Lord," wisdom and pride are incompatible. When human beings withdraw from their Creator, they become shameless and presumptuous, trusting in themselves, their own power and judgement. As the author argues, this denial of God's lordship is a form of self-deception which ultimately leads to disaster.[47]

Standing somewhat apart from these poems is a series of hymns in praise of personified Wisdom, particularly as God's mediator in creation; their distinctive content and composition has been substantially influenced by Egyptian wisdom as well as Jewish prophecy.[48] In Proverbs 8, for instance, Wisdom, poised at the entrance to the holy city, exhorts its citizens to heed her appeal. In this highly artistic composition, the poet enumerates Wisdom's benefits, which, in addition to its primacy in creation, include the prosperity,

---

[46] Translation: Skehan and DiLella, *Ben Sira*, 222.

[47] Skehan and DiLella, *Ben Sira*, 225-226.

[48] William F. Albright, "Some Canaanite-Phoenician Sources of Hebrew Wisdom," in Noth and Thomas, *Wisdom in Israel*, 1-15; Christa Kayatz, *Studien zu Proverbien 1-9: Eine form- und motivgeschichtliche Untersuchung unter Einbeziehung ägyptischen Vergleichsmaterials* (WMANT 22; Neukirchen-Vluyn: Neukirchener Verlag, 1966) 76-134; Johann Marböck, *Weisheit im Wandel: Untersuchungen zur Weisheitstheologie bei Ben Sira* (BBB 37; Bonn: Hanstein, 1971) 17-96; Maurice Gilbert, "L'éloge de la Sagesse (Siracide 24)," *RTL* 5 (1974) 326-348; Crenshaw, "Wisdom," 248-249; Hans-Jürgen Hermisson, "Observations on the Creation Theology in Wisdom," in Gammie, *Israelite Wisdom*, 43-57. There is a special set of problems regarding the Wisdom of Solomon in this respect, see Chrysostome Larcher, *Le Livre de la Sagesse ou la Sagesse de Salomon* (EBib 1, 3, 5; 3 vols.; Paris: Gabalda, 1983-1985) 2.561-605; Reese, *Hellenistic Influence*, 42-50, 105-109; Burton L. Mack, *Logos und Sophia: Untersuchungen zur Weisheitstheologie im hellenistischen Judentum* (SUNT 10; Göttingen: Vandenhoeck & Ruprecht, 1973) 63-78. Also, some of the hymns of the New Testament exhibit sapiential features, see, for example, Elisabeth Schüssler Fiorenza, "Wisdom Mythology and the Christological Hymns of the New Testament," in Wilken, *Aspects of Wisdom*, 14-41, with further references.

righteousness, and justice enjoyed by its adherents.[49] Modern critics have argued that on account of their distinctive subject matter and form this and similar hymns constitute a separate genre.

Within the Psalter there is also a small number of 'wisdom psalms', though their identification remains rather problematic.[50] These poems apparently served in cultic as well as instructional capacities.[51] Following Roland Murphy, the following may be listed with some confidence: 1, 32, 34, 37, 49, 112, 128 (= LXX 1, 31, 33, 36, 48, 111, 127); Murphy also describes a number of other psalms that incorporate sapiential elements or themes.[52] Formally, wisdom psalms have much in common with their non-wisdom neighbors, though they also exhibit special characteristics, including maxims (especially beatitudes, 'better' sayings, and numerical sayings), an address of a father or teacher to his 'son', rhetorical questions, and the loose, sometimes anthologized, organization of independent sayings, as well as acrostic arrangement. The themes of wisdom psalms are familiar from Jewish sapiential sources: the two ways, contrast of the sage and the fool, the fear of the Lord, practical ethical advice, and, most interestingly, "a preoccupation with the problem of retribution."[53]

---

[49] On Proverbs 8 see R. Stecher, "Die persönliche Weisheit in den Proverbien Kap. 8," *ZKT* 75 (1953) 41-51; R. B. Y. Scott, "Wisdom in Creation: The *AMON* of Proverbs 8.30," *VT* 10 (1960) 213-220; R. N. Whybray, "Proverbs 8.22-31 and its Supposed Prototypes," *VT* 15 (1965) 504-514 [reprint, Crenshaw, *Studies*, 390-400]; Kayatz, *Studien zu Proverbien 1-9*, 76-119; von Rad, *Wisdom in Israel*, 149-157; Maurice Gilbert, "Le discours de la Sagesse en Proverbes 8: Structure et cohérence," *La Sagesse de l'Ancien Testament* (ed. idem; BETL 51; Leuven: Leuven University Press; Gembloux: Duculot, 1979) 202-218; Patrick W. Skehan, "Structures in Poems on Wisdom: Proverbs 8 and Sirach 24," *CBQ* 41 (1979) 365-379.

[50] Hermann Gunkel and Joachim Begrich, *Einleitung in die Psalmen: Die Gattungen der religiösen Lyrik Israels* (HKAT Sup 2.19; Göttingen: Vandenhoeck & Ruprecht, 1933) 381-397; Jansen, *Psalmendichtung*, 8-55; P. A. Munch, "Die jüdischen 'Weisheitspsalmen' und ihr Platz im Leben," *AnOr* 15 (1937) 112-140; Sigmund Mowinckel, "Psalms and Wisdom," in Noth and Thomas, *Wisdom in Israel*, 205-224; idem, *The Psalms in Israel's Worship* (2 vols.; Nashville: Abingdon, 1962) 2.104-125; von Rad, *Wisdom in Israel*, 195-206; Crenshaw, "Wisdom," 249-252; idem, *Old Testament Wisdom*, 180-189; Erhard Gerstenberger, "Psalms," in Hayes, *Form Criticism*, 218-221; J. Luyten, "Psalm 73 and Wisdom," in Gilbert, *La Sagesse*, 59-81; J. P. M. van der Ploeg, "Le Psaume 119 et la Sagesse," in Gilbert, *La Sagesse*, 82-87; cf. Dieter Lührmann, "Ein Weisheitspsalm aus Qumran (11 Q Ps^a XVIII)," *ZAW* 80 (1968) 87-98.

[51] On the scholastic setting and didactic tone of these psalms see esp. Munch, "Weisheitspsalmen," 112-140; cf. Jansen, *Psalmendichtung*, 95-133; Mowinckel, *Psalms*, 2.104-125; Gerstenberger, "Psalms," 218-221.

[52] Roland E. Murphy, "A Consideration of the Classification 'Wisdom Psalms'," *VTSup* 9 (1962) 156-167 [reprint, Crenshaw, *Studies*, 456-467].

[53] Murphy, "A Consideration," 164; Crenshaw, "Wisdom," 250.

Psalm 37 (LXX 36) provides a fine illustration of this type of gnomic poem. The literary qualities, practical scope, and didactic tone of this wisdom psalm is characteristic of most gnomic poems, both Jewish and Greek. Though it exhibits a consistent theme and outlook, the hymn as a whole lacks strict logical connection between individual verses; instead they are serialized according to the purely external framework of an alphabetic acrostic. Its structure is consequently reminiscent of a collection of gnomic sayings; here are verses 1-9:

> Fret not yourself because of the wicked,
>   do not loose your temper because of sinners;
> for they will speedily fade like the grass,
>   and wither like the green herb!
> Trust in the Lord, and do good;
>   dwell in the land and keep upright in heart;
> and take delight in the Lord,
>   for he gives you the desires of your heart.
> Commit your way to the Lord
>   and trust in him; he will do it well:
> he will bring forth your salvation as the light
>   and your right as the brightness at noonday.
> Be still before the Lord, and wait patiently for him;
>   fret not yourself over him who prospers in his way,
>   over the man who carries out evil devices!
> Refrain from anger, and forsake wrath;
>   fret not yourself; it tends only to evil!
> For the wicked shall be destroyed;
>   but those who wait for the Lord, they shall inherit the land.[54]

In these lines we find a loosely organized sequence of wisdom admonitions united topically, accompanied by more-or-less relevant reasons, threats, and promises. As Artur Weiser notes, the psalmist has compiled the hymn partly from the corpus of gnomic sayings already available, partly from sayings newly composed.[55] The concepts here are familiar from the hymnic section in Ben Sira 10 cited above; the psalmist exhorts the audience to trust in God's righteousness and to wait patiently for divine judgement. Thus they are not to react with anger or envy to evil-doers but must obey the Lord and do good. The nature of the poet's perspective towards the theological issues raised here is

---

[54] Translation: Artur Weiser, *The Psalms: A Commentary* (OTL; Philadelphia: Westminster, 1962) 312.
[55] Ibidem, 312-323.

also typical of the genre: there is no critical examination of the theoretical, existential dilemma of theodicy or the inscrutable nature of divine retribution. The issue at hand is not the vindication of God, but of the practice of Jewish religion in everyday life and of the concrete response expected of the faithful to evil.[56]

In Greek literature, gnomic poetry flourished almost from the very beginning; many of the earliest poems enjoyed long careers and exercised considerable influence on later poets as models of form and style, as well as convenient sources of 'quotations'. Foremost among these were Hesiod's *Opera et Dies* and the poems of Theognis and Phocylides,[57] though other notable authors, such as Solon, Pindar, Aeschylus, Sophocles, Euripides, and Menander, indulged in the gnomic style and assimilated gnomic themes and forms into their works.[58]

During the Hellenistic era, gnomic poetry continued as a mode of ethical instruction, though prose, or prose interspersed with verse, began to overshadow the earlier genre in importance. Another significant trend was the co-optation of the genre by philosophers, who both cited the poets as evidence and composed verses of their own. As Donald R. Dudley observes, the Cynics were instrumental in this process:

> The great quantity of moralizing verse which characterizes the Hellenistic age cannot all be put down to the account of the Cynics, though it is safe to say that Cynic influence gave the first impetus to that literature. And it is noteworthy that this gnomic poetry exhibits the same features as the moralizing prose of the diatribe, the χρεία, and the ἀπομνημονεύμα [sic].[59]

---

[56] Cf. Gunkel and Begrich, *Einleitung*, 386-387; von Rad, *Wisdom in Israel*, 203-206. Similar themes also occur in LXX Psalms 1.5, 33.16-22, 91.7-9, 111.8.

[57] Isocrates *Ad Nicoclem* 43-44 (cf. 2.3) suggests the prominence of these authors; for some of the larger questions concerning their literature see Alois Rzach, "Hesiodos," *PW* 8.1 (1912) 1167-1240; P. Friedländer, "ΥΠΟΘΗΚΑΙ," *Hermes* 48 (1913) 558-616; Wolfgang Aly, "Theognis," *PW* 5.A2 (1934) 1972-1984; P. Ahlert and Wilhelm Kroll, "Phokylides," *PW* 20.1 (1941) 503-510; Aurelio Peretti, *Teognide nella tradizione gnomolica* (Classici e Orientali 4; Pisa: Libreria goliardiea, 1953); idem, "Calchi gnomici nella silloge teognidea," *Maia* 8 (1956) 197-217; Martin L. West, *Hesiod: Works and Days* (Oxford: Clarendon, 1978); Thomas J. Figueira and Gregory Nagy, eds., *Theognis of Megara: Poetry and the Polis* (Baltimore, London: Johns Hopkins University Press, 1985).

[58] In addition to the standard works on these authors see Horna, "Gnome," 76-78; Ernst Ahrens, *Gnomen in griechischer Dichtung (Homer, Hesiod, Aeschylus)* (Halle: Triltsch, 1937); Heinrich Bischoff, *Gnomen Pindars* (Würzburg: Triltsch, 1938); Bielohlawek, *Hypotheke und Gnome*, passim; Woldemar Görler, *Menandrou Gnomai* (Berlin: Freie Universität Berlin, 1963).

[59] Donald R. Dudley, *A History of Cynicism* (London: Methuen, 1937) [reprint, Hildesheim: Olms, 1967] 113; cf. the references below in note 117. Of related interest are the

As Dudley's comments suggest, the Cynic style and themes became distinctive features of the genre. Of the Cynics themselves, only the poems of Crates of Thebes and Cercidas of Megalopolis survive in substantial quantities. The former propagated Cynicism in epics and tragedies, as well as in elegiac epigrams called ΠΑΙΓΝΙΑΙ ("Trifles").[60] Like most Cynic writings, the poems are characterized by biting satire, striking images, and pedestrian language. Among their themes are attacks on wealth and hypocrisy, often coupled with praise of the difficult though virtuous Cynic way of life. In this poem, Crates parodies the famous prayer of Solon:

ὠφέλιμον δὲ φίλοις, μὴ γλυκερὸν τίθετε.
χρήματα δ'οὐκ ἐθέλω συνάγειν κλυτά, κανθάρου ὄλβον
μύρμηκός τ' ἄφενος χρήματα μαιόμενος,
ἀλλὰ δικαιοσύνης μετέχειν καὶ πλοῦτον ἀγείρειν
εὔφορον, εὔκτητον, τίμιον εἰς ἀρετήν.

To my friends make me useful rather than agreeable.
As for money I desire not to amass conspicuous wealth,
seeking after the wealth of the beetle or the substance of the ant;
rather, I desire to possess justice and to collect riches
that are easily carried, easily acquired, of great avail for virtue.[61]

The lyrical ΜΕΛΙΑΜΒΟΙ of Cercidas convey similar ethical concepts with the same energy.[62] In tone these poems are conversational though literary, and the author frequently adapts and quotes traditional materials. The contents of the ΜΕΛΙΑΜΒΟΙ consist largely of the regular stock of Cynic topics, including an autobiographical contemplation of prudence and discipline in the face of impending death.[63]

---

poets discussed by Ewen L. Bowie, "Greek Sophists and Greek Poetry in the Second Sophistic," *ANRW* II.33.1 (1989) 209-258.

[60] Text: Hermann Diels, *Poetarum Philosophorum Fragmenta* (Berlin: Weidmann, 1901) 207-223; Ernst Diehl, *Anthologia Lyrica Graeca* (Leipzig: Teubner, 1958³) 1.120-126; for more see Gerhard, *Phoinix*, 237-238; Dudley, *Cynicism*, 42-53, 56-58; Heinrich Dörrie, "Krates 2," *KP* 3 (1969) 327-328.

[61] Fragment 1.5-9 (Diehl), from Julian *Oration* 6 ("To the Uneducated Cynics") 199D-200A; text and translation: Wilmer C. Wright, trans., *The Works of the Emperor Julian* (LCL; 3 vols.; Cambridge: Harvard University Press; London: Heinemann, 1913) 2.54-55, cf. 2.94-95.

[62] Text and translation: A. D. Knox, trans., *Herodes, Cercidas, and the Greek Choliambic Poets* (LCL; Cambridge: Harvard University Press; London: Heinemann, 1967) 189-221, with the *Cercidea*, 228-239; for more see Gerhard, *Phoinix*, 237; J. U. Powell and E. A. Barber, *New Chapters in the History of Greek Literature* (Oxford: Clarendon, 1921) 2-12; Dudley, *Cynicism*, 74-84, 93-94; Knox, *Herodes*, xvii-xix, 222-227.

[63] Fragment 3; text and translation: Knox, *Herodes*, 200-205.

Other gnomic poets, though not Cynics, were influenced by the movement, or at least their writings manifest Cynic themes. Leonidas of Tarentum, for example, was a popular and influential epigrammatist of the third century B.C. His works are noteworthy for their clash of elaborate style and diction with mundane subject matter. Some of his poems, which often sketch scenes of ordinary working life, exhibit gnomic features, and the themes of these and other epigrams attest to the influence of Cynic ideas.[64] The repertoire of Sotades of Maroneia (third century B.C.), an ethical critic and satirist, also included gnomic poetry. In addition to an acrostic of gnomic verses, Stobaeus attributes to him several gnomic compositions.[65] One poem raises a prevalent gnomic topic, the unforeseeable and capricious nature of human existence:

Τῆς τύχης σκοπεῖν δεῖ τὸ μέγιστον ὡς ἔλαττον·
καὶ τὸ μὴ παρὸν μὴ θέλειν, οὐδὲ γὰρ σόν ἐστιν.
ἀμφότερα μένειν οὐκ οἶδεν· ἔστηκε γὰρ οὐδέν.
ἂν πλούσιος ὢν καθ' ἡμέραν σκοπῆς τὸ πλεῖον,
ἐς τοσοῦτον εἶ πενιχρός, ἐς ὅσον εἶ περισσός.
ὡς πένης θέλει σχεῖν καὶ πλούσιος πλέον σχεῖν,
ἴσον ἔχουσιν αὐτῶν αἱ ψυχαὶ τὸ μεριμνᾶν.

One must pay heed to the great things of fortune like the lesser;
don't desire what was before, for it is not your own.
Neither of these things knows how to remain; for nothing has been established.
Being wealthy, you may see more everyday;
in the same span of time you may be penniless, or have a surplus.
Poor and rich alike desire to have more;
the souls of both have the same anxieties.[66]

Other writers that could be included in this discussion are Chares and Phoenix of Colophon.[67] Several scholars have also speculated as to the Cynic

---

[64] E.g. *Anthologia Graeca* 6.302; 7.67, 452, 472, 648, 660, 665, 726, 731, 736; 9.99, 335; text: Gow and Page, *Hellenistic Epigrams*, 1.107-139; also see Gerhard, *Phoinix*, 240, 242; Dudley, *Cynicism*, 114-115; Gow and Page, *Hellenistic Epigrams*, 2.307-398; Rudolf Keydell, "Leonidas 9," *KP* 3 (1969) 567-568.

[65] The title of one of his poems was Εἰς Ἅιδου κατάβασις. Cf. Gerhard, *Phoinix*, 243-244, 266, 277; Dudley, *Cynicism*, 114.

[66] Stobaeus *Anthologium* 3.1.66; text: Otto Hense, ed., *Johannis Stobaei Anthologium* (5 vols.; Berlin: Weidmann, 1884-1912) [reprint 1958] 3.27; my translation.

[67] On Chares see Douglas Young, ed., *Theognis* (BT; Leipzig: Teubner, 1971²) 113-118; cf. Jaekel, *Sententiae*, 26-30; also Gerhard, *Phoinix*, 264; idem, ΧΑΡΗΤΟΣ ΓΝΩΜΑΙ (Sitzungsberichte der Heidelberger Akademie der Wissenschaften, Philosophisch-historische Klasse 3.13; Heidelberg: Carl Winter, 1912); Otto Hense, "Chares und Verwandtes,"

background of some of the gnomic poems in the *Theognidea*.[68]

While a great deal of Hellenistic gnomic poetry may be attributed, directly or indirectly, to the Cynics, they by no means exercised a monopoly on the genre. In fact, writers connected with virtually every philosophical school, and some connected with no school at all, took advantage of this medium of ethical expression and instruction. Such widespread use testifies to the genre's popularity and flexibility.

The works of Timon of Phlius (c. 320-230 B.C.) have some affinity with Cynicism, though the author's true allegiance belonged to Pyrrho of Elis, the forerunner of Skepticism.[69] While Timon was reputed to have published in a wide range of prose and poetic forms, the extant fragments are predominantly from two works, the ΣΙΛΛΟΙ ("Lampoons") in hexameters, and the ΙΝΔΑΛΜΟΙ ("Images") in elegiacs. The poems are abundant with philosophical invective, parody, and humor; they apparently served as a means of popularizing Pyrrho's philosophy while at the same time casting aspersions on his competitors.

Of the surviving nine poems of Cleanthes of Assos (died 232 B.C.), the best-known is the *Hymn to Zeus*, an eloquent Stoic statement of theology and ethics composed in dactylic hexameters.[70] This hymn draws upon much traditional poetic language and its thought is indebted to the (largely gnomic) philosophy of Heraclitus. Another poem, in iambs, portrays a dialogue between Reason and Passion.[71] While Cleanthes wrote predominantly in prose, he occasionally

---

Rheinisches Museum 72 (1917-18) 14-34; Powell and Barber, *New Chapters*, 18; Dudley, *Cynicism*, 114. On Phoenix see esp. Gerhard, *Phoinix*, passim; also Powell and Barber, *New Chapters*, 12-16; Dudley, *Cynicism*, 89, 114; Knox, *Herodes*, xvi-xvii, 242-263.

[68] For example 83-86, 731-752, 1135-1150, 1191-1194; Gerhard, *Phoinix*, 257-264; Dudley, *Cynicism*, 113-114; cf. Martin L. West, *Studies in Greek Elegy and Iambus* (Berlin, New York: de Gruyter, 1974) 40-64; Gregory Nagy, "Theognis and Megara: A Poet's Vision of his City," in Figueira and Nagy, *Theognis*, 46-51.

[69] Text: Diels, *Poetarum Philosophorum Fragmenta*, 173-206; for more see Gerhard, *Phoinix*, 242-243, 250-251; Dudley, *Cynicism*, 107-108, 114; Heinrich Dörrie, "Timon 3," *KP* 5 (1975) 847; A. A. Long, "Timon of Phlius: Pyrrhonist and Satirist," *Proceedings of the Cambridge Philological Society* 204 (1978) 68-91.

[70] Text: Hans F. A. von Arnim, ed., *Stoicorum Veterum Fragmenta* (4 vols.; Leipzig: Teubner, 1905-1924) 1.121-123 (# 537); text and translation: A. A. Long and D. N. Sedley, *The Hellenistic Philosophers* (2 vols.; Cambridge: Cambridge University Press, 1987) 1.326-327, 2.326-327; further see Ernst Neustadt, "Der Zeushymnos des Kleanthes," *Hermes* 66 (1931) 387-401; Max Pohlenz, "Kleanthes' Zeushymnus," *Hermes* 75 (1940) 117-123; J. D. Meerwaldt, "Cleanthea I, II," *Mnemosyne* 4 (1951) 40-69, 5 (1952) 1-12; Günther Zuntz, "Zum Kleanthes-Hymnus," *HSCP* 63 (1958) 289-308; Ernst G. Schmidt, "Kleanthes," *KP* 3 (1969) 226; Wlodzimierz Appel and Carolinae Holzman, "Zur Interpretation des 4.Verses Kleanthes' Hymnus auf Zeus," *Eranos* 82 (1984) 179-183; P. A. Meijer, "Γέρας in the Hymn of Cleanthes on Zeus," *Rheinisches Museum für Philologie* 129 (1986) 31-35.

[71] Arnim, *Fragmenta*, 1.570.

interspersed poetic lines, deeming their clarity and dignity a more apt means of expressing ultimate truths.[72]

Like Cleanthes, the most substantial remains of the Epicurean Philodemus of Gadara (born c. 110 B.C.) are prose; among these works are treatises on rhetoric and poetry as well as philosophy and ethics. However, we also possess approximately thirty-five of his epigrams preserved in the *Anthologia Graeca*.[73] Most of these poems are witty and erotic, though some express serious ethical ideas, for example *Anthologia Graeca* 5.112:

ἠράσθην· τίς δ' οὐχί; κεκώμακα· τίς δ' ἀμύητος
  κώμων; ἀλλ' ἐμάνην· ἐκ τίνος; οὐχὶ θεοῦ;
ἐρρίφθω· πολιὴ γὰρ ἐπείγεται ἀντὶ μελαίνης
  θρὶξ ἤδη, συνετῆς ἄγγελος ἡλικίης.
καὶ παίζειν ὅτε καιρός, ἐπαίξαμεν· ἡνίκα καὶ νῦν
  οὐκέτι, λωϊτέρης φροντίδος ἁψόμεθα.

I loved, as who has not? I revelled, and who is not initiate
in revelry? But I went mad,--by whose will, if not a god's?
Let it all go; already gray hair comes hurrying in place
of black, announcer of discretion's years.
When it was time for play, we played; now that it is
no longer so, we will apply ourselves to higher thoughts.[74]

The ideas and methods of this poem are illustrative of the genre for several reasons. First, the epigram's dialogical style, which bears some resemblance to the give and take of the diatribe, is similar to that of many other gnomic poems. The poem is also typical in the way that it personalizes the discussion of its gnomic themes by speaking in an emotional, first-person voice and by interjecting rhetorical questions. Finally, one of the important concepts guiding the poet's thoughts here--the need to understand what is appropriate or timely, καιρός, and act accordingly--is a cardinal principle of numerous gnomic texts.[75]

---

[72] Arnim, *Fragmenta*, 1.486; cf. Seneca *Epistulae Morales* 108.9-10.

[73] Text and translation: Gow and Page, *Garland*, 1.351-369, cf. 2.371-400; further see esp. Elizabeth Asmis, "Philodemus' Epicureanism," *ANRW* II.36.4 (1990) 2369-2406, with references; also Ernst G. Schmidt, "Philodemos," *KP* 4 (1972) 759-763.

[74] Text and translation: Gow and Page, *Garland*, 1.360-363, 2.387.

[75] For example Ben Sira 4.20, 11.25-28, 20.1, 22.6, 24.7; Galatians 6.9-10; Pseudo-Phocylides 82, 121; Sextus *Sententiae* 160, 163; *Gnomologium Democrateum* 71, 94, 236; Pittacus 1; Theognis 401-402; Pseudo-Isocrates *Ad Demonicum* 41; *Gnomica Homoeomata* 32, 59, 73, 74b, 123, 134; Babrius *Mythiamboi* 96 etc.; cf. von Rad, *Wisdom in Israel*, 138-143.

The *Carmen Aureum*, "Golden Verses," (perhaps third century A.D.) is a relatively long and rather eclectic gnomic poem composed in dactylic hexameters; it may have been employed in an academic setting for the instruction of recent initiates to the Pythagorean school.[76] The author or editor has divided the composition into two parts. The opening section of the poem (1-49), which consists mainly of gnomic admonitions, recommends a specific philosophical way of life to the reader, focusing on practical virtues and ethical reflection. The second section (50-71) buttresses the first by pointing to the ultimate goals of this way of life and by promising benefits to the obedient.[77]

Gnomic poetry also enjoyed a rigorous life outside the realm of philosophy. The *Mimes* of Herodes (third century B.C.), for instance, depict short colorful scenes of daily life in choliambic verse. These poems, which may have been intended for dramatic production, employ popular language, maxims, and proverbial expressions to amuse and entertain the audience, as well as to make some serious ethical points.[78] Fables, with their joint aims of entertainment and instruction, might also be considered a type of gnomic poetry. In the first century A.D., Babrius compiled an anthology of Aesopic fables, MYΘIAMBOI, rewriting them into choliambic verse.[79] Many of the fables conclude with a maxim which encapsulates the moral of the story.[80] Finally, mention should be made of the vast *Carmina Moralia* of Gregory of Nazianzus.[81] This is an anthology of ethical poems and maxims, including several gnomologia[82] and an

---

[76] Text: Young, *Theognis*, 86-94; also see Mario Meunier, *Pythagore: Les Vers d'or. Hiéroclès: Commentaire sur les vers d'or des Pythagoriciens. Traduction nouvelle avec prolégomènes et notes* (Paris: L'Artisan du Livre, 1925) 23-31; P. C. van der Horst, *Les Vers D'Or Pythagoriciens: Études avec une introduction et un commentaire* (Leiden: Brill, 1932) esp. xxv-xxxiii; Küchler, *Weisheitstraditionen*, 251-252, 271-272; Kloppenborg, *The Formation of Q*, 300.

[77] See Johan C. Thom, *The Golden Verses of Pythagoras: A Critical Investigation of its Literary Composition and Religio-historical Significance* (Ph.D. Dissertation, University of Chicago, 1989).

[78] Text: I. C. Cunningham, ed., *Herodae Mimiambi* (BT; Leipzig: Teubner, 1987); text and translation: Knox, *Herodes*, 80-175; also see Powell and Barber, *New Chapters*, 112-123; Rudolf Keydell, "Herodas," *KP* 2 (1967) 1090; Knox, *Herodes*, xix-xxiv, 74-79, 177-185.

[79] Text and translation: Otto Crusius, ed., *Babrii Fabulae Aesopeae* (BT; Leipzig: Teubner, 1897); Ben Edwin Perry, trans., *Babrius and Phaedrus* (LCL; Cambridge: Harvard University Press; London: Heinemann, 1984); also see Gerhard, *Phoinix*, 246-247, 267-269.

[80] E.g. *Mythiamboi* 5, 6, 13, 14, 18, 20, 21, 22, 24, 29, 31, 33, 37, 44, 47, 50, 52, 56, 58, 59, 64-67, 69, 71, 79, 81-85, 87, 92, 94, 96, 98, 103, 111, 112, 116, 119, 127; cf. Perry, *Babrius*, xiv-xvi.

[81] Text: *PG* 37.521-968.

[82] Ibidem, 910-915, 916-927, 927-945.

alphabetic acrostic of gnomic verses.[83] While it appears that Gregory himself is responsible for the composition of the poems in the *Carmina Moralia*, he draws extensively from the works of well-known poets such as Theognis, Euripides, and Callimachus, as well as from the available fund of proverbial lore and popular philosophy.[84]

Generally speaking, gnomic poems became an effective and popular genre in the ancient world largely because they joined ethical instruction with the aesthetic pleasure associated with reading or hearing a work of poetry. The potential of poetic expression enabled authors to lend a certain dignity to their subject matter and to make their messages more striking and memorable. The prologue to the *Comparatio Menandri et Philistionis II* summarizes the ethos of the genre:

Ὁ πᾶσιν ἀρέσας ἐν σοφοῖς ποιήμασιν
ὁ τοῦ βίου τὴν πρᾶξιν ἐπιδείξας σοφοῖς,
Μένανδρος ὁ σοφὸς νῦν πάλιν παραινέσω,
χαίρειν προ(σ)τάξας τοῖς ἀκούουσιν νέοις,
ὅπως ἕκαστος ἀκούων μου μανθάνῃ
τὴν τοῦ βίου εὐθεῖαν, ἣν ὑμῖν φράσω,
παρηγορῶν ἕκαστον ἐς τὸ συμφέρον,
ἔχων ἀγῶνα πρὸς Φιλιστίωνα νῦν,
τὸν τερπνὸν καὶ φιλητὸν καὶ βιωφελῆ,
ἐκ τῶν κατὰ μέρος ἐκλεγέντων πραγμάτων.

He who pleases all with wise poems,
and displays the praxis of life to the wise,
I, Menander the wise, shall once more prescribe
instructions to delight the youth who listen,
so that each, hearing me, will learn
the straight way of life, which I will recommend to you,
exhorting each to what is useful,
now holding a contest against Philistion,

---

[83] Ibidem, 908-910.
[84] Gerhard, *Phoinix*, 255, 275; Vetschera, *Paränese*, 27-29; Henry Chadwick, "Florilegium," *RAC* 7 (1969) 1145-1146; D. A. Sykes, "The *Poemata Arcana* of St. Gregory Nazianzen: Some Literary Questions," *Byzantinische Zeitschrift* 72 (1979) 6-15; idem, "Gregory Nazianzen as Didactic Poet," *Studia Patristica* 16 (1985) 433-437; Bernhard Wyß, "Gregor II (Gregor von Nazianz)," *RAC* 12 (1983) 793-863, esp. 808-814, 839-859. Also, Book 8 of the *Anthologia Graeca* is attributed to Gregory.

the pleasant and beloved and beneficent,
on chosen issues, each in turn.[85]

This introduction indicates the connection often made between learning and pleasure in gnomic poems. Menander's exhortations are associated with paraenesis (line 3); they are wise, practical, and useful, and they teach "the straight way of life" (line 6). At the same time, they please and delight the reader, and the whole atmosphere of the ἀγών seems more playful than studious. Following the prologue are a series of instructional paragraphs in meter and organized by topics on which Menander and Philistion offer their wise counsel; in substance, perspective, and length they are representative of the genre.

It is prudent to avoid rigid distinctions in describing the composition or purpose of gnomic poetry.[86] The genre exhibits a wide variety of literary styles and structures as well as topics and perspectives. One indication of this formal and material variety is the extent to which these authors employ, or chose not to employ, gnomic sayings. Individual poems may also differ with respect to their uniformity of subject matter and to the rigor with which their contents are logically arranged. In addition, the literature is ethically motivated to varying degrees and in differing ways, and on occasion the edificational or persuasional objectives seem subsumed under aesthetic ones.

Gnomologia

The need to preserve and collect well-known, useful, or artistic sayings, verses, quotations, and so forth must have been felt from almost the beginning of human literary activity. Ancient *florilegia*, of which Stobaeus' *Anthologium* is an example, gathered material on a wide range of themes and from a wide range of sources, including gnomic sources.[87] A special manifestation of this activity is the *gnomologium*, an anthology or collection composed entirely (or almost entirely) of gnomic sayings. Such texts demonstrate little logical or

---

[85] Text: Jaekel, *Sententiae*, 102; my translation. Also see Wilhelm Meyer, "Die athenische Spruchrede des Menander und Philistion," *Abhandlung der Bayerischen Akademie der Wissenschaften* 19 (1891) 227-295; Gerhard, *Phoinix*, 264-267, 274-275, 280.

[86] Cf. Gerhard, *Phoinix*, 228-234.

[87] Kurt Wachsmuth, *Studien zu den griechischen Florilegien* (Berlin: Weidmann, 1882); Henri-Marie Rochaise, "Florilèges Latins," *DSp* 5 (1964) 435-460; Philippe Delhaye, "Florilèges Mediévaux D'Ethique," *DSp* 5 (1964) 460-475; Marcel Richard, "Florilèges Grecs," *DSp* 5 (1964) 475-512; Chadwick, "Florilegium," 1131-1160.

material means of comprehensive organization; they ordinarily consist of a series of largely unconnected entries without any overarching order or plan. Thus a gnomologium lacks a 'macro-argument', as it were, though it may contain any number of 'micro-arguments', relatively short sequences of related sayings loosely strung together.

While the term gnomologium refers principally to anthologies of Greek provenance, similar collections were clearly important in ancient Near Eastern societies as well.[88] In the Hebrew Bible an anthology of gnomic verses has been preserved in Proverbs 10.1ff.[89] Like other ancient anthologies, this collection represents a multiplicity of sayings spanning the intellectual activity of several centuries and incorporating the experiential insights of different social groups. The maxims here counsel and admonish, but chiefly they provide illustrations of various types of behavior and their consequences. Although explicit concepts appear only infrequently, Proverbs 10.1ff. betrays a thoroughly Jewish ethos, and for its authors conformity to the order of creation appears to be consistent with the will of God. Sometime during the first century B.C., perhaps in Alexandria, translators rendered the Hebrew book of Proverbs into Greek. Significantly, this rendition exhibits considerable Hellenization and

---

[88] For examples see: E. I. Gorden and T. Jacobsen, *Sumerian Proverbs* (Philadelphia: University Museum of the University of Pennsylvania, 1959); W. G. Lambert, *Babylonian Wisdom Literature* (Oxford: Clarendon, 1960) 92-117, 213-282; James B. Pritchard, ed., *Ancient Near Eastern Texts Relating to the Old Testament* (Princeton: Princeton University Press, 1969³) 425-427, 593-594; McKane, *Proverbs*, 183-208; Brendt Alster, *Studies in Sumerian Proverbs* (Coppenhagen: Akademisk Forlag, 1975); Miriam Lichtheim, *Late Egyptian Wisdom Literature* (OBO 52; Freiburg: Universitätsverlag; Göttingen: Vandenhoeck & Ruprecht, 1983) 7-10; cf. Küchler, *Weisheitstraditionen*, 167-175; Waltrand Guglielmi, "Sprichwort," *LÄ* 5 (1984) 1219-1222.

[89] The collection is normally subdivided as follows: 1) 10.1-22.16, "The Proverbs of Solomon"; 2) 22.17-24.22, "The Sayings of the Wise," which correspond with the Instruction of Amenemope; 3) 24.23-34, "More Sayings of Wise Men"; 4) 25.1-29.27, "More Proverbs of Solomon transcribed by the Men of Hezekiah king of Judah"; 5) 30.1-33, "The Sayings of Agur son of Jakeh from Massa"; 6) 31.1-31, "The Sayings of Lemuel king of Massa which his Mother taught him," which is paralleled in Egyptian royal instructions. There are, of course, a host of complex and unresolved problems regarding the content, background, purpose, and setting of the book of Proverbs; see, for instance, Udo Skladny, *Die ältesten Spruchsammlungen in Israel* (Göttingen: Vandenhoeck & Ruprecht, 1962); Berend Gemser, *Sprüche Salomos* (HAT 1.16; Tübingen: Mohr-Siebeck, 1963²); R. N. Whybray, *Wisdom in Proverbs: The Concept of Wisdom in Proverbs 1-9* (SBT 45; Naperville: Allenson; London: SCM, 1965); Hermisson, *Studien zur israelitischen Spruchweisheit*, passim; McKane, *Proverbs*, passim; von Rad, *Wisdom in Israel*, 74-96; Roland E. Murphy, *The Forms of the Old Testament Literature, Volume 13: Wisdom Literature* (Grand Rapids: Eerdmans, 1981). Also see the discussion of LXX Proverbs 3.11-35 in Chapter Three.

deviates from its original more than any other document of the Septuagint, as Sidney Jellicoe observes:

> To a still greater extent [than the translator of Job] the translator of Proverbs adapts his original to its new environment. Maxims of purely Greek origin are incorporated and 'tags of rough hexameters and iambics abound'. Greek rather than Hebrew standards determine the style.[90]

The translators of the LXX Proverbs felt free to replace Hebrew sayings with their Greek equivalents and they often had recourse to poetic and other literary methods familiar from Greek gnomologia, particularly the Greek *paroemiographia*, such as the ΕΠΙΤΟΜΗ of Zenobius (second century A.D., but based on earlier collections).[91] This suggests that those who originally used the LXX Proverbs understood their gnomic collection in the same terms as those familiar to them from Greek sources and intended their translation to stand together with comparable gnomologia. So while the LXX Proverbs possesses distinct formal and material qualities, this is also true of other gnomic collections, and there are sufficient similarities for it to be considered in the basic investigation of ancient gnomologia.

In Greece, anthologies of this type were compiled beginning at least as early as the fourth century B.C. and endured as a vital though peripheral genre in education, literature, ethics, and philosophy throughout antiquity and beyond. The compilations normally consisted of sayings excerpted from the works of

---

[90] Sidney Jellicoe, *The Septuagint and Modern Study* (Oxford: Clarendon, 1968) 317-318; cf. McKane, *Proverbs*, 33-47; further see Emanuel Tov, "Jewish Greek Scriptures," in Kraft and Nickelsburg, *Early Judaism*, 221-237; idem, "The Septuagint," *Mikra: Text, Translation, Reading, and Interpretation of the Hebrew Bible in Ancient Judaism and Early Christianity* (ed. Martin J. Mulder; CRINT 2.1; Assen, Maastricht: Van Gorcum; Philadelphia: Fortress, 1988) 159-188.

[91] H. J. Thackeray, "The Poetry of the Greek Book of Proverbs," *JTS* 13 (1911-12) 46-66; cf. Gillis Gerleman, "The Septuagint Proverbs as a Hellenistic Document," *OTS* 8 (1950) 15-27; idem, "Studies in the Septuagint: Religion and Ethics in the LXX Proverbs," *LUÅ* 1.52.3 (1956) 36-63; John G. Gammie, "The Septuagint of Job: Its Poetic Style and Relationship to the Septuagint of Proverbs," *CBQ* 49 (1987) 14-31; von Lips, *Weisheitliche Traditionen*, 103-105. For more on Zenobius consult the articles by Otto Crusius in vol. 3 of *Corpus Paroemiographorum Graecorum* (ed. Ernst L. Leutsch and F. G. Schneidewin; 2 vols.; Göttingen: Vandenhoeck & Ruprecht, 1839-1851) [reprint with vol. 3, Hildesheim: Olms, 1958]; cf. Jürgen Werner's review of Winfried Bühler, ed., *Griechische Sprichwörter: Zenobii Athoi proverbia* (4 vols.; Göttingen: Vandenhoeck & Ruprecht, 1982) in *Göttingische Gelehrte Anzeigen* 240 (1988) 92-96 with references. Further see Karl Rupprecht, "Paroimiographoi," *PW* 18.4 (1949) 1735-1778; also cf. H. Attridge, "Fragments of Pseudo-Greek Poets," *The Old Testament Pseudepigrapha* (ed. James H. Charlesworth; 2 vols.; Garden City, New York: Doubleday, 1983, 1985) 2.821-830.

one or more sages, poets, or philosophers.[92] As Dimitri Gutas observes, the gnomologial corpus possessed two distinct yet complementary social identities:

> The gnomologia were popular in the true sense of the term: they were designed for public consumption, and as such were on the border line between folk literature, like proverbs, tales, etc., which is mostly oral, and scholarly philosophical and ethical literature. On the one hand they commanded greater respect than folk literature because the sayings and anecdotes were ascribed to venerable figures, and on the other they were not as forbidding as philosophical treatises because their contents were simple, easily understood and memorized.[93]

On account of this 'border line' existence, the gnomic anthologies as a whole display great range with respect to their traditional content, philosophical inclination, and literary quality.

Gnomic collections carry with them, like any other genre, a host of philological and literary problems. In addition to the usual questions of authorship, date, provenance, and the status of the text, special complications arise concerning gnomologia with regard to the analysis of sources, textual history, original purpose, and subsequent functions. While the anthologies are normally ascribed to a particular figure, and may preserve some authentic sayings, their contents are by and large pseudepigraphical. It is important to bear in mind that most ancient gnomologia enjoyed constant circulation and use; over the course of centuries any number of additions, abridgements, or re-arrangements could be made to a collection, all at the hands of anonymous writers and editors according to their particular needs.[94] With the notable exception of Anton Elter's investigations, the modern analysis of these formidable complexities has been limited in scope and quality.[95]

---

[92] For general comments on the Greek gnomologia see Horna, "Gnome," 78-82; J. Barnes, "A New Gnomologium, with some remarks on Gnomic Anthologies," *CQ* 44 (1950) 126-137, 45 (1951) 1-19; Spoerri, "Gnome," 825-829; Chadwick, "Florilegium," esp. 1152-1156; Dimitri Gutas, *Greek Wisdom Literature in Arabic Translation: A Study of the Graeco-Arabic Gnomologia* (AOS 60; New Haven: American Oriental Society, 1975); Küchler, *Weisheitstraditionen*, 236-302, cf. 157-235, 303-414; Kloppenborg, *The Formation of Q*, 289-306, 337-341.

[93] Gutas, *Greek Wisdom Literature*, 1-2.

[94] Horna, "Gnome," 82-84; Gutas, *Greek Wisdom Literature*, 1-5, 9-35, 436-438; Küchler, *Weisheitstraditionen*, 258-261. The various gnomic collections attributed to Menander are typical of this phenomenon, see Görler, *Menandrou Gnomai*, 102ff.

[95] See the references to Elter's works in the bibliography. A recent gnomologial study of interest is Alessandra B. Malgarini, "ΑΡΧΑΙΩΝ ΦΙΛΟΣΟΦΩΝ ΓΝΩΜΑΙ ΚΑΙ ΑΠΟΦΘΕΓΜΑΤΑ in un Manoscritto di Patmos," *Elenchos* 5 (1984) 153-200.

One reason for the difficulty in studying gnomologia is the remarkable diversity they exhibit in form, content, and function. Their morphology, to begin with, may be described with respect to two rudimentary characteristics: the types of sayings that occur in a collection and the means utilized by an author or editor to organize the sayings.

Evidence suggests that the earliest gnomologia were in verse; this was no doubt a reflection of the poetic inclinations of the earliest gnomic authors.[96] Yet while several of the surviving anthologies contain largely metrical sayings, most are in prose. The majority of gnomologia consist solely of a sequence of independent maxims; these may be predominantly wisdom admonitions or wisdom sentences, though typically it is a fair mixture of both.[97] A small number of collections, for instance the *Gnomologium Vaticanum* and the *Gnomologium Epictetum*, may supplement particular entries with explanations, illustrations, or supporting arguments, and so might be better understood as collections of enthymemes rather than gnomologia in the ordinary sense. Perhaps the specialized nature of these collections precipitated the need for such expansions. A related practice, common in Pseudo-Phocylides, is to combine several related maxims together with motive clauses or examples in various ways in order to produce discrete thematic units. In this case the gnomologium bears some resemblance to a collection of gnomic poems such as we find in the *Theognidea*.[98] Different too is the rabbinic tractate *Pirke 'Abot,* a multi-authored collection that consists largely of proverbs and maxims, though these are often accompanied by explanations, proof-texts, and various instructional materials.[99]

---

[96] Horna, "Gnome," 76-78; Barnes, "Gnomologium," 132-137; Spoerri, "Gnome," 824; Chadwick, "Florilegium," 1131-1136.

[97] Cf. Kloppenborg, *The Formation of Q*, 298-299; cf. also Küchler's grammatical analysis of the maxims in Pseudo-Phocylides (*Weisheitstraditionen*, 266-272).

[98] Cf. van der Horst, *Pseudo-Phocylides*, 77-80.

[99] Text and translation: R. Travers Herford, *Pirke Aboth. The Ethics of the Talmud: Sayings of the Fathers* (New York: Jewish Institute of Religion, 1945) [reprint, New York: Schocken, 1962]. Further see esp. M. B. Lerner, "The Tractate Avot," *The Literature of the Sages, First Part: Oral Tora, Halakha, Mishna, Tosefta, Talmud, External Tractates* (ed. Shmuel Safrai; CRINT 2.3.1; Assen, Maastricht: Van Gorcum; Philadelphia: Fortress, 1987) 262-281; also Louis Finkelstein, "Introductory Study to Pirke Aboth," *JBL* 57 (1938) 13-50 [reprint in idem, *Pharisaism in the Making* (New York: KTAV, 1972) 121-158]; Jacob Neusner, "Types and Forms of Ancient Jewish Literature: Some Comparisons," *HR* (1971-72) 354-390; Henry A. Fischel, "The Transformation of Wisdom in the World of Midrash," in Wilken, *Aspects of Wisdom*, 67-101; Küchler, *Weisheitstraditionen*, 176-198, cf. 199-206; Zeller, *Mahnsprüche*, 42-46; Kloppenborg, *The Formation of Q*, 293-294. Related to this tractate is its companion volume, the *'Abot de Rabbi Nathan*; see Anthony J. Saldarini, *The Fathers According to Rabbi Nathan (Abot de Rabbi Nathan): Version B* (SJLA 11; Leiden: Brill, 1975); idem, *Scholastic Rabbinism: A Literary Study of the Fathers According*

Gnomologia ordinarily display little logical or material organization with respect to their overall structure. The sequence from one maxim to the next often appears to be illogical or inconsistent, and sayings with differing literary structures, subject matter, and ethical viewpoints are situated side-by-side. Because normal rational connections and transitions are absent, individual sayings stand more or less in isolation and their application seems arbitrary and impersonal. Thus maxims in this sort of setting lack ordinary contexts and their projected meanings and functions are obscure or indeterminate. It remains for the reader of the anthology to remove these ambiguities by contextualizing individual sayings in specific situations or by imposing some sense of rational order on the collection as it stands.[100]

Because the gnomologial style draws together disparate ideas and themes in this way, a sequence of maxims in an anthology often has the disrupting effect of jolting the reader from one topic or perspective to the next. Such an unexpected pattern deviates from the logic anticipated of a conventional text, presenting contradictions and inconsistencies without ever seeming to resolve them. The result of anthologizing is often confrontational and disorienting; the document challenges the reader to become more constructively and imaginatively engaged in its exegesis. By construing meaning in this way, the readers become more self-conscious of the hermeneutical principles involved in their understanding of the text, and there is a greater than normal risk of individualized or idiosyncratic interpretations. A related phenomenon is the 'antilogical' tendency at work in some gnomologia; occasionally editors would juxtapose maxims conveying opposing points of view on the same subject. One rationale for this procedure is provided by Plutarch in *Moralia* 20c-22a: the contrast of differing views helps formulate a more balanced judgement, sharpens the critical faculties, and serves as preparation for future argument and debate.[101]

---

to *Rabbi Nathan* (BJS 14; Chico, CA: Scholars Press, 1982); Küchler, *Weisheitstraditionen*, 176-198, cf. 199-206; M. B. Lerner, "Avot de-R. Natan," in Safrai, *The Literature of the Sages*, 369-379.

[100] Further see Requadt, "Das Aphoristische Denken," 331-377; Barley, "Structural Approach," 737-750; Lewis, "The Discourse of the Maxim," 41-48; Krikmann, "Denotative Indefiniteness," 71-91; Barnes, "Aphorism and Argument," 91-109; van Leeuwan, *Context and Meaning*, 29-37; cf. Kahn, *Heraclitus*, 87-95.

[101] The title of the treatise is *Quomodo adolescens poetas audire debeat*. For text and translation see Babbitt, *Plutarch*, 1.71-197. As Barnes observes ("Gnomologium," 2-4), this sort of reasoning from both sides of an issue bears some resemblance to sophistic argumentation, and he in fact argues that the sophistic movement made use of such gnomologia.

This is not to say, however, that the constituent elements of a gnomic anthology necessarily lack arrangement altogether. Two means are most often employed to organize sayings. First, editors sometimes consistently utilize some arbitrary system such as alphabetization in order to serialize all the maxims in a collection. Second, in order to link together small clusters of sayings various techniques may be deployed, including catchword, linkword, inclusio, ring composition, formal analogy, and arrangement by topic.[102] While these features are extremely common they only rarely unite substantial portions of text or are applied consistently throughout a collection. An exception to this rule is Pseudo-Phocylides, which is arranged by topic throughout. In addition, some gnomologia exhibit a high degree of formal consistency in their sayings beyond any metrical requirements, for example Proverbs 10-15, a collection of mostly antithetically-formulated sayings, and the prologue to the *Dicta Catonis*, a collection of mostly two and three-word sayings.[103] Significantly, the patterns of arrangement characteristic of gnomologia are often based upon certain concrete verbal qualities of the sayings, such as their morphology or language. This is hardly unexpected, given the maxim's deliberate and artistic literary style, and the presence of such patterns underscores the form-intensive nature of gnomic wisdom.

Some typical examples of the sorts of organizational structures and devices that gnomologia characteristically deploy can be found in Sextus *Sententiae* 414-425:[104]

```
        χαίρειν ἔθιζέ σου τὴν ψυχὴν ἐφ' οἷς καλὸν χαίρειν.
415a    ψυχὴ χαίρουσα ἐπὶ μικροῖς ἄτιμος παρὰ θεῷ.
415b    σοφοῦ ψυχὴ ἀκούει θεοῦ.
        σοφοῦ ψυχὴ ἁρμόζεται πρὸς θεὸν ὑπὸ θεοῦ.
        σοφοῦ ψυχὴ ἀεὶ θεὸν ὁρᾷ.
```

---

[102] By *catchword* I mean the connection of a saying with the one that immediately precedes it by means of the repetition of a word or short phrase; *linkword* refers to a similar connection of three or more sayings which are not necessarily contiguous; *inclusio* is the use of the same term, concept, etc. at or near both the beginning and end of a passage; *ring composition* is the sustained chiastic structure of a passage, e.g. A B C B' A', where the correspondence of structural pairs can depend on such things as wording, topic, formal analogy, etc. Cf. Horna, "Gnome," 79; Küchler, *Weisheitstraditionen*, 260-261, cf. 265-274; Skehan and DiLella, *Ben Sira*, s.v. mot crochet, chiastic patterns; Kloppenborg, *The Formation of Q*, 299.

[103] Text and translation: J. Wight Duff and Arnold M. Duff, trans., *Minor Latin Poets* (LCL; Cambridge: Harvard University Press; London: Heinemann, 1935[2]) 592-629; cf. Otto Skutsch, "Dicta Catonis," *PW* 5.1 (1903) 358-370.

[104] For a recent discussion of the Sentences of Sextus see Robert L. Wilken, "Wisdom and Philosophy in Early Christianity," in idem, *Aspects of Wisdom*, 143-168.

	ψυχὴ σοφοῦ σύνεστιν ἀεὶ θεῷ.
	καρδία θεοφιλοῦς ἐν χειρὶ θεοῦ ἵδρυται.
420	ψυχῆς ἄνοδος πρὸς θεὸν διὰ λόγου θεοῦ.
	σοφὸς ἕπεται θεῷ καὶ ὁ θεὸς ψυχῇ σοφοῦ.
	χαίρει τῷ ἀρχομένῳ τὸ ἄρχον, καὶ ὁ θεὸς οὖν σοφῷ χαίρει.
	ἀχώριστόν ἐστιν τοῦ ἀρχομένου τὸ ἄρχον, καὶ θεὸς οὖν τοῦ σοφοῦ προνοεῖ καὶ κήδεται.
	ἐπιτροπεύεται σοφὸς ἀνὴρ ὑπὸ θεοῦ, διὰ τοῦτο καὶ μακάριος.
425	ψυχὴ σοφοῦ δοκιμάζεται διὰ σώματος ὑπὸ θεοῦ.
	Accustom your soul to rejoice in whatever it should rejoice.
415a	A soul which rejoices over trivial matters is dishonored before God.
415b	The soul of the sage hearkens to God.
	Through God the soul of the sage is attuned to God.
	The soul of the sage always perceives God.
	The soul of the sage is always in union with God.
	The heart of one who loves God is secure in the hand of God.
420	Through God's word the soul ascends to God.
	The sage accompanies God and God accompanies the soul of the sage.
	Anything that rules takes pleasure in what it rules, and so God takes pleasure in the sage.
	Anything that rules is inseparable from what it rules, and so God watches over and cares for the sage.
	The wise man is governed by God and so is blessed.
425	Through the body the sage's soul is tested by God.[105]

While these maxims are united by theme and perspective, there is no real progression of thought in the passage from beginning to end. The unit is organized by means of a number of interlocking, inconsistently applied devices, including catchword,[106] linkword,[107] anaphora,[108] and inclusio,[109] as well as an apparent attempt to group sayings according to length. A more sophisticated and sustained formal device commonly employed in gnomologia is ring-composition. Pseudo-Phocylides 9-21 provides an example; the structure here

---

[105] Text and translation: Edwards and Wild, *The Sentences of Sextus*, 66-69.
[106] 414-415a (χαίρω), 417-418 (ἀεί), 422-423 (ἀρχομέν- τὸ ἄρχον).
[107] 414-418, 420-421, 425 (ψυχή); 415b-418, 421, 425 (ψυχὴ σοφοῦ); 415a-425 (θεός); 421-425 (σοφός).
[108] 415b-417.
[109] χαίρ- appears at the beginning and end of 414 and 422; also ψυχὴ σοφοῦ ... θεῷ (418) and ψυχὴ σοφοῦ ... θεοῦ (425).

is supported by the linkword and inclusio created by the δικ- stems in lines 9-12, 14, and 21:

      πάντα δίκαια νέμειν, μὴ δὲ κρίσιν ἐς χάριν ἕλκειν.
10   μὴ ῥίψῃς πενίην ἀδίκως, μὴ κρῖνε πρόσωπον·
      ἢν σὺ κακῶς δικάσῃς, σὲ θεὸς μετέπειτα δικάσσει.
      μαρτυρίην ψευδῆ φεύγειν· τὰ δίκαια βραβεύειν.
      παρθεσίην τηρεῖν, πίστιν δ' ἐν πᾶσι φυλάσσειν.
      μέτρα νέμειν τὰ δίκαια, καλὸν δ' ἐπίμετρον ἁπάντων.
15   σταθμὸν μὴ κρούειν ἑτερόζυγον, ἀλλ' ἴσον ἕλκειν.
      μὴ δ' ἐπιορκήσῃς μήτ' ἀγνῶς μήτε ἑκοντί·
      ψεύδορκον στυγέει θεὸς ἄμβροτος ὅστις ὀμόσσῃ.
      σπέρματα μὴ κλέπτειν· ἐπαράσιμος ὅστις ἕληται.
      μισθὸν μοχθήσαντι δίδου, μὴ θλῖβε πένητα.
20   γλώσσῃ νοῦν ἐχέμεν, κρυπτὸν λόγον ἐν φρεσὶν ἴσχειν.
      μήτ' ἀδικεῖν ἐθέλῃς μήτ' οὖν ἀδικοῦντα ἐάσῃς.

      Always dispense justice and stretch not judgement for a favour.
10   Cast the poor not down unjustly, judge not partially.
      If you judge evilly, God will judge you thereafter.
      Flee false witness; arbitrate justice.
      Watch over a deposit, and in everything keep faith.
      Give a just measure, good is an extra full measure of all things.
15   Make a balance not unequal, but weigh honestly.
      Do not commit perjury, neither ignorantly nor willingly.
      The immortal God hates a perjurer, whosoever it is who has sworn.
      Do not steal seeds; cursed is whosoever takes them.
      Give the labourer his pay, do not afflict the poor.
20   Take heed of your tongue, keep your word hidden in your heart.
      Neither wish to do injustice, nor therefore allow another to do injustice.[110]

Here the ring composition effectively organizes and binds together the individual admonitions and sentences, all of which address the theme of justice and injustice in ethical behavior. The passage begins and ends with broad thematic statements that form a frame around the more concrete appeals in lines 10-19:

---

[110] Text and translation: van der Horst, *Pseudo-Phocylides*, 88-89, cf. 117-128.

9	A. On striving for justice
10	B. Against abusing the poor
11	C. God's punishment of injustice
12	D. Against false witness
13-15	E. On fair dealing
16	D'. Against perjury
17	C'. God's anger with perjurers
18-19	B'. Against abusing the poor
20-21	A'. Against injustice

Like most ring compositions found in gnomic wisdom, the arrangement of this passage does not rely on precise formal or ideational connections and the correspondence of structural pairs relies upon differing aspects of the maxims: theme is most important, but wording, morphology, and logical development also figure into the overall design.

The subject matter, provenance, and intended audience of the gnomologial genre, like its morphology, is wanting for consistency. A number of largely overlapping functions may be identified. The anthologies offered a means of preserving worthwhile observations and judgements in order to facilitate their later enjoyment and use. In this preservational and referential function, the maxims of a gnomologium represent excerpts culled from earlier works, quotations of famous figures, or the apt observations of a wise sage. It is in their capacity as repositories of valuable, as well as accessible, sayings that the use of gnomic anthologies in elementary education is best understood. The anthologies, particularly those in verse, served as copy-books or primers for instruction in pronunciation, orthography, spelling, and grammar, and as a means of exposing students to material of special literary and cultural merit. For more advanced students, compilations were made with an eye to their ethical and didactic content, and were frequently arranged topically. Because the study of maxims was generally deemed to be a valuable avenue to cultural awareness, social initiation, and personal improvement, gnomologia often became a basis of moral instruction in the ancient world. The gnomic anthologies preserved fundamental social norms and ethical attitudes, enabling them to be transmitted to different cultures and subsequent generations. This helped to insure the gnomologial genre of a wide audience and long life.[111]

---

[111] Horna, "Gnome," 78; Henri I. Marrou, *A History of Education in Antiquity* (New York: Sheed and Ward, 1956) 150-159, 234-235; Barnes, "Gnomologium," 132-137, 5-8; Chadwick, "Florilegium," 1131-1133; Gutas, *Greek Wisdom Literature*, 451; Kloppenborg, *The Formation of Q*, 295, 299; cf. Quintilian *Institutio Oratoria* 1.9.3-4; Abraham J. Malherbe, *Social Aspects of Early Christianity* (Philadelphia: Fortress, 1983^2) 41-45.

The progymnasmata offer evidence that maxims played a part in rhetorical training as well. Students were expected to memorize sayings of the poets and then to write their own explanations and elaborations of the sayings. They may also have been required to compile their own gnomic collections as part of their preparation.[112] It seems clear that for advanced students, and even experienced orators, gnomologia provided a convenient resource for both public and private speaking, as this excerpt from the prologue to Epicharmus' gnomic anthology suggests:

τεῖδ' ἔνεστι πολλὰ καὶ παν[τ]οῖα, τοῖς χρήσαιό κα
ποτὶ φίλον, ποτ' ἐχθρόν, ἐν δίκαι λέγων, ἐν ἁλίαι,
ποτὶ πονηρόν, ποτὶ καλόν τε κἀγαθόν, ποτὶ ξένον,
ποτὶ δύσηριν, ποτὶ πάροινον, ποτὶ βάναυσον, αἴτε τις
ἄλλ' ἔχει κακόν τι, καὶ τούτοισι κέντρα τεῖδ' ἔνο.
ἐν δὲ καὶ γνῶμαι σοφαὶ τεῖδ', αἶσιν αἱ πίθοιτό τις,
δεξιώτερός τέ κ' εἴη βελτίων τ' ἐς πά[ν]τ' ἀνήρ.
κο]ὔτι πολλὰ δεῖ λέγειν, ἀλλ' ἓν μόνον [τ]ούτων ἔπος,
ποττὸ πρᾶγμα περιφέροντα τῶνδ' ἀεὶ τὸ συμφέρον.

Within this book are many and manifold advices for you to use
towards a friend or foe, while speaking in the courts, or the assembly,
towards the rogue or the gentleman, towards the stranger,
towards the quarrelsome, the drunkard, and the vulgar, or any other
plagues that you may find--for them too there's a sting within my book.
Within it too are maxims wise; obey them,
and you will be a cleverer and a better man for all events.
You need no lengthy speech, only a single one of these sayings;
bring round to your subject whichever of them is apt.[113]

These statements testify to the effectiveness and flexibility of gnomic forms; they were not only potential ammunition in a wide range of rhetorical situations but also a means of personal betterment.

The decisive impetus for the growth of gnomologia in the Hellenistic era came from the philosophical schools, particularly the Stoics and Cynics, though

---

[112] See the references given in Fiore, *Personal Example*, 42-44; also see Horna, "Gnome," 75, 79; Barnes, "Gnomologium," 9-14.

[113] Epicharmus (c) 1-9; text and translation: Denys L. Page, trans., *Select Papyri III: Literary Papyri and Poetry* (LCL; Cambridge: Harvard University Press, 1970) 440-443. The text is from *P. Hibeh* 1, which is dated between 280 and 240 B.C.; the anthology may have been edited by Axiopistus; cf. Walther Kraus, "Epicharmos," *KP* 2 (1967) 302-303; Kloppenborg, *The Formation of Q*, 297.

anthologies were employed by the Epicureans, the Pythagoreans, and other groups as well.[114] Within the schools it is possible to identify two broad and overlapping motives for the anthologizing activities. First, philosophers would compile collections of sayings from previous authors, especially the well-known poets, for use in their own compositions. Chrysippos in particular took part in this sort of production, and the example he set had considerable influence on later Stoics.[115] The motives behind this practice are articulated by Sextus Empiricus, who reports the common opinion that "the best and character-forming philosophy had its original roots in the gnomic sayings of the poets, and on this account the philosophers, when giving exhortations, always stamped, as it were, their injunctions with phrases from the poets."[116] The Cynic tradition, beginning apparently from the earliest stages of its development, also participated in compiling gnomologia.[117] These stores of maxims provided them with a resource that was appropriate to their message, style, and audience. Regarding the collections and their relationship with philosophical movements, J. Barnes writes:

> We may assume that they were approved or used by philosophers who set a high value upon literary education and inquiry and were tolerant of, or actively interested in, *rhetoric* from Antisthenes onwards. In fact it is difficult to see how the writers of diatribes (for instance) would have fared without such assistance as a gnomologium, compiled beforehand either by themselves or by others, could afford.[118]

Thus gnomic anthologies served as a medium through which Greek literature and rhetoric influenced the development of Hellenistic philosophy.

The second area of anthologizing activity was conducted by the followers of the philosophers, who culled the treatises of their masters for precepts that

---

[114] On the connection between gnomologia and philosophy see Horna, "Gnome," 79-82; Barnes, "Gnomologium," 4-14; Chadwick, "Florilegium," 1136-1143; Spoerri, "Gnome," 825-826; Wilken, "Wisdom and Philosophy," 158-164; Küchler, *Weisheitstraditionen*, 250-261; Gutas, *Greek Wisdom Literature*, 451-457, cf. 9-35.

[115] Elter, *Gnomologium*, passim; Horna, "Gnome," 80-81; Barnes, "Gnomologium," 10; Gutas, *Greek Wisdom Literature*, 452-453.

[116] Sextus Empiricus *Adversus Mathematicos* 1.271; text and translation: R. G. Bury, trans., *Sextus Empiricus* (LCL; 4 vols.; Cambridge: Harvard University Press; London: Heinemann, 1933-1949) 3.152-153.

[117] Zeph Stewart, "Democritus and the Cynics," *Harvard Studies in Classical Philology* 63 (1958) 179-191; Gutas, *Greek Wisdom Literature*, 453-457, also s.v. Cynicism; cf. Kurt von Fritz's additions to Horna, "Gnome," 87-89; Dudley, *Cynicism*, 110-116; Jan F. Kindstrand, "The Cynics and Heraclitus," *Eranos* 82 (1984) 149-178.

[118] Barnes, "Gnomologium," 9 [his italics].

epitomized the ethical system of their philosophical school. Collections such as the *Kyriai doxai*, *Gnomologium Vaticanum*, *Gnomologium Epictetum*, and the Pythagorean *Symbola* functioned as both catechisms for recent initiates and convenient summaries for more advanced members of the community. In so far as their contents were less intimidating and more easily remembered than full-blown philosophical tractates, these texts expedited efforts to attract and instruct new students. They also represented a means of preserving and handing down the master's teachings, adding stability and continuity to the school.[119] Most of these collections, because of their more restricted pool of sources and more focused audience, bear the distinctive stamp of their particular philosophical movement or teacher. Thus correct interpretation is often contingent upon knowledge of the philosophical doctrines, or at least a familiarity with the maxims' original context and purpose. Yet at the same time, some of the schools, particularly the Cynics, preserved not only the sayings of their own teachers but anything they deemed useful or adaptable to their purposes. Thus a philosophical gnomologium may exhibit a broader and more elementary outlook than the philosophical treatises from which it draws.

Finally, it should be emphasized that while gnomologia played a role in individual indoctrination and training within philosophical schools, for the most part they were not intended for mere memorization or unquestioned acceptance. All in all, gnomic anthologies encouraged students to further study and reflection, challenging them to interpret the maxims and apply them in varying circumstances. Skills developed in this manner no doubt aided students as they internalized the school's teachings, identity, and perspective. As John Kloppenborg observes, referring to Ben Sira 39.1-3, the wisdom associated with many gnomic collections entails not only a knowledge of the sayings in a document, but also the nurturing of the reflective and creative abilities involved in the utilization of gnomic wisdom: "The goal of this mode of wisdom is to produce those who, through their assimilation of the sapiential ethos, become exponents of that ethos and sources of new wisdom."[120] So although gnomic anthologies are conservative, in so far as they transmit established ideas and preserve the ethical agendas of previous generations, they are at the same time

---

[119] Cf. Ilona Opelt, "Epitome," *RAC* 5 (1962) 944-973; Kloppenborg, *The Formation of Q*, 300-301; Gutas, *Greek Wisdom Literature*, 451-457. Also see Hans Dieter Betz, *Essays on the Sermon on the Mount* (trans. L. L. Welborn; Philadelphia: Fortress, 1985) 1-16.

[120] Kloppenborg, *The Formation of Q*, 306; cf. Grenzmann, "Probleme," 140-144; Sheppard, *Wisdom as a Hermeneutical Construct*, 100-119; Lewis, "The Discourse of the Maxim," 41-48; Williams, *Those Who Ponder Proverbs*, 47-57, 89-101; van Leeuwan, *Context and Meaning*, 29-37.

self-generating and self-correcting, in that they continually promote critical re-evaluation as well as personal additions and adaptations.[121]

Wisdom Instruction

Near Eastern wisdom instructions were a stable and influential genre beginning as early as the third millennium B.C. They offered practical guidance and ethical advice in the form of an authoritative speech, ostensibly given by a father to his son. The setting of the literature is clearly didactic, and there is a stress on order and tradition, as well as prudential behavior, proper discretion, and intellectual discipline. Instruction in its earliest form was intended for a political and intellectual elite--future rulers, scribes, and statesmen. Thus many of the texts are ascribed to kings and other famous figures. However, some instructions, particularly those of a later date, have a wider audience in view, and they address matters of daily life and conduct more than affairs of the court.[122] While in some respects they represent a counterpart to gnomologia, wisdom instructions differ from the anthologies in at least four important respects: 1) their chief provenance is the Near East, particularly Egypt, and not the Greek-speaking world; 2) their morphology and function remain relatively stable through the centuries; 3) the authors of these texts normally make a more serious effort to provide a coherent structure for their material; 4) while maxims may comprise a significant portion of an instructional text, they never account for it entirely but instead are employed in conjunction with complementary and non-wisdom forms and ideas as well.

---

[121] Cf. Niebuhr, *Gesetz und Paränese*, 5-72.

[122] On the content, setting, and purpose of Near Eastern instructions see Kayatz, *Studien zu Proverbien 1-9*, 76-134; Hans H. Schmid, *Wesen und Geschichte der Weisheit: Eine Untersuchung zur altorientalischen und israelitischen Weisheitsliteratur* (BZAW 101; Berlin: Töpelmann, 1966) 9-16; Helmut Brunner, *Altägyptische Erziehung* (Wiesbaden: Harrassowitz, 1957); idem, "Erziehung," *LÄ* 2 (1977) 22-27; idem, "Lehren," *LÄ* 3 (1980) 964-968; idem, *Altägyptische Weisheit: Lehren für das Leben* (Die Bibliothek der Alten Welt; Zürich, München: Artemis, 1988); McKane, *Proverbs*, 51-182; Bernhard Lang, *Die weisheitliche Lehrrede: Eine Untersuchung von Sprüche 1-7* (SBS 54; Stuttgart: KBW, 1972) esp. 27-60; Kenneth A. Kitchen, "Basic Literary Forms and Formulations of Ancient Instructional Writing in Egypt and Western Asia," *Studien zu altägyptischen Lebenslehren* (ed. Erik Hornung and Othmar Keel; OBO 28; Freiburg: Universitätsverlag; Göttingen: Vandenhoeck & Ruprecht, 1979) 235-282; Leo G. Perdue, "Liminality as the Social Setting of Wisdom Instructions," *ZAW* 93 (1981) 114-126; Kloppenborg, *The Formation of Q*, 264-294, 329-336.

The typical morphology of wisdom instruction may be sketched as follows.[123] For the most part, instructions open with a title, ascribing the speech to an authoritative figure. This is often followed by a prologue, frequently with some narrative description of the setting or occasion, which calls upon the reader to pay heed and promises benefits to the obedient. In some instructional texts the same themes may be raised again in an epilogue.[124] The body of the document consists of a sequence of instructional units or paragraphs, composed and arranged in a more or less careful manner according to subject matter.[125] The length of each these units varies from, say, five to fifty lines. The topical and structural divisions may be especially pronounced, as in Amenemope and *P. Insinger*, which are divided into numbered 'chapters', but are normally somewhat more relaxed and may occasionally disappear altogether.

The rigor with which the instructional units are arranged in a text varies considerably. In Amenemope and *P. Insinger*, for instance, the topical units are logically integrated, and there seems to be a clear progression of thought from beginning to end.[126] Other texts, such as Ptahhotep and Ben Sira, display some overall plan but it is rather loose and may break down in places.[127] Some authors, like Shuruppak, have organized substantial passages, but the structure

---

[123] On the literary structure of instructions see the references in the last note, in particular Kayatz, *Studien zu Proverbien 1-9*, passim; Schmid, *Wesen und Geschichte*, 8-84; Brunner, "Die Lehren," 113-139; idem, *Weisheit*, 75-87; McKane, *Proverbs*, 51-182; Kitchen, "Literary Forms," 249-279; Kloppenborg, *The Formation of Q*, 265-272, 276-282.

[124] The Instruction of Any has an unusual epilogue in which father and son debate the utility of the text's contents; translation: Miriam Lichtheim, *Ancient Egyptian Literature: A Book of Readings* (3 vols.; Berkeley, Los Angeles, London: University of California Press, 1975-1980) 2.135-146; cf. Brunner, *Altägyptische Weisheit*, 196-214.

[125] Lichtheim (*Late Egyptian Wisdom*, 6-7) observes that virtually all pre-Demotic instructions consist of integrated speeches of varying length, composed of maxims and other kinds of sentences.

[126] "The style of Amenemope is rich in similes and metaphors which are sustained at length and with skill. The work as a whole is carefully composed and unified, both through the device of thirty numbered chapters and through concentration on two basic themes: first, the depiction of the ideal man, the 'silent man,' and his adversary, the 'heated man'; second, the exhortation to honesty and warnings against dishonesty." Lichtheim, *Ancient Egyptian Literature*, 2.147 (with a translation of the text on pp. 148-163); cf. McKane, *Proverbs*, 102-117; Brunner, *Altägyptische Weisheit*, 234-256; Irene Grumach-Shirun, "Lehre des Amenemope," *LÄ* 3 (1980) 971-974. On *P. Insinger*: Lichtheim, *Late Egyptian Wisdom*, 109-116 (with a translation of the text on pp. 197-234); cf. idem, "Observations on Papyrus Insinger," in Hornung and Keel, *Studien*, 284-305; Karl-Theodor Zauzich, "Pap. Dem. Insinger," *LÄ* 4 (1982) 898-899; Brunner, *Altägyptische Weisheit*, 295-349.

[127] On the literary composition of Ben Sira see Wolfgang Roth, "On the Gnomic-Discursive Wisdom of Jesus Ben-Sirach," *Semeia* 17 (1980) 59-79; Kloppenborg, *The Formation of Q*, 281-282.

is not sustained throughout the entire document.[128] Perhaps the rabbinic tractates *Derek Eres Rabbah* and *Derek Eres Zuta* fall within the parameters of this category of instructional texts, though we should note that there are a number of special issues involved in the classification and description of these documents.[129] The instructional paragraphs of a final group, which includes the Sayings of Ahiqar, are apparently serialized with little regard to any plan.[130] Such loose structure suggests the potential for rearranging instructional units, or for removing them to be deployed in new contexts.

Within the thematic units considerable care is often given to their literary and rhetorical composition. The binary wisdom admonition predominates, either standing on its own or in conjunction with other admonitions which may be linked logically or by formal devices such as catchword. The admonitions are also combined with conditional, motive, and final clauses, as well as explanations, illustrations, and extended motivations, in order to create complex arguments. Wisdom sentences, particularly in the later texts, may be employed independently or to buttress the admonitions. For a representative illustration of these compositional techniques, we may turn to the Counsels of Wisdom 31-65, a passage that unites a number of prominent sapiential themes: the pacification of enemies, kindness to those in need, warnings against arrogance, and fear of the deity.

> Do not frequent a law court,
> Do not loiter where there is a dispute,
> For in the dispute they will have you as a testifier,
> Then you will be made their witness
> And they will bring you to a lawsuit not your own to affirm.
> When confronted with a dispute, go your way; pay no attention to it.
> Should it be a dispute of your own, extinguish the flame!
> Disputes are a covered pit,

---

[128] Cf. Brendt Alster, *The Instructions of Shuruppak: A Sumerian Proverb Collection* (Copenhagen: Akademisk Forlag, 1974).

[129] Text and translation: M. Ginsberg, trans., *Hebrew-English Edition of the Babylonian Talmud: Minor Tractates* (ed. Abraham Cohen; London: Soncino, 1984) 55b-59a; further see M. B. Lerner, "The Tractates Derekh Erets," in Safrai, *The Literature of the Sages*, 379-389, with further bibliography; also Zeller, *Mahnsprüche*, 46-47.

[130] Cf. Frederick C. Conybeare, J. R. Harris, A. S. Lewis, *The Story of Ahikar from Aramaic, Syriac, Arabic, Ethiopic, Old Turkish, Greek and Slavonic Versions* (Cambridge: Cambridge University Press, 1913²); McKane, *Proverbs*, 156-182; Küchler, *Weisheitstraditionen*, 319-413; James M. Lindenberger, *The Aramaic Proverbs of Ahiqar* (Baltimore, London: Johns Hopkins University Press, 1983); idem, "Ahiqar," in Charlesworth, *Pseudepigrapha*, 2.479-507.

A strong wall that scares away its foes.
They remember what a man forgets and lay the accusation.
Do not return evil to the man who disputes with you;
Requite with kindness your evil-doer,
Maintain justice to your enemy,
Smile on your adversary.

... [the text is damaged at this point] ...

Do not insult the downtrodden and [...]
Do not sneer at them autocratically.
With this a man's god is angry,
It is not pleasing to Samas, who will repay him with evil.
Give food to eat, beer to drink,
Grant what is asked, provide for and honor.
In this a man's god takes pleasure,
It is pleasing to Samas, who will repay him with favour.
Do charitable deeds, render service all your days.[131]

Non-instructional materials, such as narrative descriptions, hymns, or autobiographical elements may also be incorporated.[132] Programmatic or concluding statements, and even repeating formulae, may be employed to frame the paragraphs. Another feature common to most instructions is the propensity to cite or rework sayings from earlier sources of wisdom, sources which were no doubt familiar to their original audiences. This is especially clear in texts like Ankhsheshonqy, *P. Insinger*, Ben Sira, and the Teachings of Silvanus, which draw not only from their own traditions, but from the corpus of Greek wisdom as well.[133]

---

[131] Text and translation: Lambert, *Wisdom Literature*, 100-103; cf. McKane, *Proverbs*, 153-156.

[132] See, for example, Brunner, *Altägyptische Weisheit*, 81-87.

[133] On Ankhsheshonqy and *P. Insinger*: Lichtheim, *Late Egyptian Wisdom*, 28-37, 43-52, 65, 112-169, 184-196; cf. Heinz-Josef Thissen, "Lehre des Anch-Scheschonqi," *LÄ* 3 (1980) 974-975. Ben Sira: Jack T. Sanders, *Ben Sira and Demotic Wisdom* (SBLMS 28; Chico, CA: Scholars Press, 1983); Skehan and DiLella, *Ben Sira*, 40-50 and passim; cf. E. G. Bauckmann, "Die Proverbien und die Sprüche des Jesus Sirach: Eine Untersuchung zum Strukturwandel der Israelitischen Weisheitslehre," *ZAW* 72 (1960) 33-63. The Teachings of Silvanus: Malcolm L. Peel and Jan Zandee, "The Teachings of Silvanus from the Library of Nag Hammadi," *NovT* 14 (1972) 294-311; idem, "The Teachings of Silvanus (VII, 4)," *The Nag Hammadi Library in English* (ed. James M. Robinson; San Francisco: Harper & Row, 1988[3]) 346-361; Schoedel, "Jewish Wisdom," 169-199; Jan Zandee, "The Teachings of Silvanus (NHC VII,4) and Jewish Christianity," *Studies in Gnosticism and Hellenistic*

Many of the same types of linguistic and literary devices that were discussed above with regard to gnomic anthologies, such as catchword, linkword, anaphora, inclusio, isocolon, and so forth, are also present in wisdom instructions, though their application is generally more sophisticated and more intentional. Ring composition also occurs on a regular basis, for instance in Ben Sira 27.16-21:

16 ὁ ἀποκαλύπτων μυστήρια ἀπώλεσεν πίστιν
    καὶ οὐ μὴ εὕρῃ φίλον πρὸς τὴν ψυχὴν αὐτοῦ.
17 στέρξον φίλον καὶ πιστώθητι μετ' αὐτοῦ·
    ἐὰν δὲ ἀποκαλύψῃς τὰ μυστήρια αὐτοῦ,
    μὴ καταδιώξῃς ὀπίσω αὐτοῦ.
18 καθὼς γὰρ ἀπώλεσεν ἄνθρωπος τὸν νεκρὸν αὐτοῦ,
    οὕτως ἀπώλεσας τὴν φιλίαν τοῦ πλησίον·
19 καὶ ὡς πετεινὸν ἐκ χειρός σου ἀπέλυσας,
    οὕτως ἀφῆκας τὸν πλησίον καὶ οὐ θηρεύσεις αὐτόν.
20 μὴ αὐτὸν διώξῃς, ὅτι μακρὰν ἀπέστη
    καὶ ἐξέφυγεν ὡς δορκὰς ἐκ παγίδος.
21 ὅτι τραῦμα ἔστιν καταδῆσαι,
    καὶ λοιδορίας ἔστιν διαλλαγή,
    ὁ δὲ ἀποκαλύψας μυστήρια ἀφήλπισεν.

16 Whoever betrays a secret destroys confidence;
    he will never find an intimate friend.
17 Cherish your friend, keep faith with him,
    but if you betray his secret, follow him not;
18 For as one might kill another,
    you have killed your neighbor's friendship.
19 Like a bird released from the hand,
    you have let your friend go and you cannot recapture him.
20 Follow him not, for he is far away;
    he has escaped like a gazelle from the snare.
21 A wound can be bound up, and railing speech forgiven,
    but whoever betrays secrets does hopeless damage.[134]

The basic ideas of the paragraph, which consists of exhortation against betraying the confidence of friends, can be outlined as follows:

Religions Presented to Gilles Quispel on the Occasion of his 65th Birthday (ed. R. van den Broek and M. J. Vermaseren; EPRO 91; Leiden: Brill, 1981) 498-584.
[134] Translation: Skehan and DiLella, *Ben Sira*, 354, cf. 357-358.

16   A. Description of the damage caused by betrayal
17   B. Advice not to follow a betrayed friend
18   C. Simile describing the betrayal of a friend
19   C'. Simile describing the betrayal of a friend
20   B'. Advice not to follow a betrayed friend
21   A'. Description of the damage caused by betrayal

The employment of similar terms in corresponding verses strengthens the material and functional connections of the structure here, for instance ὁ ἀποκαλύπτων μυστήρια / ὁ δὲ ἀποκαλύψας μυστήρια and πίστιν / ἀφήλπισεν in 27.16 and 21 (A and A'), μὴ καταδιώξῃς / μὴ αὐτὸν διώξῃς in 27.17 and 20 (B and B'), and καθὼς ... οὕτως / καὶ ὡς ... οὕτως in 27.18 and 19 (C and C'). As with most ring compositions, the relationships between the different structural counterparts in the passage (A and A', etc.) are not all of the same type; the interconnections may depend on such varying considerations as content, terminology, literary form and function, cause-and-effect, logical development, and so forth.

With respect to literary style, Miriam Lichtheim has argued that the genre of wisdom instruction, although it is not technically poetry, also defies classification as prose. The sayings portions of the instructions (as opposed to the prologues or narrative sections) are written in a "third style," which she describes as "orational," a term suggestive of their oral qualities.[135] These writers achieve rhythm and poetic effect in ways other than by meter, mainly by parallelism, balance, and economy of language. Other literary devices commonly utilized in the instructional sayings include metrical effects, alliteration, assonance, word play, and chiasmus. As Lichtheim observes, this orational style is closely akin to that which characterizes the Hebrew Bible's Book of Proverbs.[136]

These literary features of the instructions indicate that they were designed to be recited and memorized. But, as with gnomic anthologies, the success of a particular instructional text depended to a great extent upon the development of certain skills and abilities beyond a knowledge of the text itself. William McKane's comments concerning Ptahhotep are instructive:

> The educational process goes much deeper than the memorizing of the principles, and whoever would model himself on those who have succeeded

---

[135] Lichtheim, *Ancient Egyptian Literature*, 1.5-12; cf. Robb, "Linguistic Art," esp. 174-179. On prose rhythm in the Wisdom of Solomon see Chrysostome Larcher, *Etudes sur le Livre de la Sagesse* (Paris: Gabalda, 1969) 1.88-89.

[136] Cf. above n. 91.

best in life must assimilate the spirit of their approach to statesmanship and acquire the insight, discipline and precision which brought them their success.[137]

So the instructions were not intended solely as a step-by-step guide to proper behavior in specific situations or as a blueprint for a successful life. Rather, they afford the reader some essential glimpses of the "process" and "insight" of the exemplary speaker, who represents not only the experience and authority of a father or ruler but also the time-tested wisdom of many generations. These and some other cardinal aspects of the genre's ethos are summarized in the conclusion to the Instructions of Amenemope (chapter 30):

Mark for yourself these thirty chapters:
   They please, they instruct,
They are the foremost of all books;
   They teach the ignorant.
If they are read to an ignorant man,
   He will be purified through them.
Seize them; put them in your mind
   And have men interpret them, explaining them as a teacher.
As a scribe who is experienced in his position,
   He will find himself worthy of being a courtier.[138]

The chapter resembles the prologue to the *Comparatio Menandri et Philistionis II* in that the author understands the contents of his manual as possessing both instructional and aesthetic functions, and that these functions are meant to work in tandem. Significantly, the text projects itself as being employed in a didactic setting; its sayings are meant to be studied, interpreted, and explained. Those who do so successfully can expect professional advancement, personal enrichment, and gains in social stature and respect. Most interestingly, the author associates his work with the 'purification' of the ignorant: the author's object is apparently not just the acquisition of information *per se*, but a qualitative change in the moral character and perspective of the serious student.[139]

---

[137] McKane, *Proverbs*, 60, cf. 51-65; also cf. Helmut Brunner, "Lehre des Ptahhotep," *LÄ* 3 (1980) 989-991; idem, *Altägyptische Weisheit*, 104-109.
[138] Translation: William K. Simpson, trans., *The Literature of Ancient Egypt: An Anthology of Stories, Instructions, and Poetry* (New Haven, London: Yale University Press, 1973²) 265; cf. Pritchard, *Ancient Near Eastern Texts*, 424.
[139] Cf. Kloppenborg, *The Formation of Q*, 284-287.

Concluding Remarks

By way of conclusion, we should note that the formal distinctions between gnomic poetry, gnomic anthologies, and wisdom instructions are often difficult to make. This is particularly true of late texts such as the Demotic Ankhsheshonqy, whose author (or editor) was influenced by the compositional techniques of both the Greek gnomologial and Near Eastern instructional genres.[140] Ankhsheshonqy contains a preponderance of wisdom sentences and independent, linear maxims; further, it exhibits no overall structure and only a few thematic units. Yet, though it betrays these traits of the gnomological style, the document is still technically wisdom instruction and refers to itself as such. Thus it is possible to speak of a number of ambiguous or 'hybrid' forms. On the other hand, some gnomic anthologies, most notably Pseudo-Phocylides, come close in form and composition to gnomic poems as well as the instructional genre.[141] Pseudo-Phocylides is topically organized throughout, each unit is carefully structured and stylized, and there seems to be at least a modest effort to organize the units according to some plan. Pseudo-Isocrates *Ad Demonicum* represents a final hybrid example. As various modern critics have observed, this writing is not a gnomologium but rather a moral treatise or instructional speech whose composition has been substantially influenced by the popularity of gnomologia.[142] The treatise includes an extended introduction and conclusion specifying its occasion and purpose which create a frame for a lengthy anthology of maxims organized by topic. While the structure within and among the topical units is weak, some of the paragraphs are composed in a thoughtful manner and it is possible to detect a basic arrangement of the units. This treatise, then, provides evidence that at least some texts of Greek provenance exhibit material and compositional features comparable with Near Eastern wisdom instructions.

---

[140] Lichtheim, "Papyrus Insinger," 284-305; idem, *Late Egyptian Wisdom*, 13-65; Kloppenborg, *The Formation of Q*, 269-271; cf. Berend Gemser, "The Instructions of 'Onchsheshonqy' and Biblical Wisdom Literature," *VTSup* 7 (1960) 102-128 [reprint, Crenshaw, *Studies*, 134-160]; McKane, *Proverbs*, 117-150.

[141] Cf. van der Horst, *Pseudo-Phocylides*, 77-80; Küchler, *Weisheitstraditionen*, 261-302; Niebuhr, *Gesetz und Paränese*, 5-31, 42-44, 57-72.

[142] On the contents and composition of *Ad Demonicum* see Bernhard Rosenkranz, "Die Struktur der Pseudo-Isokrateischen Demonicea," *Emerita* 34 (1966) 95-129; also Wendland, *Anaximenes*, 81-84, cf. 85-101; Carl Wefelmeier, *Die Sentenzensammlung der Demonicea* (Athens: Rossolatos, 1962) 65-81; Küchler, *Weisheitstraditionen*, 248-250; Fiore, *Personal Example*, 56-67; Lichtheim, *Late Egyptian Wisdom*, 25; Berger, "Hellenistische Gattungen," 1068-1069.

Such descriptive complications are symptomatic of the underlying similarities of the three sapiential genres discussed above. It is possible to identify a number of ways in which they resemble one another. First, the three appear to draw from more-or-less the same pool of ideas and topics; the focus on such themes as practical conduct, proper social behavior, and correct self-understanding constitutes a regular feature of the three genres. Second, most of these texts envision for themselves a didactic setting; consequently they possess a decidedly pedagogical or persuasive tone. In connection with this, each genre strives to join its ethical and didactic aims with aesthetic or artistic features in order to make the ethical concepts more striking and memorable. Third, a significant number of these authors draw from pre-existing sapiential materials; consequently, the effectiveness of their compositions relies in part upon the readers' familiarity with those materials and their ability to perceive how they have been manipulated. This characteristic underscores the more fundamental observation that the success of gnomic discourse is often predicated to a significant extent upon the oral and literary culture as well as the shared ethical experiences and values of the group or society in which the author and audience participate. Fourth, in light of these first three similarities (as well as the comments of the previous chapter) it follows that maxims figure as basic components in the composition of each of these three modes of sapiential discourse. Finally, it should be noted that the logical and literary structures of these texts are often based upon distinct thematic sections of a paragraph or so in length. This is true of most gnomic poems *per se* as well as the individual units of wisdom instructions, and even in gnomologia it is possible to detect comparable topical sequences.

These formal and functional similarities no doubt abetted the employment of two or more of these sapiential genres in the same text. The Book of Proverbs, for instance, begins with a prologue consisting of wisdom instructions and gnomic poems (chapters 1-9) followed by a gnomic collection (chapters 10ff.). It was also possible for ancient authors to join one or more of these genres with non-wisdom literary forms. Thus in Ben Sira, for example, the encomiastic Hymn in Praise of the Fathers (chapters 44-50) is attached to the wisdom instructions and gnomic poems that make up the bulk of the book (chapters 1-43).[143] Instructional or gnomic paragraphs could also be incorporated into

---

[143] Thomas R. Lee (*Studies in the Form of Sirach 44-50* [SBLDS 75; Atlanta: Scholars Press, 1986]) argues that the hymn is consciously patterned after the Hellenistic encomium; cf. Burton L. Mack, *Wisdom and the Hebrew Epic: Ben Sira's Hymn in Praise of the Fathers* (Chicago Studies in the History of Judaism; Chicago, London: University of Chicago Press, 1985); Skehan and DiLella, *Ben Sira*, 497-555.

larger non-sapiential genres. Tobit 4.3-20, for example, is a wisdom passage embedded in a narrative folktale.[144] Similar integrations occur in the literature of early Christianity. As John Kloppenborg has argued, the formative literary structure of Q was a series of wisdom instructions;[145] these were later supplemented with biographical elements and eventually incorporated into the Gospels of Matthew and Luke. Another early Christian text, the Letter of James, embodies a number of instructional paragraphs within an epistolary framework. Examples such as these indicate both the prevalence of gnomic forms in Hellenistic Judaism and early Christianity as well as their literary and rhetorical adaptability.[146]

---

[144] Cf. Paul Deselaers, *Das Buch Tobit: Studien zu seiner Entstehung, Komposition und Theologie* (OBO 43; Göttingen: Vandenhoeck & Ruprecht, 1982) 374-425.

[145] Kloppenborg (*The Formation of Q*, 171-245) identifies six "sapiential speeches": Q 6.20b-49; 9.57-62, 10.2-11, 16; 11.2-4, 9-13; 12.2-7, 11-12; 12.22-31, 33-34; 13.24, 14.26, 27, 17.33; cf. Zeller, *Mahnsprüche*, passim; Piper, *Wisdom in the Q-Tradition*, passim; von Lips, *Weisheitliche Traditionen*, 197-227.

[146] To these examples Didache 1-6 and the Epistle of Barnabas 18-20, which contain a relatively large number of gnomic sayings, could be added; cf. Küchler, *Weisheitstraditionen*, 567-571.

Chapter Three

The Literary Composition of Romans 12.1-21

One aim of the discussion so far has been to indicate both the impressive range of forms and functions that maxims themselves possess, as well as the variety of ways in which they may be organized and combined with other non-gnomic elements in order to design more complex arguments. While diversity is the rule with gnomic materials, it is possible to detect similar literary and rhetorical strategies at work in some of these texts in addition to certain organizational schemes and logical patterns that govern their structure. In this chapter, we will investigate the literary composition of Romans 12.1-21 against the background of such strategies and patterns. Careful comparison of chapter 12 with certain other ancient exhortatory texts that also make extended use of gnomic materials facilitates an improved understanding of the character of its overall design, mode of argumentation, and material content; it also sheds some light on the manner in which Paul has linked exhortation that is largely gnomic (vv. 9-21) with material that is not primarily gnomic (vv. 1-8) in making his ethical appeal to the Roman Christians. The point is not to demonstrate Paul's dependence on any specific text or group of texts but to investigate the extent to which Romans 12 conforms with the conventions observed in the composition of sapiential materials.

The most effective means of clarifying the relationship of Romans 12 with wisdom literature is to inspect the chapter side-by-side with specific and relevant comparative sources. Extensive research has unearthed a number of ancient texts of varying provenances and dates that exhibit noteworthy formal and thematic parallels with Romans 12. Of these, four in particular warrant closer investigation on account of the nature and extent of their similarities with the chapter: LXX Proverbs 3.11-35, Ben Sira 6.18-37, Pseudo-Phocylides 70-96, and the Testament of Naphtali 2.2-3.5.[1] Significantly, each of these texts is

---

[1] While these Hellenistic-Jewish texts represent the most useful comparative materials for examining the structure and argument of Romans 12, it should be noted that a number of other passages also exhibit pertinent features in these regards, and that some of these texts are not

part of the literature of Hellenistic Judaism, the type of Judaism from which Paul himself came, and three of the four texts also belong to the corpus of Jewish sapiential writings. The most pertinent characteristic of these passages for our comparative analysis, however, is the nature of their overall literary structure, in particular, that each passage imparts a self-contained ethical exhortation that has been sub-divided into three distinct formal and functional units; these may be conveniently designated as: 1) the programmatic statement, 2) the descriptive section, and 3) the prescriptive section. In so far as these four Hellenistic-Jewish texts share a basic literary pattern and rhetorical strategy they may be effectively compared with Romans 12 and so be of use in clarifying the nature of its composition and argument.

My plan for Chapter Three is as follows. By way of introduction, the main features of this proposed literary structure, and in particular the characteristics of its three formal units, will be sketched in broad terms. Second, we will investigate how this structure informs the composition and message of each of the four Hellenistic-Jewish texts listed above. Finally, Romans 12 itself will be examined in comparison with both the structure as described generally and with the four particular texts in which it occurs.

General Description of the Sources

As a preliminary observation, it should be emphasized that both individually and as a group none of the four Hellenistic-Jewish texts surveyed below are generically consistent. While each passage could be identified as wisdom instruction and examined as such, in every case certain modifications and relaxations of the instructional form appear, especially in the descriptive section, where the gnomic and exhortatory features are far less pronounced than in the programmatic statement or prescriptive section. Thus for the sake of accuracy a more comprehensive term, namely, *sapiential discourse*, will be employed to describe them. This will allow us to take into account the compositional and material qualities unique to each text as well as any similarities that they may exhibit with gnomic poetry, gnomologia, or other literary genres. In addition, and as we will see in greater detail below, the larger texts in which these four passages occur (LXX Proverbs, Ben Sira, Pseudo-Phocylides, and the Testament of Naphtali) vary as to literary genre,

---

Jewish or Christian, for example, Ankhsheshonqy 8.13-25, Pseudo-Isocrates *Ad Demonicum* 12-17, and Porphyry *Ad Marcellam* 11-12.

and so with respect to context the sapiential discourses in question are not generically restricted and may be utilized in both sapiential and non-sapiential environments. As noted above, the unifying characteristic of these four texts is not genre but their division into three formal parts: 1) a programmatic statement, 2) a descriptive section, and 3) a prescriptive section.[2] It will be useful to begin by describing these different parts and their functions.

The first part, the programmatic statement, expresses the ethical objectives and didactic perspective of the entire passage in a short and striking manner.[3] The author directly addresses and challenges the audience, demanding acceptance of his authority and agenda and issuing a broad and goal-oriented call to action. This challenge may be accompanied by some sort of explanation, motive, or reason, perhaps entailing a promise of benefits to be enjoyed by those who obey. Within the programmatic statement we ordinarily encounter the most fundamental--and most abstract--concepts of the passage. Everything that follows in the remainder of the sapiential discourse will, in varying ways, serve to expand, explain, and motivate these basic ideas and objectives.

The main purpose of the second part, the descriptive section, is to establish and depict some model of ethical behavior pertinent to the special concepts and concerns stated in the programmatic statement.[4] Here there is little direct address or exhortation; instead, hymnic and poetic techniques such as parallelism come to the fore. While the different descriptive sections exhibit considerable diversity with regard to composition, they all share two important formal components. The first is a maxim, which may be employed to summarize the section's message or to focus attention on one noteworthy ethical quality or virtue of the model. The second is a representative list of different parts or aspects of the model, which may serve to catalogue some specific, concrete illustrations of how this quality or virtue manifests itself in the model. In some instances the model provided by the author portrays the audience itself, usually in an idealized way, and so it contributes to each reader's self-understanding and self-identity. In other cases the model is drawn from some apt or well-known example external to the rhetorical situation that may function as a guide. Either way, the author suggests a tangible or observable

---

[2] With regard to this entire approach compare the recent investigations of the literary structure of Christian sapiential materials by Kloppenborg (*The Formation of Q*, 171-245) and Piper (*Wisdom in the Q-Tradition*, esp. 14-99).

[3] For the use of programmatic statements in early Christian wisdom texts see Kloppenborg, *The Formation of Q*, 172-173, 187-190, 206-216, 234-237, 342-345; Piper, *Wisdom in the Q-Tradition*, 61-77.

[4] For a discussion of the relationship between descriptive and prescriptive language in paraenetic texts see Cancik, *Untersuchungen*, 16-35; cf. Betz, *Galatians*, 253-254.

goal, a point towards which he hopes to move the audience or a standard by which they may better comprehend themselves and their ethical progress.

Once the readers have been engaged in evaluating and internalizing this model of behavior, the author is in a position to resume the direct address, teaching, exhorting, and encouraging them. Wisdom admonitions predominate, though wisdom sentences, examples, promises, and so forth may also be key elements, in the third, or prescriptive, section. This segment is normally the longest and most varied, and it exhibits the clearest gnomic features and didactic intentions. Here the author identifies certain concrete ethical strategies and specific patterns of behavior that derive from the general plan that had been announced in the programmatic statement and illustrated in the descriptive model. The prescriptive section affords the author an opportunity to articulate some of the fundamental presuppositions, principles, and motivations of the ethical program being presented, and to appeal for the audience to accept these as the basis of their future ethical decision-making. The various precepts and admonitions of the section reveal the ethical perspective and moral ideals that the author desires for the audience, but they accomplish this not so much through the exhaustive treatment of a particular topic or theme but by suggesting a number of different actions and attitudes that typify the author's ethical program.

A number of the basic formal and structural characteristics found in the four prescriptive sections will be of special interest for the analysis of Romans 12; in particular the presence of the following features should be noted:

1) In every discourse, the prescriptive section opens with what will be called a *protreptic maxim*; this is a two-part wisdom admonition, antithetically formulated, that exhorts the reader to accept one over-riding proposition or principle regarding the conduct of life and to reject its opposite.[5]

2) Immediately following the protreptic maxim there may be a series of parallel or coordinated statements that spell out a number of its implications or consequences. In this explanatory function the sequence specifies some of the concrete ethical responsibilities expected of the audience.

3) Near the center of the prescriptive section the author may state a relatively crucial goal or motivation of his ethical program; this *central statement*, as it will be called, is sometimes expressed in the form of a maxim. In this capacity the central statement may represent the literary or rhetorical culmination of the exhortation that precedes; it may also serve as a turning-

---

[5] "Protreptic" is used here only to describe the maxims' function and not necessarily to suggest any formal connection with the more complex, more diverse body of philosophical literature examined by, among others, Jordan, "Ancient Philosophic Protreptic," 309-333.

point in the section's argument, governing the direction of the material that follows. On an ideational level, the central statement may express a religious presupposition or self-evident truth for the audience that undergirds the message of the entire section.

4) The central statement may be followed by a number of more concrete injunctions, motivations, examples, and so forth. These materials may be considered subordinate to the central statement in that they specify some of its results or serve in part as proof or clarification of its assertion. By and large, however, they are logically and thematically independent, owing only their basic theme and outlook to the central statement.

5) As the prescriptive section progresses, the number of imperative admonitions decreases. This may indicate a corresponding movement from more obvious and straight-forward exhortation to instruction that is more problematic, requiring reasons and explanations with indicative statements.

6) The section often concludes with a striking maxim that summarizes the passage's message. Frequently the conclusion will form some sort of inclusio with another part of the discourse, helping to unify the passage and underscoring the sense of finality at this point.

Two additional literary features, which pertain to all three segments of the sapiential discourses, should be noted. First, all these authors make purposeful use of various literary and poetic devices. Among these are inclusio, ring composition, parallelism, antithesis, chiasmus, isocolon, enumeration, catchwords, linkwords, asyndeton, anaphora, alliteration, and metrical effects. Second, the authors also regularly quote, modify, or allude to certain traditional texts or sources, sapiential and otherwise. These references often play a role as evidence or as proof-texts, reminding the audience that the author's exhortation is grounded in certain shared cultural presuppositions and literary traditions.

Analysis of the Discourses

Now that some of the more salient features of the four discourses have been identified and described in general terms, it is possible to examine them individually and in greater detail. My plan for the survey is to begin the discussion of each passage with some brief opening remarks and an outline of the discourse's literary composition; this will be followed by the text of the discourse itself, a translation, and finally some specific observations regarding its structure and argument.

LXX Proverbs 3.11-35

The various literary units found in Proverbs 1-9 were perhaps the most influential and most typical representatives of Jewish wisdom instruction and wisdom poetry. While many of these sections bear strong formal and material resemblances to the Near Eastern instructional genre described above, the authors, editors, and translators of the LXX Proverbs have also incorporated pieces which represent relaxations or modifications of the instructional style, as well as non-instructional forms such as wisdom hymns. Similar integrations are apparent in the Near Eastern texts as well, and it seems clear that these differing modes of sapiential communication were intended to complement each other, working in concert to present eloquent and effective arguments.[6]

One such passage may be Proverbs 3.11-35, which unites a wisdom hymn (3.13-20) and an instructional unit (3.21-35). A preliminary interpretive problem concerns the literary boundaries of the discourse. While the break between 3.35 and 4.1ff. is clear enough, it is difficult to determine with certainty if 3.11-12 concludes 3.1-10, introduces 3.13ff., or perhaps both.[7] While most modern commentators opt for the first possibility, there are several factors that commend the latter two. First, v. 11 contains the personal address, "my son," often, though not invariably, employed as a formal marker at the beginning of a new section. Second, the content of vv. 11-12, an explanation of the suffering and chastisement endured by the faithful, represents something of a departure, and is only weakly connected with the preceding section, 3.1-10,

---

[6] McKane (*Proverbs*, 7), for instance, divides Proverbs 1-9 as follows: 1) passages that are strictly instruction (1.8-19; 3.1-12, 21-35; 4; 5; 6.1-5, 20-35; 7.1-5, 24-27); 2) those where there is a development and slackening of the formal structure of instruction (2; 3.13-20; 6.6-11; 7.6-23); 3) various non-instructional units (1.1-7, 20-33; 6.12-19; 8; 9). Cf. Scott, *Proverbs*, 14-17; Whybray, *Wisdom in Proverbs*, 37-62; Murphy, *Wisdom Literature*, 54-63. For more general discussion see Kayatz, *Studien zu Proverbien 1-9*, 1-75; R. N. Whybray, "Some Literary Problems in Proverbs 1-9," *VT* 16 (1966) 482-496; Lang, *Lehrrede*, 27-36.

[7] Some scholars see a formal and logical break after 3.10; most of these understand 3.11-12 as a transition or a digression, for example: Crawford H. Toy, *The Book of Proverbs* (ICC; New York: Scribner's Sons, 1899) 64-66; Julius H. Greenstone, *Proverbs, with Commentary* (Philadelphia: Jewish Publication Society of America, 1950) 28-29; Edgar Jones, *Proverbs and Ecclesiastes: Introduction and Commentary* (Torch Bible Commentaries; London: SCM, 1961) 70; Whybray, *Wisdom in Proverbs*, 42-43; Helmer Ringgren, *Sprüche* (ATD 16.1; Göttingen: Vandenhoeck & Ruprecht, 1981³) 79-84. Among those who see instead a break after 3.12 are Scott, *Proverbs*, 14-17; H. Schneider, *Die Sprüche Salomos* (HB 7.1; Freiburg: Herder, 1962) 14-18, 61-62; Gemser, *Sprüche Salomos*, 27-31; André Barucq, *Le Livre des Proverbes* (SB; Paris: Gabalda, 1964) 50-55; McKane, *Proverbs*, 289-294; Otto Plöger, *Sprüche Salomos (Proverbia)* (BKAT 17; 5 parts; Neukirchen-Vluyn: Neukirchener Verlag, 1984) 32-35; cf. Arndt Meinhold, "Gott und Mensch in Proverbien III," *VT* 37 (1987) 468-477.

Analysis of the Discourses

which stresses the positive benefits and material prosperity enjoyed by those who pursue wisdom. Third, and as a counterpart to this, the dilemma addressed by 3.11-12 anticipates the ideas expressed in many of the verses of the ensuing section, especially 3.24-26 and 31.

If we choose to subdivide the chapter after 3.10 rather than 3.12, remaining fully aware of the problems involved with this decision, then 3.11-12 may be understood as a programmatic statement governing a discrete literary unit, 3.11-35, which can be outlined as follows:

11-12	I. Programmatic Statement (two parallel sentences)
11	A. Personal address and appeal
	1. Personal address: υἱέ ("my son")
	2. Appeal to accept the παιδεία κυρίου ("Lord's training")
12	B. Motive: this discipline is proof of the Lord's ἀγάπη ("love")
13-20	II. Descriptive Section: A hymn on σοφία ("wisdom")
13	A. Maxim: a macarism on the individual who finds σοφία and knows φρόνησις ("prudence")
14-18	B. List of seven motive clauses describing the attributes of wisdom
19-20	C. Description of wisdom's mediation in God's act of creation
21-35	III. Prescriptive Section
21-25	A. Direct appeal and list of consequences
21	1. Personal address: υἱέ ("my son")
	2. Protreptic maxim: admonition to observe the author's βουλή ("counsel")
22-25	3. List of ten benefits connected to the protreptic maxim by ἵνα
26	B. Central statement: assertion that the Lord will be present for those who obey
27-35	C. Exhortation
27-31	1. Obligations (imperatives with qualifications and reasons)
27-28	a. Obligations to render aid to the needy
29-31	b. Obligations to refrain from evil
32-34	2. Extended motivation (antithetical wisdom sentences)
32	a. transgressors vs. the righteous
33	b. curse of God vs. blessing of God
34	c. the proud vs. the humble
35	3. Concluding maxim on the σοφοί ("wise") (inclusio with 3.13) and the ἀσεβεῖς ("ungodly")

Text:[8]

11 υἱέ, μὴ ὀλιγώρει παιδείας κυρίου
    μηδὲ ἐκλύου ὑπ' αὐτοῦ ἐλεγχόμενος·
12 ὃν γὰρ ἀγαπᾷ κύριος παιδεύει,
    μαστιγοῖ δὲ πάντα υἱὸν ὃν παραδέχεται.
13 μακάριος ἄνθρωπος ὃς εὗρεν σοφίαν
    καὶ θνητὸς ὃς εἶδεν φρόνησιν·
14 κρεῖττον γὰρ αὐτὴν ἐμπορεύεσθαι
    ἢ χρυσίου καὶ ἀργυρίου θησαυρούς.
15 τιμιωτέρα δέ ἐστιν λίθων πολυτελῶν,
    οὐκ ἀντιτάξεται αὐτῇ οὐδὲν πονηρόν·
    εὔγνωστός ἐστιν πᾶσιν τοῖς ἐγγίζουσιν αὐτῇ,
    πᾶν δὲ τίμιον οὐκ ἄξιον αὐτῆς ἐστιν.
16 μῆκος γὰρ βίου καὶ ἔτη ζωῆς ἐν τῇ δεξιᾷ αὐτῆς,
    ἐν δὲ τῇ ἀριστερᾷ αὐτῆς πλοῦτος καὶ δόξα·
    ἐκ τοῦ στόματος αὐτῆς ἐκπορεύεται δικαιοσύνη,
    νόμον δὲ καὶ ἔλεον ἐπὶ γλώσσης φορεῖ.
17 αἱ ὁδοὶ αὐτῆς ὁδοὶ καλαί,
    καὶ πάντες οἱ τρίβοι αὐτῆς ἐν εἰρήνῃ·
18 ξύλον ζωῆς ἐστι πᾶσι τοῖς ἀντεχομένοις αὐτῆς,
    καὶ τοῖς ἐπερειδομένοις ἐπ' αὐτὴν ὡς ἐπὶ κύριον ἀσφαλής.
19 ὁ θεὸς τῇ σοφίᾳ ἐθεμελίωσεν τὴν γῆν,
    ἡτοίμασεν δὲ οὐρανοὺς ἐν φρονήσει·
20 ἐν αἰσθήσει ἄβυσσοι ἐρράγησαν,
    νέφη δὲ ἐρρύησαν δρόσους.
21 υἱέ, μὴ παραρρυῇς,
    τήρησον δὲ ἐμὴν βουλὴν καὶ ἔννοιαν,
22 ἵνα ζήσῃ ἡ ψυχή σου,
    καὶ χάρις ᾖ περὶ σῷ τραχήλῳ.
    ἔσται δὲ ἴασις ταῖς σαρξί σου
    καὶ ἐπιμέλεια τοῖς σοῖς ὀστέοις,
23 ἵνα πορεύῃ πεποιθὼς ἐν εἰρήνῃ πάσας τὰς ὁδούς σου,
    ὁ δὲ πούς σου οὐ μὴ προσκόψῃ.
24 ἐὰν γὰρ κάθῃ, ἄφοβος ἔσῃ,
    ἐὰν δὲ καθεύδῃς, ἡδέως ὑπνώσεις·
25 καὶ οὐ φοβηθήσῃ πτόησιν ἐπελθοῦσαν

---

[8] Text: Alfred Rahlfs, ed., *Septuaginta* (2 vols.; Stuttgart: Württembergische Bibelanstalt, 1959[6], 1962[7]) 2.187-188.

	οὐδὲ ὁρμὰς ἀσεβῶν ἐπερχομένας·
26	ὁ γὰρ κύριος ἔσται ἐπὶ πασῶν ὁδῶν σου
	καὶ ἐρείσει σὸν πόδα, ἵνα μὴ σαλευθῇς.
27	μὴ ἀπόσχῃ εὖ ποιεῖν ἐνδεῆ,
	ἡνίκα ἂν ἔχῃ ἡ χείρ σου βοηθεῖν·
28	μὴ εἴπῃς Ἐπανελθὼν ἐπάνηκε καὶ αὔριον δώσω,
	δυνατοῦ σου ὄντος εὖ ποιεῖν·
	οὐ γὰρ οἶδας τί τέξεται ἡ ἐπιοῦσα.
29	μὴ τεκτήνῃ ἐπὶ σὸν φίλον κακὰ
	παροικοῦντα καὶ πεποιθότα ἐπὶ σοί.
30	μὴ φιλεχθρήσῃς πρὸς ἄνθρωπον μάτην,
	μή τι εἰς σὲ ἐργάσηται κακόν.
31	μὴ κτήσῃ κακῶν ἀνδρῶν ὀνείδη
	μηδὲ ζηλώσῃς τὰς ὁδοὺς αὐτῶν·
32	ἀκάθαρτος γὰρ ἔναντι κυρίου πᾶς παράνομος,
	ἐν δὲ δικαίοις οὐ συνεδριάζει.
33	κατάρα θεοῦ ἐν οἴκοις ἀσεβῶν,
	ἐπαύλεις δὲ δικαίων εὐλογοῦνται.
34	κύριος ὑπερηφάνοις ἀντιτάσσεται,
	ταπεινοῖς δὲ δίδωσιν χάριν.
35	δόξαν σοφοὶ κληρονομήσουσιν,
	οἱ δὲ ἀσεβεῖς ὕψωσαν ἀτιμίαν.

Translation:[9]

11	My son, do not make light of the training of the Lord,
	and do not fail when rebuked by Him;
12	for whom the Lord loves, he disciplines,
	and he scourges every son whom he receives.
13	Blessed is the man who finds wisdom,
	and the mortal who knows prudence.
14	For it is better to traffic for her
	than for treasures of gold and silver.
15	And she is more valuable than precious stones;
	no base thing shall resist her;
	she is well known to all that come near her,
	and no precious thing is her equal in value.
16	For length of existence and years of life are in her right hand;

---

[9] My translation.

	and in her left hand are wealth and glory;
	out of her mouth proceeds righteousness,
	and she bears law and mercy upon her tongue.
17	Her ways are good ways,
	and all her paths are peaceful.
18	She is a tree of life to all that lay hold of her;
	and to those that lean on her, as on the Lord, she is steadfast.
19	God by wisdom founded the earth,
	and he prepared the heavens with prudence.
20	In understanding the depths were shattered,
	and the clouds gushed water.
21	My son, do not let them slip by,
	but observe my counsel and understanding.
22	In order that your soul may live,
	and that there may be grace round your neck;
	and it will be healing for your flesh,
	and care for your bones;
23	in order that you may walk confidently in peace all your ways,
	and that your foot may not stumble.
24	For if you rest, you will be fearless;
	and if you sleep, you will slumber sweetly.
25	And you will not have fear of alarm coming upon you,
	nor of approaching attacks of ungodly people.
26	For the Lord will be in all of your ways,
	and he will establish your foot so that you are not moved.
27	Do not abstain from doing good to the needy,
	whenever your hand is able to help.
28	Do not say, 'Come back another time, tomorrow I will give,'
	while being able to do good;
	for you do not know what the next day will bring.
29	Do not devise evil against your friend,
	living nearby and trusting in you.
30	Do not be eager to do violence to a man without cause,
	lest he do some evil thing to you.
31	Do not procure the reproaches of evil men,
	and do not covet their ways.
32	For unclean before the Lord is each transgressor,
	and he does not sit among the righteous.
33	The curse of God is in the houses of the ungodly,
	but the habitations of the righteous are blessed.

34 The Lord resists the proud,
    but to the humble he gives grace.
35 The wise shall inherit glory,
    but the ungodly great dishonor.

This discourse exhorts the reader to accept and endure "the training of the Lord" that the author presents since this discipline leads to wisdom and its benefits. As the outline above indicates, it is possible to analyze the passage in terms of the three literary and rhetorical divisions described in general terms above. In this case, LXX Proverbs 3.11-12 is the programmatic statement, 3.13-20 is the descriptive section, and 3.21-35 is the prescriptive section.

Formally, the programmatic statement opens with a personal address, υἱέ ("my son"), introducing two negatively-formulated admonitions (3.11), buttressed by a two-part motive clause connected by γάρ (3.12).[10] In terms of function, these verses specify the theme of the passage and establish its material and hermeneutical foundations, stipulating a comprehensive ethical program, its motivations and objectives. The author calls this program the παιδεία κυρίου ("Lord's training"); the programmatic statement encourages the reader to undertake this divine instruction and correction despite the hardship it entails, since this discipline is proof of the Lord's ἀγάπη ("love"). The remainder of the discourse (3.13ff.) will be devoted to articulating the precise benefits and obligations that ensue from the reader's decision to accept this training.

The formal qualities of the second section of the passage, 3.13-20, depart significantly from those of the instructional genre; thus there is no direct address and no imperatives are utilized. Instead, the section incorporates a hymn describing the positive qualities of σοφία ("wisdom") as a semi-divine entity and the blessedness enjoyed by those who have acquired her. With respect to its literary quality and style the passage is reminiscent of a number of wisdom psalms.[11] Here the author demonstrates that to submit to the discipline of God, as the programmatic statement had exhorted the reader to do, is to find wisdom, the greatest of all treasures. The section begins with a maxim, a

---

[10] On 3.11-12, in addition to the commentaries, see Kayatz, *Studien zu Proverbien 1-9*, 32-35; von Rad, *Wisdom in Israel*, 198-201; Nel, *Structure and Ethos*, 37, 86-87.

[11] As von Rad observes (*Wisdom in Israel*, 151 n. 4), 3.13-26 resembles the didactic poem in Proverbs 8; cf. Kayatz, *Studien zu Proverbien 1-9*, 50-51. Hans Dieter Betz has pointed out that 3.13-20 is also similar to Hellenistic hymns, which normally have three parts: introitus, aretalogy, conclusion; here the last part is omitted because it carries over into the prescriptive section (Private communication, 9/21/89), cf. Berger, "Hellenistische Gattungen," 1149-1169; idem, *Formgeschichte*, 239-247, with references.

macarism or beatitude, which establishes the theme of the entire hymn: the individual who obtains wisdom and knows prudence is blessed (3.13).[12] By means of this saying the author extols two concepts fundamental to the administration of the παιδεία κυρίου: σοφία and φρόνησις ("prudence"). The question of precisely how the wise and prudent man becomes blessed is answered by a succession of seven motive clauses (the MT has five) introduced by γάρ that specify some of the excellent qualities of wisdom (vv. 14-18). While no direct demand is made, the wise sage in 3.13 obviously functions as a paradigmatic figure for the reader to identify with and emulate, and wisdom, a semi-divine being, is intended as the means by which the reader will know the Lord's instruction and the Lord's blessing. The third and final part of the hymn (3.19-20), following closely on the descriptions in the second, depicts wisdom as a mediator in God's act of creation.[13] The formulation here re-emphasizes the two critical terms presented in v.13 (σοφία and φρόνησις in v. 19), thus creating an inclusio that contributes to the unity of the section and underscores the topical connection of this part of the hymn with the opening maxim.

As William McKane in particular has demonstrated, 3.21-35, labelled here the prescriptive section, bears a strong likeness to Near Eastern wisdom instruction by virtue of its formal characteristics.[14] Thus we meet with wisdom admonitions in vv. 21, 27, 28, 29, 30, and 31, deployed in conjunction with motive clauses, qualifying statements, and supporting wisdom sentences. In addition to this generic consistency, a number of formal devices, including catchword, linkword, and isocolon, augment the section's structural unity.[15] Here the author makes a direct and distinctive appeal, demonstrating precisely what the παιδεία κυρίου involves with respect to the reader's ethical behavior and particular goals. The main argument may be summarized as follows: after a general injunction for the audience to obey (v. 21), the results of obedience

---

[12] On the beatitude as a sapiential form see Burkhard Gladigow, "Zum Makarismos des Weisen," *Hermes* 95 (1967) 404-433.

[13] Some modern commentators view these lines as a separate hymn or part of a separate hymn, for example Toy, *Proverbs*, 70-73; Greenstone, *Proverbs*, 31-32; Whybray, *Wisdom in Proverbs*, 42-43; Scott, *Proverbs*, 47; cf. Plöger, *Sprüche*, 36-37; Peter Doll, *Menschenschöpfung und Weltschöpfung in der alttestamentlichen Weisheit* (SBS 117; Stuttgart: Katholisches Bibelwerk, 1985) 48-51; Meinhold, "Gott und Mensch," 468-469; also Hermisson, "Creation Theology in Wisdom," 43-57; also cf. the discussion of Jewish gnomic poems in Chapter Two.

[14] McKane, *Proverbs*, 289-290, 297-302; see also Kayatz, *Studien zu Proverbien 1-9*, 66-68; Lang, *Lehrrede*, 76-77, 81-82; Nel, *Structure and Ethos*, 47, 60.

[15] For example φιλ- in vv. 29a and 30a; κακ- in vv. 29a, 30b, 31a; note also the thematic linkword εὖ ποιεῖν (vv. 27 and 28) and βοηθεῖν (v. 28), and the various references to walking, etc. in vv. 23, 26, and 31; isocolon is esp. evident in vv. 31 and 33.

are spelled out, first with respect to the benefits (vv. 22-25), the chief of which is God's aid (v. 26), then with respect to responsibilities (vv. 27-31); the section draws to a close with a series of wisdom sentences that contrast the fate of those who obey with that of those who do not (vv. 32-34), and finally a culminating summary of the section in the form of a contrastive maxim (v. 35).

The section opens with a form of personal address, υἱέ ("my son"), attached to a protreptic maxim demanding personal acceptance of wisdom and of the author's instruction (v. 21): do not allow this opportunity to pass by but observe my βουλή ("counsel") and ἔννοια ("understanding").[16] This initial saying defines the contents of the entire section and establishes its rhetorical stance. Functionally, the verse has also been carefully interconnected with the preceding materials and plays a decisive role in the logical development and ethical impact of the discourse. Thus the glory of the παιδεία κυρίου (the theme of the programmatic statement) is visible in the individual who has found σοφία (the theme of the descriptive section) and is made accessible in a concrete way to the reader through the personal βουλή of the author (the theme of the prescriptive section). In this way the author demonstrates the character and authority of the instruction and provides a material and hermeneutical context within which the direct demands made upon the "son" in the prescriptive section are intelligible and meaningful.

A sequence of ten parallel clauses (3.22-25), introduced by ἵνα (3.22), undergirds the protreptic maxim by offering an account of some of the benefits that accrue to the obedient reader; among these are ζωή ("life"), χάρις ("grace"), ἴασις ("healing"), and ἐπιμέλεια ("care").[17] The final and climactic benefit is a promise of the Lord's aid and guidance in 3.26, connected to 3.22-25 by γάρ. On account of its literary position and material prominence the verse has been designated the central statement. Indeed, it is this benefit above all that will ensure that those listed in vv. 22-25 can be realized. In addition, while v. 26 plainly concludes vv. 22-26, it is also important to recognize its impact on the verses that follow. The assertion regarding God's presence at this point underscores an essential theological value and moral ideal shared by both the writer and reader. In this capacity it determines the tone and direction of the material that follows in the remainder of the discourse.

The third and final main sub-division of the prescriptive section, 3.27-35,

---

[16] The protreptic maxim is linked with the descriptive section by means of catchword: ἐρρύησαν (v. 20) and παραρρυῆς (v. 21).

[17] The connection of the prescriptive section with the descriptive section is underscored here by the formal and material similarities between the lists in vv. 22-25 and in vv. 14-18: the benefits that the sage in v. 13 already enjoys through wisdom are the same as those potentially available to the reader through the author's counsel.

carries the argument of the discourse further through specific exhortation and encouragement. In 3.27-31, the author brings to bear several concrete admonitions that stipulate some of the ethical responsibilities tied to his program; this is buttressed by extended motivation in the form of antithetical wisdom sentences (vv. 32-34) and the discourse's conclusion (v. 35).

The direct address of the protreptic maxim (3.21) is resumed in 3.27-31 with five wisdom admonitions, each formulated negatively and beginning with μή.[18] Here the author provides a sample of his βουλή and specifies the sorts of obligations that it entails. Some of the maxims are accompanied by reasons that offer motives for the enjoined activities (3.28c, 30b); others include qualifications that take into account the reader's limited abilities or particular circumstances (3.27b, 28b, 30a). With regard to subject-matter, the author first commends benevolence for those in need (3.27-28) and then urges against evil conduct in dealing with friends (3.29), people in general (3.30), and even bad men (3.31).

The next sub-division, 3.32-34, is an extended motivation connected to the preceding imperatives by γάρ and consisting entirely of bilinear wisdom sentences.[19] These sayings depend primarily upon the admonitions in vv. 27-31, but also function as support for the advice of the entire discourse. Here the author compares the divinely-determined fate of those who accept wisdom and obey the Lord with that of ungodly and arrogant transgressors. All three sentences are formulated antithetically, raising some prominent sapiential contrasts: transgressors vs. the righteous (v. 32), cursing vs. blessing (v. 33), and the proud vs. the humble (v. 34). Significantly, references to divine judgements or reactions figure prominently in all of the sayings; here the author suggests what obedience and disobedience mean in terms of one's relationship with God.[20]

The section concludes with one last antithetical maxim where the author provides a summary and final confirmation, juxtaposing the σοφοί ("wise") and the δόξα ("glory") that they inherit with the plight of the unfaithful. The formulation of the concluding proverb recalls language used in the descriptive

---

[18] Note also the extensive use of parallelism and isocolon, esp. in v. 31.

[19] In addition to antithesis and isocolon (esp. in v. 33), these lines exhibit similar beginnings (-κ- in vv. 32a, 32b, 33a, 34a) and endings (-ει and -αι in vv. 32b, 33b, 34a).

[20] Kloppenborg (*The Formation of Q*, 186-187) observes that sapiential instructions frequently conclude with references to the rewards which await those who attend to the exhortation and the consequences for those who do not; he cites Proverbs 1.29-33, 2.20-22, 4.18-19, 5.22-23, 7.24-27, 8.32-36; Ben Sira 6.32-37 (see below), 24.19-22, as well as Q 6.46-49.

section (σοφία in 3.13, 19; δόξα in 3.16) and creates an inclusio that contributes to the unity of the discourse. It also brings to mind again the model of the descriptive section and highlights the significance of the discourse's central theological and ethical concept, wisdom.

One final note on LXX Proverbs 3.11-35 concerns its poetic style. In his study of the poetry of the LXX Proverbs, H. J. Thackeray observed that something in the neighborhood of 200 lines in the book exhibit metrical effects, roughly divided between hexameter (e.g. 3.28) and iambic (e.g. 3.15) variations, with a predilection for metrical endings. Only a very small number of these verses entail complete metrical lines, and so it is more accurate to speak of them as 'rhythmical' or 'metrical' than poetic in the strict sense. Of the translator of LXX Proverbs Thackeray writes: "the impression produced is that he was content with a partial approximation to poetry, and did not always trouble to produce finished lines."[21] In the passage above, Thackeray cited the following verses as displaying metrical effects: 3.13, 15, 22, 28, and 34, to which 3.30 should be added.[22] As he demonstrated, these are the same sort of rhythms familiar from the ancient Greek proverb collections and it seems likely that the translator(s) of LXX Proverbs made conscious use of such meters.[23]

Ben Sira 6.18-37

The textual boundaries of this passage are more easily fixed that those of Proverbs 3.11-35 and most modern critics concur regarding its unity.[24] The

---

[21] Thackeray, "Poetry," 56.
[22] Ibidem, 49, 56-58, 60.
[23] Ibidem, esp. 46-48, 63-66; see also the references cited above p. 70 n. 91; also cf. Stanislav Segert, "Semitic Poetic Structures in the New Testament," *ANRW* II.25.2 (1984) 1433-1462.
[24] For modern discussion of the meaning and composition of 6.18-37 see esp. Skehan and DiLella, *Ben Sira*, 190-196; also Rudolf Smend, *Die Weisheit des Jesus Sirach erklärt* (Berlin: Reimer, 1906) 57-62; Marböck, *Weisheit*, 113-118; O. Rickenbacher, *Weisheitsperikopen bei Ben Sira* (OBO 1; Freiburg: Universitätsverlag; Göttingen: Vandenhoeck & Ruprecht, 1973) 55-72; Georg Sauer, *Jesus Sirach* (JSHRZ 3.5; Gütersloh: Mohn, 1981) 519-521; John G. Snaith, *Ecclesiasticus, or the Wisdom of Jesus, Son of Sirach* (Cambridge Biblical Commentary; Cambridge: Cambridge University Press, 1974) 37-40. For more on Ben Sira in general see Bauckmann, "Die Proverbien," 33-63; Norbert Peters, *Das Buch Jesus Sirach oder Ecclesiasticus* (EHAT 25; Münster i.W.: Aschendorff, 1913); A. Eberharter, *Das Buch Jesus Sirach oder Ecclesiasticus* (HSAT 6.5; Bonn: Hanstein, 1925); Vinzenz Hamp, *Sirach* (Echter Bibel AT 13.2; Würzburg: Echter Verlag, 1951); R. P. C. Spicq, "L'Ecclésiastique," *La Sainte Bible* (ed. Louis Pirot and Albert Clamer; Paris:

discourse serves as a "programmatic prologue" to the third major sub-division of Ben Sira (6.18-14.19), a unit that concentrates on ethically and socially-oriented exhortation. In this introductory position, 6.18-37 specifies some fundamental themes and basic presuppositions regarding the text's goals and perspectives and so serves as a foundation for the series of sapiential passages in 7.1-14.19.[25] For the most part, these subsequent passages address relatively specific issues and concrete problems, such as social conduct and political responsibility (see especially 7.1-17, 8.1-19, and 9.17-10.18), and they exhibit varying literary structures (for instance the gnomic poem in 10.14-18 discussed in Chapter Two).[26] The following outline is proposed for 6.18-37:

18-19	I. Programmatic Statement
18a	A. Personal address: τέκνον ("My son")
	B. Appeal: ἐπίλεξαι παιδείαν ("to gather instruction")
18b	C. Motive: the reader shall find σοφία ("wisdom")
19	D. Appeal and motive restated metaphorically
20-22	II. Descriptive Section
20-21	A. Two parallel statements on the ἀπαίδευτοι ("unlearned") and the ἀκάρδιος ("heartless")
22	B. Maxim: conclusion about wisdom drawn from the descriptions
23-35	III. Prescriptive Section
23-31	A. Direct appeal and list of consequences
23a	1. Personal address: τέκνον ("my son")
23	2. Protreptic maxim: appeal to obey the author's γνώμη ("advice") and συμβουλία ("counsel")
24-27	3. Description of ten burdens that result from obedience
28-31	4. Description of rewards that result from obedience
32-37	B. Exhortation on pursuing wisdom
32-33	1. Central statement: four conditional sentences

Letouzey et Ané, 1951[2]) 6.529-841; Othmar Schilling, *Das Buch Jesus Sirach* (HB 7.2; Freiburg: Herder, 1956); Hilaire Duesberg and Paul Auvray, *Le livre de l'Ecclésiastique* (SBJ; Paris: Cerf, 1958[2]); von Rad, *Wisdom in Israel*, 240-262; Th. Middendorp, *Die Stellung Jesus ben Siras zwischen Judentum und Hellenismus* (Leiden: Brill, 1973); Edmond Jacob, "Wisdom and Religion in Sirach," in Gammie, *Israelite Wisdom*, 235-245; Maurice Gilbert, "Wisdom Literature," *Jewish Writings of the Second Temple Period: Apocrypha, Pseudepigrapha, Qumran Sectarian Writings, Philo, Josephus* (ed. Michael E. Stone; CRINT 2.2; Assen, Maastricht: Van Gorcum; Philadelphia: Fortress, 1984) 290-301, 322-323; Schnabel, *Law and Wisdom*, 10-92.

[25] Cf. Roth, "Gnomic-Discursive Wisdom," 60, 74-75.
[26] Cf. Baumgartner, "Gattungen," 161-198.

Analysis of the Discourses

	challenging the reader to accept instruction and so become wise
34-36	2. Supporting admonitions on gaining instruction through social interaction
37	3. Concluding statement
37a	a. appeal to ponder the ordinances of the Lord
37b	b. promise: the Lord will establish the reader's heart (inclusio with v. 20), and the desire for wisdom will be granted (inclusio with v. 18)

Text:[27]

18	Τέκνον, ἐκ νεότητός σου ἐπίλεξαι[28] παιδείαν,
	καὶ ἕως πολιῶν εὑρήσεις σοφίαν.
19	ὡς ὁ ἀροτριῶν καὶ ὁ σπείρων πρόσελθε αὐτῇ
	καὶ ἀνάμενε τοὺς ἀγαθοὺς καρποὺς αὐτῆς·
	ἐν γὰρ τῇ ἐργασίᾳ αὐτῆς ὀλίγον κοπιάσεις
	καὶ ταχὺ φάγεσαι τῶν γενημάτων αὐτῆς.
20	ὡς τραχεῖά ἐστιν σοφία τοῖς ἀπαιδεύτοις,
	καὶ οὐκ ἐμμενεῖ ἐν αὐτῇ ἀκάρδιος·
21	ὡς λίθος δοκιμασίας ἰσχυρὸς ἔσται ἐπ' αὐτῷ,
	καὶ οὐ χρονιεῖ ἀπορρῖψαι αὐτήν.
22	σοφία γὰρ κατὰ τὸ ὄνομα αὐτῆς ἐστιν
	καὶ οὐ πολλοῖς ἐστιν φανερά.
23	ἄκουσον, τέκνον, καὶ ἔκδεξαι γνώμην μου
	καὶ μὴ ἀπαναίνου τὴν συμβουλίαν μου·
24	εἰσένεγκον τοὺς πόδας σου εἰς τὰς πέδας αὐτῆς
	καὶ εἰς τὸν κλοιὸν αὐτῆς τὸν τράχηλόν σου·
25	ὑπόθες τὸν ὦμόν σου καὶ βάσταξον αὐτήν
	καὶ μὴ προσοχθίσῃς τοῖς δεσμοῖς αὐτῆς·
26	ἐν πάσῃ ψυχῇ σου πρόσελθε αὐτῇ
	καὶ ἐν ὅλῃ δυνάμει σου συντήρησον τὰς ὁδοὺς αὐτῆς·
27	ἐξίχνευσον καὶ ζήτησον, καὶ γνωσθήσεταί σοι,
	καὶ ἐγκρατὴς γενόμενος μὴ ἀφῇς αὐτήν·
28	ἐπ' ἐσχάτων γὰρ εὑρήσεις τὴν ἀνάπαυσιν αὐτῆς,
	καὶ στραφήσεταί σοι εἰς εὐφροσύνην·
29	καὶ ἔσονταί σοι αἱ πέδαι εἰς σκέπην ἰσχύος

---

[27] Text: Joseph Ziegler, ed., *Sapientia Iesu Filii Sirach* (Septuaginta, Vetus Testamentum Graecum 12.2; Göttingen: Vandenhoeck & Ruprecht, 1965) 152-156.

[28] Ziegler (*Sirach*, 152) prints ἐπίδεξαι, but ἐπίλεξαι seems the better choice.

	καὶ οἱ κλοιοὶ αὐτῆς εἰς στολὴν δόξης.
30	κόσμος γὰρ χρύσεός ἐστιν ἐπ' αὐτῆς,
	καὶ οἱ δεσμοὶ αὐτῆς κλῶσμα ὑακίνθινον·
31	στολὴν δόξης ἐνδύσῃ αὐτὴν
	καὶ στέφανον ἀγαλλιάματος περιθήσεις σεαυτῷ.
32	ἐὰν θέλῃς, τέκνον, παιδευθήσῃ,
	καὶ ἐὰν ἐπιδῷς τὴν ψυχήν σου, πανοῦργος ἔσῃ·
33	ἐὰν ἀγαπήσῃς ἀκούειν, ἐκδέξῃ,
	καὶ ἐὰν κλίνῃς τὸ οὖς σου, σοφὸς ἔσῃ.
34	ἐν πλήθει πρεσβυτέρων στῆθι·
	καὶ τῇ σοφίᾳ αὐτῶν προσκολλήθητι.
35	πᾶσαν διήγησιν θείαν θέλε ἀκροᾶσθαι,
	καὶ παροιμίαι συνέσεως μὴ ἐκφευγέτωσάν σε.
36	ἐὰν ἴδῃς συνετόν, ὄρθριζε πρὸς αὐτόν,
	καὶ βαθμοὺς θυρῶν αὐτοῦ ἐκτριβέτω ὁ πούς σου.
37	διανοοῦ ἐν τοῖς προστάγμασιν κυρίου
	καὶ ἐν ταῖς ἐντολαῖς αὐτοῦ μελέτα διὰ παντός·
	αὐτὸς στηριεῖ τὴν καρδίαν σου,
	καὶ ἡ ἐπιθυμία τῆς σοφίας δοθήσεταί σοι.

Translation:[29]

18	My son, from your youth gather instruction
	and until old age you will find wisdom.
19	As one that plows and sows approach her,
	and wait for her good fruits;
	for in doing her work you will toil little,
	and soon you will eat of her fruits.
20	As something harsh is wisdom to the unlearned,
	and one who is heartless will not remain with her.
21	As a severe stone of trial she will be on him,
	and before long he will cast her aside.
22	For wisdom is according to her name,
	and to many she is not manifest.
23	Listen, my son, and accept my advice,
	and do not refuse my counsel.
24	Put your feet into her fetters,
	and your neck into her chain.

---

[29] My translation, cf. Skehan and DiLella, *Ben Sira*, 190-191.

25	Bow down your shoulder, and bear her,
	and do not be grieved with her bonds.
26	With your whole soul approach her,
	and with all you power keep her ways.
27	Search and seek, and she shall be made known to you;
	and when you have gained hold of her, do not let her go.
28	For in the end you will find her rest,
	and that shall be turned to your joy.
29	And for you her fetters will be a strong defence,
	and her chains a robe of glory.
30	For there is a golden ornament upon her,
	and her bands are purple lace.
31	You shall put her on, a robe of glory,
	and you shall wear her about yourself, a crown of exultation.
32	If you are willing, my son, you will be taught;
	and if you give your soul, you will be clever.
33	If you love to hear, you will receive,
	and if you bend your ear, you will be wise.
34	Stand in the throng of elders,
	and associate with those who are wise.
35	Be willing to hear every godly discourse,
	and do not let sage proverbs escape you.
36	And if you see someone with understanding,
	awake early to go to him,
	and let your foot wear out the steps to his door.
37	Think over the ordinances of the Lord,
	and on his injunctions meditate constantly;
	he will establish your heart,
	and your desire for wisdom will be granted.

With the exception of the descriptive section (6.20-22), this sapiential text bears numerous similarities in form and substance to LXX Proverbs 3.11-35. Like the previous discourse, it confronts the reader with an appeal to pursue the παιδεία that the author provides, endorsing both its responsibilities and its rewards, and so achieve wisdom. The literary scheme embraces the same three-fold division: 6.18-19 is the programmatic statement, 6.20-22 the descriptive section, and 6.23-35 the prescriptive section.

After a personal address, τέκνον ("my son"), the programmatic statement presents a direct call for action that exhorts the reader to ἐπίλεξαι παιδεία ("to gather instruction") from his youth (cf. LXX Proverbs 3.11). The author motivates the plea to take on instruction despite the effort involved by indicating its positive outcome: the audience will find wisdom (εὑρήσεις σοφίαν) and enjoy its benefits throughout their lives (cf. LXX Proverbs 3.13). These ideas are restated metaphorically in v. 19, likening the work and rewards of the sapiential vocation to those of a farmer.[30]

The descriptive section of the discourse, 6.20-22, portrays the ἀπαίδευτος ("untrained man")[31] and the ἀκάρδιος ("heartless man"). In the programmatic statement, the author had asserted that παιδεία was the reader's means of finding wisdom. In order to dramatize this point, he describes the man who lacks παιδεία: to him σοφία is harsh and severe, and so she is soon cast aside. The reason for this is suggested by the maxim in 6.22; to those without παιδεία or καρδία, wisdom is not φανερά ("manifest"). As the author had stated in v. 19b, the toil for wisdom is minor and lasts only a short while, but to the individual without παιδεία this toil is meaningless and unbearable because the necessary insight and attitude are lacking. In contrast with the other descriptive sections, 6.20-22 projects a model that is for the most part negative. The intention, however, is principally the same. The audience, in dismissing or criticizing the ἀπαίδευτος and the ἀκάρδιος, comes to a better appreciation of what the author intends for their self-understanding and behavior.

In the prescriptive section, 6.23-35, the author elaborates on the characteristics of both παιδεία and σοφία and the relationship of the two as they pertain to the reader. Throughout this segment the author maintains a careful balance between command and appeal on one hand and motivation and explanation on the other. The section begins with an admonition to accept the author's advice and counsel; the implications of this advice for the reader are then depicted, first the burdens (vv. 24-27), then the rewards (vv. 28-31). Next comes a challenge to accept παιδεία and thus become wise (vv. 32-33), supported by several admonitions that specify how this is accomplished (vv. 34-36), and finally a culminating statement consisting of a further appeal and promise (v. 37).

To begin with, the section confronts the reader directly with a call to hear (ἄκουσον) and a personal address (τέκνον), coupled with a protreptic maxim (6.23) that gives the theme and function of the verses that follow. The παιδεία of wisdom discussed in the programmatic statement and descriptive section is

---

[30] Note also the erotic element of the imagery, cf. 6.27, 32b, 33a, 37d.
[31] The term is normally used to describe someone who is generally uneducated or unskilled, also someone who is untrained in a particular thing, cf. LXX Proverbs 5.23, 8.5, 15.12, 14, 17.21, 24.7, 27.20; Ben Sira 8.4, 10.3, 20.19, 24, 22.3; Sextus *Sententiae* 285; *Gnomica Homoeomata* 10a, 22, 27, 29, 29a, 39, 42, 45, 61, 67, 109c, 173, 182.

here termed the author's own γνώμη ("advice") and συμβουλία ("counsel"). These are the direct and immediate means by which the reader will gain access to instruction (cf. v. 32), and by which wisdom will be known and achieved (cf. vv. 27, 33). In terms of its logical place and function within the discourse, the protreptic maxim in v. 23 resembles its counterpart in LXX Proverbs 3.21.[32]

The sharply-stated entreaty in 6.23 is then expanded by means of a sequence of ten short and largely parallel admonitions (6.24-27). The injunctions here list a number of the obligations and burdensome activities that derive from and correspond to the γνώμη and συμβουλία of v. 23. In this way the author dramatizes what the protreptic maxim entails and stipulates what is expected of the reader if he accepts the instruction. The author invokes a fair amount of figurative language and parabolic imagery in these verses, particularly that of a "prisoner" or "slave" of wisdom (vv. 24-25). The undertakings enjoined in the sequence are endorsed by a description of their rewards in vv. 28-31, introduced by ἐπ' ἐσχάτων γάρ ("for at the last ... ").[33] The list of benefits takes up the "prisoner" imagery introduced earlier (v. 29, cf. vv. 24-25); there is also a description of σοφία as a decorated statue (v. 30), and as a robe and crown to be worn by the reader (v. 31).

Beginning with 6.32, the author resumes the direct plea, first with a group of second-person conditional sentences (vv. 32-33), then with imperatives (vv. 34-36). The pointed emphasis on the reader's personal decision and on the potentiality of his circumstances in the first set of appeals (vv. 32-33) suggests that these verses represent the rhetorical crux and literary climax of the prescriptive section; thus they have been designated as the central statement in the outline above. The use of τέκνον and the reference to teaching (παιδευθήσῃ) in 6.32 recalls the programmatic statement (vv. 18-19), signaling the beginning of new formal unit and indicating the importance of the specified activities: a willingness to be taught (v. 32a), the giving up of one's soul (v. 32b), and a desire to listen attentively (v. 33).[34] The second set of exhortations (vv. 34-36), linked with the first by catchword (σοφός in vv. 33 and 34), extends the personal appeal to pursue wisdom by specifying social interaction with the wise as a means of achieving it.

The final segment of the prescriptive section, 6.37, continues the appeal to pursue wisdom and constitutes a summary and conclusion for the section as well as the whole passage. The segment consists of two parallel injunctions to

---

[32] The specific formulation of 6.23 is modeled after Proverbs 4.10; cf. Skehan and DiLella, *Ben Sira*, 193-194.

[33] Cf. ἕως πολιῶν κτλ. in v. 18.

[34] Cf. Skehan and DiLella, *Ben Sira*, 195.

ponder the προστάγματα ("ordinances") and ἐντολαί ("injunctions") of the Lord, perhaps indicating the content of the discourses and teachings referred to in 6.32-36. These admonitions are affirmed by a culminating promise in v. 37b that the Lord will establish the heart of the reader (cf. the ἀκάρδιος in v. 20) and that the reader's desire for wisdom will be granted. The reference to σοφία here recalls the motive clause of the programmatic statement. This forms an effective inclusio[35] that buttresses a ring composition structuring the entire discourse:

6.18-19	A.	promise of wisdom
6.20-22	B.	the untrained
6.23	C.	appeal to accept instruction
6.24-27	D.	list of wisdom's duties
6.28-31	D'.	list of wisdom's benefits
6.32-33	C'.	appeal to accept instruction
6.34-36	B'.	the wise
6.37	A'.	promise of wisdom

Besides contributing to the literary quality and rhetorical cohesion of the discourse, the juxtaposition of structural pairs in the ring composition reinforces the overall message and creates new possibilities of interpretation. It is important to observe that the corresponding elements of the ring composition hardly represent mere restatements or rewordings of each other; so, for instance, B and B', as well as D and D', address virtually opposite subjects. In contrast with LXX Proverbs 3.11-35, here it is only in the concluding lines of the passage (v. 37) that the author makes explicit use of the Lord as a focal point of the discussion and as motivator for the instruction.

Pseudo-Phocylides 70-96

The gnomic and poetic features of the ΦΩΚΥΛΙΔΟΥ ΓΝΩΜΑΙ ("Maxims of Phocylides"), or Pseudo-Phocylides, composed in rough dactylic hexameters, are immediately obvious. As I suggested above in Chapter Two, Pseudo-Phocylides represents a generic 'hybrid' exhibiting literary characteristics familiar from all three of the prominent gnomic genres: gnomic poetry,

---

[35] Cf. ibidem, 196; also s.v. inclusio.

gnomologia, and wisdom instruction.[36] The maxims in this document have been organized into a number of thematic units; one such unit is lines 70-96, which Pieter van der Horst prints as a group entitled "The Danger of Envy and Other Vices."[37] I propose the following outline for its contents:

70	I. Programmatic Statement: admonition against φθόνος ("envy")
71-75	II. Descriptive Section: the example of the cosmos
71	A. An assertion regarding the lack of envy among the οὐρανίδαι ("heavenly ones")
72-74a	B. Three specific illustrations of this assertion
74b	C. Another assertion regarding the ὁμόνοια ("concord") of the heavenly ones
75	D. A concluding maxim emphasizing the absence of ἔρις ("strife") among the μάκαρες ("blessed ones")
76-96	III. Prescriptive Section: exhortation on σωφροσύνη
76-78	A. The fundamental ethical principles: three antithetical maxims
76	1. Protreptic maxim: command to practice σωφροσύνη and to refrain from shameful deeds
77	2. Command to refrain from retaliation and to support justice
78	3. Supporting wisdom sentence introduced by γάρ: negotiation is better than ἔρις (cf. line 75)
79-96	B. A series of subordinate maxims illustrating how to practice self-restraint, organized by ring composition
79	1. Central Statement: initial maxim on self-restraint in trusting others
80-94	2. Further maxims on self-restraint regarding various referents
95-96	3. Concluding maxims on not trusting the λαός ("people")

---

[36] There is as yet no adequate treatment of the literary composition of Pseudo-Phocylides; van der Horst, for instance, divides the text into fifteen thematic units (including the prologue and epilogue) though he does not discuss the literary design of these units or how they are connected to one another; cf. Küchler, *Weisheitstraditionen*, 262-274, 301-302.

[37] On lines 70-96 see esp. van der Horst, *Pseudo-Phocylides*, 161-178, cf. 3ff.; Nikolaus Walter (with Ernst Vogt), *Poetische Schriften* (JSHRZ 4.3; Gütersloh: Mohn, 1983) 182-216, esp. 204-206. Further on Pseudo-Phocylides in general see Küchler, *Weisheitstraditionen*, 261-302; Pieter W. van der Horst, "Pseudo-Phocylides," in Charlesworth, *Pseudepigrapha*, 2.565-582; idem, "Pseudo-Phocylides Revisited," *JSP* 3 (1988) 3-30; Gilbert, "Wisdom Literature," 313-316; P. Derron, *Pseudo-Phocylide: Sentences* (Paris: Les Belles Lettres, 1986); Niebuhr, *Gesetz und Paränese*, 5-31, 42-44, 57-72.

Text:[38]

70 μὴ φθονέοις ἀγαθῶν ἑτάροις, μὴ μῶμον ἀνάψῃς.
ἄφθονοι οὐρανίδαι καὶ ἐν ἀλλήλοις τελέθουσιν.
οὐ φθονέει μήνη πολὺ κρείσσοσιν ἠλίου αὐγαῖς,
οὐ χθὼν οὐρανίοισ' ὑψώμασι νέρθεν ἐοῦσα,
οὐ ποταμοὶ πελάγεσσιν. ἀεὶ δ' ὁμόνοιαν ἔχουσιν·
75 εἰ γὰρ ἔρις μακάρεσσιν ἔην οὐκ ἂν πόλος ἔστη.
σωφροσύνην ἀσκεῖν, αἰσχρῶν δ' ἔργων ἀπέχεσθαι.
μὴ μιμοῦ κακότητα, δίκῃ δ' ἀπόλειψον ἄμυναν.
πειθὼ μὲν γὰρ ὄνειαρ, ἔρις δ' ἔριν ἀντιφυτεύει.
μὴ πίστευε τάχιστα, πρὶν ἀτρεκέως πέρας ὄψει.
80 νικᾶν εὖ ἔρδοντας ἐπὶ πλεόνεσσι καθήκει.
καλὸν ξεινίζειν ταχέως λιταῖσι τραπέζαις
ἢ πλείσταις δολίαισι βραδυνούσαις παρὰ καιρόν.
μηδέποτε χρήστης πικρὸς γένῃ ἀνδρὶ πένητι.
μηδέ τις ὄρνιθας καλιῆς ἅμα πάντας ἑλέσθω,
85 μητέρα δ' ἐκπρολίποις, ἵν' ἔχῃς πάλι τῆσδε νεοσσούς.
μηδέποτε κρίνειν ἀδαήμονας ἄνδρας ἐάσῃς.
[μηδὲ δίκην δικάσῃς, πρὶν ⟨ἂν⟩ ἄμφω μῦθον ἀκούσῃς.]
τὴν σοφίην σοφὸς εὐθύνει, τέχνας δ' ὁμότεχνος.
οὐ χωρεῖ μεγάλην διδαχὴν ἀδίδακτος ἀκουή.
90 οὐ γὰρ δὴ νοέουσ' οἱ μηδέποτ' ἐσθλὰ μαθόντες.
μὴ δὲ τραπεζοκόρους κόλακας ποιεῖσθαι ἑταίρους·
πολλοὶ γὰρ πόσιος καὶ βρώσιός εἰσιν ἑταῖροι
καιρὸν θωπεύοντες, ἐπὴν κορέσασθαι ἔχωσιν,
ἀχθόμενοι δ' ὀλίγοις καὶ πολλοῖς πάντες ἄπληστοι.
95 λαῷ μὴ πίστευε, πολύτροπός ἐστιν ὅμιλος·
λαὸς ⟨γὰρ⟩ καὶ ὕδωρ καὶ πῦρ ἀκατάσχετα πάντα.

Translation:[39]

70 Do not envy others their goods, do not fix reproach upon them.
The heavenly ones also are without envy toward each other.
The moon envies not the sun his much stronger beams,
nor the earth the heavenly heights though it is below,
nor the rivers the seas. They are always in concord.
75 For if there were strife among the blessed ones, heaven would not

---

[38] Text: van der Horst, *Pseudo-Phocylides*, 92, 94; cf. Young, *Theognis*, 101-103.
[39] Translation: van der Horst, *Pseudo-Phocylides*, 93, 95.

Analysis of the Discourses 115

     stand firm.
     Practise self-restraint, and abstain from shameful deeds.
     Do not imitate evil, but leave vengeance to justice.
     For persuasiveness is a boon, but strife begets only strife.
     Trust not too quickly, before you shall see exactly the end.
80   It is proper to surpass your benefactors with still more benefactions.
     It is better to present guests with a simple meal quickly than
     with a large number of elaborate courses drawn out beyond the
     proper time.
     Never be a relentless creditor to a poor man.
     One should not take all the birds from a nest at the same time;
85   but leave the mother-bird behind, in order to get young from her
     again.
     Never allow ignorant men to sit in judgement.
     [Do not pass a judgement before you have heard the word of both
     parties.]
     A wise man keeps straight wisdom, and a fellow-craftsman crafts.
     An untrained ear cannot grasp important teaching.
90   For those who have never learned good things do not understand.
     Make not parasitic flatterers your friends.
     For there are many friends of eating and drinking,
     who are time-servers whenever they can satiate themselves,
     but discontented all of them with little and insatiable with much.
95   Trust not the people, the mob is fickle.
     For the people and water and fire are all uncontrollable.

This sapiential discourse differs from the previous two in that it is structurally less developed and sophisticated; its formal parts are comparatively terse and stiff, and many of the transitional and rhetorical features familiar from the other texts are subdued. Another distinction regarding this passage is the nature of its message. In contrast with LXX Proverbs 3.11-35 and Ben Sira 6.18-37 the author (or editor) of this passage has not assigned an all-encompassing term such as παιδεία to describe its contents. Instead, the theme and purpose here is more focused; the passage consists of exhortation to avoid envy and strife through ethical self-restraint and moderation. Despite these differences, the author has accommodated this exhortation to the same three-part literary scheme: line 70 is the programmatic statement, lines 71-75 are the descriptive section, and lines 76-96 are the prescriptive section.

    The programmatic statement, line 70, consists of a pair of parallel wisdom admonitions against φθόνος ("envy") in social relations.[40] In contrast with the programmatic statements of the previous discourses, the personal address is absent and no reasons are introduced to augment the imperatives. The admonitions here establish the theme and purpose of the discourse; in the ensuing lines the author endeavors to equip the audience with reasons and motivations as well as specific recommendations on how they may evade jealousy and the personal conflicts that it breeds.

The basis of the injunction against envy in line 70 is supplied by the ethical model of the cosmos, a common theme in ancient paraenesis and the subject of the descriptive section, lines 71-75.[41] Because the οὐρανίδαι ("heavenly ones") always exhibit ὁμόνοια ("harmony") and are without φθόνος and ἔρις ("strife"), the audience must imitate their example and pursue these same qualities. The passage starts with a general assertion regarding the οὐρανίδαι (line 71) linked to the programmatic statement logically with καί ("also"). The underlying argument here is that the readers must not envy others because they do not. The author demonstrates this claim by offering three specific illustrations of harmony in the universe: the moon does not envy the sun, nor the earth the heaven, nor the rivers the seas (lines 72-74a). This is followed by another ethical assertion regarding the heavenly ones, this time formulated positively: since there is no jealousy or resentment among them, the heavenly ones constantly enjoy harmony and concord. In line 75 the author draws a conclusion from the discussion in 71-74 in the form of a gnomic saying which claims that if there was rivalry or contention among the members of the cosmos, heaven itself--and by implication the human race--could not endure.[42] The maxim here, like those employed in the other descriptive sections, focuses the readers' attention on a special aspect of the model's ethical behavior and magnifies the seriousness of the moral issues involved.

In the prescriptive section (lines 76-96), the central message is that the

---

[40] On this topic in ancient ethics see Ernst Milobenski, *Der Neid in der griechischen Philosophie* (Klassisch-Philologische Studien 29; Wiesbaden: Harrassowitz, 1964); van der Horst, *Pseudo-Phocylides*, 161-162; Ceslaus Spicq, *Notes de lexicographie neó-testamentaire* (OBO 22; 3 vols.; Fribourg: Editions Universitaires; Göttingen: Vandenhoeck & Ruprecht, 1978-1982) 2.919-921; cf. Luke T. Johnson, "James 3.13-4.10 and the *Topos* ΠΕΡΙ ΦΘΟΝΟΥ," *NovT* 25 (1983) 327-347.

[41] For more on this theme see van der Horst, *Pseudo-Phocylides*, 163-165. The descriptive section here is linked with the programmatic statement in line 70 by means of catchword: φθονέοις in 70, ἄφθονοι in 71, φθονέει in 72.

[42] On maxims beginning with "if" or "for if" cf. LXX Proverbs 2.20, 11.31, 22.27, 23.1, 18, 24.14, 22d, 27.22, 29.20; Qohelet 4.10-12, 6.6, 10.4; Ben Sira 2.1, 5.12, 6.7, 12.1, 16.11, 22.26; Pseudo-Phocylides 160-161; Sextus *Sententiae* 342; Menander *Sententiae* 238, 245, 246.

means by which reader can avoid envy and strife, and so imitate the οὐρανίδαι, is to σωφροσύνην ἀσκεῖν ("practice self-restraint"), an injunction that serves as a theme for the section and names its governing virtue. These lines consist of direct and extended exhortation in which the author elicits ethical commands from the descriptive model, indicating the nature of the audience's personal responsibilities in definite terms. In this way he indicates some of the distinct ethical actions and attitudes that derive from the broader goals articulated in the programmatic statement. The section is composed of a number of admonitions (lines 76, 77, 79, 83, 86, 87, 91, 95) accompanied by wisdom sentences (lines 78, 80, 81-82, 88, 89, 90, 96), examples and illustrations (lines 84-85, 91-94). Frequent use is also made of traditional Greek and Jewish gnomic materials.[43] The exhortation here has been divided into two parts, a concise introduction of the section's fundamental ethical principles cast in the form of three antithetical maxims (lines 76-78), and a series of subordinate maxims that illustrate these basic principles with specific commands on self-restraint (lines 79-96).

The author articulates the basic ethical principles for conducting one's life free of envy in lines 76-78. Above all, it is σωφροσύνη, which appears as the first word of the protreptic maxim (as well as of the entire section), that functions as the governing virtue for the prescriptive section and serves as a theme for the advice that it contains. The contrasts made in the first three lines are fundamental to the ethos that the passage extols; together they develop an image of σωφροσύνη in broad terms and so establish a moral common ground for concrete action. The audience is commanded to practice self-restraint and to refrain from shameful acts (line 76); they are to renounce vengeance and retaliation and to allow justice to takes its course (line 77); and they are to value πειθώ ("persuasiveness") and shun conflict (line 78, cf. line 75).

Lines 79-86 provide a series of more specific, paradigmatic injunctions and illustrations that correspond with the essential ideals of lines 76-78 and suggest some of the precise ways the reader is to practice self-restraint. In this way the foundational concepts of lines 76-78 are both clarified and applied. The advice offered in 79-96 pertains to a wide range of referents: benefactors (80), guests (81), the poor (83-85), ignorant men (86), the wise (88), the uneducated (89-90), friends (91-94), and the people (95-96). Although the themes of self-restraint and moderation run as a thread through these lines, there is little logical organization discernible within the sub-section and no apparent attempt has been made to create sub-categories depending on specific topics. In addition, the progression of thought from the subject of any one maxim or

---

[43] Line 92, for instance, is borrowed from Theognis 115; for a complete discussion of the passage's sources see van der Horst, *Pseudo-Phocylides*, 161-178.

illustration to that of the next is often loose or unclear. Yet while the author has not provided a tight linear argument or a systematic treatment of σωφροσύνη, the maxims in lines 79-86 have been organized according to a literary pattern common in gnomic materials, viz., ring composition.[44] The main exhortatory themes of the exhortation here can be arranged in the following manner:

79-80	A.	Don't trust too quickly (but be generous with those who have demonstrated trust in you)
81-82	B.	Give guests a simple meal
83-85	C.	Show restraint in collecting debts
86-87	D.	Don't allow the ignorant (or uninformed) to be judges
88	E.	On the discipline of the wise sage
89-90	D'.	The uneducated cannot understand (what the sage does)
91	C'.	Don't take on "parasites" as friends
92-94	B'.	Against over-indulgence in eating and drinking
95-96	A'.	Don't trust the mob

As with most gnomic ring compositions, the correlation of structural pairs here relies upon varying material and literary aspects of the particular lines and the relationships are not precise in every case. The injunctions to show restraint in trusting others found in lines 79-80 (A) and 95-96 (A') take on special prominence on account of their respective positions, and together they set the tone and direction of the entire sub-section;[45] thus line 79 is named the central statement in the outline provided above. Both B (lines 81-82) and B' (lines 92-94) refer to moderation in eating and drinking.[46] The common idea in C (lines 83-85) and C' (line 91) is the importance of restraint in taking from others: in lines 83-85 the author encourages the audience to show mercy in collecting debts from the poor; in line 91 they are exhorted not to accept as associates individuals whom the author calls "parasites," i.e., those who are unrestrained in taking the sustenance of others. D (lines 86-87) and D' (lines 89-90) share similar referents: ignorant men and the uninformed in D, and the uneducated and those who have never learned good things in D'. At the center of the ring composition the author has placed a wisdom sentence on the discipline of the σοφός (line 88), whose wisdom is compared (or contrasted) with the skillful work of a craftsman.[47] Given the sapiential qualities of Pseudo-Phocylides as a

---

[44] Note also the use of catchword in lines 91-92 and 95-96.
[45] The inclusio created by μὴ πίστευε in lines 79 and 95 reinforces the boundaries of this ring composition.
[46] Note also the use of καιρόν in lines 82 and 93.
[47] On the different possibilities of interpretation for this line see van der Horst, *Pseudo-*

whole, the references to wisdom and the wise sage at this pivotal point in the sub-section are both appropriate and effective. The σοφός serves as paradigm of the ethos that the passage is striving to develop, and the wisdom that he possesses ensures that his moral conduct and outlook is proper and disciplined, in keeping with σωφροσύνη.

The Testament of Naphtali 2.2-3.5

In Chapter Two it was observed that on many occasions gnomic materials are found embedded within longer passages or texts that are not generically sapiential. This discourse, the Testament of Naphtali 2.2-3.5, represents another example of this phenomenon; here, as elsewhere in the Testaments of the Twelve Patriarchs, an exhortation with numerous gnomic qualities functions within a διαθήκη ("testament"), a non-sapiential genre. Most modern critics recognize 2.2-3.5 as a logical and thematic unit, with 2.1 serving as a narrative frame.[48] The following outline is proposed for the passage:

2.2-5	I. Programmatic Statement (two parallel sentences, each with explanation)
2.2	A. Maxim likening the Lord and the creation of the human body to a potter and his vessel
2.3	B. Explanation of the maxim expressing a general rule about the orderliness of the Lord's creation
2.4	C. Another maxim using the Lord / potter imagery

Phocylides, 174-175.

[48] On the Testament of Naphtali 2-3 see esp. Harm W. Hollander and Marinus de Jonge, *The Testaments of the Twelve Patriarchs: A Commentary* (SVTP 8; Leiden: Brill, 1985) 302-308; also Joachim Becker, *Untersuchungen zur Entstehungsgeschichte der Testamente der zwölf Patriarchen* (AGJU 8; Leiden: Brill, 1970) 214-228; idem, *Die Testamente der Zwölf Patriarchen* (JSHRZ 3.1; Gütersloh: Mohn, 1974) 12-14, 160-165, 181-184; Küchler, *Weisheitstraditionen*, 499-513, cf. 431-545. For more on the Testaments of the Twelve Patriarchs in general see Walther Eltester, ed., *Studien zu den Testamenten der Zwölf Patriarchen* (BZNW 36; Berlin: Töpelmann, 1969); Marinus de Jonge, ed., *Studies on the Testaments of the Twelve Patriarchs. Text and Interpretation* (SVTP 3; Leiden: Brill, 1975); Anders Hultgård, *L'Eschatologie des Testaments des Douze Patriarches* (Acta Universitatis Upsaliensis, Historia Religionum 6; 2 vols.; Stockholm: Almqvist & Wiksell, 1977, 1982); Eckhard von Nordheim, *Die Lehre der Alten: Vol. 1, Das Testament als Literaturgattung im Judentum der Hellenistisch-Römischen Zeit* (ALGHJ 13; Leiden: Brill, 1980); H. C. Kee, "The Testaments of the Twelve Patriarchs," in Charlesworth, *Pseudepigrapha*, 1.775-828; John J. Collins, "Testaments," in Stone, *Jewish Writings*, 331-344, cf. 325-355.

2.5	D. Explanation of the maxim expressing a general rule about the Lord's omniscience
2.6-8	II. Descriptive Section: the order discernible in human creation
2.6	A. On the correspondence of a person's inner dispositions and visible actions
2.7	B. On the dualism that distinguishes men and women
2.8a	C. Explanatory maxim: God made all things good in order
2.8b-c	D. On the parts of the human body and their functions vis-à-vis the whole
2.9-3.5	III. Prescriptive Section: exhortation on τάξις ("order")
2.9-10	A. Direct appeal expressed in general terms
2.9a	1. Personal address: τέκνα μου ("my children")
2.9	2. Protreptic maxim: admonition to be in order and to do nothing disorderly
2.10	3. Explanation connected to the maxim by γάρ
3.1-5	B. Subordinate exhortation (introduced by οὖν)
3.1a	1. Injunction against covetousness and vain speech
3.1b	2. Central statement: the choice between the will of God and the will of the devil
3.2	3. A positive example: the order of the cosmos
3.3	4. A negative example: the disorder of the Gentiles
3.4a	5. Another reference to the order discernible in creation
3.4b-5	6. Two more negative examples: the disorder of Sodom and of the Watchers

Text:[49]

2.2 καθὼς γὰρ ὁ κεραμεὺς οἶδε τὸ σκεῦος, πόσον χωρεῖ, καὶ πρὸς αὐτὸ φέρει πηλόν,
οὕτω καὶ ὁ κύριος πρὸς ὁμοίωσιν τοῦ πνεύματος ποιεῖ τὸ σῶμα,
καὶ πρὸς τὴν δύναμιν τοῦ σώματος τὸ πνεῦμα ἐντίθησι,

2.3 καὶ οὐκ ἔστι λεῖπον ἓν ἐκ τοῦ ἑνὸς τρίτον τριχός·
σταθμῷ γὰρ καὶ μέτρῳ καὶ κανόνι πᾶσα κτίσις ὑψίστου.

2.4 καὶ καθάπερ οἶδεν ὁ κεραμεὺς ἑνὸς ἑκάστου τὴν χρῆσιν, ὡς ἱκανή·
οὕτω καὶ ὁ κύριος οἶδε τὸ σῶμα, ἕως τίνος διαρκέσει ἐν ἀγαθῷ,

---

[49] Text: de Jonge, *Testaments*, 114-117.

Analysis of the Discourses 121

καὶ πότε ἄρχεται ἐν κακῷ.
2.5 ὅτι οὐκ ἔστι πᾶν πλάσμα καὶ πᾶσα ἔννοια ἣν οὐκ ἔγνω κύριος·
πάντα γὰρ ἄνθρωπον ἔκτισε κατ' εἰκόνα ἑαυτοῦ.
2.6 ὡς ἡ ἰσχὺς αὐτοῦ, οὕτω καὶ τὸ ἔργον αὐτοῦ·
καὶ ὡς ὁ νοῦς αὐτοῦ, οὕτω καὶ ἡ τέχνη αὐτοῦ·
καὶ ὡς ἡ προαίρεσις αὐτοῦ, οὕτω καὶ ἡ πρᾶξις αὐτοῦ·
ὡς ἡ καρδία αὐτοῦ, οὕτω καὶ τὸ στόμα αὐτοῦ·
ὡς ὁ ὀφθαλμὸς αὐτοῦ, οὕτω καὶ ὁ ὕπνος αὐτοῦ·
ὡς ἡ ψυχὴ αὐτοῦ, οὕτω καὶ ὁ λόγος αὐτοῦ,
ἢ ἐν νόμῳ κυρίου ἢ ἐν νόμῳ βελιάρ.
2.7 καὶ ὡς κεχώρισται ἀνάμεσον φωτὸς καὶ σκότους, ὁράσεως καὶ ἀκοῆς·
οὕτω κεχώρισται ἀνάμεσον ἀνδρὸς καὶ ἀνδρός,
καὶ ἀνάμεσον γυναικὸς καὶ γυναικός·
καὶ οὐκ ἔστιν εἰπεῖν ὅτι ἕν τῷ ἑνὶ τοῖς προσώποις ἢ τῷ νοΐ ὅμοιον.
2.8 πάντα γὰρ ἐν τάξει ἐποίησεν ὁ θεὸς καλά·
τὰς πέντε αἰσθήσεις ἐν τῇ κεφαλῇ
καὶ τὸν τράχηλον συνάπτει τῇ κεφαλῇ καὶ τρίχας πρὸς δόξαν,
εἶτα καρδίαν εἰς φρόνησιν, κοιλίαν εἰς διάκρισιν στομάχου,
κάλαμον πρὸς ὑγίειαν, ἧπαρ πρὸς θυμόν,
χολὴν πρὸς πικρίαν, εἰς γέλωτα σπλῆνα,
νεφροὺς εἰς πανουργίαν, ψύας εἰς δύναμιν,
πλευρὰς εἰς θήκην, ὀσφὺν εἰς ἰσχὺν καὶ τὰ ἑξῆς.
2.9 οὕτως οὖν, τέκνα μου, ἐν τάξει ἐστὲ εἰς ἀγαθά, ἐν φόβῳ θεοῦ,
καὶ μηδὲν ἄτακτον ποιεῖτε ἐν καταφρονήσει μηδὲ ἔξω καιροῦ αὐτοῦ.
2.10 ὅτι ἐὰν εἴπῃς τῷ ὀφθαλμῷ ἀκοῦσαι, οὐ δύναται·
οὕτως οὐδὲ ἐν σκότει δυνήσεσθε ποιῆσαι ἔργα φωτός.
3.1 μὴ οὖν σπουδάζετε ἐν πλεονεξίᾳ διαφθεῖραι τὰς πράξεις ὑμῶν,
ἢ ἐν λόγοις κενοῖς ἀπατᾶν τὰς ψυχὰς ὑμῶν,
ὅτι σιωπῶντες ἐν καθαρότητι καρδίας συνήσετε
τὸ θέλημα τοῦ θεοῦ κρατεῖν καὶ ἀπορρίπτειν τὸ θέλημα τοῦ διαβόλου.
3.2 ἥλιος καὶ σελήνη καὶ ἀστέρες οὐκ ἀλλοιοῦσι τάξιν αὐτῶν·
οὕτως καὶ ὑμεῖς μὴ ἀλλοιώσητε νόμον θεοῦ ἐν ἀταξίᾳ πράξεων ὑμῶν.
3.3 ἔθνη πλανηθέντα καὶ ἀφέντα τὸν κύριον ἠλλοίωσαν τάξιν αὐτῶν,

	καὶ ἐπηκολούθησαν λίθοις καὶ ξύλοις, ἐξακολουθήσαντες πνεύμασι πλάνης.
3.4	ὑμεῖς δὲ μὴ οὕτως, τέκνα μου, γνόντες ἐν στερεώματι, ἐν γῇ καὶ ἐν θαλάσσῃ καὶ πᾶσι τοῖς δημιουργήμασι κύριον τὸν ποιήσαντα ταῦτα πάντα, ἵνα μὴ γένησθε ὡς Σόδομα, ἥτις ἐνήλλαξε τάξιν φύσεως αὐτῆς.
3.5	ὁμοίως δὲ καὶ οἱ ἐγρήγοροι ἐνήλλαξαν τάξιν φύσεως αὐτῶν, οὓς καὶ κατηράσατο κύριος ἐπὶ τοῦ κατακλυσμοῦ, δι' αὐτοὺς ἀπὸ κατοικεσίας καὶ καρπῶν τάξας τὴν γῆν ἀοίκητον.

Translation:[50]

2.2	For as the potter knows the vessel, how much it is to contain and applies clay to that purpose, so also does the Lord make the body after the likeness of the spirit and according to the capacity of the body does he implant the spirit.
2.3	And the one does not fall short of the other by a third part of a hair; for by weight and measure and rule every creation of the Most High is (made).
2.4	And as the potter knows the use of each (vessel), what it is suitable for, so also does the Lord know the body, how far it will persist in goodness and when it begins in evil.
2.5	For there is nothing that is moulded and no thought which the Lord does not know; for he created every man after his own image.
2.6	As a man's strength, so also is his work; and as his mind, so also his skill; and as his deliberate choice, so also is his achievement; as his heart, so also is his mouth; as his eye, so also is his sleep; as his soul, so also is his word, either in the law of the Lord or in the law of Beliar.
2.7	And as there is a division between light and darkness, seeing and hearing, so there is a division between man and man, and between woman and woman; and it is not to be said that the one is like the other in appearance or in mind;

---

[50] Translation: Hollander and de Jonge, *Commentary*, 300-301.

2.8	for God made all things good, in order: the five senses in the head and hair for glory, then the heart for understanding, the belly for secretion of the stomach, calamus for health, the liver for wrath, the gall for bitterness, the spleen for laughter, the reins for craftiness, the muscles of the loins for power, the sides for lying down, the loin for strength, and so on.
2.9	So then, my children, be in order unto good, in the fear of God and do nothing disorderly in scorn or out of its due season.
2.10	For if you tell the eye to hear, it cannot; so neither will you able to do works of light while in darkness.
3.1	Be, therefore, not eager to corrupt your activities through covetousness, or to beguile your souls with vain words. because if you keep silence in purity of heart you will understand how to hold fast to the will of God and to cast away the will of the devil.
3.2	Sun and moon and stars do not change their order; so you also, do not change the law of God in the disorderliness of your activities.
3.3	The Gentiles changed their order, having gone astray and having forsaken the Lord and they followed after stones and sticks, having followed after spirits of deceit.
3.4	But you shall not be so, my children, having recognized in the firmament, in the earth and in the sea and in all created things the Lord who made all these things, so that you will not become as Sodom which changed the order of its nature.
3.5	In like manner also the Watchers changed the order of their nature, whom the Lord also cursed at the Flood on their account making the earth uninhabited without inhabitants and fruits.

These two chapters constitute the first and main exhortatory section of the Testament of Naphtali; the other paraenetic section is 8.4-10, for which 2.2-3.5 serves in part as an introduction. The subtitle of the testament, περὶ φυσικῆς ἀγαθότητος ("concerning natural goodness"), indicates the central theological and paraenetic theme of this discourse: the goodness of φύσις ("nature") as created by God, particularly the τάξις ("order") discernible in it, has fundamental consequences for the ethical behavior of mankind. Since God (and only God) has made all things good and in order, the appropriate moral response is to "be in order unto good, in the fear of God" (2.9). The threat of dualism and the basic choice that confronts humanity between obeying God or obeying Beliar pervades these chapters (2.4, 6, 7, 9, 10, 3.1, etc.). In order to comply with God's will and to repudiate the evil and unnatural corruption that the devil represents, the author argues that the readers must conduct their lives in order. The meaning and motivation of this ethical imperative is the subject of this discourse, which is organized as follows: programmatic statement (2.2-5), descriptive section (2.6-8), and prescriptive section (2.9-3.5).

The programmatic statement (2.2-5) is composed of two parallel gnomic sayings in the form of similitudes (2.2, 4), each with an accompanying explanation (2.3, 5). Here the author draws from the famous potter's parable,[51] likening the Lord and the creation of the human body to a potter and the vessel that he makes. In contrast with the other sapiential discourses, the programmatic statement in the Testament of Naphtali contains no personal address and no imperatives; thus a call for action is made only implicitly. The programmatic statement is furthered distinguished on account of its length and detail. This part of the discourse has been expanded almost to the point where it could be called an exordium rather that a statement. Nevertheless the function of these verses is essentially the same as elsewhere, and the author's point is clear enough: since the Lord's knowledge and handiwork are manifest in the physical and spiritual aspects of all human beings, the required response is one of reverence to the Creator and respect for the order of creation. In this way the author's theological presuppositions and ethical themes are stated at the outset. These basic principles for ethical conduct will be expanded and applied to the readers in the descriptive and prescriptive sections.

2.6-8 presents a sequence of three descriptive formulations, each designed with extensive recourse to parallelism, asyndeton, and isocolon. The underlying theme is the goodness and order present in God's creation of the human body, its individual parts and aspects, and the basic choice between good and evil that confronts and divides human beings. The author first demonstrates how the inner dispositions of human beings determine their visible actions (2.6). This correspondence may take place ἢ ἐν νόμῳ κυρίου ἢ ἐν νόμῳ βελιάρ ("either in the law of the Lord or in the law of Beliar"). A

---

[51] Cf. Psalm 2.9; Isaiah 29.16, 41.25, 45.9, 64.8; Jeremiah 18.1-11; Wisdom of Solomon 15.7-13; Ben Sira 33.13; Romans 9.20-23.

simile in the second piece of the descriptive section (2.7) compares the divisions between light and dark, seeing and hearing with the dualism among men and women. The third descriptive formulation depicts God's purposeful organization of the body's parts and the harmony of their respective functions in relation to the whole. This verse, in turn, is composed of two distinct rosters separated by εἶτα ("then"); thus 2.8b lists seven body parts, 2.8c lists ten. A gnomic saying in 2.8a underscores the apologetic intent and instructional thrust of the section: it is God who has established the goodness and order visible in these different descriptive examples.

In the prescriptive section (2.9-3.5), the ethical consequences of the observations and assertions made by the author in 2.2-8 are spelled out for the audience by way of direct address and applied examples, first with a general appeal (2.9-10), then with more specific admonitions and illustrations (3.1-5). The section as a whole is unified by various literary devices, including linkword (τάξις in 2.9, 3.2, 3, 4, and 5, cf. 2.8) and inclusio (τέκνα μου in 2.9 and 3.4).

The section opens with a protreptic maxim (2.9), accompanied by a form of familiar address (τέκνα μου), that establishes the theme and purpose of the section. The use of οὕτως οὖν ("so then") and the direct address at this point make it plain that the audience is to learn from and emulate the order of God's creation described in programmatic statement and descriptive section. Consequently they must fear God and μηδὲν ἄτακτον ποιεῖτε ("do nothing disorderly"). The protreptic maxim is accompanied by a justifying wisdom sentence connected by ὅτι (2.10). This saying underscores the absurdity of disorderly actions with images (seeing / hearing and light / darkness) drawn from the descriptive section (2.7).

3.1-5, introduced with οὖν, supports and expands upon the general appeal in 2.9-10 with a number of more concrete admonitions and examples, all of which exhort the readers to shun disorder in their ethical behavior. The author begins this part of the section with injunctions against covetousness and harmful speech (3.1a). The motivation for these commands is given in 3.1b, the section's central statement: if the audience keeps silence ἐν καθαρότητι καρδίας ("in purity of heart")[52] they will know how to obey τὸ θέλημα τοῦ θεοῦ ("the will of God") and to cast aside the way of the devil. The remainder of the section, 3.2-5, enlists some specific illustrations of these opposing ways of life. The first example is drawn from the harmony of the heavenly bodies (3.2a), which is applied to the audience in 3.2b.[53] The next example is negative: because the Gentiles have disobeyed God, their lives are full of conflict and vanity (3.3).

---

[52] Cf. Ben Sira 6.37.
[53] Cf. Pseudo-Phocylides 71-75.

This illustration is applied to the audience in 3.4, where the model of the cosmos is raised again, this time as proof of God's power and lordship in the order of the created world. The discourse concludes with two final negative examples, the disorderly nature of Sodom (3.4d) and of the Watchers (3.5), who were severely punished by God and responsible for the destruction of the Flood. The antithesis of blessing (implicit in 3.4) and cursing (3.5b) forms an effective conclusion for the passage, and contrasts of this sort are typical of the sapiential idiom (cf. LXX Proverbs 3.33).

Analysis of Romans 12.1-21

The survey conducted above provides us with a context for interpreting the literary composition and rhetorical design of Paul's exhortation in Romans 12.1-21. The format for the analysis of the chapter will be essentially the same as that employed with the four Hellenistic-Jewish discourses; after some preliminary remarks on Romans 12 and its place in Paul's epistle to the Romans, an outline, text, and translation of the chapter will be provided, followed by some more detailed comments on its structure and meaning.

It is widely acknowledged that of his surviving correspondence Paul's epistle to the Romans represents the final and most careful and thorough statement of his theology.[54] In contrast with previous letters, Paul here addresses an audience that is for the most part personally unfamiliar with him, and it is unlikely that Paul will have an opportunity to visit them anytime in the near future, although he earnestly desires to do so.[55] Thus for the Roman Christians the letter serves both as an introduction to Paul himself and as their first direct and extended exposure to his teachings as a Christian apostle. Given the sweeping nature of the epistle's central purpose, it follows that a number of

---

[54] The modern literature exhibits a wide range of views regarding the purpose, theme, and composition of the letter, see esp. the commentaries; for further bibliography see James D. G. Dunn, "Paul's Epistle to the Romans: An Analysis of Structure and Argument," *ANRW* II.25.4 (1987) 2884-2890, and idem, *Romans*, 1.liv-lv, lviii-lix, to which should be added Peter Stuhlmacher, "The Theme of Romans," *AusBR* 36 (1988) 31-44; Hans Dieter Betz, "The Foundations of Christian Ethics According to Romans 12.1-2," *Witness and Existence: Essays in Honor of Schubert M. Ogden* (ed. Philip E. Devenish and George L. Goodwin; Chicago, London: University of Chicago Press, 1989) 55-72, esp. 61-66 [originally, "Das Problem der Grundlagen der paulinischen Ethik (Röm 12.1-2)," *ZTK* 85 (1988) 199-218]; A. J. M. Wedderburn, *The Reasons for Romans* (SNTW; Edinburgh: T. and T. Clark, 1989).

[55] See esp. Romans 1.8-15, 15.22-29, and 16.1-19, and the commentaries on these passages.

more specific and complex subordinate functions are also discernible.[56] In Romans 12, as well as the chapters that follow, the exhortatory, or deliberative, concerns are generally the most conspicuous. Yet the material here must also be interpreted in light of the epistle's other functions. Perhaps the most significant of these is the apologetic purpose. It appears that the letter serves as Paul's reasoned response to specific criticisms of his ministry that had been circulating among the (most likely Jewish-Christian) congregations in Rome.[57] For the most part, it is impossible to reconstruct the precise nature of the charges that had been leveled against Paul and the reasons why his message was controversial. Judging from the argument of the letter, however, it seems that Paul replies at least in part to criticisms that his advocacy of freedom from the Jewish Torah undermined the validity of God's covenant with Israel and entailed the abandonment of Judaism. Consequently, in the eyes of his critics Paul's gospel lacked a proper moral foundation and standard. His attempt to address these issues and the close relationship of deliberative and apologetic functions in chapter 12 are important aspects of the passage's message that must be kept in mind as it is investigated below.

Romans 12 is situated at the beginning of a distinct and major sub-division of the epistle, chapters 12-15, where Paul turns directly to the issue of Christian ethics for the first time. Although the chapter marks an important shift in the letter's argument, it is logically and thematically connected not only to the ensuing paraenesis but also to the foregoing theological discussion in chapters 1-11. While a thorough treatment of the theological basis of Paul's ethics in Romans is beyond the scope of the present study, it should be emphasized here that the whole issue of ethical responsibility constitutes a natural and necessary component to the exposition of his gospel that Paul provides the Romans.[58]

---

[56] Dunn ("Paul's Epistle to the Romans," 2843-2844, and *Romans*, 1.lv-lviii), for instance, discusses the missionary, apologetic, and pastoral purposes of the letter (with numerous references to other modern opinions), emphasizing the complementary nature of these three functions. For some other recent reviews of these issues see Dieter Zeller, *Juden und Heiden in der Mission des Paulus: Studien zum Römerbrief* (FB 8; Stuttgart: KBW, 1976[2]) 38-44; Markku Kettunen, *Der Abfassungszweck des Römerbriefs* (Annales Academiae Scientiarum Fennicae, Dissertationes Humanarum Litterarum 18; Helsinki: Suomalainen Tiedeakatemia, 1979) 7-26; Wedderburn, *The Reasons for Romans*, 1-21.

[57] See Dunn, *Romans*, 1.lvi, and the references given there; also Peter Stuhlmacher, "Der Abfassungszweck des Römerbriefs," *ZNW* 77 (1986) 180-193; idem, "The Theme of Romans," 31-44; Betz, "The Foundations of Christian Ethics," 61-66; Wedderburn, *The Reasons for Romans*, 75-87, 92-142; cf. Kettunen, *Der Abfassungszweck des Römerbriefs*, esp. 176-193.

[58] On this issue see, for instance, Victor P. Furnish, *Theology and Ethics in Paul* (Nashville: Abingdon, 1968) 98-106; Ortkemper, *Leben aus dem Glauben*, 1-4; Dunn, *Romans*, 2.705-706. For the larger questions concerning the theological basis of Pauline

Thus we should not think of this exhortation as a mere afterthought or a formal consideration dictated by Paul's epistolary style. Evidence for this comes first of all from remarks made previously in the letter.[59] The clearest indication, however, is from the introduction to Paul's ethical program, 12.1-2, which begins as follows: παρακαλῶ οὖν ὑμᾶς, ἀδελφοί, διὰ τῶν οἰκτιρμῶν τοῦ θεοῦ ... ("I therefore exhort you, brothers, by the mercies of God ... "). The use of παρακαλῶ,[60] of οὖν,[61] and the reference to οἰκτιρμοί[62] suggest that Paul understands the potential of Christian ethical conduct as being rooted in God's mercy, a topic that had dominated his earlier arguments (particularly 3.21ff.) and which must be understood in relation to the epistle's overarching theme, δικαιοσύνη θεοῦ ("God's justice"), stated in 1.16-17. The formulation of 12.1 indicates that Paul's exhortation in chapters 12-15 develops out of the themes and arguments that precede, and contributes to the overall argument of the letter in a fundamental way.

Romans 12 is also closely related to chapters 13-15. In its initiatory position, chapter 12 establishes a general material and hermeneutical foundation for the concrete paraenesis that follows.[63] As such, the chapter represents the Roman Christians' first specific and extended exposure to Paul's understanding and proclamation of Christian ethics and, as we shall see in greater detail below, it is clear that he has given considerable thought to its content and presentation. Romans 12 serves as a comparatively broad and extensive introduction for the Roman Christians to Paul's ethical teaching and moral outlook as an apostle. It also constitutes his attempt to establish an ethical agenda and a basic ethical perspective for the Romans, broad in scope and complete with well-defined motivations and means. Thus the chapter not only creates a basis for the more concrete exhortation of chapters 13-15, but it also

---

ethics see Wolfgang Schrage, *The Ethics of the New Testament* (trans. David E. Green; Philadelphia: Fortress, 1982) 167-186 and the sources cited on pp. 164-165.

[59] See esp. 6.4-6, 12-13, 19, 7.6, 8.2-6, 11-13 and the commentaries on these verses.

[60] Besides the commentaries see Carl J. Bjerkelund, *Parakalô: Form, Funktion und Sinn der parakalô-Sätze in den paulinischen Briefen* (Bibliotheca Theologica Norvegica 1; Oslo: Universitetsforlaget, 1967) 156-173, cf. 112-117.

[61] Besides the commentaries see W. Nauck, "Das οὖν-paraeneticum," *ZNW* 49 (1958) 134-135.

[62] Cf. Wedderburn, *The Reasons for Romans*, 75-91.

[63] Significantly, the topics raised in Romans 12-15 all revolve around the issue of ethical obligation, a subject that would have been of special interest to a Roman audience; in addition to the commentaries see Betz, "The Foundations of Christian Ethics," 65-66; Wedderburn, *The Reasons for Romans*, 75-87; von Lips, *Weisheitliche Traditionen*, 384-387. For discussion of the wider contexts against which this issue would have been understood see Richard P. Saller, *Personal Patronage under the Early Empire* (Cambridge, New York: Cambridge University Press, 1982) with further references.

makes a significant contribution to Paul's portrayal to the Romans of his theology and mission, and to his self-presentation as an authoritative and trustworthy teacher and leader in the Christian church.

With respect to the argument of chapter 12 itself, Paul's appeal begins with a programmatic introduction of the foundations of his ethics (12.1-2), accompanied by an explanation and application of its essential principles: the Christian community as the body of Christ (12.3-8) and ἀγάπη ("love") as the basic moral perspective and goal of Christian ethical conduct (12.9-21).

Paul establishes the foundation of his ethical program in 12.1-2.[64] Significantly, he does not merely prescribe a certain type of behavior or a specific set of actions. Instead, he formulates a fundamentally new ethical program as well as a new social medium within which moral responsibilities are to be determined and carried out. The motives for Christian ethical action are not to be predicated upon popular Hellenistic morality, the Torah, or even the teachings of Jesus, but upon the righteousness of God, revealed in his mercy, which empowers those who are justified to dedicate themselves to him and to do his will in their daily lives.

In view of God's act of salvation in Christ, the only appropriate response on the part of the faithful is the self-offering to God of one's life in its entirety. This complete and ongoing self-devotion is the religious ritual that Paul envisions for the Christian community in Rome. This is an enlightened, rational religion that lays significant emphasis on the reason and intellect of each individual. Yet this religion and the life that it offers is possible only through the personal renewal that God's mercy and guidance achieves. Hence in these verses Paul articulates a very careful balance between individual achievement and the divine empowerment upon which it ultimately depends. We should quickly add, however, that Paul does not propose a merely personal, intellectual, or spiritual program. Indeed, the main thrust of chapter 12, as well as the ensuing exhortation, concerns the practical, social implications of the

---

[64] In addition to the commentaries see esp. Betz, "The Foundations of Christian Ethics," 61-66, whose observations are followed rather closely here; also Wolfgang Schrage, *Die konkreten Einzelgebote in der paulinischen Paränese: Ein Beitrag zur neutestamentlichen Ethik* (Gütersloh: Mohn, 1961) 49-53, 163-174; Raymond Corriveau, *The Liturgy of Life: A Study of the Ethical Thought of St. Paul in his Letters to the Early Christian Communities* (Studia, Travaux de recherche, 25; Bruxelles: Desclée de Brouwer, 1970) esp. 155-185; Heinrich Schlier, "Vom Wesen der apostolischen Ermahnung nach Römerbrief 12.1-2," *Die Zeit der Kirche* (Freiburg: Herder, 1972[5]) 74-89; Christopher Evans, "Romans 12.1-2: The True Worship," *Dimensions de la vie chrétienne: Rm 12-13* (ed. Lorenzo De Lorenzi; Série monographique de Benedictina, section Biblico-Oecuménique, 4; Rome: Abbaye de S. Paul, 1979) 7-33; Ortkemper, *Leben aus dem Glauben*, 19-41; Walter Radl, "Kult und Evangelium bei Paulus," *BZ* 31 (1987) 58-75.

ethical course chosen by those who have been justified. The sacrificial ritual that Paul had in mind was no doubt intended in part as a means of marking group identity, as rituals frequently did in the ancient world, and of manifesting each individual's inner commitment in concrete, visible terms. Thus in the programmatic statement Paul has also given consideration to the balance required in Christian life between rational discernment and individual accomplishment, on one hand, and practical, social obligations on the other.

The remainder of chapter 12 introduces the basic principles of Paul's ethics as they are realized in the practical life of the Christian congregations. In the first section, vv. 3-8, Paul depicts a model of corporate identity and community purpose--the church as the body of Christ--which identifies the social context for establishing Christian ethical priorities.[65] As with the ritual imagery of 12.1-2, Paul's understanding of the people of God as the body of Christ has ramifications for both personal self-understanding and rational perception, as well as group identity and concrete social responsibilities. As the formulation, especially v. 6, emphasizes, the χάρισμα (a spiritual gift manifested in practical words and actions) of each individual derives from and relies upon God's grace. Hence, for the righteous, personal motives in one's ethical conduct are subordinate to those of the new community that God's mercy through Christ has made possible. So, as v. 3 makes clear, in mutual relationships within the church there is no place for presumptuous or self-serving attitudes; all of the various practical functions exercised by individual Christians are to be directed towards the edification of the entire group.[66]

Having portrayed his ideal of the Christian community and the place of individual gifts within it, Paul exhorts the Romans to make genuine love the essential principle governing its relationships (12.9-21). For the Christian, ἀγάπη is the basic ethical perspective; it both establishes the goals of one's conduct and dictates the manner in which they are to be achieved. As James

---

[65] On 12.3-8, in addition to the commentaries, see the bibliography provided by Dunn, *Romans*, 2.718-719, esp. Josef Hainz, *Ekklesia: Strukturen paulinischer Gemeinde-Theologie und Gemeinde-Ordnung* (Münchener Universitäts-Schriften, Biblische Untersuchungen 9; Regensburg: Pustet, 1972) 181-193; Ulrich Brockhaus, *Charisma und Amt: Die paulinische Charismenlehre auf dem Hintergrund der frühchristlichen Gemeindefunktionen* (Wuppertal: Brockhaus, 1975²) 193-202; Jorge S. Bosch, "Le Corps du Christ et les charismes dans l'épître aux Romains," in Lorenzi, *Dimensions*, 51-83; Norbert Baumert, "Charisma und Amt bei Paulus," in Vanhoye, *L'Apôtre Paul*, 203-228. See also Karl Kertelge, "Das Apostelamt des Paulus," *BZ* 14 (1970) 161-181; idem, *Gemeinde und Amt im Neuen Testament* (München: Kösel, 1972); idem, "Der Ort des Amtes in der Ekklesiologie des Paulus," in Vanhoye, *L'Apôtre Paul*, 184-202, with further references.

[66] As Wedderburn (*The Reasons for Romans*, 76) notes, 12.3 carries forward the "renewed mind" concept of v. 2.

Dunn observes, Paul's injunctions here are motivated by the ideal of a true and selfless commitment to the welfare of the church, and indeed of all people:

> The sequence of thought implies that Paul saw a danger that charisms become merely mechanistic, reflex actions patterned on remembered spontaneities, routinized by regularity--a danger threatening to all regular ministries, of service as well as of speech (vv. 6-8). To be effective they need to be exercised in love. The problem, as Paul no doubt also saw all too well, is that love itself can become formalized in expression, a cloak of pretense hiding an insensitive lack of genuine concern, a pretentious claim as manipulative as any coercive (pseudo-) charism, an outward form for a judgmental and condemnatory spirit.[67]

Paul's concept of genuine love applies in the first place to mutual respect, acceptance, and commitment within the Christian community. In this regard Paul's connection of ἀγάπη with charisms and the imagery of the body of Christ is analogous to the argument in 1 Corinthians 12-13. However, in Romans 12, Paul explicitly extends the application of ἀγάπη to one's dealings with outsiders, people in general, even enemies and persecutors. If love is to be genuine, it must apply to all people and all situations; no personal distinctions or rationalizations are allowed. Precisely what this entails is indicated by 12.14-21: Christians must respond to hatred with love (vv. 14, 21); they aid and identify with those in need (vv. 15, 20); because they modestly recognize their own human shortcomings they do not stand aloof from others (v. 16) and they fear God and respect his prerogative to judge (v. 19b); thus they reject violence and personal vengeance (vv. 17-19a). While the chapter conveys a distinctively Christian (or Pauline) perspective--particularly the importance allotted to ἀγάπη--this is verified and expanded primarily by means of exhortation drawn from a number of traditional sources, particularly Jewish sapiential sources.

Paul's ethical appeal in Romans 12 is designed according to the same basic literary format and argumentative strategy detected in the four Hellenistic-Jewish sapiential discourses surveyed above. In terms of structure, function, content, style, length, and rhetorical stance, the three divisions of chapter 12 (vv. 1-2, 3-8, and 9-21) correspond with the programmatic statement, descriptive section, and prescriptive section as defined and discussed above. While it is plain that no one of these discourses served as a model for Paul's composition, taken together they do provide some insights as to how gnomic exhortation was conducted in Paul's time, and the rhetorical and literary

---

[67] Dunn, *Romans*, 752.

characteristics of each may be effectively compared with Romans 12. Of course, these four texts hardly exhaust the gnomic materials that form part of the relevant background for interpreting Romans 12, and the analysis that follows will also afford an opportunity to point out some of the more specific sapiential themes and perspectives that the chapter exhibits. Bear in mind that treatment of many of the gnomic features of 12.9-21 will be suspended until Chapter Four. Here is the outline proposed for Romans 12:

1-2	I. Programmatic Statement (two parallel sentences)
1	A. Personal address; appeal with explanation
	1. Personal address: ἀδελφοί ("brothers")
	2. Appeal for the readers to present their bodies as a living sacrifice to God
	3. Explanation: this is their λογικὴ λατρεία ("rational worship")
2	B. Antithetical admonition with motivation
	1. Commands not to conform to worldly standards but to be transformed though a renewal of the mind
	2. Motivation: to discern the will of God
3-8	II. Descriptive Section: the Christian church as the body of Christ
3	A. Maxim, with introductory formula and explanation
	1. Introductory formula emphasizing Paul's authority
	2. Maxim on τὸ σωφρονεῖν
	3. Explanation: they must think of themselves in accordance with what God has provided
4-8	B. The descriptive model: ἓν σῶμα ... ἐν Χριστῷ ("one body in Christ")
4	1. Description of the body / members imagery
5	2. Application to the audience
6-8	3. List of seven individual parts or functions
9-21	III. Prescriptive Section on the theme of ἀγάπη
9-13	A. Direct appeal and list of consequences
9a	1. Thesis statement on ἀγάπη
9b	2. Protreptic maxim
10-13	3. List of ten resulting obligations
14-21	B. Exhortation based on ἀγάπη: a series of maxims organized by ring composition
14	1. Central statement on blessing persecutors
15-20	2. Supporting maxims and proof-texts
21	3. Summarizing maxim

Text:

1 παρακαλῶ οὖν ὑμᾶς, ἀδελφοί,
διὰ τῶν οἰκτιρμῶν τοῦ θεοῦ παραστῆσαι τὰ σώματα ὑμῶν
θυσίαν ζῶσαν ἁγίαν εὐάρεστον τῷ θεῷ,
τὴν λογικὴν λατρείαν ὑμῶν·
2 καὶ μὴ συσχηματίζεσθε τῷ αἰῶνι τούτῳ,
ἀλλὰ μεταμορφοῦσθε τῇ ἀνακαινώσει τοῦ νοὸς
εἰς τὸ δοκιμάζειν ὑμᾶς τί τὸ θέλημα τοῦ θεοῦ,
τὸ ἀγαθὸν καὶ εὐάρεστον καὶ τέλειον.
3 λέγω γὰρ διὰ τῆς χάριτος τῆς δοθείσης μοι παντὶ τῷ ὄντι ἐν ὑμῖν
μὴ ὑπερφρονεῖν παρ' ὃ δεῖ φρονεῖν
ἀλλὰ φρονεῖν εἰς τὸ σωφρονεῖν,
ἑκάστῳ ὡς ὁ θεὸς ἐμέρισεν μέτρον πίστεως.
4 καθάπερ γὰρ ἐν ἑνὶ σώματι πολλὰ μέλη ἔχομεν,
τὰ δὲ μέλη πάντα οὐ τὴν αὐτὴν ἔχει πρᾶξιν,
5 οὕτως οἱ πολλοὶ ἓν σῶμά ἐσμεν ἐν Χριστῷ,
τὸ δὲ καθ' εἷς ἀλλήλων μέλη.
6 ἔχοντες δὲ χαρίσματα κατὰ τὴν χάριν τὴν δοθεῖσαν ἡμῖν διάφορα,
εἴτε προφητείαν κατὰ τὴν ἀναλογίαν τῆς πίστεως,
7 εἴτε διακονίαν ἐν τῇ διακονίᾳ,
εἴτε ὁ διδάσκων ἐν τῇ διδασκαλίᾳ,
8 εἴτε ὁ παρακαλῶν ἐν τῇ παρακλήσει·
ὁ μεταδιδοὺς ἐν ἁπλότητι,
ὁ προϊστάμενος ἐν σπουδῇ,
ὁ ἐλεῶν ἐν ἱλαρότητι.
9 ἡ ἀγάπη ἀνυπόκριτος.
ἀποστυγοῦντες τὸ πονηρόν, κολλώμενοι τῷ ἀγαθῷ,
10 τῇ φιλαδελφίᾳ εἰς ἀλλήλους φιλόστοργοι,
τῇ τιμῇ ἀλλήλους προηγούμενοι,
11 τῇ σπουδῇ μὴ ὀκνηροί,
τῷ πνεύματι ζέοντες,
τῷ κυρίῳ δουλεύοντες,
12 τῇ ἐλπίδι χαίροντες,
τῇ θλίψει ὑπομένοντες,
τῇ προσευχῇ προσκαρτεροῦντες,
13 ταῖς χρείας τῶν ἁγίων κοινωνοῦντες,
τὴν φιλοξενίαν διώκοντες.

14 εὐλογεῖτε τοὺς διώκοντας [ὑμᾶς],
    εὐλογεῖτε καὶ μὴ καταρᾶσθε.
15 χαίρειν μετὰ χαιρόντων,
    κλαίειν μετὰ κλαιόντων.
16 τὸ αὐτὸ εἰς ἀλλήλους φρονοῦντες,
    μὴ τὰ ὑψηλὰ φρονοῦντες ἀλλὰ τοῖς ταπεινοῖς συναπαγόμενοι.
    μὴ γίνεσθε φρόνιμοι παρ' ἑαυτοῖς.
17 μηδενὶ κακὸν ἀντὶ κακοῦ ἀποδιδόντες,
    προνοούμενοι καλὰ ἐνώπιον πάντων ἀνθρώπων·
18 εἰ δυνατὸν τὸ ἐξ ὑμῶν,
    μετὰ πάντα ἀνθρώπων εἰρηνεύοντες·
19 μὴ ἑαυτοὺς ἐκδικοῦντες, ἀγαπητοί,
    ἀλλὰ δότε τόπον τῇ ὀργῇ,
    γέγραπται γάρ· ἐμοὶ ἐκδίκησις, ἐγὼ ἀνταποδώσω, λέγει κύριος.
20 ἀλλὰ ἐὰν πεινᾷ ὁ ἐχθρός σου, ψώμιζε αὐτόν·
    ἐὰν διψᾷ, πότιζε αὐτόν·
    τοῦτο γὰρ ποιῶν ἄνθρακας πυρὸς σωρεύσεις ἐπὶ τὴν κεφαλὴν αὐτοῦ.
21 μὴ νικῶ ὑπὸ τοῦ κακοῦ
    ἀλλὰ νίκα ἐν τῷ ἀγαθῷ τὸ κακόν.

Translation:[68]

1   I therefore exhort you, brothers,
    by the mercies of God to present your bodies,
    a sacrifice, living, holy, acceptable to God,
    which is your reasonable worship.
2   Do not be conformed to this age,
    but be transformed by the renewal of (your) mind,
    so that you may ascertain what is the will of God,
    what is good, acceptable, and perfect.
3   For I say, through the grace given to me, to all who are among you,
    do not think too highly (of yourselves) beyond what one ought to think,
    but think in accord with moderate thinking,
    as God has measured to each a measure of faith.

---

[68] My translation; cf. Betz, "The Foundations of Christian Ethics," 61; Dunn, *Romans*, 707, 719, 736-737.

4	For just as in one body we have many members,
	and all the members do not have the same function,
5	so we all are one body in Christ,
	and individually members of one another--
6	having charisms that differ in accordance with the grace given to us,
	whether prophecy in accordance with the proportion of faith,
7	or service in service,
	or he who teaches in teaching,
8	or he who encourages in encouraging,
	he who shares with sincerity,
	he who cares with zeal,
	he who does acts of mercy with cheerfulness.
9	Let love be without pretense.
	Hate what is evil, cling to what is good.
10	Be devoted to one another in brotherly love;
	show the way to one another in respect;
11	be not negligent in zeal;
	be aglow with the Spirit;
	serve the Lord;
12	rejoice in hope;
	be steadfast in affliction;
	be persistent in prayer;
13	share in the needs of the saints;
	aspire to hospitality.
14	Bless those who persecute (you),
	bless and do not curse.
15	Rejoice with those who rejoice,
	weep with those who weep.
16	Be of the same mind among yourselves;
	do not think proud thoughts but associate with the lowly;
	do not be wise in your own estimation.
17	Repay no one evil for evil;
	take into consideration what is good in the sight of all men;
18	if possible, so far as it depends on you,
	be at peace with all men;
19	do not avenge yourselves, beloved,
	but give opportunity for God's wrath;
	for it is written: "Vengeance is mine, I will repay," says the Lord.
20	But if your enemy is hungry, feed him;

>   if he is thirsty, give him to drink;
>   for in so doing you will heap coals of fire on his head.
> 21   Do not be overcome by evil,
>   but overcome evil with good.

<u>Romans 12.1-2</u>: As noted above, these verses represent a highly condensed formulation expressing the foundation of Paul's ethical program; they take up and intensify issues raised previously in the epistle and pave the way for the exhortation in chapters 12-15. Formally, vv. 1-2 are composed of two parallel sentences, each of which contains a call to action supported with reasons. The first sentence concentrates on the religious and cultic aspects of Christian ethics, the second on its rational and theological ones. The composition of vv. 1-2 resembles in particular the programmatic statements in Proverbs 3.11-12 and Ben Sira 6.18-19. All three passages confront the reader with a balance of imperative and indicative statements presented in parallel sentences and joined to a form of familiar address. Like its Jewish counterparts, the programmatic statement in Romans 12.1-2 stipulates both the ends and the means of an ethical program and exhorts the audience to adhere to it, accepting the discipline that it entails.

Paul's statement opens with a direct appeal, παρακαλῶ ... ὑμᾶς ("I exhort you"), coupled with a form of familiar address, ἀδελφοί ("brothers"), appropriate to Paul's relationship with the Romans (12.1a).[69] The substance of Paul's entreaty is expressed in 12.1b: the Romans are to present their bodies as a sacrifice that is living, holy, and pleasing to God. This concept of sacrifice is further clarified in v. 1d, where it is identified as the Romans' λογικὴ λατρεία ("rational worship"). As Paul's composition of 12.1 stipulates, such a dedication is made possible διὰ τῶν οἰκτιρμῶν τοῦ θεοῦ ("through the mercies of God"). Like the initial verse, 12.2, connected by καί, presents a balance of imperatives and indicatives. Here the ethical command is presented first, in the form of two antithetical injunctions; the readers must not allow themselves to be conformed to the conventional moral standards of the outside world (v. 2a), but must rather be transformed τῇ ἀνακαινώσει τοῦ νοὸς ("through a renewal of the mind," v. 2b). The end of these complementary processes is given in v. 2c-d, introduced by εἰς ("so that"). The renewal and metamorphosis of which Paul speaks results in the ability to "test" or "discern" τί τὸ θέλημα τοῦ θεοῦ ("what is the will of God"). This concept is in turn clarified by the appositive τὸ ἀγαθὸν καὶ εὐάρεστον καὶ τέλειον ("what is good and acceptable and perfect," v. 2d).

---

[69] On this form of address see Dunn, *Romans*, 1.31-32, with references.

The sapiential features of the programmatic statement are hardly limited to its analogies with the four texts surveyed in the previous chapter. Besides these formal similarities, two of the concepts introduced in 12.1-2--the moral application of cultic language, and the goal of rationally ascertaining what is God's will--bear resemblance to wisdom teachings.

Both the ethical criticism of a false reliance on sacrifice and the use of cultic language in ethical contexts are evident in various Jewish and Greek texts from the ancient world.[70] Among the important witnesses to this development within the Jewish tradition is the corpus of wisdom literature;[71] perhaps the most developed treatment of the issue is Ben Sira 34.21-35.13.[72] Passages of this sort, like Romans 12.1-2, critically reformulate the concept of ritual sacrifice in two closely related ways. On one hand, there is the argument that sacrifice is ineffectual if not motivated by faith and guided by the rational mind. On the other, while refusing to eliminate ritual these texts tend to transpose the idea from the cultic to the everyday, ethical realm. On account of the latter characteristic, the parallels found in wisdom texts constitute a more relevant background for interpreting 12.1-2 than, say, those culled from the *Corpus Hermeticum* or Philo, which concentrate on the spiritual or intellectual critique of ritual sacrifice.[73]

---

[70] For bibliography see Dunn, *Romans*, 2.706-707; also Josef M. Nielen, *Gebet und Gottesdienst im Neuen Testament: Eine Studie zur biblischen Liturgie und Ethik* (Freiburg: Herder, 1963²); Johannes Behm, "θύω κτλ.," *TDNT* 3 (1965) 186-189; Everett Ferguson, "Spiritual Sacrifice in Early Christianity and its Environment," *ANRW* II.23.2 (1980) 1151-1189; F. T. van Straaten, "Gifts for the Gods," *Faith, Hope and Worship: Aspects of Religious Mentality in the Ancient World* (ed. H. S. Versnel; Studies in Greek and Roman Religion 2; Leiden: Brill, 1981) 65-151; Betz, *2 Corinthians 8 and 9*, 47-48, 126-128.

[71] Johannes Fichtner, *Die altorientalische Weisheit in ihrer israelitisch-jüdischen Ausprägung* (BZAW 62; Giessen: Töpelmann, 1933) 36-46; Leo G. Perdue, *Wisdom and Cult: A Critical Analysis of the Views of Cult in the Wisdom Literature of Israel and the Ancient Near East* (SBLDS 30; Missoula: Scholars Press, 1977) esp. 345-362; cf. von Rad, *Wisdom in Israel*, 186-189; von Lips, *Weisheitliche Traditionen*, 46-51. Some examples: Proverbs 15.8, 27b, 16.6, 17.1, 21.3, 21.27; Tobit 4.10-11; Wisdom of Solomon 18.9; Ben Sira 3.30; Pseudo-Phocylides 228-230; *Epistula Aristeas* 234; Sextus *Sententiae* 23, 46b, 47, 102, 103, 371; *Teachings of Silvanus* 104; *P. Insinger* 16.11-14; cf. Qohelet 5.1-7; Philo *De Plantatione* 30; Isocrates *Ad Nicoclem* 20.

[72] The passage begins with an attack on abuses in offering sacrifices (34.21-27) and on insincerity in performing certain religious acts (34.28-31); afterwards there is the argument that keeping the law is the greatest form of divine worship (35.1-5) and then a depiction of how true believers sacrifice (35.6-13). The entire section is closely connected with exhortation to practice social justice, esp. with regard to the disadvantaged (35.14-22a) and with a warning about God's justice, which is revealed above all in vengeance against the merciless and proud (35.22b-26). Cf. Skehan and DiLella, *Ben Sira*, 411-423.

[73] Further on this issue in Romans 12.1-2: Josef M. Nielen, "Die paulinische Auffassung der λογική λατρεία (rationabile obsequium; Röm 12.1) in ihrer Beziehung zum kultischen

The purpose and promise of 12.1-2 are expressed by εἰς τὸ δοκιμάζειν ὑμᾶς τί τὸ θέλημα τοῦ θεοῦ ("so that you may ascertain what is the will of God"). The personal transformation and intellectual renewal of which Paul has spoken is directed by a cognizance of God's moral purpose; thus one's judgement and conduct must be ethically responsible. What Paul intends is perhaps "more charismatically immediate than formal;"[74] because God's ethical requirements are not a mere given, one must discern with correct understanding what is appropriate in light of the concrete circumstances. Jewish attempts to reduce God's will to a legal code, as comparison with Romans 2.18 suggests, are for Paul unacceptable. The appositive τὸ ἀγαθὸν καὶ εὐάρεστον καὶ τέλειον not only defines God's will, but names the end products of a rational and ongoing process that is predicated upon constant inner renewal and a restructuring of daily life.[75]

The value Paul attaches to rational discernment and intellectual development in determining ethical responsibilities shares something on a basic level with the perspective of wisdom. While never qualifying the law or denying the necessity of "fear of the Lord" as an absolute standard, the authors of Jewish sapiential texts were quick to recognize the contingency and ambiguity involved in ethical decision-making. The potential for living an upright life was based upon the divine gift of wisdom as well as the pious and unquestioning obedience of the individual to God's will and law. Yet at the same time the intelligent capacity of human beings to interpret a given situation, reflect upon possibilities and implications, and ascertain the proper course played a relatively important role in the wisdom tradition, and this was one feature that somewhat distinguished it from other aspects of ancient Judaism.[76] Wisdom's emphases in this regard may have appealed to Paul as he grappled with the question of

---

Gottesdienst," *TGl* 18 (1926) 693-701; Philipp Seidensticker, *Lebendiges Opfer (Röm 12.1): Ein Beitrag zur Theologie des Apostels Paulus* (Münster: Aschendorff, 1954); Josef Blank, "Zum Begriff des Opfers nach Röm 12.1-2," *Paulus: Von Jesus zum Urchristentum* (Munich: Kösel, 1982) 169-191; Evans, "Romans 12.1-2," 7-33; Radl, "Kult und Evangelium," 58-75.

[74] Dunn, *Romans*, 2.714, referring to Oscar Cullmann, *Christ and Time: The Primitive Christian Conception of Time and History* (London: SCM, 1962³) 228.

[75] The term τὸ ἀγαθόν in particular has a strong background in Jewish wisdom literature, for example: LXX Proverbs 1.7, 2.9, 20, 4.2, 5.1, 6.11-12, 8.21, 9.10a, etc.; further see E. Hatch and H. A. Redpath, *A Concordance to the Septuagint* (2 vols.; Oxford: Clarendon, 1897) s.v. ἀγαθός. Cf. Michel, *Brief*, 262-263; Ortkemper, *Leben aus dem Glauben*, 39-40. In the immediate context Paul also uses the term in Romans 12.9, 21, 13.3-4.

[76] See esp. Proverbs 1.1-7, 2.1-15; Ben Sira 39.1-11. Further, von Rad, *Wisdom in Israel*, 53-73; Whybray, *Intellectual Tradition*, 6-14; Williams, *Those Who Ponder Proverbs*, 35-55; Collins, "Proverbial Wisdom," 1-17.

Christian ethical conduct within the context of Judaism,[77] and there are several clues in the formulation of the programmatic statement itself that indicate as much. So, for instance, an ethical and theological objective similar to that of Romans 12.2c was observed in one of the wisdom texts investigated above, the Testament of Naphtali 3.1b.[78] Another indication of Paul's affinity with wisdom in this regard is his employment here of δοκιμάζειν ("to discern," "to ascertain"), a prominent, perhaps technical, term in a number of sapiential texts and gnomic sayings,[79] including some of Paul's.[80]

Romans 12.3-8: The structure and argument of this passage corresponds with the descriptive sections in the Hellenistic-Jewish texts analyzed above. The theme of the section is ἓν σῶμα ... ἐν Χριστῷ ("one body ... in Christ"), which Paul posits as a model of social and religious identity for his audience, as well as a criteria for establishing ethical priorities and responsibilities within the Christian community. This illustration is explicitly equated with the

---

[77] Two of Schnabel's conclusions (*Law and Wisdom*, 324) can be mentioned here: " (1) [Paul's understanding of] personal freedom in the realm of the Christian ethic can be understood, partly, on the background of the Jewish wisdom tradition, and (2) the factuality of freedom and simultaneous obedience to binding norms can be explained, partly, on the basis of the correlation of wisdom and law." Cf. 323-342. Further, Wilckens, *Weisheit und Torheit*, passim; Johann Marböck, "Gesetz und Weisheit: Zum Verständnis des Gesetzes bei Jesus Sira," *BZ* 20 (1976) 1-21; Evans, "Romans 12.1-2," 25-30; Betz, *Galatians*, 291-311; Blenkinsopp, *Wisdom and Law*, 21-27, 130-132, 155-158; Niebuhr, *Gesetz und Paränese*, 232-242.

[78] ὅτι σιωπῶντες ἐν καθαρότητι καρδίας συνήσετε τὸ θέλημα τοῦ θεοῦ κρατεῖν καὶ ἀπορρίπτειν τὸ θέλημα τοῦ διαβόλου. ("because if you keep silence in purity of heart, *you will understand how to hold fast to the will of God* and to cast away the will of the devil."); text: de Jonge, *Testaments*, 116; translation: Hollander and de Jonge, *Commentary*, 301 [my italics].

[79] In biblical wisdom: Job 34.3; Proverbs 8.10, 17.3, 27.21; Wisdom of Solomon 1.3, 2.19, 3.6, 11.10; Ben Sira 2.5, 24.12, 27.5, 34.10, 26, 39.34, 42.8; cf. Sextus *Sententiae* 425. Similar ideas can be expressed, of course, with terms other than δοκιμάζω, for instance Proverbs 16.23 and Ben Sira 39.4. Cf. Pseudo-Isocrates *Ad Demonicum* 25; Isocrates *Ad Nicoclem* 50-52; *Nicocles* 7, 44; *Comparatio Menandri et Philistionis* 1.63, 169, 199; *Gnomologium Epictetum* 54; *Gnomologium Vaticanum* 28; Aesop *Proverbia* 171; Pseudo-Anacharsis *Epistle* 1.24-26.

[80] Paul uses δοκιμάζω in formulating maxims on scrutinizing oneself or one's conduct, e.g. Romans 14.22b: μακάριος ὁ μὴ κρίνων ἑαυτὸν ἐν ᾧ δοκιμάζει. Also 2 Corinthians 13.5; Galatians 6.4; 1 Thessalonians 5.21-22; cf. 1 Corinthians 3.13, 11.28, 16.3; 2 Corinthians 8.8, 22, 10.18. Thus its application in Romans 12.2, in the sense of discerning something divine, is somewhat different, cf. Romans 1.28, 2.18; Ephesians 5.10, 17; Philippians 1.9-10; Hebrews 3.9; also Wisdom of Solomon 1.3; Ben Sira 39.33-34. Further, Walter Grundmann, "δόκιμος κτλ.," *TDNT* 2 (1964) 260; Gérard Therrien, *Le Discernement dans les Ecrits Pauliniens* (EBib; Paris: Gabalda, 1973) 139-148; Markus Barth, *Ephesians: Translation and Commentary* (AB 34; 2 vols.; Garden City, New York: Douleday, 1974) 2.568-569, 604-606; Betz, *Galatians*, 302.

audience, which is likened to a human body with its individual parts, the same metaphor employed by the author of the Testament of Naphtali 2.8. As elsewhere, the description here serves as a clear point of departure for each reader's self-understanding and self-identification, and offers in principle a goal towards which the ensuing instruction is aimed. Thus the audience is invited not merely to emulate or identify with the example but to *be* the example; in this regard the purpose of Romans 12.3-8 most closely approximates that of Proverbs 3.13-18 and the Testament of Naphtali 2.6-8.

Formally the section consists of a maxim with an introductory formula and brief explanation (v. 3) followed by a description of the model itself (vv. 4-8). The gnomic saying in 12.3 is somewhat distinguished from those encountered above on account of its personalized introductory formula,[81] though its purpose is quite comparable; here, as in all of the descriptive passages, the maxim clarifies the ethical and didactic point of the model by focusing attention on its distinguishing characteristic or virtue. In Romans 12.3, Paul calls upon the members of the church, as parts of the body of Christ, to exercise moderation (σωφροσυνεῖν) in their relationships with one another (cf. Pseudo-Phocylides 76). In terms of form and content the maxim resembles a number of wisdom sayings familiar from a wide variety of gnomic sources, sapiential and otherwise, for example Pseudo-Diogenes *Epistle* 22.19-20, Pseudo-Socrates *Epistle* 34.7-8, and Menander *Sententiae* 1:

... καὶ σοὶ παραγγέλλω μὴ πλέον ἀνθρώπον φρονεῖν.
... and I enjoin you not to be overwise for a mortal.[82]

ἐὰν δὲ τὰ ἄλλα σωφρονῇς κἀγώ σοι συσσωφρονήσω.
But if you show discretion in the other matters, I shall join you in showing discretion.[83]

ἄνθρωπον ὄντα δεῖ φρονεῖν τἀνθρώπινα.
Being mortal one must think as a mortal.[84]

By introducing the concept of σωφροσύνη at this point, Paul connects his ethical teaching to the Romans with a distinctively Greek ideal, an ideal which

---

[81] The locution λέγω ὑμῖν and related formulas may introduce sapiential instruction, see Zeller, *Mahnsprüche*, 155-157; further see Frans Neirynck, "Recent Developments in the Study of Q," *Logia: Les Paroles de Jésus--The Sayings of Jesus. Mémorial Joseph Coppens* (ed. Joël Delobel; BETL 59; Leuven: Leuven University Press, 1982) 56-69.

[82] Text and translation: Malherbe, *Cynic Epistles*, 114-115.

[83] Text: Malherbe, *Cynic Epistles*, 306-307; my translation.

[84] Text: Jaekel, *Sententiae*, 33; my translation.

relates both to proper self-understanding and to restraint in moral conduct. Significantly, the term is frequently associated in ancient paraenesis with appeals to order and harmony.[85] As he indicates in 2 Corinthians 5.13-14, for Paul σωφροσύνη opposes arrogance and self-importance; those who are 'moderate' concern themselves with the common good and they are urged on in this regard by the ἀγάπη of Christ.[86]

Having made this assertion concerning an intrinsic quality of the Christian community in v. 3, Paul introduces the imagery of the human body and its individual members (v. 4) and applies this imagery to the members of the audience, identifying them as one body in Christ (v. 5). He then expands the description by cataloguing some of the profitable activities expected of the congregation (vv. 6-8): prophecy, service, teaching, and so forth. The list is neither standardized nor exhaustive and it appears that Paul has given some thought to both the specific 'offices' mentioned and to the order in which they are presented.[87] The number of functions, or charisms, that Paul names is seven, a figure that also played a compositional role in Proverbs 3.14-18 and the Testament of Naphtali 2.8b.[88] The representative list in Romans 12.6-8 serves both to describe the model and to extend its application to specific groups or members in the audience. It also buttresses the maxim in v. 3 by illustrating in concrete, personal terms how σωφροσύνη is to manifest itself outwardly in various charisms of the church. Like the other descriptive sections (particularly LXX Proverbs 3.13-20 and the Testament of Naphtali 2.6-8), 12.3-8 is characterized by balanced structure and careful style. Among the literary devices that elevate the section's expression are the rhythmic and parallel structure of vv. 3-5 (two sets of four lines) and of vv. 6b-8 (seven

---

[85] See Helen North, *Sophrosyne: Self-Knowledge and Self-Restraint in Greek Literature* (Cornell Studies in Classical Philology 35; Ithaca: Cornell University Press, 1966) 316-319 and passim; Vincent L. Wimbush, "Sophrosyne: Greco-Roman Origins of a Type of Ascetic Behavior," in Goehring, *Gnosticism and the Early Christian World*, 89-102. Most important is the discussion of the term in the Platonic dialogues, esp. the *Charmides*, see North, *Sophrosyne*, 150-196, also Charles L. Griswold, *Self-knowledge in Plato's Phaedrus* (New Haven, London: Yale University Press, 1986). Further, Ulrich Luck, "σώφρων κτλ.," *TDNT* 7 (1971) 1097-1104; Spicq, *Notes*, 2.867-874. For some additional examples of the term in sapiential sources cf. Wisdom of Solomon 8.7; 4 Maccabees 1.18 (where σωφροσύνη is posited as one of the four forms of σοφία); Sextus *Sententiae* 13, 235, 273, 399, 412; Heraclitus 4, 29, 32; *Gnomologium Democrateum* 67, 95; Menander *Sententiae* 246, 336, 350, 545, 581, 606; *Comparatio Menandri et Philistionis* 1.256-257; *Gnomologium Epictetum* 4, 10; Cleitarchus *Chreiai* 61, 138. Cf. Stobaeus *Anthologium* 3.5, passim.

[86] Cf. Victor P. Furnish, *Second Corinthians* (AB 32A; Garden City, New York: Doubleday, 1984) 305-337.

[87] In addition to the commentaries see Wedderburn, *The Reasons for Romans*, 79-81.

[88] Cf. Karl H. Rengstorf, "ἑπτά κτλ.," *TDNT* 2 (1964) 627-635.

lines), as well as paronomasia (vv. 3 and 7-8a), isocolon (vv. 3-5 and 6-8), asyndeton (vv. 6-8), and anaphora (vv. 6b-8a and 8b-d). We should also note that the focus of this section on community-oriented behavior and on the enumeration of social duties or obligations is materially consistent with that of many ancient sapiential texts, including some of those already discussed.[89]

Romans 12.9-21: This section consists of a complex string of admonitions in which Paul exhorts the Romans to implement his ethical program and fulfill their ethical responsibilities as Christians. The specific actions and attitudes that Paul believes his readers should aspire to are all grounded in the perspective and motivation of ἀγάπη, which is established as the section's main theme in the initial saying, v. 9a. The sequence of admonitions that follows, taken together, illustrate this fundamental principle of Christian ethical conduct, and demonstrate how it is to manifest itself in the behavior and demeanor of the members of the audience. In this way Paul carries the argument of the chapter forward: after introducing his ethical agenda in rather abstract terms (12.1-2) and suggesting the social identity and social context appropriate for deciding ethical priorities (12.3-8), Paul prescribes the sort of specific conduct which is the outcome of this new way of life.

The formal and rhetorical similarities that Romans 12.9-21 exhibits with the prescriptive sections of the four sapiential texts surveyed above are numerous. Like its counterparts, this section is the longest and most varied of the chapter's three parts, and it is composed primarily of wisdom admonitions, which exhibit a rather loose thematic unity and logical progression of thought. The following chart summarizes the main structural analogies:

---

[89] The emphasis of Ben Sira 7.1-14.19 on social conduct and responsibilities was noted above, see esp. 7.18-36, where the author lists a number of social duties as they relate to different members of the household and community, see Skehan and DiLella, *Ben Sira*, 203-208. This passage and others like it often place a high value on social *order*, see von Rad, *Wisdom in Israel*, 74-96, with examples; also McKane, *Proverbs*, 10-22, 413ff., esp. the discussion of "Class B" proverbs. Further see the references given above p. 15 n. 12 and p. 18 n. 24, also Fontaine, *Traditional Sayings*, 28-71 and passim. Kloppenborg (*The Formation of Q*, 171-245) observes that the sapiential speeches in Q generally address community issues; also much of the gnomic wisdom in the Epistle of James is directed towards conduct within the community, in addition to the commentaries see Schrage, *Ethics*, 279-293, with bibliography on p. 280.

	Romans	Proverbs	Ben Sira	Ps-Phoc.	Test. Naph.
Protreptic Maxim	12.9b	3.21	6.23	76	2.9
List of Consequences	12.10-13	3.22-25	6.24-27 (6.28-31)	77-78	(3.1a)
Central Statement	12.14	3.26	6.32-33	79	3.1b
Explanatory Admonitions	12.15-20	3.27-34	6.34-36	80-94	3.2-5
Summarizing Maxim	12.21	3.35	6.37	95-96	(3.4-5)

Although each prescriptive section is distinct with regard to subject matter, the five texts share this same basic literary design and rhetorical character.

Immediately after the thematic statement (12.9a),[90] the prescriptive section in Romans opens with a protreptic maxim (12.9b). Like all protreptic maxims, this saying exhorts the reader to accept one general attitude regarding ethical conduct and to reject its opposite. Thus it lays out the most fundamental decision confronting the audience, establishing a basic direction as well as a sense of urgency for the remainder of the section. Paul's maxim is most like those found in Pseudo-Phocylides 76 and the Testament of Naphtali 2.9, which do not refer to the author's instruction *per se*, as Proverbs 3.21 and Ben Sira 6.23 do, but to the behavior of the audience that derives from it.

By reason of their literary form and specificity relative to v. 9, the ten admonitions in 12.10-13 comprise a distinct unit. Modern scholars differ as to whether the sequence is best read as five pairs of admonitions,[91] or in groups of 2, 3, 3, and 2, in accordance with the verse divisions.[92] Rather than sub-dividing the paragraph, it may be more profitable to view it as a whole, with ten

---

[90] While none of the sapiential discourses examined above have thematic statements like Romans 12.9a, there are certain key terms that function as themes in the same way that ἀγάπη does for Romans 12.9-21, for example, σωφροσύνη in Pseudo-Phocylides 76-96 and τάξις in the Testament of Naphtali 2.9-3.5.

[91] Michel, *Brief*, 269-273; Cranfield, *Romans*, 2.631-640; Talbert, "Tradition and Redaction," 84-85; cf. David A. Black, "The Pauline Love Command: Structure, Style, and Ethics in Romans 12.9-21," *Filologia Neotestamentaria* 1 (1989) 5-9.

[92] Käsemann, *Romans*, 347; Dunn, *Romans*, 2.738.

members united by a number of interlocking literary features, such as isocolon, asyndeton, and anaphora. The inclusio created by the φιλ- stems in vv. 10a and 13b reinforces a more basic thematic ring: vv. 10 and 13 mention treatment of others, while vv. 11-12 do not, concentrating more on personal qualities.[93] As observed frequently in the discussions above, inclusio and ring composition of the same type found here are employed regularly by gnomic authors. Together, Paul's sequence of ten parallel admonitions serves to catalogue the sort of activities or responsibilities that Paul ties to the implementation of v. 9 and so elaborates on some of the distinctive characteristics of ἀγάπη. The impact of the sequence is reminiscent of Pseudo-Phocylides 79-96, where the injunctions are not directed so much at a particular class of activities or type of referent but are rather aimed towards the development of an ethical perspective applicable in all social situations. In both passages the sequence spells out some of the concrete consequences of the protreptic maxim but its recommendations are more suggestive and representative than comprehensive.[94]

For the closest formal analogies to 12.10-13, however, we must turn to LXX Proverbs 3.22-25 and Ben Sira 6.24-27. In all three of these passages the list of consequences derives from and is somewhat subordinate to the protreptic maxim; at the same time the list creates a climactic, step-ladder effect that leads up to the section's central statement, which in turn is supported by a number of explanatory admonitions. Also, in each instance the number ten figures prominently in the composition of the sequence (cf. Testament of Naphtali 2.8c). In Romans 12.10-13, the extensive use of participles intensifies this suspense, as the reader anticipates the grammatical resolution and material culmination of the paragraph, which occurs in v. 14, the central statement. Ben Sira 6.24-27 in particular provides an interesting contrast to Romans 12.10-13. Like Romans, the members of its sequence are ethical injunctions, not a list of benefits, as in Proverbs 3.22-25. Like Romans, of its ten exhortations nine are positive, one negative. The organization in Ben Sira also exhibits ring composition: 6.24-25 and 27 refer to visible, physical actions, while v. 25 mentions only inner dispositions. A crucial difference, however, is that the sequence in Ben Sira 6.24-27 is followed not by the passage's central statement, but by a corresponding list of eight advantages or rewards (6.28-31) that will accrue to the listeners if they obey the ten admonitions. In Romans 12, on the other hand, there is neither here, nor anywhere else in the chapter, a promise or

---

[93] Michel, *Brief*, 270-271; Talbert, "Tradition and Redaction," 84; Ortkemper, *Leben aus dem Glauben*, 88; Dunn, *Romans*, 2.754.

[94] The sequence in 12.10-13 also exhibits partial formal similarities with vv. 6-8; cf. the relationship between LXX Proverbs 3.22-25 and 3.14-18.

even expectation of personal benefits. Instead, at the point where Ben Sira presents a list of rewards, Paul places the central statement (12.14), the most challenging admonition of the entire chapter.

On account of its grammatical formulation (the first finite verbs of the section) and its striking concepts, the admonition in 12.14 stands apart from its immediate context. While still materially subordinate to the thematic statement and protreptic maxim in v. 9, this verse marks something of a turning point in the section, governing the thought and direction of the exhortation that follows in vv. 15-21. As we will see in Chapter Four, this verse also occupies a key position in the passage structurally, operating as the first maxim of the ring composition in 12.14-21 (cf. Pseudo-Phocylides 79-96). While the injunctions of the entire section set forth the special marks of ἀγάπη, it appears that of them all the commands here most dramatically characterize this ethical perspective and so most clearly distinguish the conduct of those who endorse it as their guiding norm. The compositional role that v. 14 plays in the prescriptive section, as well as its general content, are comparable with those observed with the central statements of the texts surveyed above. In two of these passages the central statement associates the author's instruction with the guidance and authority of the Lord (LXX Proverbs 3.26; Testament of Naphtali 3.1b); the other two name a prominent virtue or quality to be pursued and valued by those who obey the instruction (Ben Sira 6.32-33; Pseudo-Phocylides 79). Each central statement is then followed by various explicating and motivating maxims, as well as other materials, which expand upon these ideas and carry the argument of the section forward in a somewhat new direction. In two of the survey texts (Proverbs and Ben Sira; cf. Pseudo-Phocylides), these explanatory sayings lead to a summarizing maxim that concludes the entire passage. Romans 12.21 clearly functions in a similar fashion; its broad outlook and antithetical structure is reminiscent of the summarizing maxim in Proverbs 3.35.

In drawing this discussion to a close mention should also be made of some other minor ways in which the composition of Romans 12 bears a likeness to the Hellenistic-Jewish texts surveyed above. First, there is a movement from mostly imperative (12.14-19a) to mostly indicative (12.19b-21) sentences; this corresponds with similar shifts observed in Proverbs (3.27-31 » 3.32-35), Pseudo-Phocylides (76-87 » 88-96) and the Testament of Naphtali (3.1-2 » 3.3-5). Second are the various stylistic features employed throughout the section.[95] Among these are parallelism (vv. 9b-12), isocolon (vv. 9b, 11-12, 13, 14, 15), asyndeton (vv. 9-15), anaphora (vv. 10-13, 14), paronomasia (vv. 13-14, 16,

---

[95] In addition to the commentaries see Black, "The Pauline Love Command," 9-13.

21) and rhythmical effects.[96] Third, Paul exhibits a disposition throughout the section to quote and rework traditional materials; this is one of the important features that distinguishes vv. 9-21 from its immediate context, chapters 12-15. Not surprisingly, foremost among these traditional texts is LXX Proverbs.[97] Fourth, as mentioned above, Romans 12 serves as a general literary and material introduction to the concrete paraenesis of chapters 13-15. Comparable contextual functions may also attributed Proverbs 3.11-35 (which together with the rest of Proverbs 1-9 introduces Proverbs 10ff.), Ben Sira 6.18-37 (which is a prologue for Ben Sira 6.18-14.19), and the Testament of Naphtali 2.2-3.5 (which serves in part as an introduction to 8.4-10). Finally, we should note several thematic parallels. Paul's admonition in 12.10b ("show the way to one another in respect"), for instance, agrees with Pseudo-Phocylides' recommendation to surpass one's benefactors with still more benefactions (80). The book of Proverbs' injunctions to assist the needy (3.27-28) are comparable with the maxims in Romans 12.13 and 16. More to the point, however, are admonitions in the survey texts to refrain from violence (Proverbs 3.23, 29-30), not to take revenge (Pseudo-Phocylides 77-78), to be humble (Proverbs 3.34),

---

[96] The rhythmical effects in Romans 12.9-21 are comparable with those observed by Thackeray ("Poetry," 46-66) in the LXX Proverbs and the ancient Greek Proverb collections, particularly the different variations of the *versus paroemiacus*, an anapaestic rhythm which approximates the second half of a dactylic hexameter: ⏓ – | ⏑ ⏑ – | ⏑ ⏑ – | x. As it happens, similar rhythms are esp. detectable at key junctures in the composition, 12.9a, 16d, and 21b:

– ⏑⏑ – ⏑ ⏑ – ⏑⏑   – ⏑ – – ⏑ ⏑ – ⏑ ⏑ – –
ἡ ἀγάπη ἀνυπόκριτος   μὴ γίνεσθε φρόνιμοι παρ' ἑαυτοῖς

– – ⏑ ⏑ – ⏑ ⏑ –
... ἐν τῷ ἀγαθῷ τὸ κακόν.

To be sure, these do not represent complete metrical lines; rather it appears that Paul associated certain rhythms or rhythmical effects with the composition of gnomic sayings and that these were the same rhythms familiar to him from the LXX Proverbs, and perhaps certain pagan proverbs or proverb collections as well. Cf. Martin L. West, *Greek Metre* (Oxford, New York: Clarendon, 1983) 53-54, 174. On the effective use of meter in prose see Dionysius of Halicarnassus *De Compositione Verborum* 25; Aristotle *Rhetorica* 3.8; cf. Kennedy, *New Testament Interpretation*, 59.

[97] Cf. Proverbs 3.4 and Romans 12.17b; Proverbs 3.7 and Romans 12.16d; Proverbs 25.21-22a and Romans 12.20; also Deuteronomy 32.35 and Romans 12.19c; further, see Piper, *Love Command*, 111-114. For an important discussion of the use of "quotations" in the New Testament (many of them gnomic) see Robert Reneham, "Classical Greek Quotations in the New Testament," *The Heritage of the Early Church: Essays in Honor of Georges V. Florovsky* (ed. David Neiman and Margaret Schatkin; Orientalia Christiana Analecta 195; Rome: Institutum Studiorum Orientalium, 1973) 17-46.

and to fear God's judgement (Proverbs 3.33-34; cf. Testament of Naphtali 3.5); all of these topics are prominent in the paraenesis in Romans 12.14-21.

Concluding Remarks

While the five authors discussed in this chapter all participate in the same general theological and ethical traditions common to Hellenistic Judaism and early Christianity, the nature and extent of the parallels detected among these passages hardly justifies any theory of direct literary dependence.[98] Rather, it appears that each author has enlisted a more-or-less conventional literary design and argumentative strategy for addressing his audience. This suggests that the rhetorical and ethical situations that these writers confront as well as the broader means and objectives which they have in mind in addressing these situations are comparable. The overarching aim in the case of each sapiential discourse is to identify an ethical program or agenda and to depict its purpose and content (articulating obligations and benefits) in both abstract or theoretical as well as concrete and methodological terms. In this respect each author endeavors to teach and inform his audience, conveying both a body of ethical material as well as an appropriate hermeneutical stance. At the same time, each writer strives to persuade the readers to take on the responsibilities of the program and to accept its ideals as their own moral standards and goals. The author's intention is for the audience to inculcate the ethos which he presents and describes and to take on the specific ethical actions and perspectives which it entails. In this sense the author serves as an ethical leader, and he himself becomes an example of the sort of person he exhorts his readers to become.

Thinking of these five passages in terms of the literary structure described above also underscores the organic quality and linear structure of each argument. Thus a series of injunctions and admonitions such as those found in Romans 12.9-21 lacks direction and persuasiveness without some explanation of the in principle model in terms of which it is to be interpreted and applied (provided in 12.3-8). And this model will only appear to be an end in itself unless the author has focused the audience's attention on the more fundamental objectives and principles of his ethical system (explained in 12.1-2). For the most part, modern commentators have recognized both the literary integrity of Romans 12.1-21 and its major subdivisions of vv. 1-2, 3-8, and 9-21. The analysis provided here, however, represents something of an advance over previous critical discussions

---

[98] Though we can be certain at least that Paul knows LXX Proverbs 3 (he cites, either directly or indirectly, LXX Proverbs 3.7 in 12.16).

of the chapter's literary composition in so far as it is conducted by means of specific and extended reference to comparative materials that form part of Paul's historically relevant theological and literary environment.

In connection with this, the analysis conducted above also makes it possible at this point to utilize some more specific terminology in describing Paul's message in Romans 12.1-21. Above, the four Hellenistic-Jewish texts discussed for comparative reasons were labelled *sapiential discourses* on account of the various literary, material, and rhetorical features that they share both with one another and with some of the prominent sapiential genres of antiquity.[99] In light of the nature and the extent of the similarities that Romans 12 demonstrates with these four texts, it seems warranted to conclude that this passage may be refered to as a sapiential discourse as well, and that an appropriate title for the chapter might be 'Paul's sapiential discourse on Christian ethics', a title suggesting not only its form but also its content and purpose. Refering to the chapter in this way is useful because it indicates on a specific level the nature of the formal design, literary medium, and rhetorical stance of Paul's exhortation here. It also suggests in a more general way the religious, ethical, and literary traditions within which Paul appears to be participating in his composition of Romans 12. As we will see in Chapter Four, the kind of analysis employed above can be extended beyond consideration of the overall design of Romans 12.1-21 to a more detailed investigation of the special gnomic qualities and specific ethical characteristics of 12.9-21.

---

[99] On the term 'sapiential discourse' see above pp. 92-93.

Chapter Four

Analysis of Romans 12.9-21

As the analysis in Chapter Three has shown, the nature of the literary design and mode of argumentation in Romans 12.1-21 conforms to a significant extent with that found in the four Hellenistic-Jewish texts presented, each of which is also characterized by the substantial use of gnomic forms and themes. Thus the manner in which Paul has situated (or 'contextualized') the sequence of maxims in 12.9-21 is intelligible in light of the literary conventions and paraenetic strategies employed by other ancient gnomic writers. The investigation also suggested that 12.9-21, designated as the prescriptive section, represents the most plainly gnomic and decidedly exhortatory part of the chapter; it is also the longest and most structurally and materially complex. Of the three modes of sapiential communication examined in Chapter Two, the section seems to come closest generically to wisdom instruction, though it also bears some resemblance to certain gnomic poems such as LXX Psalm 36. The constituent literary forms of 12.9-21 are predominantly wisdom admonitions, organized under a common theme and combined with other gnomic and non-gnomic forms in order to create a coherent and convincing ethical argument of about a paragraph in length. Comparison with the four Jewish sapiential discourses also made it possible to clarify the basic literary structure of this section: it opens with a protreptic maxim (v. 9b) and a list of ethical responsibilities that derive from it (vv. 10-13); this is followed by the central statement (v. 14), which sets the tone and direction of the series of subordinate admonitions that follow (vv. 15-20); and the passage concludes with a summarizing maxim (v. 21). However, although 12.9-21 shares this general compositional outline with the other texts investigated, it was also emphasized in Chapter Three that vv. 9-21, like any of the other prescriptive sections, exhibits a host of unique characteristics with respect to such features as its design, style, and content. Indeed, though the mien of the passage is quite traditional, and intentionally so, its precise ideas and formulations betray Paul's hand in a number of ways.

The purpose of the analysis that follows is to consider some of these special features of 12.9-21 against the background of the sorts of ancient gnomic materials discussed in Chapters One and Two. While a number of the section's characteristics will be evaluated, the following objectives will figure prominently in the investigation: 1) beyond the formal observations already made, to consider in greater detail the literary composition of the passage, particularly the structure of 12.14-21; 2) to examine the formal and material characteristics of the specific maxims and other forms utilized the passage; 3) to discuss the broader themes, sources, and ethical perspective of 12.9-21 in comparison with ancient wisdom literature; 4) to address some of the important interpretive problems normally involved with the exegesis of the passage, particularly Paul's use of imperatival participles in 12.9b-13, 16-19a, and the relationship of 12.14 with similar commands known from the synoptic tradition. My plan for the investigation in Chapter Four is rather straightforward; the passage will be considered verse-by-verse, pausing at certain points to discuss some of the more general issues connected with its interpretation.

Romans 12.9: The Thematic Statement and Protreptic Maxim

The more abstract concepts, the change in style, and the address with (implied) imperatives in 12.9 clearly indicate a break with the preceding verses and the beginning of a new literary unit,[1] the prescriptive section, vv. 9-21. The first paragraph of the section, vv. 9-13, consists of the section's thematic heading, v. 9a, accompanied by a series of participial clauses that elaborate on the theme, first in general terms (v. 9b), then with more specific injunctions (vv. 10-13).

The initial maxim, ἡ ἀγάπη ἀνυπόκριτος ("Let love be without pretense") fills the role of a thesis statement: everything that follows can be subsumed under this theme.[2] In its capacity as an appeal for love and a warning against deceit, the saying conveys both positive and negative aspects, and each of these will be developed through the exhortations that follow.[3] The form of the

---

[1] Contra Talbert, "Tradition and Redaction," 85.

[2] Contra Michel, *Brief*, 269-270; Käsemann, *Romans*, 343; cf. Schlier, *Römerbrief*, 373; Dunn, *Romans*, 2.738-739. Paul also had occasion to formulate other gnomic sayings using ἀγάπη in 1 Corinthians 8.1 and 13.13, cf. Philippians 2.1-2.

[3] Luther was quick to identify these two aspects of the command, and his comments on 12.9-21 are insightful; after noting the connection between v. 9 and the verses that precede, he writes: "For just as nothing ought to be more free of dissimulation than love, so nothing can

saying--simply a noun plus an adjective--is similar to numerous other maxims from antiquity, especially some of those found in the ΤΩΝ ΕΠΤΑ ΣΟΦΩΝ ΑΠΟΦΘΕΓΜΑΤΑ ("The Sayings of the Seven Sages"), for instance Cleobulus 1, Solon 1, Thales 11-13, Pittacus 11, and Periander 2-4.[4] In so far as v. 9a functions as a definition of love it is also comparable with the gnomic sayings found in the ΒΙΟΣ ΣΕΚΟΥΝΔΟΥ ΦΙΛΟΣΟΦΟΥ ("The Life of Secundus the Philosopher"), which offers a series of responses to twenty different inquiries regarding the identity of a variety of ethical and other subjects.[5]

Although the precise terms employed in this saying--ἀγάπη and ἀνυπόκριτος--should be understood as conveying a distinctively Christian meaning, each of them also possesses some background in Jewish wisdom literature. As numerous modern studies have demonstrated, the early Christians invested the term ἀγάπη with a far greater significance and decidedly more theological meaning than it had possessed previously.[6] The most important witness for the word's employment prior to the writings of the New Testament is the Septuagint, where it frequently refers to sexual love or the love of a married couple. There are, however, at least a few anticipations of

---

be more polluted by dissimulation than love. Nothing so shrinks from dissimulation as love, and nothing suffers so much from dissimulation as love." Translation: Hilton C. Oswald, trans., *Luther's Works, Volume 25: Lectures on Romans* (ed. Jaroslav Pelikan and Helmut T. Lehmann; St. Louis: Concordia, 1972) 451. It is interesting to note that his exegesis of this section in Romans is rich with various proverbs and maxims.

[4] Text: Diels and Kranz, *Die Fragmente der Vorsokratiker*, 1.62-66.

[5] The form of question and answer employed is typical of the Pythagorean ἀκούσματα, though the content of the responses is philosophically eclectic; the title of the book in some manuscripts is ΣΕΚΟΥΝΔΟΥ ΤΟΥ ΣΟΦΟΥ ΓΝΩΜΑΙ, see Perry, *Secundus*, 14; the different versions of the book also vary as to the number of questions and answers, see esp. Perry, *Secundus*, passim; also Kloppenborg, *The Formation of Q*, s.v. Secundus. The Armenian version includes a paragraph that provides different definitions of 'Love' (§ 11); for translation see Perry, *Secundus*, 114; the Greek version has a paragraph on φίλος; for text and translation see ibidem 84-85.

[6] For discussion and bibliographies see Victor Warnach, *Agape: Die Liebe als Grundmotiv der neutestamentlichen Theologie* (Düsseldorf: Patmos-Verlag, 1951) 106-144; Ceslaus Spicq, *Agapè dans le Nouveau Testament: Analyse des Textes* (EBib; 2 vols.; Paris: Librairie Lecoffre, 1958-59) 1.208-315, 2.9-305; Rudolf Bultmann, "Das christliche Gebot der Nächstenliebe," *Glauben und Verstehen: Gesammelte Aufsätze* (4 vols.; Tübingen: Mohr-Siebeck, 1965-74[6]) 1.229-244; Victor P. Furnish, *The Love Command in the New Testament* (Nashville, New York: Abingdon, 1972) 91-131; Piper, *Love Command*, 4-18, 102-118; Spicq, *Notes*, 1.15-30; James Barr, "Words for Love in Biblical Greek," *The Glory of Christ in the New Testament: Studies in Christology in Memory of George B. Caird* (ed. Lincoln D. Hurst and Nicholas T. Wright; Oxford: Clarendon, 1987) 3-18. Of related interest are the various studies on ἀγάπη in 1 Corinthians 13, see Conzelmann, *1 Corinthians*, 217-231, with references; cf. also Philippians 2.1-4 and the commentaries on this passage, esp. Joachim Gnilka, *Der Philipperbrief* (HTKNT 10.3; Freiburg, Basel, Vienna: Herder, 1968) 102-107.

its Christian use here, for instance Wisdom of Solomon 3.9 and 6.18, where ἀγάπη is an attribute of those who have faith in God and pursue wisdom.[7] The application of ἀνυπόκριτος to ἀγάπη also appears to be distinctively Christian and, as with ἀγάπη, nearly all profane examples of the term occur after the New Testament era.[8] In the Septuagint it is found only twice, and here again sapiential contexts figure prominently: in Wisdom of Solomon 5.18 and 18.16 the term describes the incorruptible and irrevocable quality of God's defence of righteousness.[9] As comparison with these wisdom texts implies, while ἀγάπη may have constituted a special theological possession of early Christianity, its intention and value clearly had universal aspects as well. Thus the term was able to embrace a wide array of positive moral qualities that were not distinctively Christian, as the paraenesis in 12.9b-21 demonstrates.

In so far as 12.9a is an assertion that ἀγάπη can not be or should not be ὑπόκριτος, the gnomic saying raises the question of whether Paul here implicitly contrasts ἀγάπη with ἔρως and φιλία, which in the evaluation of antiquity often deteriorated into self-interest and dissimulation.[10] Paul's warning against pretense and deception in love demonstrates his appreciation not only of love's power for Christian life and the intensity of the human

---

[7] Cf. Jeremiah 2.2; Ben Sira 19.18, 40.20. For more on the passages in Wisdom of Solomon see Winston, *The Wisdom of Solomon*, 124-129, 151-156; Larcher, *Le Livre de la Sagesse*, 1.284-294, 2.425-434. Also cf. Testament of Gad 6-7 (with Hollander and de Jonge, *Commentary*, 330-335); *Derek Eres Zuta* 9.2-3.

[8] Cf. 2 Corinthians 6.6; 1 Peter 1.22. In James 3.17, ἀνυπόκριτος is listed as an attribute of σοφία; further cf. 1 Timothy 1.5; 2 Timothy 1.5; Apocalypse of Sedrach 1.1-4; Ulrich Wilckens, "ἀνυπόκριτος," *TDNT* 8 (1972) 570-571; Spicq, *Notes*, 1.105-109, 3.656-657.

[9] Further on these passages see Winston, *The Wisdom of Solomon*, 144-150, 313-322; Larcher, *Le Livre de la Sagesse*, 2.386-392, 3.993-1025.

[10] Greek philosophy often made a distinction between two opposing types or aspects of ἔρως, a distinction that was picked up by some of the Jewish gnomic authors, see, for example, Pseudo-Phocylides 67 and van der Horst, *Pseudo-Phocylides*, 158-159, with references; cf. Pseudo-Phocylides 61, 193, 194, 214; Proverbs 7.18, 30.16; *Pirke 'Abot* 5.19; Sextus *Sententiae* 141; Cleitarchus *Chreiai* 25. Further: Warnach, *Agape*, 456-472; Anders Nygren, *Agape and Eros* (trans. Philip S. Watson; Philadelphia: Westminster, 1953[2]); Ceslaus Spicq, *Agapè: Prolégomènes a une Etude de Théologie Néo-Testamentaire* (Studia Hellenistica 10; Louvain: Nauwelaerts; Leiden: Brill, 1955) 1-70; idem, *Notes*, 1.15-18, 2.936-939; V. Lindström. "Eros und Agape," *RGG* 2 (1958) 603-605, cf. 1128-1132; A. H. Armstrong, "Platonic 'Eros' and Christian 'Agape'," *The Downside Review* 79 (1961) 105-121; idem, "Platonic Love: A Reply to Professor Verdenius," *The Downside Review* 82 (1964) 199-208; Carl Schneider and Andreas Rumpf, "Eros," *RAC* 6 (1966) 306-342; Rudolf Hanslik, "Eros," *KP* 2 (1967) 361-363; Robert Joly, *Le Vocabulaire chrétien de l'amour est-il original? Φιλεῖν et Ἀγαπᾶν dans le grec antique* (Bruxelles: Presses universitaires de Bruxelles, 1968); Kurt Treu, "Freundschaft," *RAC* 8 (1972) 418-434; Heinz-Horst Schrey, "Freundschaft," *TRE* 11 (1983) 590-599; Barr, "Words for Love," 3-18.

emotions involved, but also for the serious danger it posed if not exercised in truth and humility. This fear of hypocrisy in love was a perspective that Paul shared with other gnomic writers, for instance the author of LXX Proverbs 27.5:

κρείσσους ἔλεγχοι ἀποκεκαλυμμένοι κρυπτομένης φιλίας.
Open reproofs are better than concealed love.

Compare *Gnomologium Democrateum* 97 and Theognis 1219-1220:

πολλοὶ δοκέοντες εἶναι φίλοι οὐκ εἰσί,
καὶ οὐ δοκέοντες εἰσίν.
Many who seem to be friends are not,
and many who do not seem to be are.[11]

ἐχθρὸν μὲν χαλεπὸν καὶ δυσμενῆ ἐξαπατῆσαι
Κύρνε· φίλον δὲ φίλωι ῥάιδιον ἐξαπατᾶν.
It is difficult for an enemy to deceive his foe,
Cyrnus, but easy for friend to deceive friend.[12]

As these examples indicate, Paul's injunction in 12.9a has material analogues in both Jewish and Greek gnomic literature, and this maxim, as well as the exhortation associated with it in vv. 9b-21, must be interpreted in light of the larger and ongoing discussion of love and hypocrisy in Hellenistic ethical thought.[13]

It is prudent not to construe the next saying, the protreptic maxim in v. 9b-c, as a definition of ἀνυπόκριτος.[14] Yet the admonition's function as a complement of the term is clear, particularly if we recognize that ἀνυπόκριτος conveys not only the sense of "without pretense" or "sincere" but also "unqualified" and "unwavering." Thus in v. 9 Paul summons the Romans to definite and wholehearted service and recommends an uncompromising posture

---

[11] Text: Diels and Kranz, *Die Fragmente der Vorsokratiker*, 2.162.11-12; my translation; cf. *Gnomica Homoeomata* appendix 21.

[12] Text: West, *Iambi et Elegi*, 1.233; my translation.

[13] On the topic of hypocrisy in Hellenistic literature see BAGD s.v. ὑποκρίνομαι, ὑπόκρισις, ὑποκριτής; Günther Bornkamm, "Heuchelei," *RGG* 3 (1959) 305-306; Ulrich Wilckens, "ὑποκρίνομαι κτλ.," *TDNT* 8 (1972) 559-571; idem, with Alois Kehl and Karl Hoheisel, "Heuchelei," *RAC* 14 (1988) 1206-1231; Spicq, *Notes*, 3.650-657; cf. Harald Patzer's review of Bruno Zucchelli, *ΥΠΟΚΡΙΤΗΣ: Origine e storia del termine* (Brescia: Paideia, 1963) in *Gnomon* 42 (1970) 641-652 [reprinted in his *Gesammelte Schriften* (Stuttgart: Steiner, 1985) 261-272].

[14] Cranfield, *Romans*, 2.631.

towards good and evil. The form of the protreptic maxim--ἀποστυγοῦντες τὸ πονηρόν, κολλώμενοι τῷ ἀγαθῷ[15] ("hate what is evil, hold fast to what is good")--corresponds with the various protreptic maxims examined in Chapter Three as well as a number of other gnomic sayings, including maxims employed in two wisdom psalms, LXX Psalms 33.14 and 36.27.[16]

Up to this point in the letter, Paul has described ἀγάπη only in divine terms; its application to the ethical behavior of the audience in chapter 12 appears to be based upon the understanding that these earlier passages had developed.[17] Thus it seems clear that for Paul the potential of love as a human attribute is predicated upon divine mercy and divine enabling. As the argument of the chapter demonstrates, this divine enabling stands behind not only the various charisms which the members of the church enjoy but also the rational ability of its members to determine their ethical responsibilities and to discriminate between what is good and evil. There is consequently an important logical connection in the chapter between v. 9 and v. 2, a connection that is reinforced by the repetition of τὸ ἀγαθόν ("what is good").[18] The relationship between δοκιμάζειν ("to discern") in v. 2 and the distinction to be made between good and evil in v. 9, which is implicit in Romans 12, is made explicit in a gnomic saying that Paul had used in an earlier letter, 1 Thessalonians 5.21-22:[19]

---

[15] Some textual witnesses (F, G, etc.) read μισοῦντες for ἀποστυγοῦντες, which appears to have been a fairly rare word, see BAGD and LSJ s.v. ἀποστυγέω. This is the only occurrence of the term in the New Testament, the LXX, or (apparently) the Patristic literature; cf. Gregory of Nazianzus *Carmina Moralia* 768.

[16] Not only the form but also the context of these maxims is comparable (note the use of ἀγαπάω, ἀγαθός, and εἰρήνη); LXX Psalm 33.13-15:
τίς ἐστιν ἄνθρωπος ὁ θέλων ζωὴν
ἀγαπῶν ἡμέρας ἰδεῖν ἀγαθάς;
παῦσον τὴν γλῶσσάν σου ἀπὸ κακοῦ
καὶ χείλη σου τοῦ μὴ λαλῆσαι δόλον.
ἔκκλινον ἀπὸ κακοῦ καὶ ποίησον ἀγαθόν,
ζήτησον εἰρήνην καὶ δίωξον αὐτήν.
LXX Psalm 36.27-28a:
ἔκκλινον ἀπὸ κακοῦ καὶ ποίησον ἀγαθὸν
καὶ κατασκήνου εἰς αἰῶνα αἰῶνος·
ὅτι κύριος ἀγαπᾷ κρίσιν ...
Cf. Amos 5.14-15; 1 Thessalonians 5.21-22.

[17] Cf. Romans 5.5, 8, 8.35, 39; also 13.10, 14.15, 15.30.

[18] This is comparable with the function of the protreptic maxims in LXX Proverbs 3.21 and Ben Sira 6.23, see above pp. 103 and 110-111.

[19] In Romans 12 and 1 Thessalonians 5, as elsewhere in his correspondence, Paul associates the need for discrimination with the discussion of charisms and love; see also 1 Corinthians 2.12-15, 12.10; cf. Galatians 6.1.

πάντα δὲ δοκιμάζετε,
τὸ καλὸν κατέχετε,
ἀπὸ παντὸς εἴδους πονηροῦ ἀπέχεσθε.

Put everything to the test,
keep what is good,
avoid every kind of evil.

Isocrates offers comparable advice in *Nicocles* 52:

δοκιμάζετε τὰς πράξεις, καὶ νομίζετε πονηρὰς μὲν ἃς πράττοντες λανθάνειν ἐμὲ βούλεσθε, χρηστὰς δὲ περὶ ὧν ἐγὼ μέλλω πυθόμενος βελτίους ὑμᾶς νομιεῖν.

Scrutinize your actions and believe that they are evil when you wish to hide from me what you do, and good when my knowledge of them will be likely to make me think better of you.[20]

The comparable functions of these passages, as well as the similarities in language (δοκιμάζω; πονηρός), are suggestive of the more widespread value attached in ancient paraenesis to rational evaluation and self-evaluation of practical ethical values and behavior. In connection with this, a crucial objective discernible in many gnomic texts is the promotion of moral reflection and self-criticism as a means to check ignorance, laxity, and deceit in human conduct. So it seems significant that Paul does not simply state "Let there be love" in v. 9a, but rather assumes love's presence in the Roman congregations and then qualifies the term with ἀνυπόκριτος followed by the protreptic maxim. Paul understood charisms as vital to the everyday reality of the Roman Christians, but it was necessary that these gifts be honestly and constantly evaluated by the standard of ἀγάπη and directed towards the welfare of the entire community, with moral discrimination always necessary in order to determine what was true and worthwhile in any act of love and what should be rejected as vain or evil. Hence ἀγάπη, like the will of God, is not a mere given but must be rationally discerned with the correct understanding. Qualifications of this sort are common in wisdom texts, which often foster a realistic outlook regarding ulterior motives and the sometimes dubious nature of human intentions. The sages were wary of deceit and deception of all kinds, especially self-deceit.[21]

---

[20] Text and translation: Norlin, *Isocrates*, 1.106-107.
[21] For more on the topic of self-deceit in gnomic wisdom see the comments below on Romans 12.16.

Romans 12.10-13 and the Use of Imperatival Participles

The explanation of Paul's use of participles in the imperatival mood in 12.9b-13, 16-19a has proven to be a major and largely unresolved interpretive crux. Given the numerous treatments of this problem in recent literature, it is unnecessary to review the various opinions here.[22] Rather than joining the already confused fray, a more prudent approach may be instead to accept what appears to be the modern scholarly consensus; then it will be possible to carry the discussion somewhat further by considering in what way such a grammatical construction functions at this stage in the letter.

The debate centers around two related questions. First, does the employment of the participle here as a virtual imperative represent a Semitic idiom or is it a natural development of Hellenistic Greek? Though there are at least a handful of imperatival participles in the Hellenistic papyri, most scholars have opted for the former explanation.[23] Thus the closest parallels to this mode of exhortation may be found in the rabbinic materials (and perhaps also in the Qumran scrolls), where imperatival participles express general, communal rules and obligations of a secondary or derivative nature. Such commands may be a part of Jewish catechesis, in which case they denote repeated or habitual actions and prescribe behavior that is considered customary or traditional. On

---

[22] James H. Moulton, *A Grammar of New Testament Greek* (2 vols.; Edinburgh: T. & T. Clark, 1908[3]) [reprint, 1957] 1.180-184, 222-223; A. T. Robertson, *A Grammar of the Greek New Testament in Light of Historical Research* (New York: Hodder and Stoughton, 1914) 944-946, 1132-1135; David Daube, "Appended Note: Participle and Imperative in 1 Peter," in Edward G. Selwyn, *The First Epistle of St. Peter* (London: Macmillan, 1947[2]) 467-488; H. G. Meecham, "The Use of the Participle for the Imperative in the New Testament," *ExpTim* 58 (1946-47) 207-208; Charles K. Barrett, "The Imperative Participle," *ExpTim* 59 (1948) 165-166; David Daube, *The New Testament and Rabbinic Judaism* (Jordan Lectures in Comparative Religion 2; London: Athlone, 1956) 90-105; C. F. D. Moule, *An Idiom Book of New Testament Greek* (Cambridge: Cambridge University Press, 1959[2]) 179-180; BDF § 468; A. P. Salom, "The Imperatival Use of the Participle in the New Testament," *AusBR* 11 (1963) 41-49; Nigel Turner, *Grammatical Insights into the New Testament* (Edinburgh: T. & T. Clark, 1965) 165-168; Furnish, *Theology*, 39-42; Talbert, "Tradition and Redaction," 83-95; William D. Davies, *Paul and Rabbinic Judaism: Some Rabbinic Elements in Pauline Theology* (London: SPCK, 1981[4]) 130-133; Philip Kanjuparambil, "Imperative Participles in Romans 12.9-21," *JBL* 102 (1983) 285-288; cf. David Daube, "Jewish Missionary Maxims in Paul," *ST* 1 (1947) 158-169 [reprinted in his *Rabbinic Judaism*, 336-351].

[23] Esp. Daube, "Appended Note," 467-488, and *New Testament*, 90-97; Davies, *Rabbinic Judaism*, 130-133; Talbert, "Tradition and Redaction," 83-95; Kanjuparambil, "Participles," 285-288; cf. Barrett, "Participle," 165-166; Moule, *Idiom Book*, 179-180; Turner, *Insights*, 165-168. For the opposing viewpoint see esp. Moulton, *Grammar*, 1.180-184, 222-223; Salom, "Imperatival Use," 41-49; cf. Meecham, "Participle," 207-208; Ortkemper, *Leben aus dem Glauben*, 15-18.

the whole, imperatival participles in rabbinic literature do not constitute absolute commands; thus they are often accompanied by some sort of qualification or may be dependent upon more authoritative instructions.[24]

The explanation of the imperatival participle in Romans 12 as a Semitic idiom is acceptable, especially in light of the traditional Jewish content of many of these injunctions as well as their less than absolute nature. The second question regarding the imperatival participles follows from this conclusion: if this solution is approved, is it proof that these verses represent translations from comparable Hebrew or Aramaic sayings and that Paul has modeled Romans 12.9ff. (or some substantial portion of it) after a Semitic document? Charles Talbert, answering affirmatively, has conjectured as to the nature and composition of Paul's source; he understands the participial imperatives as evidence of Paul's dependence on some fixed, written Jewish ethical code.[25] Because it is impossible to demonstrate that Paul draws from any specific Semitic text, critics like Talbert have had to resort to reconstructing hypothetical documents. These attempts, however, suffer from serious methodological flaws and subsequent studies have either rejected these explanations outright or extensively qualified them.[26]

Indeed, there are a number of indications that although Paul draws extensively from various traditional sources, he is not simply translating a pre-existing Jewish code. First, regular Greek imperatives (vv. 14, 16c, 19b-21) and imperatival infinitives (v. 15) are integrated into the section. Second, several LXX citations--both direct and indirect--are also incorporated (vv. 16c, 17b, 20; cf. 19c). 12.17b, a rendering of LXX Proverbs 3.4, represents the most significant of these for the present discussion:

LXX Proverbs 3.4   προνοοῦ καλὰ ἐνώπιον κυρίου καὶ ἀνθρώπων
Romans 12.17b   προνοούμενοι καλὰ ἐνώπιον πάντων ἀνθρώπων

Most likely, Paul originally knew the proverb in a form something like the LXX version, that is, with a regular Greek imperative, and then altered the verb for its inclusion in Romans 12.17. Comparison with Paul's formulation of the proverb in 2 Corinthians 8.21, where a regular Greek verb is employed,

---

[24] Daube, "Appended Note," 472-476.
[25] Talbert, "Tradition and Redaction," 83-95; cf. Davies, *Rabbinic Judaism*, 130-133.
[26] See esp. Piper, *Love Command*, 14-15; also Furnish, *Theology*, 39-42; Käsemann, *Romans*, 345; Ortkemper, *Leben aus dem Glauben*, 15-18; Wilckens, *Brief*, 3.18-19; Zeller, *Brief*, 206; Dunn, *Romans*, 2.737-738. Similar complications arise with the redactional theories of Winsome Munro, *Authority in Paul and Peter: The Identification of a Pastoral Stratum in the Pauline Corpus and 1 Peter* (SNTSMS 45; Cambridge: Cambridge University Press, 1983); cf. Dijkman, "1 Peter," 265-271; Dunn, *Romans*, 2.737-738.

furnishes evidence of his compositional freedom vis-à-vis the tradition.[27] Third, a great deal of the terminology, style, and ordering of material in this passage appears to be consistent with that familiar from the rest of Paul's writings.[28] Especially noteworthy are parallels located within the epistle itself, for example:

Romans 12.12a-b   //   Romans 5.3-4
Romans 12.16a   //   Romans 15.5
Romans 12.16b   //   Romans 11.20
Romans 12.16c   //   Romans 11.25

In each instance, terms, ideas, and even complete sentences utilized in the paraenesis of Romans 12 are utilized in non-paraenetic sections elsewhere in the letter. Furthermore, several of the words and phrases in the section--most notably εἰ δυνατόν, τὸ ἐξ ὑμῶν (v. 18a), ἀγαπητοί (v. 19a), γέγραπται γάρ (v. 19b), λέγει κύριος (v. 19c) and ἀλλά (v. 20a)--depart somewhat from the style and form normally anticipated in such a grouping of traditional wisdom sayings and may be Paul's own additions.[29] Fourth, in several places Paul's composition apparently profits by the application of Greek catchwords: διώκοντ- in vv. 13-14, φρον- in v. 16, πάντων ἀνθρώπων in vv. 17b, 18b, and ἐκδικ- in v. 19 (also note the inclusio formed by φιλ- stems in vv. 10 and 13). It is important to note that in each case catchword links a maxim that contains an imperatival participle with a saying that either makes use of a regular Greek imperatives or that is derived from the LXX. Fifth, in support of his thesis, Talbert assumes that Paul nowhere else employs an imperatival participle. However, this is not the case; Paul's formulations in both Galatians 6.1b (a maxim)[30] and 2 Corinthians 8.24[31] take advantage of the idiom.

Finally, mention should be made of several parallels between the language and thought of Romans 12.9-21 and that of 1 Thessalonians 5.12-22 and 1 Peter 3.8-12. The agreements may be tabulated as follows:[32]

---

[27] 2 Corinthians 8.21: προνοοῦμεν γὰρ καλὰ οὐ μόνον ἐνώπιον κυρίου ἀλλὰ καὶ ἐνώπιον ἀνθρώπων. Cf. Betz, *2 Corinthians 8 and 9*, 77.

[28] In addition to the analyses of the commentaries, see Jürgen Sauer, "Traditionsgeschichtliche Erwägungen zu den synoptischen und paulinischen Aussagen über Feindesliebe und Wiedervergeltungsverzicht," *ZNW* 76 (1985) 18-19; also Ortkemper, *Leben aus dem Glauben*, 17.

[29] Cf. 12.19b with Hebrews 10.30 without the introductory or concluding formulae; cf. 1 Corinthians 14.21.

[30] Galatians 6.1b: σκοπῶν σεαυτόν, μὴ καὶ σὺ πειρασθῇς. Cf. Betz, *Galatians*, 298, esp. n. 53.

[31] Cf. *TCGNT* 582; Betz, *2 Corinthians 8 and 9*, 82-83.

[32] For a more detailed analysis of these parallels see Piper, *Love Command*, 4-18.

Romans 12	1 Thessalonians 5	1 Peter 3
9b-c ἀποστυγοῦντες τὸ πονηρόν, κολλώμενοι τῷ ἀγαθῷ	21b-22 τὸ καλὸν κατέχετε, ἀπὸ παντὸς εἴδους πονηροῦ ἀπέχεσθε	
10 τῇ φιλαδελφίᾳ ... φιλόστοργοι		8c φιλάδελφοι
11b τῷ πνεύματι ζέοντες	19 τὸ πνεῦμα μὴ σβέννυτε	
12a τῇ ἐλπίδι χαίροντες	16 πάντοτε χαίρετε	
12c τῇ προσευχῇ προσκαρτεροῦντες	17 ἀδιαλείπτως προσεύχεσθε	
14 εὐλογεῖτε ...		9b εὐλογοῦντες
16a τὸ αὐτὸ ... φρονοῦντες		8a ὁμόφρονες
16b τοῖς ταπεινοῖς συναπαγόμενοι		8d ταπεινόφρονες
17a μηδενὶ κακὸν ἀντὶ κακοῦ ἀποδιδόντες	15a ὁρᾶτε μή τις κακὸν ἀντὶ κακοῦ τινι ἀποδῷ	9a μὴ ἀποδιδόντες κακὸν ἀντὶ κακοῦ
18b μετὰ πάντων ἀνθρώπων εἰρηνεύοντες	13b εἰρηνεύετε ἐν ἑαυτοῖς	11b ζητησάτω εἰρήνην

Do these agreements offer any evidence that in Romans 12 Paul depends on a written Semitic document? A possible explanation for the parallels is that the author of 1 Peter knew Romans and drew upon it for the composition of 3.8-12. However, this is probably not the case, and so they must be explained by postulating some common source or sources.[33] As the diagram shows, the only agreement in thought and language that approximates a precise parallel is Romans 12.17a / 1 Thessalonians 5.15a / 1 Peter 3.9a. Yet, as we shall see below, this same saying can be found in a number of earlier texts from Hellenistic Judaism and it probably circulated orally as a proverb in the early church. In addition, the ζητησάτω εἰρήνην in 1 Peter 3.11b is derived from LXX Psalm 33.15, and so does not rely directly on a Semitic translation. With respect to what remains, the discrepancies in the forms of the sayings, the arrangement of ideas, and the nature of the contextual material in the three texts argues against any theory of dependence on a common *written* source. As John Piper observes, there is no convincing evidence here to postulate a fixed catechetical code lying behind these three passages, rather:

> there appears to have been a fund of oral traditional material systematized only loosely under different themes ... In these thematic groupings there was apparently much variation. From this fund of paraenetic material the New Testament writers ... drew out what was useful and within certain essential limitations adapted it freely.[34]

Individual authors, like Paul, could at different times alter or modify the language, form, and organization of sayings in order to meet their immediate literary and rhetorical needs. They could also combine materials from different sources or contribute sayings and comments of their own in order to create new literary permutations. Given the gnomic and proverbial quality of so much of the material in these three passages it seems possible, even likely, that sayings of the sort found there could circulate freely among the early congregations in an oral form and without reliance on any written source or fixed code, Semitic or otherwise.[35]

These observations, then, tend to justify the skepticism that the majority of

---

[33] For the various viewpoints see Selwyn, *1 Peter*, 190-201; Francis W. Beare, *The First Epistle of Peter* (Oxford: Blackwell, 1958[2]) 134-139; Karl H. Schelkle, *Die Petrusbriefe. Der Judasbrief* (HTKNT 13.2; Freiburg: Herder, 1961) 93-98; Leonhard Goppelt, *Der erste Petrusbrief* (MeyerK 12.1; Göttingen: Vandenhoeck & Ruprecht, 1978[8]) 48-51, 223-231; Norbert Brox, *Der erste Petrusbrief* (EKKNT 21; Zürich: Benzinger; Neukirchen-Vluyn: Neukirchener Verlag, 1979) 47-51, 151-155; Piper, *Love Command*, 7-8; idem, "Hope as the Motivation of Love: 1 Peter 3.9-11," *NTS* 26 (1979-80) 212-231; cf. Horst Goldstein, *Paulinische Gemeinde im Ersten Petrusbrief* (SBS; Stuttgart: KBW, 1975).

[34] Piper, *Love Command*, 18.

[35] Cf. Philip Carrington, *The Primitive Christian Catechism: A Study in the Epistles* (Cambridge: Cambridge University Press, 1940) passim; Selwyn, *1 Peter*, 408-413; Eduard Lohse, "Paränese und Kerygma im erstern Petrusbrief," *ZNW* (1954) 72-75; Michel, *Brief*, 305.

critics share as to whether the different strands of tradition that lie behind Romans 12 can be reconstructed, and to what extent we can differentiate the traditional sources from the material for which Paul himself is responsible. The presence of an imperatival participle in a saying, while an important indication of its traditional Jewish nature, does not prove that it is a translation of a Semitic original or that any substantial part of the chapter ultimately goes back to a Semitic source.[36] Indeed, the notion that Paul would merely translate some traditional ethical code and then insert it into his letter to the Romans hardly jibes with our growing appreciation for the apostle's literary and rhetorical abilities. More probably, he draws from a rich diversity of traditional sources in order to create his own unique composition.

If we can conclude, then, that Paul meant to apply, compose, and arrange the maxims in 12.9ff. in a skillful and purposeful way, and not merely to hand down an assortment of traditional sayings with a unifying theme or form, it is necessary to take account of what impact his choice of the imperatival participles has on the passage. At least three consequences can be observed. They pertain to: 1) the Jewish tenor of the instruction, 2) the literary structure of the passage, and 3) Paul's rhetorical stance in writing the epistle.

First, by making use of sayings with imperatival participles, or by formulating such sayings himself, Paul deliberately capitalizes on a traditional Jewish style of paraenesis. By availing himself of this Semitic practice, Paul both accentuates the Jewish complexion of the exhortation and promotes his own rhetorical self-presentation as an authoritative teacher of Jewish (or Jewish-Christian) wisdom. The Semitic style seems an appropriate corollary to the high concentration of quotations and allusions from Jewish scripture (even though it is the LXX). In accordance with this, Paul's imperatival participles appear to have the same qualified, communal, and general qualities as observed in comparable Semitic participles in the rabbinic writings.

Second, the application of imperatival participles, in conjunction with regular imperatives (both present and aorist tenses), infinitival, and adjectival imperatives, creates variety and contrast in the forms of the maxims. In this capacity they add to one of the broader features of the passage, viz., the integration of a rich diversity of sayings, not only with respect to sources, ideas, and perspectives, but also literary forms.[37] Two further compositional

---

[36] Cf. Turner, *Insights*, 168: " ... the Semitic imperatival participle of St. Peter and St. Paul need not involve a Semitic document lying behind their work. Biblical Greek may already have absorbed this construction into its system, as it had absorbed numerous other Semitisms."

[37] Cf. Betz, *Galatians*, 291-311; von Lips, *Weisheitliche Traditionen*, 380-382.

features of the participles in 12.9-13, 16-19 should be noted at this point. First of all, Paul has arranged them in three more-or-less distinct thematic and logical groups: vv. 9b-13, 16a-b, and 17-19a. The organization of participles in such clusters augments the unity and connectedness of these sayings. Second, the commands expressed by Paul with participles are essentially subordinate to the other types of imperatives in the section.[38] This is particularly apparent with the participles in vv. 9b-13, which serve, in part, as descriptive elaborations of the topic statement in v. 9a. It is important to bear in mind that the verbs here are not true imperatives but must be interpreted as such. A more literal translation of the participles in the paragraph brings out both the subordinate and descriptive qualities of the sayings in vv. 9b-13:[39]

> Love without pretense.
> Hating what is evil, clinging to what is good.
> Devoted to one another in brotherly love;
> showing the way to one another in respect;
> not negligent in zeal;
> glowing with the Spirit;
> serving the Lord;
> rejoicing in hope;
> remaining steadfast in affliction;
> being persistent in prayer;
> sharing in the needs of the saints;
> aspiring to hospitality.

Besides contributing to the thesis character of v. 9a, we should note that the sequence in this shape exhibits certain formal similarities with 12.6-8 and so the transition from the descriptive to the prescriptive section is remarkably smooth.[40] In addition, the run of participles in vv. 9-13 creates grammatical suspense, so to speak, as the reader anticipates the first finite verb of the section in v. 14, where there is a sense of climax and resolution. That such a step-ladder effect may be intentional is suggested by yet another compositional function of the participle: this time the catchword created by the participle διώκοντες in v. 13b and διώκοντας in v. 14a.

A third consequence involves the ingenious way in which the participles maintain a careful balance of imperative and indicative, prescriptive and

---

[38] Cf. Daube, "Appended Note," 473-475.
[39] Cf. Dunn, *Romans*, 2.738, who refers to Bultmann, *Der Stil der paulinischen Predigt*, 75-76.
[40] Käsemann, *Romans*, 343-344; Zeller, *Brief*, 206; Dunn, *Romans*, 2.738.

descriptive, deliberative and epideictic within the passage. As noted above, the core of the prescriptive section is ordinarily the imperatival wisdom admonition. Yet, generally speaking, the mode of appropriation that sapiential texts recommend for themselves frequently relies less on authoritative command than on the cogency of their advice and the persuasiveness of their argument. Hence their interpretation requires debate and deliberation, and there is a need for wisdom authors to supply motives, proofs, and reasons. This tension between the hermeneutic of obedience and that of critical reflection is somewhat obviated by this impersonal, gnomic formulation.[41] We should remember that in Romans Paul addresses a congregation he had not founded and an audience that is largely unacquainted with him personally. So he may have found the imperatival participles an effective means of instructing and exhorting the Romans without the same degree of forcefulness or the same expectation of obedience that normal imperatives would convey. Further, the use of the participles here is somewhat unusual and unexpected and so puts the audience off-guard. The passage compels the reader to construe meaning in a way different from elsewhere in the epistle and so serves as an indication that Paul's means of communicating with his audience, as well as his rhetorical stance, has changed.

In terms of content, the topics addressed in 12.10-13 include mutual and sincere respect, personal fortitude and zeal, and concrete assistance to the needy; most of these sayings are at home in a sapiential milieu.[42] Like 12.3 and 16, v. 10b, τῇ τιμῇ ἀλλήλους προηγούμενοι ("showing the way to one another in honor")[43] is both a warning against pride and a call for mutual edification within the community; it has analogues in numerous gnomic sayings, including Paul's maxim in Romans 13.7.[44] Commentators are quick to point

---

[41] Cf. Daube, "Appended Note," 474-476.

[42] A difficult textual problem is presented by one of the maxims in this paragraph, 12.11c, where some witnesses (D*, F, G, etc.) have καιρῷ for the somewhat better attested κυρίῳ (P46, ℵ, A, B, etc.). While there is some support for the former reading (see Käsemann, *Romans*, 346; Ortkemper, *Leben aus dem Glauben*, 93 n. 91), and such a maxim would not be without some parallels in gnomic literature (e.g. Pseudo-Phocylides 121a: καιρῷ λατρεύειν), the latter is the more acceptable choice, cf. Romans 14.18, 16.18; 1 Thessalonians 1.9. Further, Michel, *Brief*, 272; Cranfield, *Romans*, 2.634-636; Schlier, *Römerbrief*, 376-377; Wilckens, *Brief*, 3.21; Ortkemper, *Leben aus dem Glauben*, 93-96; Schmithals, *Kommentar*, 446; von Lips, *Weisheitliche Traditionen*, 402.

[43] Cf. the translation suggested by Cranfield, *Romans*, 2.632-633.

[44] See esp. Ben Sira 8.1-19, exhortation on giving due respect and fair treatment to various types of people. Cf. Proverbs 15.22-23, 17.5, 18.1, 19.26-27, 20.20, 22.1, 9-10, 26.1, 27.10, 18, 28.21, 29.2, 30.7; Ben Sira 3.1-16, 4.7, 10.28; Philippians 2.3-4; *Pirke 'Abot* 4.20; *Derek Eres Zuta* 2.8-10; Pseudo-Isocrates *Ad Demonicum* 16; Menander *Sententiae* 358, 807; *Gnomologium Epictetum* 7; *Carmen Aureum* 1-8; *Gnomologium*

out the connections between 12.11a, τῇ σπουδῇ μὴ ὀκνηροί ("not negligent in eagerness"), and wisdom literature: all the occurrences of ὀκνηρός in the LXX are found in sapiential texts.[45] The sequence of terms in v. 12a-b is clearly similar to that of Paul's gnomic *concatenation* in Romans 5.3-4: χαίρω / καυχάομαι; θλῖψις; ὑπομονή / ὑπομένω.[46] Both the need to be steadfast and disciplined in times of affliction (v. 12b)[47] and the value of prayer (v. 12c)[48] are stressed by sapiential authors. And, naturally, exhortations to render necessary assistance and support, both to the needy within the community (v. 13a) and to strangers (v. 13b), are common in wisdom texts.[49]

Since enumeration often functions as a compositional device in wisdom texts, the number of sayings in 12.10-13, ten, may be significant. In Chapter Three, we observed how this figure operated in the structure of LXX Proverbs 3.14-18, Ben Sira 6.24-27, and other sapiential materials.[50] In these and many

---

Vaticanum 15, 64; Aesop *Proverbia* 38, 65; Publilius Syrus *Sententiae* 443; Ptahhotep 22. Further, Ortkemper, *Leben aus dem Glauben*, 90-91. Cf. the discussion of 12.16 below.

[45] Proverbs 6.6, 9, 20.4, 21.25, 22.13, 26.13-16, 31.27; Ben Sira 22.1-2, 37.11; cf. *Gnomologium Vaticanum* 28. Dunn (*Romans*, 2.741-742) also refers to Philo *Heres* 254 and *Pirke 'Abot* 2.15. For σπουδή cf. Romans 12.8; 2 Corinthians 7.11-12, 8.7-8, 16; Philippians 3.1; 2 Peter 1.4; Matthew 25.26.

[46] On the form and function of the *concatenation* see Dibelius, *James*, 94-99 and the references given there. Cf. Romans 8.24-27 for a progression of thought (hope, prayer) similar to that in 12.12.

[47] ὑπομονή and ὑπομένω in biblical wisdom: Proverbs 20.22; Wisdom of Solomon 16.22, 17.5; Ben Sira 2.14, 16.13, 17.24, 22.18, 38.27, 41.2, 51.8. Further examples of endurance and patience as sapiential topics: Proverbs 3.11-12, 14.17, 19.11, 24.16, 25.15; Ben Sira 2.1ff., 4.17-19; James 1.3-4, 12, 5.7-11; Sextus *Sententiae* 15, 119, 216, 293, 301; Theognis 555-556, 657-658, 817-818, 1029-1036, 1123-1128; Publilius Syrus *Sententiae* 102, 111, 220, 293, 390, 450, 504, 512. Further see Spicq, *Notes*, 3.658-665, with references.

[48] Esp. Ben Sira and Sextus: Ben Sira 7.10, 14, 21.1, 5, 32.13, 34.29, 31, 35.21, 37.15, 38.9; Sextus *Sententiae* 80, 88, 122, 124, 125, 213, 217, 277, 372, 374, 375; cf. James 5.12-18.

[49] In the New Testament φιλοξενία occurs elsewhere only in Hebrews 13.2a, a maxim. On contributing to the needs of others, strangers in particular, see, for example: LXX Psalm 36.26; Proverbs 3.27-28, 11.24, 26, 13.11-12, 14.21, 31, 18.19, 19.7, 17, 20.13, 21.13, 26, 22.9, 22, 25.21-22, 28.3, 27; Tobit 1.3, 2.10, 3.2, 4.7-11, 12.8-9, 14.9-11; Ben Sira 3.30-4.6, 4.31, 7.32-33, 14.3-19, 18.15-18, 29.8-13, 35.3-4; Luke 6.29-36; Sextus *Sententiae* 47, 52, 266, 330, 339-342, 378; cf. Str-B 3.297. In Greek thought, Menander *Sententiae* 554 is perhaps representative (text: Jaekel, *Sententiae*, 65): ξένους ξένιζε, μήποτε ξένος γένῃ. Also 208, 542-545, 825, 827-828; *Comparatio Menandri et Philistionis* 1.85-86; Hesiod *Opera et Dies* 225, 327; Pseudo-Isocrates *Ad Demonicum* 25; *Gnomologium Epictetum* 43; *Dicta Catonis* 2.1. The 22nd chapter of *P. Insinger* (27.22-29.11) concerns strangers, cf. Lichtheim, *Late Egyptian Wisdom*, 162-163. Further see Spicq, *Notes*, 2.932-935; Hainz, *Koinonia*, 115-117; von Lips, *Weisheitliche Traditionen*, 402-403.

[50] For some further examples see Ben Sira 39.26, 40.18-27, 50.6-10; *Pirke 'Abot* 5.1-9; cf. W. M. W. Roth, *Numerical Sayings in the Old Testament: A Form-Critical Study* (VTSup

other cases ten is understood to convey a sense of completion or fulfillment. So in Philo's writings for instance, it is ἀριθμὸν τέλειον καὶ πλήρη,[51] and this connotation seems particularly apt for the composition of the Testament of Naphtali 2.8b, as we saw above.[52] The same may apply to Paul's elaboration of ἀγάπη in vv. 10-13, especially in light of the connection with τέλειος in v. 2, though we should bear in mind that these commands are not intended to represent an exhaustive list but rather they serve as illustrations of the sorts of actions Paul associates generally with unpretentious love. In this respect, the injunctions in vv. 10-13 are close in function to the lists of *exempla* recommended by the rhetorical handbooks and frequently employed in ancient paraenesis.[53]

Romans 12.14 and its Relationship with the Synoptic Gospels

The sequence of sayings in 12.9-13 culminates in 12.14, a verse that has attracted a great deal of modern critical attention. These investigations have been part of research conducted on two larger fronts: 1) the literary and historical relationship between the Pauline correspondence and the synoptic gospels (and their sources); and 2) the fate of Jesus' command to love in early Christianity. With respect to the first issue, a determination of whether any saying of Jesus familiar to us from the synoptic tradition influenced Paul's composition here, or anywhere else, cannot be made with certainty.[54] The

---

13; Leiden: Brill, 1965) 88-93.

[51] *De Specialibus Legibus* 2.201; text and translation: Colson et al., *Philo*, 7.432-433.

[52] Cf. Karl Staehle, *Die Zahlenmystik bei Philon von Alexandreia* (Leipzig, Berlin: Teubner, 1931) 53-58; Friedrich Hauck, "δέκα," *TDNT* 2 (1964) 36-37.

[53] See Michael R. Cosby, "The Rhetorical Composition of Hebrews 11," *JBL* 107 (1988) 257-273, with references.

[54] The amount of literature on this problem is immense; most important is the recent study by Frans Neirynck ("Paul and the Sayings of Jesus," in Vanhoye, *L'Apôtre Paul*, 265-321), whose results are followed rather closely here. Cf. David M. Stanley, "Pauline Allusions to the Sayings of Jesus," *CBQ* 23 (1961) 26-39; Davies, *Paul and Rabbinic Judaism*, 136-145; Furnish, *Theology*, 51-59; David L. Dungan, *The Sayings of Jesus in the Churches of Paul: The Use of the Synoptic Tradition in the Regulation of Early Church Life* (Philadelphia: Fortress; Oxford: Blackwell, 1973); Björn Fjärstedt, *Synoptic Tradition in 1 Corinthians: Themes and Clusters of Theme Words in 1 Corinthians 1-4 and 9* (Uppsala: Theologiska Institutionen, 1974); Dale C. Allison, "The Pauline Epistles and the Synoptic Gospels: The Pattern of the Parallels," *NTS* 28 (1982) 1-32; Peter Stuhlmacher, "Jesustradition im Römerbrief? Eine Skizze," *TBei* 14 (1983) 240-250; Christopher M. Tuckett, "1 Corinthians

evidence proffered by 1 Corinthians 7.10-11, 9.14, and 11.23ff. (cf. 14.37) shows that Paul played a role in maintaining and transmitting at least some portion of the traditions about Jesus and the teachings ascribed to him. In addition, we can be fairly certain that Paul was indebted at least in a general sense to Jesus' teachings on ἀγάπη and that his appreciation for the significance and meaning of the term derives ultimately from this source. But the form in which Paul was familiar with the tradition, whether written or oral, and whether Paul knew Q or some predecessor of Q, are questions that remain almost entirely unresolved. Given the paucity of convincing parallels between Paul's surviving correspondence and the synoptic gospels and the further observation that many of these parallels represent only unattributed allusions and reminiscences and not explicit quotations, skepticism is in order all along regarding the nature and extent of Paul's acquaintance with the synoptic traditions. Further, because the bulk of these allusions appear in paraenetic sections of the epistles together with a host of similar catechetical material, it is for the most part uncertain whether Paul consciously alludes to the words of Jesus or if these sayings had merely been passed on to him as an anonymous part of the exhortatory tradition of Hellenistic Judaism and early Christianity.

On the other hand, we must be quick to acknowledge that of all the possible allusions in Romans to sayings of Jesus preserved in the synoptic gospels, 12.14 constitutes the strongest candidate.[55] The pertinent texts are the following:[56]

---

and Q," *JBL* 102 (1983) 607-619; idem, "Paul and the Synoptic Mission Discourse?" *ETL* 60 (1984) 376-381; Peter Richardson, "The Thunderbolt in Q and the Wise Man in Corinth," *From Jesus to Paul: Studies in Honour of Francis Wright Beare* (ed. idem and John C. Hurd; Waterloo, Ontario: Wilfred Laurier University, 1984) 91-111; Sauer, "Traditionsgeschichtliche Erwägungen," 1-28; Nikolaus Walter, "Paulus und die urchristlichen Tradition," *NTS* 31 (1985) 498-522; David Wenham, "Paul's Use of the Jesus Tradition: Three Samples," *The Jesus Tradition Outside the Gospels: Gospel Perspectives 5* (ed. idem; Sheffield: JSOT, 1985) 7-37.

[55] See esp. Stanley, "Pauline Allusions," 26-39; Allison, "The Pattern of the Parallels," 5, 10-12, 18, 20; Stuhlmacher, "Jesustradition," 240-250; Sauer, "Traditionsgeschichtliche Erwägungen," 17-28; Walter, "Paulus und die urchristlichen Tradition," 501-503, 513-518; Wenham, "Paul's Use of the Jesus Tradition," 15-24; Neirynck, "Paul and the Sayings of Jesus," 270-271, 295-304.

[56] Cf. John S. Kloppenborg, *Q Parallels: Synopsis, Critical Notes, and Concordance* (FFNT; Sonoma, CA: Polebridge, 1988) 28-31.

Romans 12.14	εὐλογεῖτε τοὺς διώκοντας [ὑμᾶς],[57] εὐλογεῖτε καὶ μὴ καταρᾶσθε.
Luke 6.27-28	ἀγαπᾶτε τοὺς ἐχθροὺς ὑμῶν, καλῶς ποιεῖτε τοῖς μισοῦσιν ὑμᾶς, εὐλογεῖτε τοὺς καταρωμένους ὑμᾶς προσεύχεσθε περὶ τῶν ἐπηρεαζόντων ὑμᾶς.
Matthew 5.44	ἀγαπᾶτε τοὺς ἐχθροὺς ὑμῶν καὶ προσεύχεσθε ὑπὲρ τῶν διωκόντων ὑμᾶς.
Didache 1.3b	εὐλογεῖτε τοὺς καταρωμένους ὑμῖν καὶ προσεύχεσθε ὑπὲρ τῶν ἐχθρῶν ὑμῶν, νηστεύετε δὲ ὑπὲρ τῶν διωκόντων ὑμᾶς· ... ὑμεῖς δὲ ἀγαπᾶτε τοὺς μισοῦντας ὑμᾶς, καὶ οὐχ ἕξετε ἐχθρόν.
1 Corinthians 4.12b	λοιδορούμενοι εὐλογοῦμεν, διωκόμενοι ἀνεχόμεθα ...

Paul's maxim betrays clear verbal and formal similarities with both the Lukan and Matthean formulations, particularly Luke 6.28a, as well as the version of the saying in Didache 1.3b. Yet, in making these comparisons, it is important to ascertain as far as possible the literary histories and relationships of these sayings.[58] With regard to the synoptic passages, it appears that Luke 6.27b / Matthew 5.44a and Luke 6.28b / Matthew 5.44b are drawn from Q, and so represent early portions of the tradition. Yet for the latter saying it is likely that Luke preserves the older wording, and so the single term that Romans 12.14 has in common with these lines, διώκω in Matthew 5.44b, represents a redaction that should be assigned to a later stage of the tradition, either to Q^{Mt} or Matthew. This would make it far less likely that Paul could have acquired

---

[57] The ὑμᾶς in Romans 12.14a is omitted in some texts (P[46], B, etc.); perhaps later copyists (ℵ, A, D, etc.), under the influence of Luke 6.28 / Matthew 5.44 added the pronoun, cf. *TCGNT* 528. P[46] also omits the second εὐλογεῖτε.

[58] It is important to note that various explanations of the relationship of Q to the Gospels of Matthew and Luke have been offered by modern scholars; the position taken here more-or-less represents the modern consensus, but compare esp. the theories regarding the Synoptic question of Betz, *Essays on the Sermon on the Mount*, passim; idem, "The Sermon on the Mount and Q: Some Aspects of the Problem," *Gospel Origins and Christian Beginnings: In Honor of James M. Robinson* (ed. James E. Goehring, Charles W. Hedrick, Jack T. Sanders, with Hans Dieter Betz; FF 1; Sonoma, CA: Polebridge, 1990) 19-34.

the term from the synoptic tradition.[59] A complication of the same sort arises with Luke 6.27b-28a. While many modern critics would include them in their reconstructions of Q, the fact that these lines have no parallels in Matthew raises the possibility that they are later additions that should be ascribed to Q[Lk] or Luke. If this is the case, then Luke 6.28a, in which most of the similarities with Romans 12.14 are concentrated, may have entered the synoptic tradition at a comparatively late date--at any rate later than Paul's composition of Romans.[60]

Comparison of Luke 6.28a with Didache 1.3b seems to cloud the issue even further. While the debate continues, some modern critics believe that the author of Didache 1.3b-6 drew from a tradition independent of the gospels of Matthew and Luke.[61] Further, it is significant that the saying about blessing

---

[59] See Neirynck, "Paul and the Sayings of Jesus," 296-297, with references, esp. Josef Schmid, *Matthäus und Lukas: Eine Untersuchung des Verhältnisses ihrer Evangelien* (BibS (F) 23.2-4; Freiburg: Herder, 1930) 292; Jacques Dupont, *Les Béatitudes I: Le Problème littéraire--Les deux versions du Sermon sur la montagne et des Béatitudes* (EBib; Brussels: Abbaye de Saint André; Louvain: Nauwelaerts, 1958²) 155; Dieter Lührmann, *Die Redaktion der Logienquelle. Anhang: Zur weiteren Überlieferung der Logienquelle* (WMANT 33; Neukirchen-Vluyn: Neukirchener Verlag, 1969) 53-56; Heinz Schürmann, *Das Lukasevangelium* (HTKNT 3.1; Freiburg: Herder, 1969) 342-346; Athanasius Polag, *Fragmenta Q: Textheft zur Logienquelle* (Neukirchen-Vluyn: Neukirchener Verlag, 1979) 34-35; Wolfgang Schenk, *Synopse zur Redenquelle der Evangelien: Q Synopse und Rekonstruktion in deutscher Übersetzung mit kurzen Erläuterungen* (Düsseldorf: Patmos, 1981) 26-27; Zeller, *Mahnsprüche*, 101-103. Cf. Sauer, "Traditionsgeschichtliche Erwägungen," 5-17; Kloppenborg, *The Formation of Q*, 174.

[60] See Neirynck, "Paul and the Sayings of Jesus," 297-298, with references, esp. Dieter Lührmann, "Liebet eure Feinde (Lk 6.27-36 / Mt 5.39-48)," *ZTK* 69 (1972) 412-438, esp. 416; Siegfried Schulz, *Q: Die Spruchquelle der Evangelisten* (Zürich: Theologischer Verlag, 1972) 128; Joseph A. Fitzmyer, *The Gospel According to Luke* (ABS 28; 2 vols.; Garden City, New York: Doubleday, 1981, 1985) 1.638; Zeller, *Mahnsprüche*, 102, 187; Paul Hoffmann, "Tradition und Situation: Zur Verbindlichkeit des Gebots der Feindesliebe in der synoptischen Überlieferung und in der gegenwärtigen Friedensdiskussion," *Ethik im Neuen Testament* (ed. Karl Kertelge; QD 102; Freiburg: Herder, 1984) 50-118, esp. 52-53. Cf. Schürmann, *Lukasevangelium*, 346; Migaku Sato, *Q und Prophetie: Studien zur Gattungs- und Traditionsgeschichte der Quelle Q* (WUNT 2.29; Tübingen: Mohr-Siebeck, 1988) 222-224.

[61] See Neirynck, "Paul and the Sayings of Jesus," 298-299, with references. The conclusions of a recent study of Didache 1.3b by Jonathan Draper ("The Jesus Tradition in the Didache," in Wenham, *Perspectives 5*, 269-287, esp. 273-277) can be cited at this point: "Didache thus presents an independent text which cannot realistically be viewed as a harmony of the Gospels. It seems to have independent access to the tradition on which the Gospels also draw." (*op. cit.* 277) Others who favor the Didache's independence of the synoptic gospels include Richard Glover, "The Didache's Quotations and the Synoptic Gospels," *NTS* 5 (1958-59) 12-29, esp. 14, 27; idem, "Patristic Quotations and Gospel Sources," *NTS* 31 (1985) 234-251, esp. 239-240; Willy Rordorf, "Le problème de la transmission textuelle de Didachè 1.3b-2.1," *Überlieferungsgeschichtliche Untersuchungen* (ed. Franz Paschke; TU 125; Berlin: Akademie Verlag, 1981) 499-513, esp. 510; Wolf-Dietrich Köhler, *Die Rezeption*

and cursing in the Didache, like its counterpart in Romans 12, is not attributed to Jesus and it occurs in a context that is decidedly sapiential. So it may be that the author of the Didache knew the saying not as the words of Jesus but as an anonymous part of traditional Jewish (or Jewish-Christian) wisdom. This suggests the same explanation for the origin and use of parallel sayings in Paul and Luke (or perhaps Q); it was only in the latter text(s) that the maxim was attributed to Jesus.

Turning to Romans 12 itself, we find a number of clues to support this hypothesis. First, as already observed, Paul gives no explicit indication that 12.14 is in any way related to the teaching of Jesus. In order to counter this sort of difficulty, some scholars argue that Paul does not mention the Lord in connection with the possible allusion here (or elsewhere) because he can presuppose the audience's familiarity with the material.[62] This argument is flawed in at least two respects: 1) Paul is certainly in a position to assume his readers' thorough knowledge of the LXX and yet he specifically cites it frequently and at length, and often supplies introductory formulae like those found in Romans 12.19-20; 2) with respect to Romans in particular, Paul addresses a congregation to which he has never preached and which, for the most part, is unfamiliar with him; thus it is very difficult to say to what extent, if at all, he could presume the Romans' knowledge of any specific teaching of Jesus.

Second, while some interesting agreements do exist, Romans 12.14 does not constitute a precise parallel to any of the synoptic sayings. In particular, the repetition and antithesis in Paul's maxim stand in contrast to the synthetic parallelism of the sayings in Matthew, Luke, and the Didache. It is possible either that Paul knew and transmitted the saying in a form somewhat different

---

des Matthäusevangeliums in der Zeit vor Irenäus (WUNT 2.24; Tübingen: Mohr-Siebeck, 1987) 43-47; Clayton N. Jefford, *The Sayings of Jesus in the Teaching of the Twelve Apostles* (VCSup 11; Leiden: Brill, 1989) 38-48, 52-53, 90-92; Kurt Niederwimmer, *Die Didache* (Kommentar zu den Apostolischen Vätern 1; Göttingen: Vandenhoeck & Ruprecht, 1989) 100-105. Among those who view it as dependent on the synoptics are Bentley Layton, "The Sources, Date and Transmission of Didache 1.3b-2.1," *HTR* 61 (1968) 343-383; Klaus Wengst, *Didache (Apostellehre), Barnabasbrief, Zweiter Klemensbrief, Schrift an Diognetes* (Schriften des Urchristentums; Darmstadt: Wissenschaftliche Buchgesellschaft; München: Kösel, 1984) 18-20; Christopher M. Tuckett, "Synoptic Tradition in the Didache," *The New Testament in Early Christianity: La Réception des Ecrits Néotestamentaires dans le Christianisme Primitif* (ed. Jean-Marie Sevrin; BETL 86; Leuven: Leuven University Press, 1989) 197-230, esp. 214-220; cf. Jean-Paul Audet, *La Didachè* (EBib; Paris: Gabalda, 1958) 163-166.

[62] So Fjärstedt, *Synoptic Tradition*, 41-65; Allison, "The Pattern of the Parallels," 21-25; Wenham, "Paul's Use of the Jesus Tradition," 28-30; Dunn, *Romans*, 2.745. But cf. Furnish, *Theology*, 55.

than that found in Luke and the Didache, or that he has reformulated the saying in order to meet his specific needs, such as he apparently does with other traditional sayings in the chapter. Comparison with 1 Corinthians 4.12b, where the ideas of cursing, blessing, and persecution are combined in a very different literary permutation, is one clue to Paul's compositional freedom. Thus his use of regular imperatives, the emphatic repetition of εὐλογεῖτε, and the choice of διώκοντας may have been governed not by the tradition but by his own literary and rhetorical objectives.[63]

Third, both the specific terminology and basic sentiment expressed in this saying are by no means distinctively Christian and so need not necessarily go back to Jesus and the synoptic gospels. The contrast between blessing and cursing, first of all, is rather common in biblical language, for instance LXX Psalm 36.22, Proverbs 3.33 (discussed above), 30.10, Ben Sira 21.26-27, 33.12, and James 3.9-10.[64] In addition, while it is clear that early Christianity stressed and developed exhortation of the kind found in Romans 12.14, the notion of responding positively to evil had been anticipated to a significant extent by ancient Judaism. So, for instance, we encounter a call to render assistance to enemies in need in Proverbs 25.21-22a,[65] which Paul cites in Romans 12.20. The sages of the ancient Near East offered comparable advice to their readers as well; in addition to the passage from the Counsels of Wisdom 41-44 examined in Chapter Two, a number of maxims in *P. Insinger* express similar thoughts, for instance 23.6 and 27.9:

> It is better to bless someone than to do harm to one who has insulted you.
>
> When a wise man is stripped he gives his clothes and blesses.[66]

Compare Publilius Syrus *Sententiae* 142:

> Cum inimico ignoscis amicos gratis complures acquiris.
> When you forgive an enemy, you win several friends at no cost.[67]

As these examples attest, both the form and the content of 12.14, as well as Luke 6.28a, have precedents in traditional gnomic sources.[68]

---

[63] Cf. Neirynck, "Paul and the Sayings of Jesus," 299-300.

[64] Cf. Dibelius, *James*, 201-203; Ortkemper, *Leben aus dem Glauben*, 101-102; Martin, *James*, 118-120.

[65] Cf. LXX Proverbs 15.28a: δεκταὶ παρὰ κυρίῳ ὁδοὶ ἀνθρώπων δικαίων, διὰ δὲ αὐτῶν καὶ οἱ ἐχθροὶ φίλοι γίνονται. Cf. Piper, *Love Command*, 27-49.

[66] Translation: Lichtheim, *Late Egyptian Wisdom*, 221, 225.

[67] Text and translation: Duff and Duff, *Minor Latin Poets*, 32-33.

[68] Zeller (*Mahnsprüche*, 104-106; *Brief*, 210) and Kloppenborg (*The Formation of Q*,

Fourth, no evidence elsewhere in the epistle corroborates the theory that Paul depends on some part of the synoptic tradition. In particular, the parallels adduced by some scholars between Romans 12.17, 21, 14.10 and Luke 6.27-37 hardly constitute any real verbal or formal connections, just the expression of similar ideas and motives.[69] The same holds true by and large of the other alleged allusions to the sayings of Jesus in the *Corpus Paulinum*. While no survey of the passages in question is possible here, we may note the results of a recent investigation by Frans Neirynck. He observes that Paul makes only two explicit references to a command of the Lord, 1 Corinthians 7.10-11 and 9.14, but in both instances there is no 'quotation' of the saying, just an allusion or reminiscence. In the remainder of Paul's correspondence, "there is no certain trace of a conscious use of sayings of Jesus. Possible allusions to gospel sayings can be noted on the basis of similarity of form and context but a direct use of a gospel saying in the form it has been preserved in the synoptic gospels is hardly possible."[70]

So in conclusion, while the possibility that Paul depends upon the synoptic tradition here and that he intends in v. 14 an allusion to the teachings of Jesus cannot be removed entirely, it seems unlikely that this is the case. The lack of explicit attestation, the distinct form, and the traditional Jewish content and context in Romans 12 indicate that the saying is not to be understood as a quotation, either direct or indirect, of the Lord. Further, there are some doubts regarding both the dominical history of the parallel command in Luke 6.28a and at what point in time it became part of the synoptic tradition. While the presence of comparable maxims in Luke 6.28a and Didache 1.3b indicates the traditional background of Romans 12.14, they do not prove that Paul knew it as a saying of Jesus. The short, striking formulation and the memorable pairing of blessing and cursing may have enabled this saying to achieve the status of a proverb; it could have then circulated widely among early Christian congregations in a number of different forms. A feasible explanation is that Paul drew this saying, or some version of it, from the fund of traditional, anonymous, and probably oral Jewish and Jewish-Christian wisdom available to him. Then, at a later date, the traditional saying was known independently to other authors who attributed it to Jesus. Consequently there is no telling in what form or context Paul may have originally known the saying.

---

179 n. 37) cite additional parallels; both authors emphasize the traditional, sapiential nature of Luke 6.27-28 / Matthew 5.44. For more on non-violence and non-retaliation in ancient wisdom literature see the discussion of 12.17a, 19-20 below.

[69] Contra Allison, "The Pattern of the Parallels," 11-12.

[70] Neirynck, "Paul and the Sayings of Jesus," 320.

The Theme(s) and Structure of Romans 12.14-21

Most of the large number of studies on the love command in the New Testament include some treatment of Romans 12.14-21.[71] While the concept of loving (or blessing) one's enemies is not unique to early Christianity, the consensus is that the greater status allotted to this attitude in the New Testament represents something of an advance. Significantly, in chapter 12 Paul carefully integrates the treatment of enemy love with commands regarding love within the community. Yet, as most commentators acknowledge, v. 14, which contains the decisive injunction to bless persecutors, presides over the chapter's remaining verses.[72] The use of regular imperatives here for the first time in the section together with the emphatic repetition of εὐλογεῖτε attest to its prominence. The catchword, διώκοντ-, also implies that the admonition should be connected with the preceding verses as well. Thus the unpretentious love that motivates treatment of insiders in vv. 10-13 should not be distinguished from that which responds to outsiders in vv. 14-21. This compositional scheme implies that, love, if it is genuine, cannot be divided into types and subsequently prioritized, nor can it be factored into categories appropriate to differing times or situations; in this sense it is τέλειος. The formulation of the central maxim in v. 14, in particular the addition of the second line, offers another clue as to Paul's intention. Christians are not obligated merely to bless persecutors but they must also refrain from cursing them. Thus any thought of blessing now and cursing later, or of blessing publicly and then cursing privately, is removed. In this way the admonition serves not only as a call for love in the face of adversity but also as an indirect warning against insincerity and hypocrisy; for Paul there is no room for ulterior motives or half-hearted intentions.

It is noteworthy that besides the general statements in 1 Corinthians 4.12, Galatians 6.10, 1 Thessalonians 3.12, and 5.15, this is the only place where Paul extends the discussion of love to those outside the Christian community.[73] Moreover, Romans 12.14-21 is the only passage in which Paul calls on Christians to respond positively to enemies. No doubt the notion of blessing

---

[71] Spicq, *Agapè*, 2.141-157; Krister Stendahl, "Hate, Non-Retaliation, and Love: 1QS 10.17-20 and Romans 12.19-21," *HTR* 55 (1962) 343-355; Furnish, *Love Command*, 102-108; Piper, *Love Command*, 89-95; Schrage, *Ethics*, 211-217. Also see the references in note 6.

[72] Michel, *Brief*, 269-270, 273-274; Cranfield, *Romans*, 2.629; Wilckens, *Brief*, 3.18; Käsemann, *Romans*, 347; Dunn, *Romans*, 2.738; but cf. Schmithals, *Kommentar*, 444, 447-456.

[73] Cf. Betz, *Galatians*, 310-311.

one's persecutors must have been difficult for any early Christian community to accept, and this is doubly true for the Roman Christians in light of the available historical information.[74] For Paul, it seems, to comply with a command such as 12.14 would be the most visible, intense sort of manifestation of the ἀγάπη he hopes to instill in his audience; in this regard the seriousness attached in the ancient world to blessing and cursing ought to be emphasized.[75] The concentration of traditional Jewish wisdom that follows in vv. 15-21 not only explains and expands upon this demanding ethical admonition, but also serves as validation, offering authoritative reasons for its implementation. While Paul makes a number of appeals in vv. 15-21, it seems that each of the admonitions here may be understood as contributing to one of three basic themes, each of which derives from and supports the central admonition in v. 14. There is, most of all, the repudiation of vengeance and violence: Christians do not retaliate for wrongdoing (vv. 17-19a), but respond in solidarity to the needs of others (v. 15), even enemies (v. 20). Second, in conjunction with this renunciation, Paul exhorts the Romans to fear God, and in particular to recognize his exclusive prerogative to judge men; the faithful are to defer humbly to God's power, confident in his justice (v. 19b). Third, in light of the serious commitment to these first two ideals, there is clearly no place among the Romans for human pride and arrogance, which are incompatible with both peaceful co-existence and the fear of God (v. 16). These three themes or ideals, taken together, provide an effective illustration of the essential moral

---

[74] It is very unlikely that Paul has any specific persecutors in mind here. On persecution of Jews and Christians in Rome see Schmithals, *Der Römerbrief als historisches Problem*, 69-91; E. Mary Smallwood, *The Jews under Roman Rule from Pompey to Diocletian: A Study in Political Relations* (SJLA 20; Leiden: Brill, 1981²) 201-219; Peter Lampe, *Die stadtrömischen Christen in den ersten beiden Jahrhunderten: Untersuchungen zur Sozialgeschichte* (WUNT 2.18; Tübingen: Mohr-Siebeck, 1987) s.v. Verfolgung.

[75] For more on blessing and cursing in Judaism and Christianity see Lyder Brun, *Segen und Fluch im Urchristentum* (Skriften utgitt av det Norske Videnskaps-Akademi i Oslo, II, Hist.-Filos. Klasse 1; Oslo: J. Dybwad, 1932); Siegfried Morenz, F. Horst, and Helmut Koester, "Segen und Fluch," *RGG* 5 (1961) 1648-1652; Herbert C. Brichto, *The Problem of 'Curse' in the Hebrew Bible* (JBLMS 13; Philadelphia: SBL, 1963); Herman W. Beyer, "εὐλογέω κτλ.," *TDNT* 2 (1964) 754-765; Wolfgang Schenk, *Der Segen im Neuen Testament: Eine begriffsanalytische Studie* (Theologische Arbeiten 25; Berlin: Evangelische Verlagsanstalt, 1967); Willy Schottroff, *Der altisraelitische Fluchspruch* (WMANT 30; Neukirchen-Vluyn: Neukirchener Verlag, 1969); Wolfgang Speyer, "Fluch," *RAC* 7 (1969) 1160-1288; Gerhard Wehmeier, *Der Segen im Alten Testament: Eine semasiologische Untersuchung der Wurzel brk* (Theologische Dissertationen 6; Basel: Reinhardt, 1970); Betz, *Galatians*, 50-54, 142-152, 320-323; Christopher W. Mitchell, *The Meaning of BRK "To Bless" in the Old Testament* (SBLDS 95; Atlanta: Scholars Press, 1987) esp. 79-131; cf. Claus Westermann, *Blessing in the Bible and the Life of the Church* (trans. Keith Crim; Fortress: Philadelphia, 1978).

perspective of ἀγάπη that motivates an act such as blessing one's persecutors, and indeed forms the basis of all acts of sincere love and compassion.

As we shall see below, individually each of these three themes--non-violence, the fear of God, and humility--represent fairly prominent topics in sapiential exhortation. Equally pertinent are several gnomic texts in which an author presents these same concepts together, integrating them in order to create ethical messages not unlike Paul's in Romans 12.14-21. Four of these texts should be familiar from previous discussions--LXX Proverbs 3.27-35, Ben Sira 10.12-18, LXX Psalm 36, and the Counsels of Wisdom 31-65--and several others can be added to this list. In *Proverbs 3.27-35*, which represents the core of the prescriptive section in Proverbs 3.21-35, the author begins with maxims on assisting those in need (vv. 27-28), then exhortations against evil-doing, quarreling, and violence (vv. 29-31), buttressed by reminders of God's punishment of the wicked and arrogant as well as his exaltation of the righteous and humble (vv. 32-35).[76] *Ben Sira 10.12-18* includes a hymnic description of God's destruction of the proud and exaltation of the humble (vv. 14-17) framed by warnings that insolence, anger, and other vices are not allotted to humans and will be justly punished by God (vv. 12-13, 18).[77] Similar topics are raised in *Ben Sira 35.14-26*. Here the author contrasts God's special concern for the powerless and oppressed (vv. 14-22a) with the vengeance he will wreak on the merciless and proud in retribution for their wrongdoing (vv. 22b-26). The themes of *LXX Psalm 36* center on trust in God and in his providential rule. The righteous, though they are humiliated presently, should patiently wait for God's justice, when they will be delivered. The wicked, on the other hand, who practice violence and murder, and who pursue vain wealth and boast against God, will be condemned and destroyed. Consequently, the faithful, in fear of God, should not emulate the wicked; they must refrain from anger and wrath, and pursue peace and justice.[78] The same advice occurs in *LXX Psalm 33*, another wisdom psalm, where the faithful, who are humble (vv. 2, 6, 18-19) and fear the Lord (vv. 7-9), are to flee evil and pursue peace (vv. 13-14) in expectation that God will save the righteous and punish wrongdoers (vv. 4, 6-7, 15-22). The author of the *Counsels of Wisdom* begins lines 31ff. with advice to avoid legal disputes (31-40); this leads to a series of more comprehensive maxims on responding with kindness and justice to one's enemies (40ff.). Afterwards there is a warning against arrogance and insolence (57-58), which is motivated by a fear of the god's retribution (59-60); then there are several

---

[76] See above pp. 96-105.
[77] See above pp. 57-58.
[78] See above pp. 60-61.

commands to assist those in need, acts that are pleasing to the deity (61-65).[79] Mention should also be made of *Ben Sira 27.22-28.11*. The author begins this section by attacking deceitfulness and malice (27.22-24) and describing how the evil plans of the violent, proud, and vengeful will be repaid in full by the Lord: they will suffer the same fate they had intended for others (27.25-28.1). This is followed by exhortation to forgive the sins and injustices of others, and to disdain strife and hatred (28.2-11).

This brief survey reveals a more-or-less consistent pattern of thought, in which a gnomic author unites the distinct though related themes of non-retaliation, the fear of God, and humility in exhorting the audience. The underlying ethos that each of these sapiential texts recommends for its readers has three complementary aspects: the first concerns individual self-understanding; the second, one's dealings with others; the third, the relationship between human beings and God.[80] If people genuinely appreciate their personal limitations and the faults of human nature then they will naturally refrain from passing judgement on others and doing them harm. Likewise, they will be quick to acknowledge God's power and the divine prerogative to reward and punish human beings. Thus not only the specific concepts encountered in the individual precepts of Romans 12.14-21 have analogues in the sapiential literature but there are also precedents in the comparative material for the combination and co-ordinated use of these concepts in a single passage displaying a similar function.

Given these thematic connections between Romans 12.14-21 and the wisdom tradition, the question remains how Paul orders his thoughts in this paragraph. It appears that he profits by a literary device employed regularly in gnomic wisdom, ring composition. Comparable literary structures were encountered on a number of occasions in the investigations above: Ben Sira 6.18-37, 27.16-21, Pseudo-Phocylides 9-21, 79-96, Romans 12.10-13, and so forth. Noteworthy, too, is the recent study of Daniel Fredericks, who has investigated the function of similar literary devices in Qohelet 5.6-6.9.[81] The following outline is proposed for Romans 12.14-21:[82]

---

[79] Cf. Lichtheim's description of the ideal Near Eastern sage (particularly as depicted in the Instruction of Any): he is humble before God and peace-loving, "his chief characteristic is modesty" (*Ancient Egyptian Literature*, 2.146); cf. above pp. 83-84.

[80] Cf. Zeller, *Mahnsprüche*, 147-151, and the sources cited there.

[81] Daniel C. Fredericks, "Chiasm and Parallel Structure in Qoheleth 5.6-6.9," *JBL* 108 (1989) 17-35, esp. 18-28.

[82] For some other theories of ring composition in this part of the epistle see Schmithals, *Römerbrief*, 423-424 (for 12.1-15.30) and 449 (for 12.9-15); Dunn, *Romans*, 2.706 (for 12.1-15.6); Betz, "The Foundations of Christian Ethics," 65 n. 64 (for 12.9-21); Wedderburn, *The Reasons for Romans*, 76 (for 12.3-16 and 12.17-13.7). Cf. Joachim

v. 14	A.	Return evil with good
v. 15	B.	Respond to the needs of others
v. 16	C.	Know your place and be humble
vv. 17-19a	D.	Live at peace with all people
v. 19b-c	C'.	Leave vengeance to God
v. 20	B'.	Respond to the needs of enemies
v. 21	A'.	Overcome evil with good

As the chart indicates, the maxims and other materials in vv. 14-21 appear to be grouped and arranged in formal and thematic clusters, a common literary phenomenon in gnomic sources. The ring composition is carried further within the center cluster of sayings, part D (vv. 17-19a); the translation of these verses can be organized as follows:

v. 17a	E.	"Never repaying evil for evil,
v. 17b	F.	taking thought for what is good
	G.	before all men;
v. 18a	H.	if possible, so far as it depends on you,
v. 18b	G'.	with all men
	F'.	living at peace;
v. 19a	E'.	not taking your own revenge,"

These outlines are useful in so far as they illustrate the passage's careful composition and suggest one of the ways in which the various sayings and ideas in the paragraph are structured and related to one another. Thus, for instance, they reveal how v. 14 governs the thought of the passage and highlight its affinity with the summarizing maxim in v. 21. The scheme also points to the unexpected v. 18a as the focal point of the ring. The juxtaposition of different structural counterparts or pairs (A and A', etc.) is based upon varying combinations of features: formal analogy, material similarities, logical connections, and so forth. As with most ring compositions, the components of the second half of the paragraph, here vv. 18b-21, are hardly mere repetitions or rewordings of their counterparts in vv. 14-17. Rather, parts A, B, C, etc. suggest and anticipate what is said in A', B', C', which take up and elaborate on earlier themes. In this way the thought of each admonition in the paragraph is developed and expanded. The chiastic structure in the center of the ring composition, part D (vv. 17-19a) is fairly straightforward, relying on the correspondence of specific words and phrases. At the extremities of the ring

---

Jeremias, "Chiasmus in den Paulusbriefen," *ZNW* 49 (1958) 145-156.

composition both vv. 14 and 21 are marked by strong antithetical contrasts (blessing / cursing; good / evil), though there is a shift in perspective: what v. 14 exhorts in concrete terms v. 21 represents with a generalized summary that indicates the ultimate consequences of what is commanded. B and B' (vv. 15 and 20) by comparison, are largely parallel in structure, each maxim exhorting the audience to respond positively to the situations of others as circumstances dictate. While the appeals in v. 15 are rather broad, self-evident, and easily accomplished, the commands in v. 20 are specific, contrary to conventional behavior, and difficult. C and C' (vv. 16 and 19b-c) represent the most problematic pairing in the ring composition, and the relationship of these two elements will be discussed at length below. Here the connection is not based upon formal analogy or thematic agreement, but rather upon the logical correlation of the ideas expressed, i.e., the appeal to be humble and the necessity of fearing God's judgement. The meaning and implications of this connection, as well as of the entire proposed structure, will become clearer as the analysis continues.

Romans 12.15

Immediately after the command to bless persecutors in 12.14, Paul has placed another wisdom admonition, 12.15: χαίρειν μετὰ χαιρόντων, κλαίειν μετὰ κλαιόντων ("rejoice with those who rejoice, weep with those who weep").[83] The employment of imperatival infinitives in these lines represents a very old practice in Greek literature. Injunctions of this kind are employed chiefly in legal statements and wisdom sayings, and a number of gnomic texts, including Hesiod's *Opera et Dies*, the *Theognidea*, the Sayings of the Seven Sages, the *Carmen Aureum*, and the *Praecepta Delphica*, attest to the practice.[84] Among Jewish authors Pseudo-Phocylides in particular takes advantage of imperatival infinitives, and Paul employs the form in another of his gnomic sayings, Philippians 3.16.[85] The infinitive as imperative often occurs in the Homeric epics, normally after a regular imperative, so that the infinitive serves to carry on the command already given or to express what is expected of the addressee as his part in a series of acts. The author normally provides an

---

[83] Some textual witnesses (A, D², etc.) add καί after χαιρόντων, ruining the asyndeton, though most do not (P⁴⁶, B, D*, F, G, etc.).

[84] Cf. BDF § 389.

[85] Cf. Gnilka, *Der Philipperbrief*, 201-202.

infinitival command as something contingent upon an already expressed or implied state of affairs, and so stipulates conduct that is deemed fitting or obligatory in light of the previous imperatives.[86] In gnomic poems and gnomologia an admonition with the imperatival infinitive is often accompanied by another saying governed by an indicative or (regular) imperative verb, which may either immediately precede or follow the infinitival maxim (e.g. Pseudo-Phocylides 76-77). These facts suggest that v. 15 should be closely associated with v. 14, and so lends weight to the observation that χαίρειν and κλαίειν are "clearly parallel" with εὐλογεῖτε καὶ μὴ καταρᾶσθε.[87] The thoughts in v. 15, therefore, appear to develop out of, and perhaps form a corollary to, v. 14. As in Homer, the infinitives may specify behavior that is considered appropriate in light of the main imperatives in v. 14.[88]

A number of commentators have identified v. 15 as a maxim, offering Ben Sira 7.34 as the closest parallel:

μὴ ὑστέρει ἀπὸ κλαιόντων, καὶ μετὰ πενθούντων πένθησον.
Do not fail those who weep, but mourn with those who mourn.

While this hardly constitutes an exact parallel, it does indicate the traditional nature of the formulation.[89] The immediate context of the latter saying, Ben Sira 7.32-35, is an appeal to fulfill responsibilities to the poor and unfortunate. The author here also associates the command with the ethical goal of ἀγάπη (cf. ἀγαπάω in 7.35).[90] In both Ben Sira and Romans, the maxims encourage a feeling of genuine concern and sincere empathy that is to accompany certain

---

[86] D. B. Munro, *A Grammar of the Homeric Dialect* (Oxford: Clarendon, 1891) § 241.

[87] Robertson, *Grammar*, 944.

[88] In addition to these grammatical considerations, the logical connection of v. 15 to v. 14 is reflected in another gnomic text, Publilius Syrus *Sententiae* 142-143 (text: Duff and Duff, *Minor Latin Poets*, 32):
Cum inimicio ignoscis amicos gratis complures acquiris.
Contubernia sunt lacrimarum ubi misericors miserum adspicit.
In both texts there is a progression of gnomic sayings from the topic of treating one's enemies benevolently to that of a concrete expression of human solidarity. In contrast with Romans 12.14-15, here the personal benefit is made explicit.

[89] Cf. Job 30.25; Proverbs 14.13; Ben Sira 4.7-10; Tobit 13.14; Matthew 5.4, 7; 1 Corinthians 7.30, 12.26; 2 Corinthians 11.29; Philippians 2.17-18; Testament of Issachar 7.5; Testament of Zebulon 6.5, 7.3-4; Testament of Joseph 17.7; Philo *De Josepho* 94; *Derek Eres Rabbah* 7.7; *Derek Eres Zuta* 4.5; Str-B 3.298; Sextus *Sententiae* 414, 422; Pseudo-Libanius 39.3-4; Theognis 313-314, 627-628, 1217-1218; Epictetus *Dissertationes* 2.5.23, *Encheiridion* 25.1; *Gnomica Homoeomata* appendix 19; Ankhsheshonqy 12.17. Michel (*Brief*, 274) also refers to *P. Insinger* 11.9. Cf. Daube, "Missionary Maxims," 158-163; von Lips, *Weisheitliche Traditionen*, 404.

[90] Cf. Skehan and DiLella, *Ben Sira*, 203-208.

specific acts of kindness. Similar objectives appear in comparably formulated Greek maxims, such as Menander *Sententiae* 448 and Hesiod *Opera et Dies* 353:

λυποῦντα λύπει, καὶ φιλοῦνθ' ὑπερφίλει.
Give grief for grief, and more than love for love.[91]

τὸν φιλέοντα φιλεῖν, καὶ τῷ προσιόντι προσεῖναι.
Befriend the friendly, and visit him who visits.[92]

In addition to the ideas of empathy and solidarity, a guiding principle in these sayings is the necessity of reciprocity in human relationships, and of the ability to discern what is needed in a particular situation.[93] The implication of the maxim in 12.15 is that Christians must not only identify with the joys and sorrows of others, but that they must perceive their needs and respond in a positive and appropriate way.

Romans 12.16

In the next verse, 12.16, Paul has created a cluster of three related sayings: τὸ αὐτὸ εἰς ἀλλήλους φρονοῦντες, μὴ τὰ ὑψηλὰ φρονοῦντες ἀλλὰ τοῖς ταπεινοῖς συναπαγόμενοι. μὴ γίνεσθε φρόνιμοι παρ' ἑαυτοῖς ("Being of the same mind among yourselves, not thinking proud thoughts, but associating with the lowly, do not be wise in your own estimation"). The verse, above all the first saying, v. 16a, follows naturally from v. 15: the solidarity expected with people generally applies in particular to actions and attitudes within the Roman congregation itself.[94] The ordering of the sayings in the verse bears likeness to a structure encountered on occasion in sapiential writings, which is also comprised of three elements: a) an opening maxim, usually of a relatively straight-forward nature; b) a two-part explanation or expansion of part 'a', each part evaluating opposing possibilities or implications; and c) a concluding

---

[91] Text: Jaekel, *Sententiae*, 58; my translation.
[92] Text: West, *Works and Days*, 113, cf. 245; my translation.
[93] Cf. Pseudo-Isocrates *Ad Demonicum* 31.
[94] Apparently, the maxim in 12.16a had become a regular exhortation in Pauline paraenesis; parallel commands can be found in Romans 15.5; 2 Corinthians 13.11; Philippians 2.2, 4.2. Significantly, in Romans 15.5 and Philippians 2.2 it is also used in the course of warnings against presumptuousness. Cf. Matthew 5.3; 2 Clement 17.3; Josephus *Antiquitates Judaicae* 19.58, *Bellum Judaicum* 2.160; Daube, "Missionary Maxims," 162-169; Käsemann, *Romans*, 347.

statement with direct application to the audience.[95] The presence of this structure, as well as the purposeful repetition of the φρον- root, together with the choice of imperatives (participles in v. 16a and b, a regular imperative in v. 16c) suggests that the three sayings should be taken together, and that v. 16c conveys the main thought. Thus the verse constitutes a warning against arrogance and aloofness, and a call for the audience to think and act in harmony, even when this involves menial tasks or associating with people held in low esteem by society at large.[96]

Attacks on pride, often accompanied by calls for self-evaluation, are very common in gnomic literature. The Greeks viewed pride above all as a very grievous intellectual and personal flaw. The sort of 'gnomic paradox' conveyed by the admonition in v. 16c figures prominently in the writings of some of the pre-Socratics and Plato, as well as the diatribe tradition, often in connection with the interpretation of the Delphic maxim γνῶθι σαυτόν.[97] Gnomic sayings comparable to the warnings in 12.16 are also prevalent in Jewish and Christian wisdom literature. A fairly large number of these maxims tend to view pride more as an intellectual or social flaw than as a sin and an affront to God, though the distinction, perhaps, should not be pushed too far.[98] Such appeals for humility were often accompanied by or in the form of illustrations of self-deceit. For thoughts similar to Romans 12.16 see, for example, LXX

---

[95] Some examples: Matthew 6.24 / Luke 16.13; *Gnomologium Epictetum* 16, 19, 25; Moschion *Hypothekai* 17. Further on Luke 16.13 see Piper, *Wisdom in the Q-Tradition*, 86-99.

[96] On the question of whether ταπεινοῖς should be understood as neuter or masculine see Michel, *Brief*, 306-307; Barrett, *Romans*, 103; Schlier, *Römerbrief*, 380; Cranfield, *Romans*, 2.644; Wilckens, *Brief*, 3.23; Ortkemper, *Leben aus dem Glauben*, 104-105.

[97] See esp. Pierre Courcelle, *Connais-toi toi-même de Socrate à Bernard* (3 vols.; Paris: Etudes Augustiniennes, 1974-1975) passim; also Hans Dieter Betz, "The Delphic Maxim ΓΝΩΘΙ ΣΑΥΤΟΝ in Hermetic Interpretation," *HTR* 63 (1970) 465-484; idem, "The Delphic Maxim 'Know Yourself' in the Greek Magical Papyri," *HR* 21 (1981) 156-171; idem, *Der Apostel Paulus und die sokratische Tradition: Eine exegetische Untersuchung zu seiner 'Apologie' 2 Korinther 10-13* (BHTh 45; Tübingen: Mohr-Siebeck, 1972) 118-132; idem, *Plutarch's Ethical Writings*, 378-381; idem, *Galatians*, 301-303. Some examples: *Gnomologium Democrateum* 52, 84, 86, 88, 114; Cleobulus 20, Solon 13, Thales 20, Pittacus 12; Theognis 39-52, 83-86, 153-154, 833-836; Heraclitus 3-5, 22, 28-29, 36-37; Menander *Sententiae* 138, 358, 431, 510, 520, 581, 674, 762, 778, 794, 807, 814; *Comparatio Menandri et Philistionis* 1.295; Pseudo-Menander *Sententiae* 408-409; *Gnomologium Epictetum* 3, 15, 45; *Gnomologium Vaticanum* 54, 64; *Gnomica Homoeomata* 47, 63, 97, 170a, 182; Pseudo-Diogenes *Epistles* 22.19-20, 40.22-23, 49.1-10; *Anthologia Graeca* 5.256, 9.54, 10.38, 75; Stobaeus *Anthologium* 3.22, passim. See further the discussion of Romans 12.3 above.

[98] Cf. McKane, *Proverbs*, 428, 453-454, 467-468, 480, 490, 498-499, 550-551; von Rad, *Wisdom in Israel*, 74-110.

Proverbs 28.11:

σοφὸς παρ' ἑαυτῷ ἀνὴρ πλούσιος
πένης δὲ νοήμων καταγνώσεται αὐτοῦ.
A wealthy man is wise in his own estimation,
but a poor man of intelligence shall condemn him.

Or Didache 3.9b:

οὐ κολληθήσεται ἡ ψυχή σου μετὰ ὑψηλῶν,
ἀλλὰ μετὰ δικαίων καὶ ταπεινῶν ἀναστραφήσῃ.
Do not allow yourself to cleave to the proud,
but associate with the just and humble.[99]

Several maxims in Paul's previous correspondence address this issue as well, for instance 1 Corinthians 1.25, 3.18, 8.2, 2 Corinthians 10.18, Galatians 5.26 and 6.3-4.[100] The thoughts expressed in all these texts follow more-or-less the same line of argument. For human beings to consider themselves wise, powerful, or otherwise important is an objectively false claim, and so opinions of this sort represent a form of self-deception and self-deceit. Those who overestimate themselves are incapable of coming to grips with their own deficiencies and they deny their need for the guidance of others. Because of this disdainful and self-centered attitude, genuine personal progress and edifying

---

[99] Text: Wengst, *Didache*, 70; my translation; cf. Niederwimmer, *Die Didache*, 132. Further examples: Proverbs 3.5, 34, 8.13, 11.2, 12-13, 12.15-17, 13.9-10, 13, 14.3, 10, 12, 16, 30, 16.2, 5, 18-19, 25, 17.16, 18, 24, 18.12, 19.10, 18, 20.9, 21.2, 4, 8, 24, 23.4-5, 25.6-7, 14, 26.5, 12, 16, 27.1-2, 20-21, 28.11, 13, 26, 29.23, 30.8; Qohelet 7.8-9, 16, 20, 23-24, 29, 8.10-11; Tobit 4.13; Ben Sira 1.28-30, 2.17, 3.17-24, 5.1-8, 7.4-6, 16-17, 8.1-7, 10.6-18, 26-29, 11.1-6, 9, 13.20, 18.20-21, 21.4; Luke 14.11, 18.14; James 3.13; Pseudo-Phocylides 53-54, 118, 122; Didache 3.7-10; Sextus *Sententiae* 64, 138, 188, 199, 203, 284, 286, 320, 325, 333, 342, 389b, 432; Cleitarchus *Chreiai* 24, 109, 115, 132; *Teachings of Silvanus* 87, 90, 91, 95, 110-111; *Pirke 'Abot* 1.13, 2.5, 9, 16, 3.1, 4.4, 7, 9, 12, 18, 28, 5.22, 6.1, 5; *Derek Eres Rabbah* 2.1, 8, 9, 14, 22; *Derek Eres Zuta* 2.6, 3.2, 5, 11, 4.4, 8.10, 9.11. Also Ptahhotep 1-4, 9-10, 25, 52; Amenemope 25.1-15; Any 6.11-15, 8.11-12; *P. Insinger* 3.10-19, 4.13-23, 5.13, 33.13, 22.

[100] Cf. Romans 1.22, 11.20, 12.3, 14.22b, 15.1; 1 Corinthians 1.29, 3.19, 4.10, 11.28; 2 Corinthians 11.28, 31, 12.10. Attacks on presumptuousness and self-deception figure prominently in Paul's writings on a number of occasions, e.g. Romans 1-2, 1 Corinthians 1-3, 2 Corinthians 10-13. Gnomic sayings, along with the literary tactics associated with the diatribe, are often used to convey such critiques. See Dan O. Via, Jr., *Self-Deception and Wholeness in Paul and Matthew* (Minneapolis: Fortress, 1990) esp. 19-45; also Stowers, *The Diatribe*, 100-118; Christopher Forbes, "Comparison, Self-Praise and Irony: Paul's Boasting and the Conventions of Hellenistic Rhetoric," *NTS* 32 (1986) 1-30; Peter Marshall, *Enmity in Corinth: Social Conventions in Paul's Relations with the Corinthians* (WUNT 2.23; Tübingen: Mohr-Siebeck, 1987) 182-218, 364-381. Also see the references above in n. 97.

social intercourse are out of the question. In the end, their shamelessness and vain ambition will lead to ruin. Pride and self-deceit, especially in Jewish writings, are also associated with impiety and viewed as affronts to God. Arrogant people do not humbly acknowledge their utter dependence on God or properly comprehend their place in the universe; eventually they will be punished for their ὕβρις.[101] Morally opposed to this is humility (represented here by ταπεινός) and the self-knowledge that accompanies it, which frequently stand as ethical and intellectual ideals for ancient authors, gnomic and otherwise.[102]

In the ring composition for 12.14-21 proposed above, v. 19b-c, an exhortation to leave wrath and vengeance to God, was posited as the structural counterpart to v. 16. At first sight the material connection between the two verses is unclear. There are, however, several reasons for supposing that Paul's appeal for humility in v. 16 anticipates the command to respect God's prerogative to judge and to punish in v. 19b-c, and that the two concepts complement one another here as well as elsewhere in sapiential literature. The first observation to be made in this regard is that v. 16c represents a modified quotation of LXX Proverbs 3.7a; the saying in its entirety is:

---

[101] For discussion and bibliography see Georg Bertram, "ὕβρις κτλ.," *TDNT* 8 (1972) 295-307, cf. 8.525-529; Hans von Gersau, "Hybris," *KP* 2 (1967) 1257-1258; N. R. E. Fisher, *Hybris: Study in Values* (Warminster: Aris and Phillips, n.d.). Of related interest are the studies on hypocrisy, see above n. 13. For ὕβρις in Biblical wisdom see Proverbs 1.22, 8.13, 11.2, 13.10, 14.3, 10, 16.18, 19, 19.10, 18; Wisdom of Solomon 2.19, 4.18; Ben Sira 10.6, 8, 21.4; cf. Proverbs 6.17, 15.25, 27.13; Ben Sira 8.11, 32.18; Pseudo-Phocylides 62. In Greek literature see esp. Hesiod *Opera et Dies* 213-285, exhortation concerning the superiority of δίκη over ὕβρις; cf. West, *Works and Days*, 209-229; also *Gnomologium Democrateum* 111; Chilon 20; Theognis 40, 151, 153, 291, 307, 379, 541, 603, 732, 835, 1103, 1174; Heraclitus 104; Menander *Sententiae* 410, 792, 795; *Comparatio Menandri et Philistionis* 1.250.

[102] Cf. LXX Psalm 33.18; Job 5.11; Proverbs 3.34; Ben Sira 3.20, 10.15; Matthew 11.29; Luke 1.52; 2 Corinthians 7.6, 10.1; James 1.9, 4.6; 1 Peter 5.5; cf. James 1.10, 4.10; 1 Peter 3.8, 5.6; also Menander *Sententiae* 100 (app.), 850, Appendix 2.5 (p. 127 in Jaekel, *Sententiae*); for ὑψηλός vs. ταπεινός cf. Epictetus *Dissertationes* 2.6.25. Further see the commentaries, also BAGD s.v. ταπεινός, ταπεινοφρονέω, ταπεινοφρόνησις, ταπεινοφροσύνη, ταπεινόφρων, ταπεινόω, ταπείνωσις; Karl Thieme, "Die ταπεινοφροσύνη Philipper 2 und Römer 12," *ZNW* 8 (1907) 9-33; Albrecht Dihle, "Demut," *RAC* 3 (1957) 735-778; G. Mensching, E. Kutsch, A. Benoît, and R. Mehl, "Demut," *RGG* 2 (1958) 76-82; Ragnar Leivestad, "ΤΑΠΕΙΝΟΣ--ΤΑΠΕΙΝΟΦΡΩΝ," *NovT* 8 (1966) 36-47; Walter Grundmann, "ταπεινός κτλ.," *TDNT* 8 (1972) 559-571; Spicq, *Notes*, 2.878-880; Horst D. Preuß, Marianne Awerbuch, and Stefan Rehrl, "Demut," *TRE* 8 (1981) 459-468, with bibliography on p. 468; cf. Klaus Wengst, *Humility, Solidarity of the Humiliated: The Transformation of an Attitude* (trans. John Bowden; Philadelphia: Fortress, 1989).

μὴ ἴσθι φρόνιμος παρὰ σεαυτῷ,
φοβοῦ δὲ τὸν θεὸν καὶ ἔκκλινε ἀπὸ παντὸς κακοῦ.

Do not be wise in your own estimation,
but fear God and refrain from all evil.

No doubt Paul's readers, who were well-versed in the LXX, would have recognized the first line of the proverb immediately and expected its familiar conclusion. If we can assume that for early Christians (as well as Diaspora Jews) the LXX Proverbs not only constituted part of their holy scriptures but also contributed to their proverbial lore and traditional wisdom, then this conjecture seems warranted. Thus the idea of the fear of God, and the theological implications that it represented, had already been indirectly introduced into the passage by means of the quotation. In any event, the saying in 12.16c, and its connection with the fear of God, was probably already on the minds of the Roman audience, for Paul had just cited a different version of LXX Proverbs 3.7a in Romans 11.25: μὴ ἦτε παρ' ἑαυτοῖς φρόνιμοι. The context here (11.25-32) links modest self-estimation and an appreciation for one's rational limitations with recognition of the power of God's mercy and wrath as they work themselves out in his impenetrable plan for salvation. Paul here, as elsewhere, strives to check any human confidence in rationally discerning God's plans and motives.[103] Thus by calling to mind the second line of LXX Proverbs 3.7, "fear God and refrain from evil," by citing the first, Paul indirectly suggests the issues raised in v. 19b (as well as vv. 17-19a).

Another, less text-centered, clue comes from v. 16b. Similar contrasts of the proud and mighty with the low and humble are made in biblical wisdom, often accompanied by a depiction of God's judgement and his doling out of rewards and punishments.[104] A few of these texts, for instance Proverbs 3.34 and Ben Sira 10.12-18, have already been discussed. As Käsemann argues, in a Christian environment this command "is a sign of the end-time which has dawned with the crucified Christ," and "entrance into the *basileia* is denied to those who do not perceptibly take their place here," i.e., with the lowly.[105] This idea stems from the perception of God as a righteous Lord who saves the oppressed and exalts the lowly while destroying oppressors and humiliating the arrogant. In biblical literature it is precisely the ταπεινοί whom God

---

[103] In addition to the commentaries see Johnson, *Apocalyptic and Wisdom Traditions*, 160-164. For other warnings against reliance on human wisdom in Paul's letters see esp. Romans 1.18-23, 2.17-24; 1 Corinthians 1.18-3.23; 2 Corinthians 10.4-6, 11.19.

[104] Cf. Schlier, *Römerbrief*, 380. For examples see below.

[105] Käsemann, *Romans*, 348.

characteristically judges favorably and rewards.[106] In a context like Romans, the injunctions in v. 16b would have clear eschatological overtones and would provide a natural corollary to a discussion of God's wrath and vengeance.[107] That Paul understood τὰ ὑψηλὰ φρονοῦντες in v. 16b as the opposite of fearing God is made explicit in the preceding chapter, Romans 11.20b-21, where Paul addresses the newly 'grafted' Gentile members in his audience:[108]

μὴ ὑψηλὰ φρόνει ἀλλὰ φοβοῦ·
εἰ γὰρ ὁ θεὸς τῶν κατὰ φύσιν κλάδων οὐκ ἐφείσατο,
μή πως οὐδὲ σοῦ φείσεται.
Do not think proud thoughts, but fear.
For if God did not spare the natural branches,
neither will he spare you.

In advocating φόβος, Paul draws on a strong strand of Jewish piety prominent in the wisdom tradition, the fear of the Lord as the beginning of wisdom.[109]

This suggests a final observation, that in the Jewish wisdom corpus a connection is generally drawn between humility and the fear of God. For the wise sages, intellectual self-determination and an over-reliance on one's rational abilities were inimical to trust in God. In comparison with God, the strength, understanding, and perspective of human beings are in fact extremely limited and so self-deception poses a constant danger.[110] The wise, therefore, readily acknowledge their utter dependence on God not only for guidance and enlightenment, but also for life itself. In wisdom literature the proud are consistently depicted as in opposition to God's will; their ὕβρις will be punished by God, in contrast to the reward that awaits the humble:[111]

---

[106] For references see Dunn, *Romans*, 2.747.

[107] In Isaiah 5 a comparable saying, in the form of a woe indictment (v. 21), is connected with an announcement of judgement (vv. 26-30).

[108] For ὑψηλός meaning proud, cf. Proverbs 17.16; Qohelet 7.9; 1 Timothy 6.17, etc.

[109] Any substantial treatment of the importance of "the fear of God" in Jewish wisdom, and the meaning of the concept, is impossible here. To "fear" God means to acknowledge his lordship and to respect his power and wisdom to judge. Those who are fearful, therefore, obey the law and refrain from sin, and so avoid God's wrath. Passages like Proverbs 10.29, 19.23, 24.21-22; Ben Sira 1.11-30, 2.1-18, etc. are typical; further, see Josef Haspecker, *Gottesfurcht bei Jesus Sirach: Ihre religiöse Struktur und ihre literarische und doktrinäre Bedeutung* (AnBib 30; Rome: Papal Biblical Institute, 1967) esp. 209ff., 313ff.; cf. von Rad, *Wisdom in Israel*, 53-73.

[110] Cf. Proverbs 3.5, 19.21, 20.9, 24, 21.2, 4, 30-31, 29.26; Tobit 4.19; *Derek Eres Zuta* 9.11; McKane, *Proverbs*, 495-496. Further see the references in n. 92.

[111] Cf. Proverbs 3.34, 11.2, 15.25, 33, 16.2, 5, 18, 18.12, 21.8, 28.13; Wisdom of Solomon 5.8ff.; Ben Sira 1.27-39, 2.17, 3.17-24, 7.16-17, 9.12, 10.6-18, 11.1-7, 14-26, 12.6, 16.5-16, 18.21, 21.4, 27.28, 35.14-26; Luke 6.36-45; James 1.9-10, 4.6, 10; 1 Peter

ὕβρις ἄνδρα ταπεινοῖ,
τοὺς δὲ ταπεινόφρονας ἐρείδει δόξῃ κύριος.
Hybris brings a man low,
but the Lord upholds the humble-minded with honor. [Proverbs 29.23]

The imagery of God's wrath and vengeance could also serve as the basis of concrete exhortation against arrogance, self-deceit, greed, impiety, vanity, and so forth:

μὴ ἔπεχε ἐπὶ τοῖς χρήμασίν σου
καὶ μὴ εἴπῃς Αὐτάρκη μοί ἐστιν.
μὴ ἐξακολούθει τῇ ψυχῇ σου καὶ τῇ ἰσχύι σου
πορεύεσθαι ἐν ἐπιθυμίαις καρδίας σου·
καὶ μὴ εἴπῃς Τίς με δυναστεύσει;
ὁ γὰρ κύριος ἐκδικῶν ἐκδικήσει.
...
μὴ ἀνάμενε ἐπιστρέψαι πρὸς κύριον
καὶ μὴ ὑπερβάλλου ἡμέραν ἐξ ἡμέρας·
ἐξάπινα γὰρ ἐξελεύσεται ὀργὴ κυρίου,
καὶ ἐν καιρῷ ἐκδικήσεως ἐξολῇ.
Rely not on your own wealth;
and say not: "Self-sufficiency is mine."
Do not follow your own soul and strength
in pursuing your heart's desires.
And say not, "Who can prevail against me?"
for the Lord will exact punishment.
...
Delay not your conversion to the Lord
and do not put it off from day to day;
for suddenly the Lord's wrath comes forth,
at the time of vengeance you will be destroyed. [Ben Sira 5.1-3, 7]

Thus we find entreaties not to behave arrogantly in one's dealings with other people, since this will not go unpunished by God:

μὴ προσλογίζου σεαυτὸν ἐν πλήθει ἁμαρτωλῶν·
μνήσθητι ὅτι ὀργὴ οὐ χρονιεῖ.
ταπείνωσον σφόδρα τὴν ψυχήν σου,
ὅτι ἐκδίκησις ἀσεβοῦς πῦρ καὶ σκώληξ.

3.8, 5.5; *Teachings of Silvanus* 88, 104, 108, 110-112, 114, 118.

> Reckon not yourself among the throng of sinners;
> remember that (God's) wrath will not delay.
> Humble your soul exceedingly,
> for the vengeance of the ungodly is fire and worms. [Ben Sira 7.16-17]

The fear of God's judgement and punishment also motivates realistic self-evaluation and humble repentance:

> πρὸ κρίσεως ἐξέταζε σεαυτόν,
> καὶ ἐν ὥρᾳ ἐπισκοπῆς εὑρήσεις ἐξιλασμόν.
> πρὶν ἀρρωστῆσαί σε ταπεινώθητι
> καὶ ἐν καιρῷ ἁμαρτημάτων δεῖξον ἐπιστροφήν.
> Before judgement examine yourself,
> and at the time of scrutiny you will find expiation.
> Before you get sick humble yourself
> and in the time of sins show repentance. [Ben Sira 18.20-21]

For the sapiential authors, humility was a combination of virtuous actions and attitudes concerning oneself as well as others, but it especially entailed total dependence on God. So, in conclusion, while the pairing of 12.16 with 12.19b-c does not depend upon some of the more obvious qualities such as formal analogy or material agreement discernible in the other pairs of the ring composition, the topics which they raise correspond with one another, and their association seems particularly apt in a sapiential environment. As we have seen, gnomic authors frequently connected appeals for humility and correct self-understanding with warnings to fear God's judgement and wrath. Thus the thoughts of v. 16 anticipate and agree with those in v. 19b-c logically and materially. In addition, there are several clues within 12.14ff. and its immediate context, such as the citation of LXX Proverbs 3.7a, which indicate that Paul may have had such a connection in mind and that his audience would expect and understand the association.

Romans 12.17-19

As in 12.9b-13 and 16a-b, Paul has organized the imperatival participles of vv. 17-19a in a thematic cluster and they should be read together as a unit. The four sayings are united by the topic of living peacefully with all people; many of the forms and concepts here are familiar from ancient wisdom, particularly Jewish wisdom. As indicated above, these verses form the center of the ring composition in 12.14-21 and may be arranged as follows (for translation see above):

v. 17a	E. μηδενὶ κακὸν ἀντὶ κακοῦ ἀποδιδόντες,
v. 17b	F. προνοούμενοι καλὰ
	G. ἐνώπιον πάντων ἀνθρώπων·
v. 18a	H. εἰ δυνατόν, τὸ ἐξ ὑμῶν,
v. 18b	G'. μετὰ πάντων ἀνθρώπων
	F'. εἰρηνεύοντες·
v. 19a	E'. μὴ ἑαυτοὺς ἐκδικοῦντες,

Appropriately enough, as the ring composition approaches the center, the construction becomes tighter, relying more on the correspondence of specific words and phrases. E and E' constitute complete sayings with very similar, indeed almost the same, content. Both are negatively-formulated, beginning with μη- and ending with an imperatival participle. In the chart, the other two admonitions, vv. 17b and 18b, have been divided in half in order to highlight how their literary structure contributes to the effect of the ring composition. Both are positively-formulated sayings containing an imperatival participle (F and F') plus the phrase πάντων ἀνθρώπων introduced by a preposition (G and G'). Again the two sayings are alike materially, with the reference to peace in v. 18b perhaps constituting a specification of καλός ("good," "noble") in v. 17b. The cluster, as well as the entire ring composition, centers on Paul's qualification εἰ δυνατόν, τὸ ἐξ ὑμῶν in v. 18a.

The parallels for 12.17a located in 1 Thessalonians 5.15a and 1 Peter 3.9 were documented above in the discussion of imperatival participles. The presence of numerous commands in the Jewish paraenetic tradition with only slightly different permutations indicates that Paul here cites some variation of a proverb.[112] A virtually identical injunction occurs in *Joseph and Aseneth* 28.4:

... μὴ ἀποδιδόντες κακὸν ἀντὶ κακοῦ τινι ἀνθρώπῳ.
... do not return evil for evil to any person.[113]

This admonition and others like it may ultimately stem from Proverbs 17.13: ὃς ἀποδίδωσιν κακὰ ἀντὶ ἀγαθῶν, οὐ κινηθήσεται κακὰ ἐκ τοῦ οἴκου αὐτοῦ ("Whoever returns evil for good, evil shall not be removed from his house"). This saying, in turn, forms part of the very large and varied group of

---

[112] So Piper, *Love Command*, 39, 49; Sauer, "Traditionsgeschichtliche Erwägungen," 20; Neirynck, "Paul and the Sayings of Jesus," 300.

[113] Text: Marc Philonenko, *Joseph et Aséneth: Introduction, Texte Critique, Traduction et Notes* (SPB 13; Leiden: Brill, 1968) 216; my translation.

injunctions against retaliation, violence, vengeance, unjust anger, and so forth in the gnomic literature of Judaism.[114] Numerous comparable materials may also be found in the sapiential literature of the ancient Near East and the Hellenistic world as well.[115]

The next admonition, v. 17b, is a reworking of LXX Proverbs 3.4, which Paul had quoted differently in a previous letter, 2 Corinthians 8.21:

LXX Proverbs 3.4	προνοοῦ καλὰ ἐνώπιον κυρίου καὶ ἀνθρώπων
2 Corinthians 8.21	προνοοῦμεν γὰρ καλὰ οὐ μόνον ἐνώπιον κυρίου ἀλλὰ καὶ ἐνώπιον ἀνθρώπων
Romans 12.17b[116]	προνοούμενοι καλὰ ἐνώπιον πάντων ἀνθρώπων

In all three passages the focus appears to be more on the need for sensitivity to the views of others than on active material provision; Christians are to be aware of what is considered morally upright by prevailing standards and to take thought for how their actions will effect and be evaluated by others.[117] While the meanings of the three maxims are alike, it seems that in Romans 12.17b Paul has deliberately changed the verb to a participle and removed ἐνώπιον κυρίου from the proverb as he had known it, adding πάντων. These alterations create

---

[114] Some examples: Proverbs 3.29-31, 12.16, 14.29, 15.1, 18, 16.32, 17.9, 11, 14, 19, 18.14, 18, 19.7, 19, 20.3, 21.14, 22.24, 24.17-22, 29, 25.9-10, 26.21, 27, 27.3-4, 29.8, 22; Pseudo-Phocylides 32-34, 63-64, 74-75, 77, 142-143, 151; Testament of Gad 6-7; *Joseph and Aseneth* 23.9, 28.10, 14, 29.3; *Epistula Aristeas* 227; *Derek Eres Rabbah* 2.1, 13; *Derek Eres Zuta* 1.7, 8.3; in Ben Sira see esp. 27.22-28.26, and Skehan and DiLella, *Ben Sira*, 359-367. Cf. the references cited above in nn. 110-111. Further von Rad, *Wisdom*, 83ff., 128ff.; Piper, *Love Command*, 19-65; also see the remarks below on Romans 12.19. For this theme in Christian wisdom see esp. Zeller (*Mahnsprüche*, 57-58, 104-106, 115-116) who cites various parallels (including many of those given here) for Matthew 5.39-41, 44-47, 7.1-5; cf. Sextus *Sententiae* 89, 96, 105, 183-184, 210-213, 324, 327, 343, 370, 386; Cleitarchus *Chreiai* 110.

[115] For example: Hesiod *Opera et Dies* 265-266, 327; Theognis 279-282, 325-328, 365-366, 833-836, 1029-1030, 1051-1054, 1133-1134, 1223-1224; Menander *Sententiae* 5, 19, 46, 99, 269, 604, 675; *Gnomologium Epictetum* 21, 25, 27; *Carmen Aureum* 9-11, 17-18; *Gnomologium Vaticanum* 1, 62; Publilius Syrus *Sententiae* 87-88, 110, 142-143, 241, 290, 311, 344-345, 548, 550, 599, 628, 643, 680, 702; *Dicta Catonis* 1.36, 4.34. Also the instructional literature: Ptahhotep 2-4, 6, 19; Amenemope 4.10-5.19, 22.1-23.11; Any 5.6-7, 6.15-7.4, 7.11-12, 8.12, 14-16; Ahiqar 123-124; Ankhsheshonqy 6.8, 12.16, 26.10; *P. Insinger* 3.20, 23, 19.22, 23.6, 27.7, 9, 29.12ff., 33.7ff.

[116] Under the influence of LXX Proverbs 3.4 and 2 Corinthians 8.21 several copyists have apparently attempted to harmonize Romans 12.17b by inserting either ἐνώπιον τοῦ θεοῦ (A¹) or οὐ μόνον ἐνώπιον τοῦ θεοῦ ἀλλὰ καί (F, G, etc.); cf. *TCGNT* 528.

[117] Romans 1.26, 28, 2.7, 10, 14.18; Galatians 6.10; Philippians 4.5, 8; Colossians 4.5; 1 Thessalonians 3.12, 4.12, 5.15; 1 Timothy 5.8; Titus 3.2; 1 Peter 2.12, 15. Further see Str-B 1.767-768, 3.299; cf. Philo *De Ebrietate* 84; *Aesopica Fabulae* 222.5 (p. 407 in Perry, *Aesopica*); also cf. Cranfield's translation of the saying, *Romans*, 2.645-646.

a catchword with v. 18b and contribute to the ring structure and thematic unity of vv. 17-19a. The omission of any reference to the Lord here also provides an element of suspense before the saying regarding revenge in v. 19b with its λέγει κύριος.[118] The thought of v. 17b has affinities in various wisdom texts; although the sages by no means commend conformism, they still express concern for the public welfare and understand the value of a good reputation.[119] The author of the Instruction of Ankhsheshonqy 17.26, like Paul, links such a concern with an injunction against anger: "Be small of wrath so that your reputation will be great in the hearts of all men."[120]

By means of the qualification in v. 18a, εἰ δυνατόν, τὸ ἐξ ὑμῶν ("if possible, so far as it depends on you"), Paul admits that harmonious living with others might not always be possible nor lie within the power of the members of the audience; they must be cognizant of their limitations as well as their responsibilities in working for peace. Significantly, v. 18a forms the center not only of the construction in vv. 17-19a but also of the larger ring composition in vv. 14-21. Just as the structure of the passage pinwheels on εἰ δυνατόν, τὸ ἐξ ὑμῶν, so too the interpretation and application of its injunctions depend upon the willingness and ability of the Roman congregations.[121] While this particular formulation is apparently unique, qualifications of this kind are by no means absent in gnomic wisdom, for example *Carmen Aureum* 6-8a:

πραέσι δ' εἶκε λόγοις ἔργοισί τ' ἐπωφελίμοισι.
μηδ' ἔχθαιρε φίλον σὸν ἁμαρτάδος εἵνεκα μικρῆς,
ὄφρα δύνηι·

---

[118] As Dunn (*Romans*, 2.750) notes, Paul in effect treats λέγει κύριος as part of the quotation and so "Lord" refers to God; perhaps the formula in this instance comes from Paul's source, whatever it may have been. Dunn, *loc. cit.*, refers to E. E. Ellis, *Paul's Use of the Old Testament* (Grand Rapids: Eerdmans, 1957) 107-112. For the progression of thought in v. 17 cf. 1 Thessalonians 5.15.

[119] Cf. Testament of Simeon 5.2-3; *Epistula Aristeas* 225, 232; Sextus *Sententiae* 16, 38, 51, 260; *Pirke 'Abot* 2.1, 3.13; *Derek Eres Zuta* 3.8; Theognis 213-218, 301-302, 309-312, 313-314, 1071-1074; Pseudo-Isocrates *Ad Demonicum* 16-17; Isocrates *Ad Nicoclem* 50-53; *Gnomologium Epictetum* 7, 67; *Gnomologium Vaticanum* 70; Publilius Syrus *Sententiae* 99; *Dicta Catonis* 1.31, 2.7, 29; Ptahhotep 14, 35; Amenemope 10.16-17. Further see Willem C. van Unnik, "Die Rücksicht auf die Reaktion der Nicht-Christen als Motiv in der altchristlichen Paränese," *Judentum, Urchristentum, Kirche: Festschrift für Joachim Jeremias* (ed. Walther Eltester; Berlin: Töpelmann, 1960) 498-522 [reprint, *Sparsa Collecta: The Collected Essays of Willem C. van Unnik* (NovTSup 29-31; 3 vols.; Leiden: Brill, 1973, 1980, 1983) 2.307-322]; Betz, *2 Corinthians 8 and 9*, 77 n. 306.

[120] Translation: Lichtheim, *Late Egyptian Wisdom*, 82.

[121] As Käsemann (*Romans*, 349) observes: "The individual is left unusual room to maneuver within the framework of his abilities and weaknesses."

Yield to gentle words and useful deeds,
and do not hate your friend for a small fault,
for long as you can.[122]

Related to commands of this sort are maxims in which the author explicitly identifies his gnomic assertions as a personal view and so appears to be quite self-conscious regarding their subjectivity. In many other cases gnomic wisdom is clearly intended as paradigmatic and so its counsel is qualified or limited in a certain way or contingent upon certain external factors. *Gnomologium Democrateum* 102 and Sextus *Sententiae* 381 provide two illustrations:

καλὸν ἐν παντὶ τὸ ἶσον·
ὑπερβολὴ δὲ καὶ ἔλλειψις οὔ μοι δοκέει.
Equal measure is good in everything;
but excess and deficiency are not--*it seems to me.*[123]

τιμᾷ θεὸν ἄριστα ὁ τὴν ἑαυτοῦ διάνοιαν
ἐξομοιώσας θεῷ εἰς δύναμιν.
He honors God best who conforms his mind to God
as far as possible.[124]

This reflects an understanding that the various applications of a gnomic saying become clear only in action, and that modifications or corrections are often necessary. Sometimes the ultimate meaning of a maxim is not immediately apparent but it becomes useful only at a later time and in a different situation.[125] Gnomic wisdom is goal-oriented but it admits of many alternative paths leading to these goals. Those who participate in gnomic traditions must therefore remain open-minded, leaving their options open in order to react to attendant circumstances. However, it would be incorrect to understand v. 18a as a mere qualification or an 'escape clause'. Rather, it underscores the challenge involved in what Paul says. The implementation of the instruction in 12.9-21 is not a matter of simply obeying a list of precepts or following a

---

[122] Text: Young, *Theognis*, 87; my translation.
[123] Text: Diels and Kranz, *Die Fragmente der Vorsokratiker*, 2.163.5-6; my translation; cf. 2 Corinthians 8.13-15; Betz, *2 Corinthians 8 and 9*, 67-70.
[124] Text and translation: Edwards and Wild, *The Sentences of Sextus*, 64-65. For some further examples see Proverbs 3.27-28; Menander *Sententiae* 825; Aristotle *Rhetorica* 2.21.5; *Anthologia Graeca* 9.54; Galatians 6.10; cf. Betz, *Galatians*, 310-311. Also cf. Plato's famous phrase κατὰ τὸ δυνατόν: *Cratylus* 422d, 435c, *Republic* 460a, 466d, *Symposium* 207d, *Timaeus* 46c, etc.
[125] Cf. Pseudo-Isocrates *Ad Demonicum* 44.

mechanistic routine; it rather rests upon the courage and imagination of the Romans. They must make a realistic assessment of the problems to be addressed and be aware of how much each of them can do and of what sorts of things they can change. The phrase reminds them that the actualization of Paul's ethical program is not automatic, but depends upon them.

The counterpart to v. 17b is v. 18b, μετὰ πάντων ἀνθρώπων εἰρηνεύοντες ("with all people living at peace"). No doubt among those things considered noble by all men is peace, and the ability to give forethought to the ideals of others can abet the peace process (cf. Romans 14.18-19).[126] A number of parallels for Paul's saying exist in related sapiential texts. First of all, the maxim is reminiscent of admonitions Paul had formulated in previous epistles, 1 Thessalonians 5.13b (εἰρηνεύετε ἐν ἑαυτοῖς) and 2 Corinthians 13.11 (εἰρηνεύετε). The εἰρην- stem also figures prominently in two wisdom sayings of the gospel tradition, Matthew 5.9a (μακάριοι οἱ εἰρηνοποιοί)[127] and Mark 9.50c (εἰρηνεύετε ἐν ἀλλήλοις), though direct influence of these sayings on Paul is unprovable. In Jewish-Christian circles the phrase διώκω εἰρήνην seems to have constituted an idiom, perhaps derived from LXX Psalm 33.15: ἔκκλινον ἀπὸ κακοῦ καὶ ποίησον ἀγαθόν, ζήτησον εἰρήνην καὶ δίωξον αὐτήν ("Refrain from evil and do good, seek peace and pursue it").[128] It is interesting to note that the psalmist here, like Paul, associates an appeal for peace with a protreptic maxim.[129] The presence of this and similar commands in Jewish and Christian sapiential sources indicates the prevalence of the ideal of peace among the sages.[130]

12.19a, μὴ ἑαυτοὺς ἐκδικοῦντες ("not taking you own revenge"), is a

---

[126] Cf. Michel, *Brief*, 276-277; Schmithals, *Kommentar*, 452-453.

[127] For more on this saying see Friedrich A. Strobel, "Die Friedenshaltung Jesu im Zeugnis der Evangelien," *ZEE* 17 (1973) 97-106; Rudolf Schnackenburg, "Die Seligpreisung der Friedensstifter (Mt 5,9) im mattäischen Kontext," *BZ* 26 (1982) 161-178; W. D. Davies and Dale C. Allison, *The Gospel According to Matthew, Volume 1* (ICC; Edinburgh: T. & T. Clark, 1988) 457-458; cf. LXX Psalm 33.14; Proverbs 10.10; James 3.18; *Pirke 'Abot* 1.12; Str-B 1.215-218.

[128] See Romans 14.19; 2 Timothy 2.22; Hebrews 12.14; 1 Peter 3.11; cf. Epictetus *Dissertationes* 4.5.24; Piper, *Love Command*, 13-14, 64, 112.

[129] Cf. above p 154.

[130] In biblical wisdom the word stem εἰρην- occurs frequently: Job 3.26, 5.23-24, 11.18, 15.21, 16.13; LXX Psalms 33.14, 36.11; Proverbs 3.2, 17, 23, 4.27, 12.20, 16.5, 17.1; Wisdom of Solomon 3.3, 14.22; Ben Sira 1.18, 6.6, 13.18, 26.2, 28.9, 13, 38.8, 41.1, 14, 44.6, 14, 45.24, 47.13, 16, 50.23; cf. Testament of Benjamin 5.1; James 3.17-18; *Derek Eres Rabbah* 2.17, 24; *Derek Eres Zuta* 9.12; Theognis 885; Stobaeus *Anthologium* 4.14, passim. Further see Gerhard von Rad and Werner Foerster, "εἰρήνη κτλ.," *TDNT* 2 (1964) 400-420; Erich Dinkler and Erika Dinkler-von Schubert, "Friede," *RAC* 8 (1972) 434-505; Spicq, *Notes*, 3.215-230; Hans-Werner Gensichen, Hans Heinrich Schmid, Werner Thießen, Gerhard Delling, and Wolfgang Huber, "Frieden," *TRE* 11 (1983) 599-646.

virtual re-wording of v. 17a; with ἐκδικέω there is the plain implication that a (real or perceived) wrong has been done for which one retaliates in order to exact revenge.[131] The injunction clearly depends upon what follows (ἀλλὰ κτλ.); thus vv. 19b-c express the motivation and result of v. 19a, and indeed of all of vv. 17-19a. We should take note, however, of the formal and material transition that takes place between vv. 17-19a and vv. 19b-c. First, the vocative ἀγαπητοί ("beloved"), unexpected to a certain extent in a gnomic composition of this type, creates something of an interruption.[132] Also, the aorist imperative δότε ("give"), the sense of which contrasts strongly with the preceding participles (the last of the chapter's imperatival participles occurs in v. 19a), indicates a change in the mode of exhortation and a break with vv. 17-19a. More conspicuous is the thematic transition, with both v. 19b and c referring clearly to divine vengeance; while the topic of non-retaliation continues here, the argument shifts from a discussion of the Romans' relationship with other people to their relationship with God.[133] As noted above, this command to give way to God's vengeance and to respect the divine prerogative to judge and punish forms a predictable corollary to the call for humility and self-criticism in v. 16, the verse's structural counterpart.

The repudiation of vengeance, often accompanied by a call to leave judgement and punishment to God, is common in sapiential sources.[134] Of course Paul's treatment of the topic represents something of a departure, especially in so far as it possesses an obvious eschatological orientation, in

---

[131] Cf. Cranfield, *Romans*, 2.645.

[132] The form of the direct address suggests an inclusio (of sorts) with ἀγάπη in 12.9a, with the central statement, 12.14, at the approximate center (note also that the two terms form a frame around the section's seventeen imperatival participles in vv. 9b-19a); Paul uses the term elsewhere in Romans in 1.7, 11.28, 16.5, 8, 9, 12; cf. Menander *Sententiae*, Fragment 7.9 (p. 11 in Jaekel, *Sententiae*); also cf. the use of τέκνα μου in the Testament of Naphtali 2.9-3.4. Further, Oda Wischmeyer, "Das Adjectiv ΑΓΑΠΗΤΟΣ in den paulinischen Briefen: Eine traditionsgeschichtliche Miszelle," *NTS* 32 (1986) 476-480.

[133] In addition to the commentaries see Simon Légasse, "Vengeance humaine et vengeance divine en Romains 12,14-21," *La Vie de la Parole: De l'Ancien au Nouveau Testament: Etudes d'exégèse et d'herméneutique bibliques offertes à Pierre Grelot* (ed. Departement des Etudes Bibliques de l'Institut Catholique de Paris; Paris: Desclée, 1987) 281-291. Note also the concentration of explicit scripture citations and the use of indicative verbs in vv. 19b-20 as compared with what precedes.

[134] In addition to the discussion that follows see the references above in nn. 114 and 115; also Lichtheim, *Late Egyptian Wisdom*, 37-43; Williams, *Those Who Ponder Proverbs*, 18-23; A. A. DiLella, "The Problem of Retribution in the Wisdom Literature," *The Rediscovery of Scripture: Biblical Theology Today* (Report of the 46th Meeting of the Franciscan Educational Conference; Burlington, Wisconsin: Franciscan Educational Conference, 1967) 109-127; von Lips, *Weisheitliche Traditionen*, 404-405. As noted above in Chapter Two, the theme of retribution is a preoccupation of many of the Jewish wisdom psalms.

accordance with its Christian setting.[135] At the same time, there are many clear similarities between Paul's command in 12.19b-c and the wisdom corpus. A number of the ancient gnomic sayings that reject retaliation also make appeals to trust in God's justice; others express the symmetry between act and consequence.

ὁ ἐκδικῶν παρὰ κυρίου εὑρήσει ἐκδίκησιν.
The vengeful will suffer vengeance from the Lord. [Ben Sira 28.1]

μὴ εἴπῃς Τείσομαι τὸν ἐχθρόν·
ἀλλὰ ὑπόμεινον τὸν κύριον, ἵνα σοι βοηθήσῃ.
Do not say, "I shall take vengeance on the enemy;"
but wait for the Lord so that he will help you. [Proverbs 20.9c]

Compare Pseudo-Phocylides 77 and Menander *Sententiae* 675, which do not appeal to divine power and authority:

μὴ μιμοῦ κακότητα, δίκῃ δ' ἀπόλειψον ἄμυναν.
Do not imitate evil, but leave vengeance to justice.[136]

πειρῶ βλάβην σὺ μᾶλλον ἢ δίκας ἔχειν.
Try to bear wrong rather than get redress.[137]

Similar advice occurs regularly in Near Eastern instructional texts, for instance the Instruction of Any 7.11-12, 8.14-16:

Don't ever talk back to your attacker,
Do not set a trap for him;
It is the god who judges the righteous,
His fate comes and takes him away.
...
Don't rush to attack your attacker,
Leave him to the god,
Report him daily to the god,

---

[135] On the eschatological basis of Paul's ethics see Furnish, *Theology*, 214-216; Schrage, *Ethics*, 181-186, and the references given there; also Charles K. Barrett, "Ethics and Eschatology: A Résumé," in Lorenzi, *Dimensions*, 221-235; Johnson, *Apocalyptic and Wisdom Traditions*, 55-109, 123-139. The merging of sapiential and eschatological perspectives is reflected in the synoptic tradition as well, see the references provided above p. 1 n. 2; cf. von Lips, *Weisheitliche Traditionen*, 69-92, 241-254.

[136] Text and translation: van der Horst, *Pseudo-Phocylides*, 92-93, cf. 166-167.

[137] Text: Jaekel, *Sententiae*, 72.

Tomorrow being like today,
And you will see what god does,
When he injures him who injures you.[138]

In the Instructions of Amenemope 4.10-17, a reminder of divine judgement against violence serves as motivation for specific recommendations against arguing with someone who is enraged:

Don't start a quarrel with a hot-mouthed man,
Nor needle him with words.
Pause before a foe, bend before an attacker,
Sleep (on it) before speaking.
A storm that bursts like fire in straw,
Such is the heated man in his hour.
Withdraw from him, leave him alone,
The god knows how to answer him.[139]

P. Insinger 33.8-13 provides another example; here the charge of impiety is explicitly connected with warnings against violence and vengeance:

Violent vengefulness against the god brings a violent death.
Vengefulness which is very powerful brings retaliation in turn.
The god does not forget, retaliation does not rest.
The impious man does not fear it,
retaliation does not become sated with him.
But gentleness toward the weak is on the way of the man of god.
He who is arrogant in the town is one who will be weak on its ground.[140]

Like Romans 12.9-21, this passage associates the repudiation of vengeance with exhortation to assist the unfortunate and to be humble.

As most commentators have observed, Paul probably derived the idiom διδόναι τόπον in 12.19b from Jewish wisdom, and it seems clear that the ensuing ὀργή denotes divine wrath.[141] The proof-text cited in support of this admonition, 12.19c, is a quotation of Deuteronomy 32.35. The citation deviates

---

[138] Translation: Lichtheim, *Ancient Egyptian Literature*, 2.140-142; cf. Zeller, *Mahnsprüche*, 104-106, 115-116.

[139] Translation: Lichtheim, *Ancient Egyptian Literature*, 2.150; cf. McKane, *Proverbs*, 574-575.

[140] Translation: Lichtheim, *Late Egyptian Wisdom*, 232; cf. Zeller, *Mahnsprüche*, 115-116; Kloppenborg, *The Formation of Q*, 180 n. 45.

[141] See esp. Ortkemper, *Leben aus dem Glauben*, 112-119, and the references provided there.

significantly from both the MT and the LXX versions but agrees with Hebrews 10.30a (minus the introductory and concluding formulas).[142] Perhaps Paul had access to a different text, though it is also possible that he knew and quoted the verse in this form as a proverbial saying, in a manner akin to the citations in 12.16c, 17a and b.

Romans 12.20-21

12.20 is a nearly exact citation of LXX Proverbs 25.21-22a; Paul writes ψώμιζε instead of the LXX's τρέφε. The opening ἀλλά, whose adversative force (if any) is unclear,[143] connects the proverb with the previous citation. In light of God's eschatological judgement, one should not merely abstain from vengeful acts but offer positive and appropriate assistance to others in need, even to enemies. This picks-up and intensifies the maxim in v. 15, the proverb's structural counterpart, by referring to more concrete actions and by recommending that they be done to enemies as opposed to just people in general; it also carries the thought forward by indicating the motivation and the result of such behavior. The scholarly debate over whether v. 20c conveys a positive or negative connotation is long and complex.[144] With the latter opinion, "coals of fire" refers to eschatological judgement. As John Piper argues, this interpretation may not be necessarily restricted to the perception of an ulterior motive behind the actions in v. 20a-b. In this case v. 20 would have the same meaning as v. 19.[145] If v. 20c is understood in the positive sense, which seems more likely, "coals of fire" is a proverbial expression for deep shame and remorse, and so anticipates v. 21. With this option the end of the actions in v. 20a-b is the reform of one's enemy and the possibility of reconciliation. As Dieter Zeller points out, such prudent counsel would be at

---

[142] It is also close to the Targum versions, in addition to the commentaries see Str-B 3.300-301.

[143] This confusion is reflected in some of the textual witnesses which replace ἀλλὰ ἐὰν with ἐὰν οὖν (D², etc.) or ἐὰν (P⁴⁶, D*, F, G, etc.).

[144] For example: Str-B 3.301-303; Spicq, *Agapè*, 2.155-156, 207-208; Stendahl, "Hate, Non-Retaliation, and Love," 343-355; William Klassen, "Coals of Fire: Sign of Repentance or Revenge?" *NTS* 9 (1962-63) 337-350; McKane, *Proverbs*, 591-592; Léonard Ramaroson, "Charbons ardents: 'sur la tête' ou 'pour le feu' (Prov 25.22a--Rom 12.20b)," *Biblica* 51 (1970) 230-234; Furnish, *Love Command*, 107-108; Cranfield, *Romans*, 2.648-650; Ortkemper, *Leben aus dem Glauben*, 119-123; Dunn, *Romans*, 2.750-751; Schmithals, *Kommentar*, 454-455.

[145] Piper, *Love Command*, 114-119.

home in a sapiential milieu, and this meaning certainly conforms better with the main thrust of the passage.[146]

Significantly, after citing LXX Proverbs 25.21-22a in Romans 12.20 almost verbatim, Paul opts not to include the final line of the traditional gnomic saying (LXX Proverbs 25.22b): ὁ δὲ κύριος ἀνταποδώσει σοι ἀγαθά ("and the Lord shall reward you with good"). In its place he offers a maxim of his own, v. 21: μὴ νικῶ ὑπὸ τοῦ κακοῦ ἀλλὰ νίκα ἐν τῷ ἀγαθῷ τὸ κακόν (" do not be overcome by what is bad, but overcome the bad with the good"). No doubt Paul's audience, who were thoroughly acquainted with the LXX, recognized the first three lines of the Jewish proverb cited in v. 20 and would have anticipated the fourth and concluding line (note the δέ in 25.22b). Thus the effect of Paul's substitution would have been felt immediately.[147] This sort of 'correction' or modification of a proverb or cliché was a common means of generating new gnomic sayings in the ancient world. Sapiential authors could employ such expressions of popular morality as a foil against which to highlight their own positions, often with a pronounced rhetorical effect.[148] Aristotle provides an example:

οὐδὲ τὸ μηδὲν ἄγαν· δεῖ γὰρ τούς γε κακοὺς ἄγαν μισεῖν.

Not "Nothing in excess," for one should hate at least the wicked in excess.[149]

The omission of LXX Proverbs 25.22b not only makes the formulation in v. 21 more striking, but also dramatizes the absence in the prescriptive section of any promise of personal benefits for those who accept instruction. In this respect Romans 12 is distinguished from all of the Hellenistic-Jewish texts surveyed in Chapter Three.

With respect to form, content, and function, the character of 12.21 appears fairly traditional, and its specific features are familiar from a number of other gnomic sayings. Comparison with the Testament of Benjamin 4.2-3, for instance, demonstrates the traditional paraenetic character of the contrast and

---

[146] Zeller, *Brief*, 211-213; cf. idem, *Mahnsprüche*, 104-106.

[147] It is interesting to note that both LXX Proverbs 25.22b and Romans 12.21 contain ἀγαθ-, though the term is employed in quite different ways.

[148] For various discussions of how gnomic authors adapted, modified, or corrected previous sayings see, for example, Bauckmann, "Die Proverbien und die Sprüche des Jesus Sirach," 33-63; McKane, *Proverbs*, 371ff.; van der Horst, *Pseudo-Phocylides*, 64-69; Lichtheim, *Late Egyptian Wisdom*, 35-37, 167-168; Skehan and DiLella, *Ben Sira*, 40-50; Crenshaw, *Ecclesiastes*, 36-37. Some further examples from Greco-Roman sources: Heraclitus 4, 29; *Gnomologium Vaticanum* 59; *Anthologia Graeca* 9.379; Quintilian *Institutio Oratoria* 6.3.96-98.

[149] Aristotle *Rhetorica* 2.21.14; text: Freese, *Rhetoric*, 286; my translation; cf. Solon 1.

the demand that Paul makes here:

ὁ ἀγαθὸς ἄνθρωπος οὐκ ἔχει σκοτεινὸν ὀφθαλμόν·
ἐλεᾷ γὰρ πάντας, κἂν ὦσιν ἁμαρτωλοί·
κἂν βουλεύωνται περὶ αὐτοῦ εἰς κακά,
οὗτος ἀγαθοποιῶν νικᾷ τὸ κακόν, σκεπαζόμενος ὑπὸ τοῦ ἀγαθοῦ·
τοὺς δὲ δικαίους ἀγαπᾷ ὡς τὴν ψυχὴν αὐτοῦ.

The good man has not a dark eye;
for he shows mercy to all men, even though they are sinners;
even though they devise to do him harm,
by doing good he overcomes the evil, because he is shielded by the good.
But he loves the righteous as his own soul.[150]

Significantly, the context here relates the ideal of overcoming evil by doing good with the more concrete objective of responding positively to enemies, just as Paul does in 12.14-21. Both passages also somehow connect these ethical aspirations with ἀγάπη.

With respect to its literary structure, v. 21 also corresponds with various gnomic texts, and a number of other maxims also take advantage of similar sorts of word-play, or paronomasia, for instance Sextus *Sententiae* 165b:

ὁ νικῶν τῷ ἀπατᾶν νικᾶται ἐν ἤθει.
Whoever wins with deception is conquered in integrity.[151]

In addition, 12.21 also bears strong resemblance to the culminating exclamation, or ἐπιφώνημα, recommended by the rhetorical handbooks and popular with Latin orators.[152] The author of the *Rhetorica ad Alexandrum* instructs his students to conclude each sub-section of their oration with a concise and definite conclusion: "This is the way you must connect one division with another and keep up the thread of your speech."[153] While the ἐπιφώνημα may take a number of different forms, the most striking are often maxims. Comparable summarizing maxims were also detected in LXX Proverbs 3.35 and Ben Sira 6.37 (cf. Pseudo-Phocylides 95-96). These statements not only

---

[150] Text: de Jonge, *Testaments*, 170-171; translation: Hollander and de Jonge, *Commentary*, 420, cf. 421-423; also 1QS 10.17-18; Michel (*Brief*, 279 n. 3) and Schlier (*Römerbrief*, 384) also cite Polyaenus *Strategemata* 5.12; cf. Berger, "Hellenistische Gattungen," 1060-1061.

[151] Text and translation: Edwards and Wild, *The Sentences of Sextus*, 34-35. Cf. 1 Corinthians 14.38; Sextus *Sententiae* 43, 393; Solon 10; *Gnomologium Democrateum* 125; *Gnomologium Epictetum* 29; Publilius Syrus *Sententiae* 50.

[152] Cf. the discussion in Chapter Two; also Demetrius *De Elocutione* 2.106-110.

[153] Pseudo-Aristotle *Rhetorica ad Alexandrum* 39a8-39b2.

recapitulate the main theme of the section, but drive it home in a memorable way.

Concluding Remarks

In concluding the analysis of Romans 12.9-21, the unity inherent in the passage ought to be emphasized. As most commentators note, 12.21, on account of its epigrammatic composition and striking contrast, rounds of the paragraph very effectively. The strong antithetical thrust of v. 21 recalls v. 14, its structural counterpart, and the two maxims are alike formally.[154] What v. 14 had stated in vivid, particular terms v. 21 summarizes with broad language that suggests the ultimate implications involved. The formulation of v.21 is also reminiscent of the protreptic maxim in 12.9b and so serves as a framing device, summarizing and concluding not only the ring composition in 12.14-21, but also the entire prescriptive section. Indeed, though there are important variations in the actual terminology and specific ideas, the contrast of good and evil has been a consistent formal and ethical consideration, and its presence at key junctures--vv. 9b, 14, 17, and 21--serves to bind the section together. These antitheses, in conjunction with a number of other structural and stylistic devices described above, function to unify the passage from a literary standpoint.

These observations regarding the formal features of Romans 12.9-21 are also consistent with its thematic integrity and the organic quality of its argument. Although the individual admonitions in 12.9-21 are varied and more-or-less detachable, and the logical connection from one exhortation to the next can be somewhat loose or abrupt, all these ideas and injunctions are meant to be understood together and in light of one another, contributing to a single theme, namely Paul's appeal for the Romans to love without pretense. Thus the maxims that address relations within the church stand alongside those concerning outsiders, and the more-or-less conventional appeals for solidarity, sympathy, and modesty mesh with the more striking and difficult commands to bless persecutors and to return good for evil. In addition, certain shifts in Paul's flow of thought, for instance between 12.13 and 12.14, or 12.16 and 12.17, should not be interpreted as logical disruptions of the general theme;

---

[154] Cf. Matthew 5.41 / Luke 6.29, though these verses should not be construed as a source for 12.21; see the discussion of 12.14 above; cf. Sauer, "Traditionsgeschichtliche Erwägungen," 24-27; Neirynck, "Paul and the Sayings of Jesus," 302.

rather all the admonitions contribute to Paul's depiction of genuine ἀγάπη and the far-ranging implications which this has for everyday Christian life. As Paul shows, ἀγάπη has ramifications for one's relations with other Christians, with outsiders and non-believers, with enemies and persecutors, and with God; it effects one's self-understanding as well. In all these respects ἀγάπη remains constant, positive, and selfless. Paul did not view Christian life as divided neatly into different sets of attitudes and obligations appropriate to different types of people or situations. Nor did he have any thought of the Roman Christians compartmentalizing their lives into spiritual and ordinary matters, or of conducting their affairs cut off from involvement with the wider community. The same unpretentious concern and positive outgoing love must therefore be the fundamental moral imperative in all situations, and above all in the most demanding ones, otherwise it is not love at all. This type of love does not reckon on personal gain or aggrandizement or on receiving a positive response in turn. Its motivation, rather, is God's will and God's love, which manifests itself in the lives of those who have been declared righteous.

The unity discernible in Romans 12.9-21 in terms of its structure, theme, function, and mode of argumentation indicates that to a significant extent the passage possesses a literary and material integrity beyond the role it plays as the prescriptive section in what was called 'Paul's sapiential discourse on Christian ethics' in Chapter Three. In addition to this, and as demonstrated above, it is also possible to analyze 12.9-21 as a self-contained literary unit, in which case 'Paul's gnomic exhortation on love' might be an appropriate title for its contents. Because Paul's message here seems to defy classification as any one of the particular genres surveyed in Chapter Two, a general term such as 'gnomic exhortation' is apt; its broadness allows for the fact that the passage shares features with all three of the prominent gnomic genres and that it is situated in a larger literary context (i.e., Paul's letter to the Romans) that is not generically gnomic and that is not primarily sapiential in nature. Approaching Romans 12.9-21 from these different perspectives shows how the argument of the passage operates on various levels, a feature that contributes to its literary and rhetorical sophistication.

Conclusion

The investigation of Paul's gnomic wisdom against the background of ancient sapiential traditions has taken into account a fairly wide range of issues concerning the comparative materials as well as analyzing in some detail the ethical, literary, and rhetorical characteristics of Romans 12.9-21. At this point it is possible to summarize the results and briefly ponder some of the wider implications of the study for our understanding of Romans 12 and of Pauline ethics and literature.

At the outset I suggested that an analysis of Paul's gnomic wisdom could be of use in clarifying a number of the problematic literary and ethical features of his letters as well as in providing a more precise description of his relationship with ancient wisdom traditions. It was noted that although Paul's gnomic formulations often figure prominently in his ethical thought they have generated only scant scholarly interest. A relatively long and complex gnomic passage from Paul's most important surviving letter, Romans 12.9-21, was selected for investigation. It was suggested that by better understanding the nature of the formal and material relationship of the passage with ancient sapiential texts it would be possible to describe more precisely its literary and rhetorical characteristics and the manner in which it has been integrated into the larger argumentative structure of the epistle.

In order to address these problems, it was necessary to begin by exploring some of the essential prior issues associated with the investigation of ancient gnomic sources. The first topic of inquiry was the gnomic saying itself, its range of characteristic functions and structures. It appears that the composition and use of gnomic wisdom were prominent aspects of life in the ancient world. This was due, in part, to the fact that the maxim is not a strictly limited literary category but rather a flexible and multi-faceted form of communication. Thus it shares something morphologically and functionally with such related forms as the proverb, chreia, epigram, aphorism, precept, and so forth. On account of their piquancy, insight, and utility, maxims are readily transferred from one culture or time to another, and so they often constitute an essential element of traditional morality. By virtue of their specificity of imagery and subject matter and their generally flexible and open stance, maxims do not represent moral rules or laws, but rather paradigmatic ethical assertions limited in application or contingent upon certain factors. Generally, a gnomic formulation is not appropriate for every comparable situation in the same way or to the same degree, and so an amount of tentativeness and subjectivity comes into play when considering the composition, application, and interpretation of gnomic sentences. The gnomic style therefore invites ethical criticism and rational reflection, and possesses both decidedly rhetorical and heuristic aspects. Another characteristic of the gnomic style is the relatively international character and universal appeal it enjoys on both the ideational and argumentative levels. Such features were readily observable in the discussion of the morphology of Hellenistic maxims, where we observed numerous structural and rhetorical similarities in maxims of far-ranging dates, provenances, and contexts.

The second important prior issue concerning gnomic wisdom is its use in developing and supporting larger ethical exhortations and arguments and the sorts of texts in which it is characteristically employed. There are in fact a variety of ways in which maxims may be integrated into larger contexts and combined with non-gnomic forms to create more complex literary units, and the authors of numerous types of ancient literary genres utilize the gnomic style. Thus gnomic wisdom may play a role in all sorts of non-sapiential forms of communication--speeches and letters for instance. Of particular interest for the analysis of Romans 12.9-21, however, are the three main sapiential genres that are distinguished by their utilization of gnomic wisdom: gnomic poetry, gnomologia, and wisdom instruction. As the surveys in Chapter Two indicate, these were prevalent modes of gnomic communication, and it is possible to identify Greek, Jewish, and Near Eastern examples for each of them. The primary representatives of gnomic poetry are sapiential hymns and didactic poems; these compositions are highly artistic as well as unified, and they address universal ethical issues, combining maxims with other poetic forms and techniques. Gnomologia refer to loosely organized anthologies of maxims, often with no logical principle of organization or unifying ethical perspective. Instructional texts, prevalent especially in the ancient Near East, are didactic prose compositions with relatively coherent overall structures; they are usually divided into topical units that combine wisdom admonitions with other paraenetic forms. As we saw, these three genres demonstrate numerous similarities with regard to subject matter, morphology, setting, and function. So, in practice, generic identification can often prove difficult and a number of texts are best understood as 'hybrid' forms. The considerable diversity these genres may exhibit with respect to the larger literary contexts and rhetorical situations in which they are utilized was also noted.

In the second part of the investigation, Romans 12 was examined, beginning with analysis of the broader characteristics of 12.1-21 and then proceeding to consider the specific features of the gnomic passage in 12.9-21. In Chapter Three, the nature of the literary design and mode of argumentation of Romans 12 was shown to be comparable in many respects with that of the four so-called sapiential discourses, Hellenistic-Jewish texts that conform in varying degrees to one or more of the gnomic genres of antiquity. These four discourses resemble each other and Romans 12.1-21 in a number of ways, but above all in the structure and function of their three main formal divisions, which may be labelled the programmatic statement, the descriptive section, and the prescriptive section. Within each of these sub-divisions further formal and rhetorical features were also identified and described. These underscore the organic quality of Romans 12 and the linear nature of Paul's message. Thus 12.9-21 is not merely an isolated sequence of maxims, but is intended to be interpreted and applied in light of the appeal of the entire chapter.[1] An important aspect of the evaluation is that it explains the morphological and rhetorical characteristics of the passage, as well as its interaction with its literary context, in terms of sources that comprise part of Paul's pertinent historical environment. The chapter concludes by suggesting that on account of the nature of its message and the extent of its similarities with the four Hellenistic-Jewish sapiential discourses, an appropriate designation for Romans 12.1-21 might be 'Paul's sapiential discourse on Christian ethics'.

Chapter Four considered in greater detail the specific gnomic features and special exegetical problems connected with Romans 12.9-21, a passage exhibiting strong contacts with the gnomic literature with respect to its literary, material, and rhetorical complexion as well as the nature of its constituent parts. One especially noteworthy feature of the passage is the use of ring composition in 12.14-21. This literary device, a regular one in gnomic materials, structures the thought of the passage and shows how v. 14 governs its tone and direction. In addition to the compositional unity of 12.14-21, these verses are thematically coherent in a manner that is intelligible in light of the gnomic literature. As we observed, the most prominent topics here--non-retaliation, the fear of God, and humility--are also employed together in numerous other gnomic passages from antiquity, and they constitute an effective message that supports and expands upon the overarching theme of ἀγάπη.

The evidence suggests, then, that the argument of Romans 12.9-21 is carefully designed and that the passage contributes to the literary character of the epistle in a unique way. From both literary and ideational standpoints the

---

[1] Further see above pp. 147-148.

composition of the passage is unified and sophisticated. This internal unity indicates that, in addition to contributing to the chapter as a whole, the passage may also be understood as a self-contained unit, which one might call 'Paul's gnomic exhortation on love'.[2] Of course, the gnomic sayings here do not constitute a systematic treatment of ἀγάπη, much less Pauline ethics, yet neither are they simply a random assortment of moral precepts grouped under a common theme. Rather, in formulating his ethical message to the Romans, Paul has availed himself of some of the more advanced ideas and methods familiar to us from the sources of Hellenistic-Jewish wisdom, a religious, ethical, and literary tradition of decided importance to Paul as well as to his congregations. Thus it seems warranted to understand Romans 12.9-21 as on the same level of literary and material quality as comparable passages in, say, Ben Sira or Pseudo-Phocylides. At the same time, many of the features of Paul's gnomic wisdom (like that of his Hellenistic-Jewish counterparts) have significant analogues in the sapiential literature of the wider Hellenistic world. The substance and style of Paul's exhortation to the Romans conform to a large extent with the prevalent ethical expectations of contemporary Hellenistic culture, and there is much that is not exclusive to Jewish or Christian ethical thought. Thus, on a presuppositional level, both the mode of communication employed and many of the specific ideas and forms are broad-based and far-reaching, and would have been meaningful to Gentiles as well as Jews.

Generically, Romans 12.9-21 approximates some of the topical paragraphs observed in wisdom instruction, though, as we saw, it also resembles certain gnomic poems in tone and content (e.g. LXX Psalm 36), and it shares certain features familiar from the ancient gnomic anthologies as well. Thus the passage's similarities with the gnomic genres are not restricted to any particular one, but rather it seems to take advantage of certain ideas and methods common to them all. Because of this, to classify 12.9-21 as any one of these generic categories would involve a certain amount of imprecision. It should also be noted in this regard that 12.9-21 is not itself an independent, unattached text, but is embedded within a larger text (Paul's epistle to the Romans) which has its own genre, a genre that is not gnomic or sapiential. So rather than classifying the passage generically, it seems more useful to consider its gnomic style and its use of gnomic conventions, and leave the discussion of generic identification to analysis of the letter as a whole.

It should be emphasized that Paul's teaching here does not consist of his handing down *verbatim* some tried-and-true proverbs or of imitating the

---

[2] Further see above pp. 198-199.

structure or message of a well-known gnomic text.[3] His level of participation in the sapiential traditions and conventions goes far beyond quoting isolated sayings from Jewish or Christian sources; it extends to the level of composing fairly long and sophisticated ethical arguments of his own creation while making use of ideas and methods that are international in scope. It appears that for Paul, gnomic wisdom was not merely a convenient fund of popular, standardized ethical advice to be arbitrarily appended at the conclusion of a letter. He is, in fact, actively engaged in the critical interpretation and application of certain traditional gnomic sources, forms, structures, and so forth, as well as in the integration of these familiar exhortatory conventions with innovations of his own.

These distinctions or 'advancements' evident in Paul's exhortation in Romans 12.9-21 occur on various levels of the text's composition and message. So with respect to individual maxims, for example, we may find Paul on occasion directly quoting a proverbial saying (e.g. 12.20), at other points alluding to or modifying sayings (e.g. 12.17b), and in still other places he apparently composes new gnomic utterances (e.g. 12.9a). Similar observations may be made with respect to the overall composition of the section; while the nature of its argumentative strategy is plainly comparable to that of Hellenistic-Jewish wisdom, Romans 12.9-21 does depart from the patterns observed there in certain regards. Thus, for instance, the apostle's exhortation lacks any explicit reference to the personal awards that await the obedient, a feature which appears to be standard in the four Jewish sapiential discourses. This distinctive feature conforms with the more basic theological aspects of Paul's presentation of his gospel in the epistle, contributing to his broader theological aims. And finally, of course, all the various gnomic contents of the section are refocused and redirected in so far as they serve together to portray Paul's understanding of ἀγάπη and must be interpreted and applied in light of the basic concepts that he articulates in the programmatic statement (vv. 1-2) and descriptive section (vv. 3-8); these concepts, in turn, rest upon theological presuppositions substantiated previously in the letter. In these respects Paul's style is much like that of the gnomic authors discussed in Chapters Two and Three. These writers, while depending extensively on traditional sources and conventions, conditioned and refocused their materials in order to suit their specific literary or rhetorical requirements, and they felt free to borrow regularly from sources from outside their immediate cultural or literary milieu.

---

[3] It would be incorrect, of course, to suppose that at any point in his correspondence Paul simply absorbs traditional material into his exhortations uncritically; for a broader treatment of this issue see Furnish, *Theology*, 25-92.

Another significant feature of Paul's gnomic exhortation in Romans 12 is that it is not rhetorically isolated or logically inappropriate with respect to the epistle as a whole. Rather, it is clear that 12.9-21 has been carefully integrated into both its larger paraenetic and apologetic contexts in such a way that the passage is relevant to Paul's fundamental objectives in writing the letter.

The chapter serves first of all as a general material and hermeneutical foundation for chapters 13-15, in which Paul addresses specific ethical issues and controversies that would have been of particular interest to the Roman Christians as he understands their situation. As we have seen above, in this introductory function Romans 12 is analogous to the four Jewish sapiential discourses surveyed in Chapter Three, especially Ben Sira 6.18-37. Thus the paraenetic material in Romans 13-15 must be interpreted in light of the fundamental principles outlined by Paul in chapter 12, beginning with the sacrifice and renewal concepts of vv.1-2, the self-understanding of the Christian community as the body of Christ expressed in vv. 3-8, and ἀγάπη as the fundamental moral imperative of Christian conduct in vv. 9-21. In chapter 12 Paul lays the groundwork for the paraenesis that follows, establishing his ethical presuppositions and underscoring the ideals and objectives he shares with the audience. In this way he endeavors to establish guidelines and priorities that will govern the Romans' future behavior and to bring them to an improved understanding that will inform their ethical outlook and decision-making. In connection with this it should be noted that our results concerning the gnomic complexion of chapter 12 and its relationship with the material that follows raises the further question of the extent to which Paul's paraenesis in chapters 13-15 has been conditioned by sapiential ideas and methods. Some indications of this influence may be found in the employment of gnomic sayings in 13.7, 14.7, and 22b, as well as in the sapiential characteristics of Paul's appeal in 13.1-7 and 16.17-20.[4]

The chapter also contributes to the apologetic function of the letter by revealing the nature of Paul's ethics in a way that would have been intelligible and persuasive especially to Jewish, but also to Gentile members of the audience. By designing and presenting the gnomic wisdom in Romans 12.9-21 as he has, Paul demonstrates a fundamental connection of his ethical program with Judaism, particularly with its wisdom traditions. In this way he shows how his theology presupposes a strong moral basis and implies a committed and

---

[4] Cf. Romans 13.8, 14.19. On 16.17-20, in addition to the commentaries, see Walter Schmithals, "The False Teachers of Romans 16.17-20," in *Paul and the Gnostics* (Nashville: Abingdon, 1972) 219-238.

concrete moral strategy for Christian living. He thus anticipates and counters any notions circulating among the Roman Christians that, because it does not accept the Jewish law as its norm of ethical conduct, his gospel lacks a proper moral standard and agenda, and so entails the abandonment of Judaism. In this regard the exhortation in Romans 12 develops out of and supports the preceding discussions concerning Judaism, particularly in chapters 9-11, where Paul affirms to the Roman Christians his understanding of Israel's role in God's plan of salvation and recommends to the congregations there the crucial relevance of Israel's experience and testimony.[5] Paul demonstrates this relevance and extends its application in this paraenetic passage through the high concentration of citations and motifs familiar from Jewish sapiential sources as well as the Jewish nature of the chapter's composition and style.

A related component of Paul's theological argument in Romans is his assault on any ethnic, cultural, or national exclusivism deriving from possession and observance of the Jewish law. For Paul there is no place for presumptuousness or particularism on the part of Jews and Jewish-Christians over against Gentiles on the basis of any assumed special status. God's mercy and the possibility for righteousness are available to all those who accept Christ, Jews and Gentiles alike. Significantly, in critiquing certain aspects of Jewish ethical practice, Paul draws from a wisdom tradition within Judaism itself that is always looking beyond the boundaries of its own religious experience for insight from other cultures. So, to an extent, Paul's exhortation becomes part of an ongoing ethical critique within the Jewish wisdom traditions of the particularistic and legalistic features of Jewish religion. In Romans 12 Paul demonstrates that his ethical program does not involve a wholesale rejection of Judaism, but is predicated to a significant extent upon the Jewish heritage of moral values and beliefs as expressed in the authoritative texts and traditions of wisdom. At the same time, Paul's gnomic wisdom (like that of Judaism) contains many widely-recognized principles dealing with the basic issues of human existence and is formulated by means of a relatively cross-cultural means of communication. So, although it is principally Jewish in nature, Paul's paraenesis in Romans 12 has appeal and application that extend to the Gentile members of his audience. In this respect the substance and purpose of his gnomic wisdom correspond to the universal scope of his mission and gospel as described throughout the epistle to the Romans.

In accomplishing these objectives, the ethical exhortation of chapter 12

---

[5] There are clearly certain sapiential features in Romans 9-11 as well, esp. the hymn in 11.33-36, which immediately precedes chapter 12; see Johnson, *Apocalyptic and Wisdom Traditions*, 123-175, and the sources cited there; also Dunn, *Romans*, 2.697.

contributes in turn to Paul's broader apologetic objective in the epistle of providing for the Roman Christians a carefully constructed and relatively thorough treatment of his theology, responding to real or potential criticisms of himself and of the fundamental purpose of his ministry. In doing so, he offers the Romans a self-portrait of his *ethos*--his moral character and integrity--as a Christian apostle. As the argument of the epistle demonstrates, Paul views himself both as a bearer of traditional Jewish moral values and as an ethical role-model for his audience. In connection with this, Romans 12 contributes to Paul's rhetorical self-presentation as an instructor of Jewish (or Jewish-Christian) wisdom and demonstrates his acknowledgement of the responsibility he shares for the moral development of the Christians in Rome. Thus in Romans 12 Paul defines and asserts one aspect of his role as a leader and teacher in the Christian church.

A final observation regarding the purpose of Romans 12.9-21 concerns Paul's understanding and presentation of ἀγάπη itself. In so far as Paul's gnomic exhortation depicts some of the positive ethical features and implications of love and holds it up as an ideal to which the Roman Christians should aspire, 12.9-21 possesses epideictic as well as deliberative and apologetic functions. In this regard, the passage is somewhat comparable to Paul's 'hymn to love' in 1 Corinthians 13,[6] though there are a number of important differences between the two texts that ought to be emphasized. 1 Corinthians 13, in keeping with its hymnic design and style, is highly descriptive, making extensive use of such features as comparison, personification, and first-person expressions. It strives to develop in the audience a more profound appreciation for the general qualities of ἀγάπη, particularly as it relates to relationships within the church. By demonstrating its superior characteristics, the hymn encourages the audience to participate in the praise of love, and to embrace it as their highest aspiration. While Romans 12.9-21 also has as its theme ἀγάπη, its tone and style are decidedly more exhortatory and argumentative. Here Paul emphasizes the implications of love for daily conduct, and shows how it entails specific ethical responsibilities both inside and outside of the Christian community. Thus Paul's gnomic exhortation on love articulates an ethical policy or program, and, as befits its own rhetorical character, goes beyond the hymn to cultivate in the audience practical perspectives and strategies for ethical decision-making.

To sum up: Romans 12.9-21 is not a random assortment of common precepts and admonitions, but shows signs of being carefully designed and

---

[6] This text demonstrates certain connections with the sapiential traditions of Hellenistic-Judaism as well; see Conzelmann, *1 Corinthians*, 217-231, with references.

integrated by Paul into the epistle. The literary, rhetorical, and material characteristics of the passage are for the most part familiar from the gnomic wisdom of Hellenistic Judaism, though in form and content it participates in the far larger arena of literary and ethical conventions associated with ancient sapiential literature as a whole. Finally, Paul's employment of gnomic wisdom at this juncture of the epistle contributes to its discernible rhetorical and theological objectives in a logical and effective manner.

While it may be possible to take these observations concerning the nature of Paul's participation in the conventions of gnomic wisdom both as evidence of his abilities as a gnomic author and of the meaning of the gnomic style for his ethics in general, it should be emphasized that the conclusions drawn here regarding his gnomic wisdom are based upon analysis of a limited (though important) sample and may be extended to other portions of the Pauline corpus only with considerable care.[7] A thorough treatment of the significance of gnomic wisdom for Paul's ethics and theology would have to take into account not only comparable gnomic paragraphs such as Galatians 5.25-6.10[8] and 1 Thessalonians 5.13b-22,[9] but also the larger paraenetic contexts in which these passages are situated. It would also have to consider Paul's use of isolated wisdom sentences in various contexts and situations.[10] It still remains to be seen whether these gnomic formulations exhibit the same Jewish character and the

---

[7] The findings of this study tend to corroborate the work of certain New Testament scholars, Hans Dieter Betz in particular, who have argued that Paul avails himself of this mode of paraenesis elsewhere in his correspondence; for Betz's contributions see the references above p. 4 n. 8.

[8] On this passage see esp. Betz, *Galatians*, 23, 291-311; also Bernard H. Brinsmead, *Galatians: Dialogical Response to Opponents* (SBLDS 65; Chico, CA: Scholars, 1982) 163-181; Gerhard Ebeling, *The Truth of the Gospel: An Exposition of Galatians* (trans. David Green; Philadelphia: Fortress, 1985) 259-261; Günther Klein, "Werkruhm und Christusruhm im Galaterbrief und die Frage nach einer Entwicklung des Paulus: Ein hermeneutischer und exegetischer Zwischenruf," *Studien zum Text und zur Ethik des Neuen Testaments: Festschrift zum 80. Geburtstag von Heinrich Greeven* (ed. Wolfgang Schrage; Berlin, New York: de Gruyter, 1986) 196-211; John M. G. Barclay, *Obeying the Truth: A Study of Paul's Ethics in Galatians* (SNTW; Edinburgh: T. & T. Clark, 1988) 146-177.

[9] See Béda Rigaux, *Saint Paul. Les Epîtres aux Thessaloniciens* (EBib; Paris: Gabalda; Gembloux: Duculot, 1956) 575-602; Traugott Holtz, *Der erste Brief an die Thessalonicher* (EKKNT 13; Zürich: Benziger; Neukirchen-Vluyn: Neukirchener Verlag, 1986) 239-269; Bruce C. Johanson, *To All the Brethren: A Textlinguistic and Rhetorical Approach to 1 Thessalonians* (CB.NT 16; Stockholm: Almqvist & Wiksell, 1987) 136-142. For an overview of recent scholarship see Raymond F. Collins, *Studies on the First Letter to the Thessalonians* (BETL 66; Leuven: Leuven University Press, 1984) 3-75, esp. 63-69; Wolfgang Trilling, "Die beiden Briefe des Apostels Paulus an die Thessalonicher: Eine Forschungsübersicht," *ANRW* II.25.4 (1987) 3365-3403.

[10] For a list of these maxims see above p. 4 n. 6.

same degree of literary and material sophistication as Romans 12.9-21, though there are important indications that this is the case. With these caveats in mind, our study can draw to an end by suggesting in what further ways gnomic wisdom might have constituted an appropriate and effective component of Paul's ethical thought.

As the introductory chapters above have shown, on the whole gnomic wisdom addresses specific issues or instances of ethical behavior while conveying a hermeneutic that is more-or-less self-consciously paradigmatic and flexible. A mode of exhortation with such qualities must have been of use to Paul and other early Christians as they tried to address the concrete development of their new lives without resorting to the enumeration of specific duties or inclusive codes of conduct.[11] As I have argued, while Romans 12.9-21 represents largely typical or traditional paraenesis as it is frequently understood, the section is on the whole relevant to the special objectives of the epistle.[12] This does not mean, however, that we should construe each detail of the passage as a direct reflection of Paul's perception of the historical situation in Rome in the same way as, say, chapters 13-15 do.[13] Thus there is no reason to suppose that Paul had any special reason to instruct the Romans to bless persecutors, for instance, or to weep with those who weep. Rather, the particular commands expressed in gnomic form illustrate the sorts of ethical responsibilities and perspectives which Paul attributes generally to ἀγάπη and which he implores the Roman Christians to accept as valid and to inculcate into their lives. Here Paul suggests different types of behavior appropriate in a range of areas of Christian life while conveying an ethical program that is neither axiomatic nor automatic.

The gnomic features of the exhortation in this passage also demonstrate how Paul's ethics are both communicable and verifiable by means of concrete actions and obligations. Of course specific acts do not in themselves constitute evidence of the new life in Christ; rather the gnomic style underscores the fact that Christian ethics must be experiential and pragmatic. So although in Romans 12 Paul draws a broad picture of the foundations and motivations of his ethical program, this does not prevent him from spelling out some of the

---

[11] Cf. above pp. 21-24.

[12] It would be a mistake to suppose that Paul's gnomic formulations are necessarily aimed at a general audience. In principle, the extent to which his exhortation at any point is conditioned by a specific situation must be determined not only on the basis of form or style, but also the literary context and rhetorical situation; cf. Schrage, *Einzelgebote*, 37-48.

[13] It should emphasized that the analysis of Romans 12.9-21 provided above in no way rules out the possibility that Paul had composed the passage before-hand in very different circumstances and then inserted it secondarily at this point in the epistle.

specific implications of this program, often by way of example. Paul is not satisfied with an ethic that is only abstract, spiritualized, or eschatological, though all of these characteristics are present; it must also be grounded in individual acts and be responsive to changing circumstances.

Functionally, then, Paul's gnomic wisdom occupies an important middle ground, so to speak, between ethics expressed in theory (e.g. Romans 12.1-2) and explicit recommendations directed towards specific historical situations (e.g. Romans 13-15).[14] The gnomic style affords his audience a series of glimpses that depict Christian moral character in exhortation that is co-ordinated, though not exhaustive or systematic. In this way Paul provides moral legitimation, direction, and encouragement while acknowledging human limits and individual distinctions and leaving many of the specific details to the responsibility and resourcefulness of his congregations. Paul can demonstrate the *praxis* of Christian life by carefully selecting and arranging wisdom sentences that extol a number of exemplary values and attitudes as they pertain to the fundamental aspects of ethical behavior as he understands it. In this regard 12.9-21 is comparable in purpose to the gnomic materials of the four Hellenistic-Jewish sapiential discourses as well as many other ancient gnomic texts. And so, in general, the gnomic style appears to be well-suited to exhortatory tasks such as those that face Paul. This is due in part to the fact that gnomic wisdom allows for a certain degree of contingency and individualization with respect to its interpretation and application; it also allows for some freedom to adapt to new needs and situations. Yet gnomic wisdom is still concrete and practical, and it is conveyed in a traditional form that emphasizes the timeless and universal legitimacy of its ethical advice.

A crucial aspect of the ethical maneuverability associated with gnomic wisdom is the substantial role played by the rational abilities of the individual.[15] While maxims essentially represent themselves as authoritative, and so appear to demand outright obedience, they also attach significance to the role of personal insight and intuition. One of the goals of the gnomic exhortation in Romans 12 (as well as elsewhere in the Pauline corpus) is to promote in the

---

[14] A similar general development is discernible within the exhortatory section of Galatians, which moves from a theoretical exposition of ethics (5.13-24) to a sequence of gnomic sentences that depicts the practice of Christian life (5.25-6.10) to specific recommendations concerning circumcision and the law (6.11-18); cf. Betz, *Galatians*, 22-23, 253-255, 271-325; Barclay, *Obeying the Truth*, 106-177.

[15] On the importance of human reason in Paul's thought see Therrien, *Le Discernement*, esp. 139-148, 263ff. and the works cited there; Spicq, *Notes*, 3.157-165; cf. idem, *Connaissance et Morale dans la Bible* (Etudes d'Ethique Chrétienne 13; Fribourg: Editions Universitaires; Paris: Cerf, 1985).

audience constant criticism and self-evaluation, in order to maintain a high level of ethical awareness and moral responsibility.[16] Gnomic wisdom is one means at Paul's disposal for provoking his readers and stimulating their intellectual involvement, thus emphasizing and developing the rational component of ethical conduct. Paul's ultimate concern appears to be not so much with ethical obedience *per se*, or with defining any distinctively Christian ethical obligations. Instead he strives to develop in his readers a mature ethical outlook that is both practical and endowed with reason.[17]

In many respects this function of Paul's wisdom corresponds with that of his Jewish predecessors and contemporaries. The Jewish sages also accepted a serious human responsibility for acquiring knowledge (even from non-Jewish sources) and developing one's intellectual faculties. At the same time, however, they firmly believed that all true knowledge had as its point of departure not human reason or ability, but the knowledge of God. Indeed, effective knowledge about God was for them the only thing that enabled one to deal rationally with the world of experience and ethics in the first place. The Jewish wisdom writers therefore recognized the necessity of faith for knowledge, and of a reliance on God for wisdom. On account of this commitment to a theological absolute that surpasses any objective material knowledge, no conflict existed for them between their intellectual and theological perceptions of life. By indicating the proper place of reason in the sphere of human endeavor and responsibility, "faith liberates knowledge," to paraphrase Gerhard von Rad; thus "wisdom stands and falls according to the right attitude of man to God."[18]

For Paul, too, the intellectual and practical activities he promotes by means of gnomic wisdom must take as their point of departure certain theological presuppositions. Thus the recommendations that Paul makes in Romans 12.9-21 must be conducted under the theological rubrics prescribed in 12.1-8. Christian ethical action is first of all predicated upon divine enablement made available through God's mercy. This involves a fundamental transformation of mind and body, and results in a new relationship of the individual with God, a

---

[16] Cf. Betz, *Galatians*, 291-293. The objective of ethical self-evaluation also raises the issue of Paul's understanding of συνείδησις ("conscience"), see Ernst Wolf, "Gewissen," *RGG* 2 (1958) 1550-1557; Christian Mauer, "σύνοιδα, συνείδησις," *TDNT* 7 (1971) 898-919; Henry Chadwick, "Gewissen," *RAC* 10 (1978) 1025-1107, esp. 1060-1069; Hans-Joachim Eckstein, *Der Begriff der Syneidesis bei Paulus: Eine neutestamentlich-exegetische Untersuchung zum "Gewissensbegriff"* (WUNT 2.10; Tübingen: Mohr-Siebeck, 1983); Michael Wolter, "Gewissen II," *TRE* (1984) 214-217; Spicq, *Connaissance et Morale*, 68-87; idem, *Notes*, 2.854-858, with further bibliography.

[17] Cf. Betz, "The Foundations of Christian Ethics," 63-66.

[18] Von Rad, *Wisdom in Israel*, 68-69, cf. 53-73.

relationship that presents the possibility of determining God's will and carrying it out in concrete action. So in its rational or critical mode, the gnomic wisdom in Romans 12.9-21 must be understood in light of the ideal of "the renewal of the mind" raised by Paul in 12.1-2.[19] Another fundamental aspect of this wisdom is the new social circumstances that accompany this transformation. Christians do not develop morally or establish ethical priorities as individuals but as members of the Christian church, which Paul describes as the body of Christ. For those who accept his message this entails an essentially new self-understanding and new moral agenda; this explains why many of Paul's injunctions here are social in orientation. A final aspect of Paul's gnomic wisdom is his argument that genuine and selfless love must be the new standard of Christian ethical conduct. For Paul ἀγάπη governs all ethical relations and attitudes, both inside and outside the body of believers. It functions as the means by which Christians encounter God's will in concrete ethical situations and provides the criteria by which they determine the course to follow in their new lives as Christians.

---

[19] Cf. above pp. 129-130, 136-139.

Bibliography

Primary Sources

Aesop *Proverbia*
"Proverbiorum Sylloge quae inscribitur ΑΙΣΩΠΟΥ ΛΟΓΟΙ," in Ben E. Perry, ed. *Aesopica*. Urbana: University of Illinois Press, 1952. 1.265-286.

Ahiqar
Frederick C. Conybeare, J. R. Harris, A. S. Lewis. *The Story of Ahikar from Aramaic, Syriac, Arabic, Ethiopic, Old Turkish, Greek and Slavonic Versions*. Cambridge: Cambridge University Press, 1913².
James M. Lindenberger. *The Aramaic Proverbs of Ahiqar*. Baltimore: Johns Hopkins University Press, 1983.
idem, trans. "Ahiqar," in Charlesworth, *Pseudepigrapha*, 2.479-507.

Amenemope
Miriam Lichtheim, trans. *Ancient Egyptian Literature: A Book of Readings*. 3 vols. Berkeley, Los Angeles, London: University of California Press, 1975-1980. 2.146-163.

Anksheshonqy
Miriam Lichtheim. *Late Egyptian Wisdom Literature in the International Context: A Study of Demotic Instructions*. OBO 52. Freiburg: Universitätsverlag; Göttingen: Vandenhoeck & Ruprecht, 1983. 66-92.

Anthologia Graeca
Andrew S. F. Gow and Denys L. Page, eds. *The Greek Anthology: Hellenistic Epigrams*. 2 vols. Cambridge: Cambridge University Press, 1965.
idem, eds. *The Greek Anthology: The Garland of Philip and Some Contemporary Epigrams*. 2 vols. Cambridge: Cambridge University Press, 1968.
Denys L. Page, ed. *Further Greek Epigrams*. Cambridge: Cambridge University Press, 1981.

Any
Miriam Lichtheim, trans. *Ancient Egyptian Literature: A Book of Readings*. 3 vols. Berkeley, Los Angeles, London: University of California Press, 1975-1980. 2.135-146.

Aristotle *Rhetorica*
John Henry Freese, trans. *Aristotle: The "Art" of Rhetoric*. LCL. Cambridge: Harvard University Press; London: Heinemann, 1926.

Babrius ΜΥΘΙΑΜΒΟΙ
Otto Crusius, ed. *Babrii Fabulae Aesopeae*. BT. Leipzig: Teubner, 1897.
Ben E. Perry, trans. *Babrius and Phaedrus*. LCL. Cambridge: Harvard University Press; London: Heinemann, 1984.

Ben Sira
Joseph Ziegler, ed. *Sapientia Iesu Filii Sirach.* Septuaginta, Vetus Testamentum Graecum 12.2. Göttingen: Vandenhoeck & Ruprecht, 1965.

Carmen Aureum
"ΠΥΘΑΓΟΡΙΚΑ: ΧΡΥΣΑ ΕΠΗ," in Douglas Young, ed. *Theognis.* BT. Leipzig: Teubner, 1971[2]. 86-94.

Cercidas of Megalopolis and the *Cercidea*
A. D. Knox, trans. *Herodes, Cercidas, and the Greek Choliambic Poets.* LCL. Cambridge: Harvard University Press; London: Heinemann, 1967. 189-239.

Chares ΓΝΩΜΑΙ
Douglas Young, ed. *Theognis.* BT. Leipzig: Teubner, 1971[2]. 113-118.

Cleanthes of Assos
Hans F. A. von Arnim, ed. *Stoicorum Veterum Fragmenta.* 4 vols. Leipzig: Teubner, 1905-1924. 1.483-619.

Cleitarchus *Chreia*
"ΕΚ ΤΩΝ ΚΛΕΙΤΑΡΧΟΥ ΠΡΑΓΜΑΤΙΚΩΝ ΧΡΕΙΩΝ ΣΥΝΑΓΩΓΗ," in Henry Chadwick, ed. *The Sentences of Sextus: A Contribution to the Early Christian History of Ethics.* TextsS 5. Cambridge: Cambridge University Press, 1959. 73-83.

Comparatio Menandri et Philistionis
Siegfried Jaekel, ed. *Menandri Sententiae.* BT. Leipzig: Teubner, 1964. 87-120.

Counsels of Wisdom
W. G. Lambert, ed. *Babylonian Wisdom Literature.* Oxford: Clarendon, 1960. 96-107.

Crates of Thebes
Hermann Diels, ed. *Poetarum Philosophorum Fragmenta.* Berlin: Weidmann, 1901. 207-223.
Ernst Diehl, ed. *Anthologia Lyrica Graeca.* 4 vols. Leipzig: Teubner, 1958[3]. 1.120-126.

Cynic Epistles (Anacharsis, Crates, Diogenes, Heraclitus, Socrates)
Abraham J. Malherbe, et al., trans. *The Cynic Epistles: A Study Edition.* SBLSBS 12. Missoula: Scholars Press, 1977.

Demetrius *De elocutione*
W. Rhys Roberts (with W. Hamilton Fyfe), trans. *Aristotle: The Poetics. "Longinus": On the Sublime. Demetrius: On Style.* LCL. Cambridge: Harvard University Press; London: Heinemann, 1932[2]. 257-487.

Derek Eres Rabbah and *Zuta*
M. Ginsberg, trans. *Hebrew-English Edition of the Babylonian Talmud: Minor Tractates.* ed. Abraham Cohen. London: Soncino, 1984. 55b-59a.

Dicta Catonis
J. Wight Duff and Arnold M. Duff, trans. *Minor Latin Poets.* LCL. Cambridge: Harvard University Press; London: Heinemann, 1935[2]. 592-629.

Didache
Klaus Wengst, ed. *Didache (Apostellehre), Barnabasbrief, Zweiter Klemensbrief, Schrift an Diognetes.* Schriften des Urchristentums. Darmstadt: Wissenschaftliche Buchgesellschaft; München: Kösel, 1984. 66-91.

Dionysius of Halicarnassus *De compositione verborum*
Stephen Usher, trans. *Dionysius of Halicarnassus: The Critical Essays.* LCL. 2 vols. Cambridge: Harvard University Press; London: Heinemann, 1985. 2.3-243.

Epicharmus
    Denys L. Page, trans. *Select Papyri III: Literary Papyri and Poetry*. LCL. Cambridge: Harvard University Press, 1970. 438-445.

Epictetus
    William A. Oldfather, trans. *Epictetus*. LCL. 2 vols. New York: G. P. Putnam's Sons; London: Heinemann, 1926, 1928.

Epistolary Theorists
    Abraham J. Malherbe, trans. *Ancient Epistolary Theorists*. SBLSBS 19. Atlanta: Scholars Press, 1988. Originally in *Ohio Journal of Religious Studies* 5 (1977) 3-77.

Epistula Aristeas
    Moses Hadas, ed. *Aristeas to Philocrates (Letter of Aristeas)*. Jewish Apocryphal Literature, Dropsie College Edition. New York: Harper & Brothers, 1951.
    R. J. H. Shutt, trans. "Letter of Aristeas," in Charlesworth, *Pseudepigrapha*, 2.7-34.

Gnomica Homoeomata
    Anton Elter. *Gnomica Homoeomata*. 5 parts. Bonn: C. George, 1900-1904.

Gnomologium Democrateum
    "ΔΗΜΟΚΡΑΤΟΥΣ ΓΝΩΜΑΙ," in Hermann Diels and Walter Kranz, eds. *Die Fragmente der Vorsokratiker*. 3 vols. Berlin: Weidmann, 1951-52[6]. 2.153-165 (B35-115).

Gnomologium Epictetum
    "Gnomologium Epictetum Stobaei," in Heinrich Schenkl, ed. *Epicteti Dissertationes ab Arriano Digestae*. BT. Stuttgart: Teubner, 1916[2]. Reprinted 1965. 476-492.

Gnomologium Vaticanum
    "Fragmenta Epicurea: Sententiae Vaticanae," in Cyril Bailey, ed. *Epicurus: The Extant Remains*. Oxford: Clarendon, 1926. Reprint, Westport, CT: Hyperion, 1979. 106-119.
    "Gnomologium Vaticanum Epicureum," in Graziano Arrighetti, ed. *Epicuro: Opere*. Biblioteca di cultura filosofica 41. Torino: Einaudi, 1983[2]. 139-157.

Heraclitus
    Charles H. Kahn. *The Art and Thought of Heraclitus: An Edition of the Fragments with Translation and Commentary*. Cambridge, New York: Cambridge University Press, 1979.

Herodes
    A. D. Knox, trans. *Herodes, Cercidas, and the Greek Choliambic Poets*. LCL. Cambridge: Harvard University Press; London: Heinemann, 1967. 80-175.
    I. C. Cunningham, ed. *Herodae Mimiambi*. BT. Leipzig: Teubner, 1987.

Hesiod *Opera et Dies*
    Martin L. West. *Hesiod: Works and Days*. Oxford: Clarendon, 1978.

Hippocrates ΑΦΟΡΙΣΜΟΙ
    W. H. S. Jones, trans. *Hippocrates*. LCL. 4 vols. Cambridge: Harvard University Press; London: Heinemann, 1923-1931. 4.98-221.

Isocrates and Pseudo-Isocrates
    George Norlin, trans. *Isocrates*. LCL. 2 vols. Cambridge: Harvard University Press; London: Heinemann, 1928, 1929.

Joseph and Aseneth
Marc Philonenko, ed. *Joseph et Aséneth: Introduction, Texte Critique, Traduction et Notes.* SPB 13. Leiden: Brill, 1968.

Leonidas of Tarentum
Andrew S. F. Gow and Denys L. Page, eds. *The Greek Anthology: Hellenistic Epigrams.* 2 vols. Cambridge: Cambridge University Press, 1965. 1.107-139.

Menander *Sententiae*
Siegfried Jaekel, ed. *Menandri Sententiae.* BT. Leipzig: Teubner, 1964.
Menander *Sententiae* (Syriac)
T. Baarda, "The Sentences of the Syriac Menander," in Charlesworth, *Pseudepigrapha,* 2.583-606.
Moschion *Sententiae* and *Hypothekai*
Heinrich Schenkl, ed. *Epicteti Dissertationes ab Arriano Digestae.* BT. Stuttgart: Teubner, 1916[2]. Reprinted 1965. 493-496.

Papyrus Insinger
Miriam Lichtheim. *Late Egyptian Wisdom Literature in the International Context: A Study of Demotic Instructions.* OBO 52. Freiburg: Universitätsverlag; Göttingen: Vandenhoeck & Ruprecht, 1983. 197-234.
Philo
Francis H. Colson, George H. Whitaker, and Ralph Marcus, trans. *Philo.* LCL. 12 vols. New York: G. P. Putnam's Sons; London: Heinemann, 1929-1962.
Philodemus of Gadara
Andrew S. F. Gow and Denys L. Page, eds. *The Greek Anthology: The Garland of Philip and Some Contemporary Epigrams.* 2 vols. Cambridge: Cambridge University Press, 1968. 1.351-369.
Phocylides
J. M. Edmonds, trans. *Elegy and Iambus.* LCL. 2 vols. London: Heinemann; New York: G. P. Putnam's Sons, 1931. 1.172-181.
Bruno Gentili and Carolus Prato, eds. *Poetarum Elegiacorum Testimonia et Fragmenta.* BT. 2 vols. Leipzig: Teubner, 1979, 1985. 1.135-140.
Phoenix of Colophon
Gustav A. Gerhard. *Phoinix von Kolophon: Texte und Untersuchungen.* Leipzig, Berlin: Teubner, 1909.
A. D. Knox, trans. *Herodes, Cercidas, and the Greek Choliambic Poets.* LCL. Cambridge: Harvard University Press; London: Heinemann, 1967. 242-263.
Pirke 'Abot
R. Travers Herford, ed. *Pirke Aboth. The Ethics of the Talmud: Sayings of the Fathers.* New York: Jewish Institute of Religion, 1945. Reprint, New York: Schocken, 1962.
Porphyry *Ad Marcellam*
Walter Pötscher. *Porphyrios: ΠΡΟΣ ΜΑΡΚΕΛΛΑΝ.* Philosophia Antiqua 15. Leiden: Brill, 1969.
Kathleen O. Wicker, ed. *Porphyry: Ad Marcellam.* SBLTT 28. Atlanta: Scholars Press, 1987.

Progymnasmata
 Christian Walz, ed. *Rhetores Graeci.* 9 vols. Stuttgart, Tübingen: J. G. Cotta, 1835.
 Hugo Rabe, ed. *Hermogenis Opera.* BT, Rhetores Graeci 6. Leipzig: Teubner, 1913.
 Ronald F. Hock and Edward N. O'Neil, eds. *The Chreia in Ancient Rhetoric. Volume I: The Progymnasmata.* SBLTT 27. Atlanta: Scholars Press, 1986.
Pseudepigrapha
 James H. Charlesworth, ed. *The Old Testament Pseudepigrapha.* 2 vols. Garden City, New York: Doubleday, 1983, 1985.
Pseudo-Aristotle *Rhetorica ad Alexandrum*
 Harris Rackham, trans. *Aristotle: Rhetorica ad Alexandrum.* LCL. Cambridge: Harvard University Press; London: Heinemann, 1938.
Pseudo-Cicero *Rhetorica ad Herennium*
 Harry Caplan, trans. *[Cicero] Rhetorica ad Herennium.* LCL. Cambridge: Harvard University Press; London: Heinemann, 1954.
Pseudo-Phocylides
 Douglas Young, ed. *Theognis.* BT. Leipzig: Teubner, 1971[2]. 95-112.
 Pieter W. van der Horst. *The Sentences of Pseudo-Phocylides: With Introduction and Commentary.* SVTP 4. Leiden: Brill, 1978.
 idem, trans. "Pseudo-Phocylides," in Charlesworth, *Pseudepigrapha*, 2.565-582.
Ptahhotep
 William K. Simpson, et al., trans. *The Literature of Ancient Egypt: An Anthology of Stories, Instructions, and Poetry.* New Haven, London: Yale University Press, 1973[2]. 159-176.
Publilius Syrus *Sententiae*
 J. Wight Duff and Arnold M. Duff, trans. *Minor Latin Poets.* LCL. Cambridge: Harvard University Press; London: Heinemann, 1935[2]. 3-111.

Quintilian *Institutio Oratoria*
 Harold E. Butler, trans. *The Institutio Oratoria of Quintilian.* LCL. 4 vols. New York: G. P. Putnam's Sons; London: Heinemann, 1921-22.

Secundus
 Ben E. Perry, ed. *Secundus the Silent Philosopher.* APA Philological Monographs 22. Ithaca: Cornell University Press, 1964.
Seneca *Epistulae Morales*
 L. D. Reynolds, ed. *L. Annaei Senecae Ad Lucilium Epistulae Morales.* OCT. 2 vols. Oxford: Clarendon, 1965.
Septuagint
 Alfred Rahlfs, ed. *Septuaginta.* 2 vols. Stuttgart: Württemberische Bibelanstalt, 1959[6], 1962[7].
The Seven Sages (Cleobulus, Solon, Chilon, Thales, Pittacus, Bias, Periander)
 "Δημητρίου Φαληρέως Τῶν ἑπτὰ σοφῶν ἀποφθέγματα," in Hermann Diels and Walter Kranz, eds. *Die Fragmente der Vorsokratiker.* 3 vols. Berlin: Weidmann, 1951-52[6]. 1.62-66.
Sextus Empiricus
 Robert G. Bury, trans. *Sextus Empiricus.* LCL. 4 vols. New York: Putnam's Sons; London: Heinemann; Cambridge: Harvard University Press, 1933-49.

Sextus *Sententiae*
  Henry Chadwick, ed. *The Sentences of Sextus: A Contribution to the Early Christian History of Ethics*. TextsS 5. Cambridge: Cambridge University Press, 1959.
  Richard A. Edwards and Robert A. Wild, eds. *The Sentences of Sextus*. SBLTT 22. Chico, CA: Scholars Press, 1981.
Silvanus
  Malcolm L. Peel and Jan Zandee, trans. "The Teachings of Silvanus (VII, *4*)," *The Nag Hammadi Library in English*. ed. James M. Robinson. San Francisco: Harper & Row, 1988[3]. 346-361.
Stobaeus
  Otto Hense, ed. *Johannis Stobaei Anthologium*. 5 vols. Berlin: Weidmann, 1884-1912. Reprint 1958.

Testaments of the Twelve Patriarchs
  Marinus de Jonge, ed. (with Harm W. Hollander, H. J. de Jonge, Th. Korteweg) *The Testaments of the Twelve Patriarchs: A Critical Edition of the Greek Text*. PVTG 1.2. Leiden: Brill, 1978.
  Harm W. Hollander and Marinus de Jonge. *The Testaments of the Twelve Patriarchs: A Commentary*. SVTP 8. Leiden: Brill, 1985.
  H. C. Kee, trans., "Testaments of the Twelve Patriarchs," in Charlesworth, *Pseudepigrapha*, 1.775-828.
Theognis and the *Theognidea*
  Martin L. West, ed. *Iambi et Elegi Graeci ante Alexandrum Cantati*. OCT. 2 vols. Oxford: Clarendon, 1971-72. 1.172-241.
  Douglas Young, ed. *Theognis*. BT. Leipzig: Teubner, 1971[2]. 1-85.
Timon of Phlius
  Hermann Diels, ed. *Poetarum Philosophorum Fragmenta*. Berlin: Weidmann, 1901. 173-206.

Zenobius
  "ΖΗΝΟΒΙΟΥ ΕΠΙΤΟΜΗ ΕΚ ΤΩΝ ΤΑΡΡΑΙΟΥ ΚΑΙ ΔΙΔΥΜΟΥ ΠΑΡΟΙΜΙΩΝ ΣΥΝΤΕΘΕΙΣΑ ΚΑΤΑ ΣΤΟΙΧΕΙΟΝ," in Ernst L. Leutsch and F. G. Schneidewin, eds. *Corpus Paroemiographorum Graecorum*. 2 vols. Göttingen: Vandenhoeck & Ruprecht, 1839-51. Reprint [with third volume], Hildesheim: G. Olms, 1958. 1.1-175.

Secondary Sources

Abrahams, Roger D. "Introductory Remarks to a Rhetorical Theory of Folklore," *Journal of American Folklore* 81 (1968) 143-158.
Adkins, Arthur W. H. *Merit and Responsibility: A Study in Greek Values*. Oxford: Oxford University Press, 1960. Reprint, Midway Reprint. Chicago, London: University of Chicago Press, 1975.
_____. "Greek Religion," *Historia Religionum: Handbook for the History of Religions*. ed. C. J. Blecker and G. Widengren. Leiden: Brill, 1969. 1.377-441.
_____. "Orality and Philosophy," in Robb, *Language and Thought*, 207-227.
Ahlert, P., and Wilhelm Kroll. "Phokylides," *PW* 20.1 (1941) 503-510.
Ahrens, Ernst. *Gnomen in griechischer Dichtung (Homer, Hesiod, Aeschylus)*. Würzburg: Triltsch, 1937.
Albright, William F. "Some Canaanite-Phoenician Sources of Hebrew Wisdom," in Noth and Thomas, *Wisdom in Israel*, 1-15.
Allison, Dale C. "The Pauline Epistles and the Synoptic Gospels: The Pattern of the Parallels," *NTS* 28 (1982) 1-32.
Alster, Brendt . *Studies in Sumerian Proverbs*. Coppenhagen: Akademisk Forlag, 1975.
Alt, Albrecht. "Solomonic Wisdom," in Crenshaw, *Studies*, 102-112. Originally "Die Weisheit Salomos," *TLZ* 76 (1951) 139-144.
Alter, Robert. *The Art of Biblical Poetry*. New York: Basic Books, 1985.
Aly, Wolfgang. "Theognis," *PW* 5.A2 (1934) 1972-1984.
Appel, Wlodzimierz, and Carolinae Holzman. "Zur Interpretation des 4.Verses Kleanthes' Hymnus auf Zeus," *Eranos* 82 (1984) 179-183.
Armstrong, A. H. "Platonic 'Eros' and Christian 'Agape'," *The Downside Review* 79 (1961) 105-121.
_____. "Platonic Love: A Reply to Professor Verdenius," *The Downside Review* 82 (1964) 199-208.
Asemisson, Hermann U. "Notizen über Aphorismus," in Neumann, *Der Aphorismus*, 161-169. Originally in *Trivium* 7 (1949) 144-161.
Audet, Jean-Paul. *La Didachè*. EBib. Paris: Gabalda, 1958.

Baasland, Ernst. "Der Jakobusbrief als neutestamentliche Weisheitsschrift," *ST* 36 (1982) 119-139.
_____. "Literarische Form, Thematik und geschichtliche Einordnung des Jakobusbriefes," *ANRW* II.25.5 (1988) 3646-3684.
Barclay, John M. G. *Obeying the Truth: A Study of Paul's Ethics in Galatians*. SNTW. Edinburgh: T. & T. Clark, 1988.
Barley, Nigel. "A Structural Approach to the Proverb and Maxim with Special Reference to the Anglo-Saxon Corpus," *Proverbium* 20 (1972) 737-750.
Barnes, J. "A New Gnomologium, with some remarks on Gnomic Anthologies," *CQ* 44 (1950) 126-137, 45 (1951) 1-19.
Barnes, Jonathan. "Aphorism and Argument," in Robb, *Language and Thought*, 91-109.
Barr, James. "Words for Love in Biblical Greek," *The Glory of Christ in the New Testament: Studies in Christology in Memory of George B. Caird*. ed. Lincoln D. Hurst and Nicholas T. Wright. Oxford: Clarendon, 1987. 3-18.
Barrett, Charles K. "The Imperative Participle," *ExpTim* 59 (1948) 165-166.

_____. *A Commentary on the Epistle to the Romans.* HNTC. London: Black, 1957.
_____. "Ethics and Eschatology: a résumé," in Lorenzi, *Dimensions*, 221-235.
Barth, Markus. *Ephesians: Translation and Commentary.* AB 34. 2 vols. Garden City, New York: Douleday, 1974.
Barucq, André. *Le Livre des Proverbes.* SB. Paris: Gabalda, 1964.
Bauckmann, E. G. "Die Proverbien und die Sprüche des Jesus Sirach: Eine Untersuchung zum Strukturwandel der Israelitischen Weisheitslehre," *ZAW* 72 (1960) 33-63.
Baumert, Norbert. "Charisma und Amt bei Paulus," in Vanhoye, *L'Apôtre Paul*, 203-228.
Baumgartner, W. "Die literarischen Gattungen in der Weisheit des Jesus Sirach," *ZAW* 34 (1914) 161-198.
Beardslee, William A. "The Wisdom Tradition and the Synoptic Gospels," *JAAR* 35 (1967) 231-240.
_____. *Literary Criticism of the New Testament.* GBSNTS. Philadelphia: Fortress, 1969.
_____. "Uses of the Proverb in the Synoptic Gospels," *Int* 24 (1970) 61-73.
_____. "Proverbs in the Gospel of Thomas," *Studies in the New Testament and Early Christian Literature: Essays for A. P. Wikgren.* ed. David E. Aune. NovTSup 33. Leiden: Brill, 1972. 92-103.
_____. "Plutarch's Use of Proverbial Forms of Speech," *Semeia* 17 (1980) 101-112.
Beare, Francis W. *The First Epistle of Peter.* Oxford: Blackwell, 1958[2].
Becker, Joachim. *Untersuchungen zur Entstehungsgeschichte der Testamente der zwölf Patriarchen.* AGJU 8. Leiden: Brill, 1970.
_____. *Die Testamente der zwölf Patriarchen.* JSHRZ 3.1. Gütersloh: Mohn, 1974.
Behm, Johannes. "θύω κτλ.," *TDNT* 3 (1965) 186-189.
Bennett, Alva W. "Sententia and Catalogue in Propertius (3,9,1-20)," *Hermes* 95 (1967) 222-243.
Berger, Klaus. "Hellenistische Gattungen im Neuen Testament," *ANRW* II.25.2 (1984) 1031-1432.
_____. *Formgeschichte des Neuen Testaments.* Heidelberg: Quelle & Meyer, 1984.
Bertram, Georg. "ὕβρις κτλ.," *TDNT* 8 (1972) 295-307.
Betz, Hans Dieter. "The Delphic Maxim ΓΝΩΘΙ ΣΑΥΤΟΝ in Hermetic Interpretation," *HTR* 63 (1970) 465-484.
_____. *Der Apostel Paulus und die sokratische Tradition: Eine exegetische Untersuchung zu seiner 'Apologie' 2 Korinther 10-13.* BHT 45. Tübingen: Mohr-Siebeck, 1972.
_____. *Galatians: A Commentary on Paul's Letter to the Churches in Galatia.* Hermeneia. Philadelphia: Fortress, 1979.
_____. "The Delphic Maxim 'Know Yourself' in the Greek Magical Papyri," *HR* 21 (1981) 156-171.
_____. *2 Corinthians 8 and 9: A Commentary on Two Administrative Letters of the Apostle Paul.* Hermeneia. Philadelphia: Fortress, 1985.
_____. *Essays on the Sermon on the Mount.* trans. L. L. Welborn. Philadelphia: Fortress, 1985.
_____. "The Problem of Rhetoric and Theology according to the Apostle Paul," in Vanhoye, *L'Apôtre Paul*, 16-48.
_____. "The Foundations of Christian Ethics According to Romans 12.1-2," *Witness and Existence: Essays in Honor of Schubert M. Ogden.* ed. Philip E. Devenish and George L. Goodwin. Chicago, London: University of Chicago Press, 1989. 55-72. Originally "Das Problem der Grundlagen der paulinischen Ethik (Röm 12.1-2)," *ZTK* 85 (1988) 199-218.
_____. "The Sermon on the Mount and Q: Some Aspects of the Problem," *Gospel Origins and Christian Beginnings: In Honor of James M. Robinson.* ed. James E. Goehring, Charles W. Hedrick, Jack T. Sanders, with Hans Dieter Betz. FF 1. Sonoma, CA:

Polebridge, 1990. 19-34.
Betz, Hans Dieter, ed. *Plutarch's Ethical Writings and Early Christian Literature.* SHNT 4. Leiden: Brill, 1978.
Beyer, Herman W. "εὐλογέω κτλ.," *TDNT* 2 (1964) 754-765.
Bielohlawek, Karl. *Hypotheke und Gnome: Untersuchungen über die griechische Weisheitsdichtung der vorhellenistischen Zeit.* Philologus Sup 32.3. Leipzig: Dieterich'sche Verlagsbuchhandlung, 1940.
Bischoff, Heinrich. *Gnomen Pindars.* Würzburg: Triltsch, 1938.
Bjerkelund, Carl J. *Parakalô: Form, Funktion und Sinn der parakalô-Sätze in den paulinischen Briefen.* Bibliotheca Theologica Norvegica 1. Oslo: Universitetsforlaget, 1967.
Black, David A. "The Pauline Love Command: Structure, Style, and Ethics in Romans 12.9-21," *Filologia Neotestamentaria* 1 (1989) 3-22.
Blank, Josef. "Zum Begriff des Opfers nach Röm 12.1-2," *Paulus: Von Jesus zum Urchristentum.* Munich: Kösel, 1982. 169-191.
Blenkinsopp, Joseph. *Wisdom and Law in the Old Testament: The Ordering of Life in Israel and Early Judaism.* Oxford Bible Series. London, New York: Oxford University Press, 1983.
Bornkamm, Günther. "Heuchelei," *RGG* 3 (1959) 305-306.
Bosch, Jorge S. "Le Corps du Christ et les charismes dans l'épître aux Romains," in Lorenzi, *Dimensions*, 51-72.
Bowie, Ewen L. "Greek Sophists and Greek Poetry in the Second Sophistic," *ANRW* II.33.1 (1989) 209-258.
Braak, Ivo. *Poetik in Stichworten: Literaturwissenschaftliche Grundbegriffe.* Kiel: Hirt, 1969³.
Brichto, Herbert C. *The Problem of 'Curse' in the Hebrew Bible.* JBLMS 13. Philadelphia: SBL, 1963.
Brinsmead, Bernard H. *Galatians: Dialogical Response to Opponents.* SBLDS 65. Chico, CA: Scholars Press, 1982.
Brockhaus, Ulrich. *Charisma und Amt: Die paulinische Charismenlehre auf dem Hintergrund der frühchristlichen Gemeindefunktionen.* Wuppertal: Brockhaus, 1975².
Brox, Norbert. *Der erste Petrusbrief.* EKKNT 21. Zürich: Benzinger; Neukirchen-Vluyn: Neukirchener Verlag, 1979.
Brueggeman, Walter. *In Man We Trust: The Neglected Side of Biblical Faith.* Atlanta: Knox, 1972.
Brun, Lyder. *Segen und Fluch im Urchristentum.* Skriften utgitt av det Norske Videnskaps-Akademi i Oslo, II, Hist.-Filos. Klasse 1. Oslo: J. Dybwad, 1932.
Brunner, Helmut. *Altägyptische Erziehung.* Wiesbaden: Harrassowitz, 1957.
_____. "Erziehung," *LÄ* 2 (1977) 22-27.
_____. "Lehren," *LÄ* 3 (1980) 964-968.
_____. "Lehre des Ptahhotep," *LÄ* 3 (1980) 989-991.
_____. *Altägyptische Weisheit: Lehren für das Leben.* Die Bibliothek der Alten Welt. Zürich, München: Artemis, 1988.
Bryce, Glendon E. *A Legacy of Wisdom: The Egyptian Contribution to the Wisdom of Israel.* Lewisburg: Bucknell University Press; London: Associated University Presses, 1979.
Bultmann, Rudolf. *Der Stil der paulinischen Predigt und die kynisch-stoische Diatribe.* FRLANT 13. Göttingen: Huth, 1910. Reprint, Göttingen: Vandenhoeck & Ruprecht, 1984.
_____. *The History of the Synoptic Tradition.* trans. John Marsh. Oxford: Blackwell, 1968².

_____. "Das christliche Gebot der Nächstenliebe," *Glauben und Verstehen: Gesammelte Aufsätze*. 4 vols. Tübingen: Mohr-Siebeck, 1965-74[6]. 1.229-244.

Burgess, Theodore. "Epideictic Literature," *University of Chicago Studies in Classical Philology* 3 (1902) 89-261.

Callaway, Phillip R. "Deuteronomy 21.18-21: Proverbial Wisdom and Law," *JBL* 103 (1984) 341-353.

Cancik, Hildegard. *Untersuchungen zu Senecas Epistulae Morales*. Spudasmata 18. Hildesheim: Olms, 1967.

Capelle, Wilhelm, and Henri-Irenée Marrou. "Diatribe," *RAC* 3 (1957) 990-1009.

Carlston, Charles E. "Proverbs, Maxims, and the Historical Jesus," *JBL* 99 (1980) 87-105.

_____. "Wisdom and Eschatology in Q," *Les Paroles de Jésus--The Sayings of Jesus: Mémorial Joseph Coppens*. ed. Joël Delobel. BETL 59. Leuven: Leuven University Press, 1982. 101-119.

Carmichael, C. M. "Deuteronomic Laws, Wisdom, and Historical Traditions," *JSS* 12 (1967) 198-206.

Carrington, Philip. *The Primitive Christian Catechism: A Study in the Epistles*. Cambridge: Cambridge University Press, 1940.

Carson, Anne. *Eros the Bittersweet: An Essay*. Princeton: Princeton University Press, 1986.

Chadwick, Henry. "Florilegium," *RAC* 7 (1969) 1131-1160.

_____. "Gewissen," *RAC* 10 (1978) 1025-1107.

Charlesworth, James H. "Jewish Hymns, Odes, and Prayers (ca. 167 BCE--135 CE)," in Kraft and Nickelsburg, *Early Judaism*, 411-436.

Clark, Donald L. *Rhetoric in Greco-Roman Education*. New York: Columbia University Press, 1959.

Clarke, M. L. *Rhetoric at Rome: A Historical Survey*. New York: Barnes and Noble, 1953.

Coleman, Robert. "The Artful Moralist: A Study of Seneca's Epistolary Style," *CQ* 24 (1974) 276-289.

Collins, John J. "Proverbial Wisdom and the Yahwist Vision," *Semeia* 17 (1980) 1-17.

_____. "Testaments," in Stone, *Jewish Writings*, 325-355.

Collins, Raymond F. *Studies on the First Letter to the Thessalonians*. BETL 66. Leuven: Leuven University Press, 1984.

Connors, Robert J. "Greek Rhetoric and the Transition from Orality," *Philosophy and Rhetoric* 19 (1986) 38-64.

Conzelmann, Hans. "Paulus und die Weisheit," *NTS* 12 (1965-66) 231-244.

_____. *1 Corinthians: A Commentary on the First Epistle to the Corinthians*. trans. James W. Leitch. Hermeneia. Philadelphia: Fortress, 1975.

Corriveau, Raymond. *The Liturgy of Life: A Study of the Ethical Thought of St. Paul in his Letters to the Early Christian Communities*. Studia, Travaux de recherche, 25. Bruxelles: Desclée de Brouwer, 1970.

Cosby, Michael R. "The Rhetorical Composition of Hebrews 11," *JBL* 107 (1988) 257-273.

Courcelle, Pierre. *Connais-toi toi-même de Socrate à saint Bernard*. 3 vols. Paris: Etudes Augustiniennes, 1974-1975.

Cousin, Jean. *Etudes sur Quintilian*. 2 vols. Paris: Boivin, 1935-1936. Reprint, Amsterdam: Schippers, 1967.

Cranfield, C. E. B. *A Critical and Exegetical Commentary on the Epistle to the Romans*. ICC. 2 vols. Edinburgh: T. & T. Clark, 1975, 1979.

Crenshaw, James L. "Wisdom," in Hayes, *Form Criticism*, 229-236.

_____. "Prolegomenon," in Crenshaw, *Studies*, 22-35.

_____. *Old Testament Wisdom: An Introduction*. Atlanta: John Knox, 1981.

_____. "Wisdom and Authority: Sapiential Rhetoric and its Warrants," *Congress Volume: Vienna 1980*. ed. J. A. Emerton. VTSup 32. Leiden: Brill, 1981. 10-29.
Crenshaw, James L., ed. *Studies in Ancient Israelite Wisdom*. Library of Biblical Studies. New York: KTAV, 1976.
Crossan, John D. *In Fragments: The Aphorisms of Jesus*. San Francisco: Harper and Row, 1983.
Crossan, John D., ed. *Semeia 17: Gnomic Wisdom*. Chico, CA: Scholars Press, 1980.
Crüsemann, Frank. *Studien zur Formgeschichte von Hymnus und Danklied in Israel*. WMANT 32. Neukirchen-Vlyun: Neukirchener Verlag, 1969.
Cullmann, Oscar. *Christ and Time: The Primitive Christian Conception of Time and History*. London: SCM, 1962[3].

Daube, David. "Appended Note: Participle and Imperative in 1 Peter," in Edward G. Selwyn. *The First Epistle of St. Peter*. London: Macmillan, 1947[2]. 467-488.
_____. "Jewish Missionary Maxims in Paul," *ST* 1 (1947) 158-169. Reprinted in Daube, *Rabbinic Judaism*, 336-351.
_____. *The New Testament and Rabbinic Judaism*. Jordan Lectures in Comparative Religion 2. London: Athlone, 1956.
Davids, Peter H. *The Epistle of James: A Commentary on the Greek Text*. NIGTC. Grand Rapids: Eerdmans, 1982.
_____. "The Epistle of James in Modern Discussion," *ANRW* II.25.2 (1988) 3621-3645.
Davies, Stevan L. *The Gospel of Thomas and Christian Wisdom*. New York: Seabury, 1983.
Davies, William D. *Paul and Rabbinic Judaism: Some Rabbinic Elements in Pauline Theology*. London: SPCK, 1981[4].
Davies, William D., and Dale C. Allison. *The Gospel According to Matthew, Volume 1*. ICC. Edinburgh: T. & T. Clark, 1988.
Davis, James A. *Wisdom and Spirit: An Investigation of 1 Corinthians 1.18-3.20 against the Background of Jewish Sapiential Traditions in the Greco-Roman Period*. Lanham, MD: University Press of America, 1984.
De Jonge, Marinus, ed. *Studies on the Testaments of the Twelve Patriarchs: Text and Interpretation*. SVTP 3. Leiden: Brill, 1975.
Delhaye, Philippe. "Florilèges Mediévaux D'Ethique," *DSp* 5 (1964) 460-475.
Derron, P. *Pseudo-Phocylide: Sentences*. Paris: Les Belles Lettres, 1986.
Deselaers, Paul. *Das Buch Tobit: Studien zu seiner Entstehung, Komposition und Theologie*. OBO 43. Göttingen: Vandenhoeck & Ruprecht, 1982.
Dibelius, Martin. *James: A Commentary on the Epistle of James*. rev. Heinrich Greeven. Hermeneia. Philadelphia: Fortress, 1976.
Dihle, Albrecht. "Demut," *RAC* 3 (1957) 735-778.
_____. "Posidonius' System of Moral Philosophy," *JHS* 93 (1973) 50-57.
Dijkman, J. H. L. "1 Peter: A Later Pastoral Stratum?" *NTS* 33 (1987) 265-271.
DiLella, Alexander A. "The Problem of Retribution in the Wisdom Literature," *The Rediscovery of Scripture: Biblical Theology Today. Report of the 46th Meeting of the Franciscan Educational Conference*. Burlington, Wisconsin: Franciscan Educational Conference, 1967. 109-127.
Dinkler, Erich, and Erika Dinkler-von Schubert. "Friede," *RAC* 8 (1972) 434-505.
Doll, Peter. *Menschenschöpfung und Weltschöpfung in der alttestamentlichen Weisheit*. SBS 117. Stuttgart: Katholisches Bibelwerk, 1985.
Donfried, Karl P., ed. *The Romans Debate*. Minneapolis: Augsburg, 1977.
Dörrie, Heinrich. "Herakleitos," *KP* 2 (1967) 1045-1048.

_____. "Krates 2," *KP* 3 (1969) 327-328.
_____. "Timon 3," *KP* 5 (1975) 847.
Doty, William G. *Letters in Primitive Christianity.* GBSNTS. Philadelphia: Fortress, 1973.
Dover, Kenneth J. *Greek Popular Morality in the Time of Plato and Aristotle.* Berkeley: University of California Press, 1974.
Draper, Jonathan. "The Jesus Tradition in the Didache," *The Jesus Tradition Outside the Gospels: Gospel Perspectives 5.* ed. David Wenham. Sheffield: JSOT, 1985. 269-287.
Dudley, Donald R. *A History of Cynicism.* London: Methuen, 1937. Reprint, Hildesheim: Olms, 1967.
Duesberg, Hilaire, and Paul Auvray. *Le livre de l'Ecclésiastique.* SBJ. Paris: Cerf, 1958[2].
Dundes, Alan. "On the Structure of the Proverb," in Dundes and Mieder, *The Wisdom of Many*, 43-64. Originally in *Proverbium* 25 (1975) 961-973. Also reprinted in *Analytic Essays in Folklore.* ed. Alan Dundes. Studies in Folklore 2. The Hague, Paris: Mouton, 1975. 103-118.
Dundes, Alan, and Wolfgang Mieder, eds. *The Wisdom of Many. Essays on the Proverb.* Garland Folklore Classics 1. New York, London: Garland, 1981.
Dungan, David L. *The Sayings of Jesus in the Churches of Paul: The Use of the Synoptic Tradition in the Regulation of Early Church Life.* Philadelphia: Fortress; Oxford: Blackwell, 1973.
Dunn, James D. G. "Paul's Epistle to the Romans: An Analysis of Structure and Argument," *ANRW* II.25.4 (1987) 2842-2890.
_____. *Romans.* WBC 38. 2 vols. Dallas: Word Books, 1988.
Dupont, Jacques. *Les Béatitudes I: Le Problème littéraire--Les deux versions du Sermon sur la montagne et des Béatitudes.* EBib. Brussels: Abbaye de Saint André; Louvain: Nauwelaerts, 1958[2].
Düring, Ingemar. *Aristotle's Protrepticus: An Attempt at Reconstruction.* Studia Graeca et Latina Gothoburgensia 12. Göteborg: Elanders Boktryckeri Aktiebolag, 1961.

Ebeling, Gerhard. *The Truth of the Gospel: An Exposition of Galatians.* trans. David Green. Philadelphia: Fortress, 1985.
Eberharter, A. *Das Buch Jesus Sirach oder Ecclesiasticus.* HSAT 6.5. Bonn: Hanstein, 1925.
Eckstein, Hans-Joachim. *Der Begriff der Syneidesis bei Paulus: Eine neutestamentlich-exegetische Untersuchung zum "Gewissensbegriff".* WUNT 2.10. Tübingen: Mohr-Siebeck, 1983.
Eißfeldt, Otto. *Der Maschal im Alten Testament.* BZAW 24. Gießen: Töpelmann, 1913.
Ellis, E. E. *Paul's Use of the Old Testament.* Grand Rapids: Eerdmans, 1957.
Elter, Anton. *Gnomologiorum Graecorum historia atque origine.* 9 parts plus 2-part supplement. Bonn: C. George, 1893-1897.
Eltester, Walther, ed. *Studien zu den Testamenten der Zwölf Patriarchen.* BZNW 36. Berlin: Töpelmann, 1969.
Evans, Christopher. "Romans 12.1-2: The True Worship," in Lorenzi, *Dimensions,* 7-33.

Fallon, F. T., and Ron Cameron. "The Gospel of Thomas: A *Forschungsbericht* and Analysis," *ANRW* II.25.6 (1988) 4195-4251.
Ferguson, Everett. "Spiritual Sacrifice in Early Christianity and its Environment," *ANRW* II.23.2 (1980) 1151-1189.
Fichtner, Johannes. *Die altorientalische Weisheit in ihrer israelitisch-jüdischen Ausprägung.* BZAW 62. Gießen: Töpelmann, 1933.

Figueira, Thomas J., and Gregory Nagy, eds. *Theognis of Megara: Poetry and the Polis.* Baltimore, London: Johns Hopkins University Press, 1985.
Finkelstein, Louis. "Introductory Study to Pirke Aboth," *JBL* 57 (1938) 13-50. Reprinted in idem, *Pharisaism in the Making.* New York: KTAV, 1972. 121-158.
Fiore, Benjamin. *The Function of Personal Example in the Socratic and Pastoral Epistles.* AnBib 105. Rome: Biblical Institute Press, 1986.
Fiorenza, Elisabeth Schüssler. "Wisdom Mythology and the Christological Hymns of the New Testament," in Wilken, *Aspects of Wisdom,* 14-41.
Fischel, Henry A. "The Transformation of Wisdom in the World of Midrash," in Wilken, *Aspects of Wisdom,* 67-101.
Fishbane, Michael. *Biblical Interpretation in Ancient Israel.* Oxford: Clarendon, 1985
Fisher, N. R. E. *Hybris: Study in Values.* Warminster: Aris & Phillips, n.d.
Fitzmyer, Joseph A. *The Gospel According to Luke.* AB 28. 2 vols. Garden City, New York: Doubleday, 1981, 1985.
Fjärstedt, Björn. *Synoptic Tradition in 1 Corinthians: Themes and Clusters of Theme Words in 1 Corinthians 1-4 and 9.* Uppsala: Theologiska Institutionen, 1974.
Fontaine, Carol R. *Traditional Sayings in the Old Testament: A Contextual Study.* BLS 5. Sheffield: Almond, 1982.
Forbes, Christopher. "Comparison, Self-Praise and Irony: Paul's Boasting and the Conventions of Hellenistic Rhetoric," *NTS* 32 (1986) 1-30.
Fredericks, Daniel C. "Chiasm and Parallel Structure in Qoheleth 5.6-6.9," *JBL* 108 (1989)17-35.
Friedländer, P. "ΥΠΟΘΗΚΑΙ," *Hermes* 48 (1913) 558-616.
Frontenrose, Joseph. *The Delphic Oracle: Its Responses and Operations.* Berkely: University of California Press, 1978.
Furnish, Victor P. *Theology and Ethics in Paul.* Nashville: Abingdon, 1968.
_____. *The Love Command in the New Testament.* Nashville, New York: Abingdon, 1972.
_____. *Second Corinthians.* AB 32A. Garden City, New York: Doubleday, 1984.

Gaiser, Konrad. *Protreptik und Paränese bei Platon: Untersuchungen zur Form des Platonischen Dialogs.* Tübinger Beiträge zur Altertumswissenschaft 40. Stuttgart: Kohlhammer, 1959.
Gammie, John G. "The Septuagint of Job: Its Poetic Style and Relationship to the Septuagint of Proverbs," *CBQ* 49 (1987) 14-31.
Gammie, John G., Walter A. Brueggemann, W. Lee Humphreys, and James M. Ward, eds. *Israelite Wisdom: Theological and Literary Essays in Honor of Samuel Terrien.* New York: Union Theological Seminary; Missoula: Scholars Press, 1978.
Gärtner, Hans. "Die Sieben Weisen," *KP* 5 (1975) 177-178.
Gemser, Berend. "The Instructions of 'Onchsheshonqy' and Biblical Wisdom Literature," *VTSup* 7 (1960) 102-128. Reprinted in Crenshaw, *Studies,* 134-160.
_____. *Sprüche Salomos.* HAT 1.16. Tübingen: Mohr-Siebeck, 1963².
_____. "The Spiritual Structure of Biblical Aphoristic Wisdom," in Crenshaw, *Studies,* 208-219. Originally in *Adhuc Loquitur: Collected Essays of Dr. Berend Gemser.* ed. A. van Selms and A. S. van der Woude. Leiden: Brill, 1968. 138-149.
Gensichen, Hans-Werner, Hans Heinrich Schmid, Werner Thießen, Gerhard Delling, and Wolfgang Huber. "Frieden," *TRE* 11 (1983) 599-646.
Gerhard, Gustav A. *Phoinix von Kolophon: Texte und Untersuchungen.* Leipzig: Teubner, 1909.
_____. ΧΑΡΗΤΟΣ ΓΝΩΜΑΙ. Sitzungsberichte der Heidelberger Akademie der Wissenschaften, Philosophisch-historische Klasse 3.13. Heidelberg: Winter, 1912.

Gerleman, Gillis. "The Septuagint Proverbs as a Hellenistic Document," *OTS* 8 (1950) 15-27.
_____. "Studies in the Septuagint: Religion and Ethics in the LXX Proverbs," *LUÅ* 1.52.3 (1956) 36-63.
Gerstenberger, Erhard. *Wesen und Herkunft des apodiktischen Rechts*. WMANT 20. Neukirchen-Vluyn: Neukirchener Verlag, 1965.
_____. "Psalms," in Hayes, *Form Criticism*, 218-221.
Gese, H. "Weisheitsdichtung," *RGG* 6 (1962) 1577-1581.
Gilbert, Maurice. "L'éloge de la Sagesse (Siracide 24)," *RTL* 5 (1974) 326-348.
_____. "Le discours de la Sagesse en Proverbes 8: Structure et cohérence," in Gilbert, *La Sagesse*, 202-218.
_____. "Wisdom Literature," in Stone, *Jewish Writings*, 283-324.
Gilbert, Maurice, ed. *La Sagesse de l'Ancient Testament*. BETL 51. Leuven: Leuven University Press; Gembloux: Duculot, 1979.
Gladigow, Burkhard. "Zum Makarismos des Weisen," *Hermes* 95 (1967) 404-433.
Glover, Richard. "The Didache's Quotations and the Synoptic Gospels," *NTS* 5 (1958-59) 12-29.
_____. "Patristic Quotations and Gospel Sources," *NTS* 31 (1985) 234-251.
Gnilka, Joachim. *Der Philipperbrief*. HTKNT 10.3. Freiburg, Basel, Vienna: Herder, 1968.
Goehring, James E., Charles W. Hedrick, Jack T. Sanders, with Hans Dieter Betz, eds. *Gnosticism and the Early Christian World: In Honor of James M. Robinson*. FF 2. Sonoma, CA: Polebridge, 1990.
Goldstein, Horst. *Paulinische Gemeinde im Ersten Petrusbrief*. SBS. Stuttgart: KBW, 1975.
Goppelt, Leonhard. *Der erste Petrusbrief*. MeyerK 12.1. Göttingen: Vandenhoeck & Ruprecht, 1978[8].
Görler, Woldemar. *Menandrou Gnomai*. Berlin: Freie Universität Berlin, 1963.
Greenstone, Julius H. *Proverbs, with Commentary*. Philadelphia: Jewish Publication Society of America, 1950.
Grenzmann, Wilhelm. "Probleme des Aphorismus," in Neumann, *Der Aphorismus*, 17-208.
Griswold, Charles L. *Self-Knowledge in Plato's Phaedrus*. New Haven, London: Yale University Press, 1986.
Grumach-Shirun, Irene. "Lehre des Amenemope," *LÄ* 3 (1980) 971-974.
Grundmann, Walter. "δόκιμος κτλ.," *TDNT* 2 (1964) 260.
_____. "ταπεινός κτλ.," *TDNT* 8 (1972) 559-571.
Guglielmi, Waltrand. "Sprichwort," *LÄ* 5 (1984) 1219-1222.
Guillemin, Anne Marie. *Pline et la vie littéraire de son temps*. Collection d'études latines 4. Paris: Société d'édition "Les Belles Lettres," 1929.
Gunkel, Hermann, and Joachim Begrich. *Einleitung in die Psalmen: Die Gattungen der religiösen Lyrik Israels*. HKATSup 2.19. Göttingen: Vandenhoeck & Ruprecht, 1933.
Gutas, Dimitri. *Greek Wisdom Literature in Arabic Translation: A Study of the Graeco-Arabic Gnomologia*. AOS 60. New Haven: American Oriental Society, 1975.

Hainz, Josef. *Ekklesia: Strukturen paulinischer Gemeinde-Theologie und Gemeinde-Ordnung*. Münchener Universitäts-Schriften, Biblische Untersuchungen 9. Regensburg: Pustet, 1972.
_____. *Koinonia: "Kirche" als Gemeinschaft bei Paulus*. Biblische Untersuchungen 16. Regensburg: Pustet, 1982.

Hamp, Vinzenz. *Sirach*. Echter Bibel AT 13.2. Würzburg: Echter Verlag, 1951.
Hanslik, Rudolf. "Eros," *KP* 2 (1967) 361-363.
Hasluck, F. W. "Inscriptions from the Cyzicus District," *JHS* 27 (1907) 62-63.
Haspecker, Josef. *Gottesfurcht bei Jesus Sirach: Ihre religiöse Struktur und ihre literarische und doktrinäre Bedeutung*. AnBib 30. Rome: Papal Biblical Institute, 1967.
Hauck, Friedrich. "δέκα," *TDNT* 2 (1964) 36-37.
Hayes, John H., ed. *Old Testament Form Criticism*. Trinity University Monograph Series in Religion. San Antonio: Trinity University Press, 1974.
Hellwig, Antje. *Untersuchungen zur Theorie der Rhetorik bei Platon und Aristoteles*. Hypomnemata 38. Göttingen: Vandenhoeck & Ruprecht, 1973.
Hense, Otto. "Chares und Verwandtes," *Rheinisches Museum* 72 (1917-18) 14-34.
Hermisson, Hans-Jürgen. *Studien zur israelitischen Spruchweisheit*. WMANT 28. Neukirchen-Vlyun: Neukirchener Verlag, 1968.
_____. "Observations on the Creation Theology in Wisdom," in Gammie, *Israelite Wisdom*, 43-57.
Hoffmann, Paul. "Tradition und Situation: Zur "Verbindlichkeit" des Gebots der Feindesliebe in der synoptischen Überlieferung und in der gegenwärtigen Friedensdiskussion," *Ethik im Neuen Testament*. ed. Karl Kertelge. QD 102. Freiburg: Herder, 1984. 50-118.
Holbeck, Bengt. "Proverb Style," *Proverbium* 15 (1970) 470-472.
Holtz, Traugott. *Der erste Brief an die Thessalonicher*. EKKNT 13. Zürich: Benziger; Neukirchen-Vluyn: Neukirchener Verlag, 1986.
Hoppe, Rudolf. *Der theologische Hintergrund des Jakobusbriefes*. FB 28. Würzburg: Echter Verlag, 1977.
Horna, Konstantin. "Gnome, Gnomendichtung, Gnomologien," *PWSup* 6 (1935) 74-87 [with additional notes by Kurt von Fritz, 87-89].
Hornung, Erik, and Othmar Keel, eds. *Studien zu altägyptischen Lebenslehren*. OBO 28. Freiburg: Universitätsverlag; Göttingen: Vandenhoeck & Ruprecht, 1979.
Horsley, Richard A. "Wisdom of Word and Words of Wisdom in Corinth," *CBQ* 39 (1977) 224-239.
Hultgård, Anders. *L'Eschatologie des Testaments des Douze Patriarches*. Acta Universitatis Upsaliensis, Historia Religionum 6. 2 vols. Stockholm: Almqvist & Wiksell, 1977, 1982.

Jacob, Edmond. "Wisdom and Religion in Sirach," in Gammie, *Israelite Wisdom*, 235-245.
Jacobson, Arland D. "Proverbs and Social Control: A New Paradigm for Wisdom Studies," in Goehring, *Gnosticism and the Early Christian World*, 75-88.
Jansen, H. Ludin. *Die spätjüdische Psalmendichtung. Ihr Entstehungskreis und ihr "Sitz im Leben": Eine literaturgeschichtlich-soziologische Untersuchung*. Skrifter utgitt av Det Norske Videnskaps-Akademi i Oslo II.3. Oslo: Jacob Dybwad, 1937.
Jason, Heda. "Proverbs in Society: The Problem of Meaning and Function," *Proverbium* 17 (1971) 617-623.
Jefford, Clayton N. *The Sayings of Jesus in the Teaching of the Twelve Apostles*. VCSup 11. Leiden: Brill, 1989.
Jellicoe, Sidney. *The Septuagint and Modern Study*. Oxford: Clarendon, 1968.
Jeremias, Joachim. "Chiasmus in den Paulusbriefen," *ZNW* 49 (1958) 145-156.
Johanson, Bruce C. *To All the Brethren: A Textlinguistic and Rhetorical Approach to 1 Thessalonians*. CB.NT 16. Stockholm: Almqvist & Wiksell, 1987.
Johnson, E. Elizabeth. *The Function of Apocalyptic and Wisdom Traditions in Romans 9-11*. SBLDS 109. Atlanta: Scholars Press, 1989.
Johnson, Luke T. "James 3.13-4.10 and the Topos ΠΕΡΙ ΦΘΟΝΟΥ," *NovT* 25 (1983) 327-

347.

Jolles, André. *Einfache Formen*. Tübingen: Niemeyer, 1965³.

Joly, Robert. *Le Vocabulaire chrétien de l'amour est-il original? Φιλεῖν et 'Αγαπᾶν dans le grec antique*. Bruxelles: Presses universitaires de Bruxelles, 1968.

Jones, Edgar. *Proverbs and Ecclesiastes: Introduction and Commentary*. Torch Bible Commentaries. London: SCM, 1961.

Jordan, Mark D. "Ancient Philosophic Protreptic and the Problem of Persuasive Genres," *Rhetorica* 4 (1986) 309-333.

Kanjuparambil, Philip. "Imperatival Participles in Romans 12.9-21," *JBL* 102 (1983) 285-288.

Karathanasis, Demetrios K. *Sprichwörter und sprichwörtliche Redensarten des Altertums in den rhetorischen Schriften*. Speyer am Rhein: Pilger, 1936.

Käsemann, Ernst. *Commentary on Romans*. trans. and ed. Geoffrey W. Bromiley. Grand Rapids: Eerdmans, 1980.

Kayatz, Christa. *Studien zu Proverbien 1-9: Eine form- und motivgeschichtliche Untersuchung unter Einbeziehung ägyptischen Vergleichsmaterials*. WMANT 22. Neukirchen-Vluyn: Neukirchener Verlag, 1966.

Kennedy, George A. *The Art of Persuasion in Greece*. Princeton: Princeton University Press, 1963.

_____. *New Testament Interpretation through Rhetorical Criticism*. Studies in Religion. Chapel Hill, London: University of North Carolina Press, 1984.

Kertelge, Karl. "Das Apostelamt des Paulus," *BZ* 14 (1970) 161-181.

_____. *Gemeinde und Amt im Neuen Testament*. München: Kösel, 1972.

_____. "Des Ort des Amtes in der Ekklesiologie des Paulus," in Vanhoye, *L'Apôtre Paul*, 184-202.

Kettunen, Markku. *Der Abfassungszweck des Römerbriefs*. Annales Academiae Scientiarum Fennicae, Dissertationes Humanarum Litterarum 18. Helsinki: Suomalainen Tiedeakatemia, 1979.

Keydell, Rudolf. "Herodas," *KP* 2 (1967) 1090.

_____. "Leonidas 9," *KP* 3 (1969) 567-568.

Kidd, I. G. "The Relation of Stoic Intermediates to the *Summum Bonum*, With Reference to Change in the Stoa," *CQ* 5 (1955) 181-194. Reprinted as "Stoic Intermediates and the End for Man," *Problems in Stoicism*. ed. A. A. Long. London: University of London, Athlone Press, 1971. 150-172.

_____. "Moral Actions and Rules in Stoic Ethics," *The Stoics*. ed. John M. Rist. Berkeley, Los Angeles: University of California Press, 1978. 247-258.

Kindstrand, Jan F. "The Cynics and Heraclitus," *Eranos* 82 (1984) 149-178.

Kirk, J. A. "The Meaning of Wisdom in James: Examination of a Hypothesis," *NTS* 16 (1969-70) 24-38.

Kirshenblatt-Gimblett, Barbara. "Toward a Theory of Proverb Meaning," in Dundes and Mieder, *The Wisdom of Many*, 111-121. Originally in *Proverbium* 22 (1973) 821-827.

Kitchen, Kenneth A. "Basic Literary Forms and Formulations of Ancient Instructional Writing in Egypt and Western Asia," in Hornung and Keel, *Studien,* 235-282.

Klassen, William. "Coals of Fire: Sign of Repentance or Revenge?" *NTS* 9 (1962-63) 337-350.

Klein, Günther. "Werkruhm und Christusruhm im Galaterbrief und die Frage nach einer Entwicklung des Paulus: Ein hermeneutischer und exegetischer Zwischenruf," *Studien zum Text und zur Ethik des Neuen Testaments: Festschrift zum 80. Geburtstag von Heinrich Greeven*. ed. Wolfgang Schrage. Berlin, New York: de Gruyter, 1986. 196-

211.
Kloppenborg, John S. *The Formation of Q: Trajectories in Ancient Wisdom Collections.* Studies in Antiquity and Christianity. Philadelphia: Fortress, 1987.
_____. *Q Parallels: Synopsis, Critical Notes, and Concordance.* FFNT. Sonoma, CA: Polebridge, 1988.
Koch, Klaus. "Gibt es ein Vergeltungsdogma im Alten Testament?" *Um das Prinzip der Vergeltung in Religion und Recht des Alten Testaments.* WF 125. Darmstadt: Wissenschaftliche Buchgesellschaft, 1972. 130-180. Originally in *ZTK* 52 (1955) 1-42.
Köhler, Wolf-Dietrich. *Die Rezeption des Matthäusevangeliums in der Zeit vor Irenäus.* WUNT 2.24. Tübingen: Mohr-Siebeck, 1987.
Kraft, Robert A., and George W. E. Nickelsburg, eds. *Early Judaism and its Modern Interpreters.* SBLBMI 2. Philadelphia: Fortress; Atlanta: Scholars Press, 1986.
Krappe, Alexander H. *The Science of Folklore.* London: Methuen, 1930.
Kraus, Walther. "Epicharmos," *KP* 2 (1967) 302-303.
Krikmann, Arvo. "On Denotative Indefiniteness of Proverbs," *Proverbium: Yearbook of International Proverb Scholarship* 1 (1984) 47-91.
_____. "Some Additional Aspects of the Semantic Indefiniteness of Proverbs," *Proverbium: Yearbook of International Proverb Scholarship* 2 (1985) 58-85.
Krüger, Heinz. *Studien über den Aphorismus als philosophische Form.* Frankfurt am Main: Nest, 1957.
Küchler, Max. *Frühjüdische Weisheitstraditionen. Zum Fortgang weisheitlichen Denkens im Bereich frühjüdischen Jahweglaubens.* OBO 26. Freiburg: Universitätsverlag; Göttingen: Vandenhoeck & Ruprecht, 1979.
Kuntz, J. Kenneth. "The Canonical Wisdom Psalms of Ancient Israel: Their Rhetorical, Thematic, and Formal Dimensions," *Rhetorical Criticism: Essays in Honor of James Muilenburg.* ed. Jared J. Jackson and Martin Kessler. Pittsburgh: Pickwick, 1974. 186-222.

Labarbe, Jules. "Aspects gnomiques de l'épigramme grecque," *Foundation Hardt pour L'Etude de L'Antiquité Classique, Entriens* 14 (1967) 349-383.
Lampe, Peter. *Die stadtrömischen Christen in den ersten beiden Jahrhunderten: Untersuchungen zur Sozialgeschichte.* WUNT 2.18. Tübingen: Mohr-Siebeck, 1987.
Lang, Bernhard. *Die weisheitliche Lehrrede: Eine Untersuchung von Sprüche 1-7.* SBS 54. Stuttgart: KBW, 1972.
Laporte, Jean. "Philo in the Tradition of Biblical Wisdom Literature," in Wilkin, *Aspects of Wisdom*, 103-141.
Larcher, Chrysostome. *Le Livre de la Sagesse ou la Sagesse de Salomon.* EBib 1,3,5. 3 vols. Paris: Gabalda, 1983-1985.
Lausberg, Heinrich. *Handbuch der literarischen Rhetorik.* Munich: Hueber, 1973^2.
Layton, Bentley. "The Sources, Date and Transmission of Didache 1.3b-2.1," *HTR* 61 (1968) 343-383.
Lee, Thomas R. *Studies in the Form of Sirach 44-50.* SBLDS 75. Atlanta: Scholars Press, 1986.
Leeman, A. D. "Posidonius the Dialectician in Seneca's Letters," *Mnemosyne* 7 (1954) 233-240.
Légasse, Simon. "Vengeance humaine et vengeance divine en Romains 12,14-21," *La Vie de la Parole: De l'Ancien au Nouveau Testament: Etudes d' exégèse et d'herméneutique bibliques offertes à Pierre Grelot.* ed. Departement des Etudes Bibliques de l'Institut Catholique de Paris. Paris: Desclée, 1987. 281-291.
Leivestad, Ragnar. "ΤΑΠΕΙΝΟΣ--ΤΑΠΕΙΝΟΦΡΩΝ," *NovT* 8 (1966) 36-47.

Lerner, M. B. "The Tractate Avot," in Safrai, *The Literature of the Sages*, 262-281.
_____. "Avot de-R. Natan," in Safrai, *The Literature of the Sages*, 369-379.
_____. "The Tractates Derekh Erets," in Safrai, *The Literature of the Sages*, 379-389.
Lewis, Philip E. "The Discourse of the Maxim," *Diacritics* 2 (1972) 41-48.
Lichtheim, Miriam. "Observations on Papyrus Insinger," in Hornung and Keel, *Studien*, 284-305.
_____. *Late Egyptian Wisdom Literature in the International Context: A Study of Demotic Instructions*. OBO 52. Freiburg: Universitätsverlag; Göttingen: Vandenhoeck & Ruprecht, 1983.
Lietzmann, Hans. *An die Römer*. HNT 8. Tübingen: Mohr-Siebeck, 1933[4], 1971[5].
Lindström, V. "Eros und Agape," *RGG* 2 (1958) 603-605.
Lohse, Eduard. "Paränese und Kerygma im ersten Petrusbrief," *ZNW* 45 (1954) 68-89.
Long, A. A. "Timon of Phlius: Pyrrhonist and Satirist," *Proceedings of the Cambridge Philological Society* 204 (1978) 68-91.
Lorenzi, Lorenzo De, ed. *Dimensions de la vie chrétienne: Rm 12-13*. Série monographique de Benedictina, section Biblico-Oecuménique, 4. Rome: Abbaye de S. Paul, 1979.
Luck, Ulrich. "'Weisheit' und Leiden: Zum Problem Paulus und Jakobus," *TLZ* 92 (1967) 252-258.
_____. "Der Jakobusbrief und die Theologie des Paulus," *TGl* 61 (1971) 161-179.
_____. "σώφρων κτλ.," *TDNT* 7 (1971) 1097-1104.
_____. "Die Theologie des Jakobusbriefes," *ZTK* 81 (1984) 1-30.
Lührmann, Dieter. "Ein Weisheitspsalm aus Qumran (11 Q Ps^a XVIII)," *ZAW* 80 (1968) 87-98.
_____. *Die Redaktion der Logienquelle. Anhang: Zur weiteren Überlieferung der Logienquelle*. WMANT 33. Neukirchen-Vluyn: Neukirchener Verlag, 1969.
_____. "Liebet eure Feinde (Lk 6.27-36/Mt 5.39-48)," *ZTK* 69 (1972) 412-438.
Luyten, J. "Psalm 73 and Wisdom," in Gilbert, *La Sagesse*, 59-81.

Mack, Burton L. *Logos und Sophia: Untersuchungen zur Weisheitstheologie im hellenistischen Judentum*. SUNT 10. Göttingen: Vandenhoeck & Ruprecht, 1973.
_____. *Wisdom and the Hebrew Epic: Ben Sira's Hymn in Praise of the Fathers*. Chicago Studies in the History of Judaism. Chicago, London: University of Chicago Press, 1985.
Mack, Burton L., and Roland E. Murphy. "Wisdom Literature," in Kraft and Nickelsburg, *Early Judaism*, 371-410.
Malgarini, Alessandra B. "ΑΡΧΑΙΩΝ ΦΙΛΟΣΟΦΩΝ ΓΝΩΜΑΙ ΚΑΙ ΑΠΟΦΘΕΓΜΑΤΑ in un Manoscritto di Patmos," *Elenchos* 5 (1984) 153-200.
Malherbe, Abraham J. *Social Aspects of Early Christianity*. Philadelphia: Fortress, 1983[2].
_____. *Moral Exhortation: A Greco-Roman Sourcebook*. LEC 4. Philadelphia: Westminster, 1986.
_____. *Paul and the Thessalonians: The Philosophic Tradition of Pastoral Care*. Philadelphia: Fortress, 1987.
_____. *Paul and the Popular Philosophers*. Minneapolis: Fortress, 1989.
Maloney, Gilles, Paul Potter, and Winnie Frohn-Villeneuve. *Répartition des oeuvres hippocratiques pars genres littéraires*. Québec: Université Laval, 1979.
Marböck, Johann. *Weisheit im Wandel: Untersuchungen zur Weisheitstheologie bei Ben Sira*. BBB 37. Bonn: Hanstein, 1971.
_____. "Gesetz und Weisheit: Zum Verständnis des Gesetzes bei Jesus Sira," *BZ* 20 (1976) 1-21.
Margolius, Hans. "System und Aphorismus," in Neumann, *Der Aphorismus*, 280-292. Originally in *Schopenhauer-Jahrbuch* 41 (1960) 117-124.

_____. "On the Uses of Aphorisms in Ethics," *The Educational Forum* 28 (1963) 79-85. Reprinted as "Aphorismen und Ethik," in Neumann, *Der Aphorismus*, 293-304.

Marshall, Peter. *Enmity in Corinth: Social Conventions in Paul's Relations with the Corinthians*. WUNT 2.23. Tübingen: Mohr-Siebeck, 1987.

Martin, Josef. *Antike Rhetorik: Technik und Methode*. Handbuch der Altertumswissenschaft 2.3. Munich: Beck, 1974.

Martin, Ralph P. *James*. WBC 48. Waco, Texas: Word Books, 1988.

Mauer, Christian. "σύνοιδα, συνείδησις," *TDNT* 7 (1971) 898-919.

Mautner, Franz H. "Der Aphorismus als literarische Gattung," in Neumann, *Der Aphorismus*, 19-74. Originally in *Zeitschrift für Aesthetik und Allgemeine Kunstwissenschaft* 27 (1933) 132-175.

McDonald, James I. H. *Kerygma and Didache: The Articulation and Structure of the Earliest Christian Message*. SNTSMS 37. Cambridge: Cambridge University Press, 1980.

McKane, William. *Proverbs: A New Approach*. OTL. Philadelphia: Westminster, 1970.

Meecham, H. G. "The Use of the Participle for the Imperative in the New Testament," *ExpTim* 58 (1946-47) 207-208.

Meerwaldt, J. D. "Cleanthea I, II," *Mnemosyne* 4 (1951) 40-69, 5 (1952) 1-12.

Meijer, P. A. "Γέρας in the Hymn of Cleanthes on Zeus," *Rheinisches Museum für Philologie* 129 (1986) 31-35.

Meinhold, Arndt. "Gott und Mensch in Proverbien III," *VT* 37 (1987) 468-477.

Mensching, G., E. Kutsch, A. Benoît, and R. Mehl. "Demut," *RGG* 2 (1958) 76-82.

Meunier, Mario. *Pythagore: Les Vers d'or. Hiéroclès: Commentaire sur les vers d'or des Pythagoriciens. Traduction nouvelle avec prolégomènes et notes*. Paris: L'Artisan du Livre, 1925.

Meyer, Wilhelm. "Die athenische Spruchrede des Menander und Philistion," *Abhandlung der Bayerischen Akademie der Wissenschaften* 19 (1891) 227-295.

Michel, Otto. *Der Brief an die Römer*. MeyerK 4. Göttingen: Vandenhoeck & Ruprecht, 1955[10], 1978[14].

Middendorp, Th. *Die Stellung Jesu ben Siras zwischen Judentum und Hellenismus*. Leiden: Brill, 1973.

Milobenski, Ernst. *Der Neid in der griechischen Philosophie*. Klassisch-Philologische Studien 29. Wiesbaden: Harrassowitz, 1964.

Mitchell, Christopher W. *The Meaning of BRK "To Bless" in the Old Testament*. SBLDS 95. Atlanta: Scholars Press, 1987.

Moore, Carey A. *Daniel, Esther, and Jeremiah: The Additions. A New Translation with Introduction and Commentary*. AB 44. Garden City, New York: Doubleday, 1977.

Morenz, Siegfried, F. Horst, and Helmut Koester. "Segen und Fluch," *RGG* 5 (1961) 1648-1652.

Moule, C. F. D. *An Idiom Book of New Testament Greek*. Cambridge: Cambridge University Press, 1959[2].

Moulton, James H. *A Grammar of New Testament Greek*. 2 vols. Edinburgh: T. & T. Clark, 1908[3]. Reprinted 1957.

Mouraviev, S. "Gnome," *Glotta* 51 (1973) 69-78.

Mowinckel, Sigmund. "Psalms and Wisdom," in Noth and Thomas, *Wisdom in Israel*, 205-224.

_____. *The Psalms in Israel's Worship*. 2 vols. Nashville: Abingdon, 1962.

Mulder, Martin J., ed. *Mikra: Text, Translation, Reading, and Interpretation of the Hebrew Bible in Ancient Judaism and Early Christianity*. CRINT 2.1. Assen, Maastricht: Van Gorcum; Philadelphia: Fortress, 1988.

Munch, P. A. "Die jüdischen 'Weisheitspsalmen' und ihr Platz im Leben," *AnOr* 15 (1937) 112-140.

Munro, D. B. *A Grammar of the Homeric Dialect*. Oxford: Clarendon, 1891.
Munro, Winsome. *Authority in Paul and Peter: The Identification of a Pastoral Stratum in the Pauline Corpus and 1 Peter*. SNTSMS 45. Cambridge: Cambridge University Press, 1983.
Murphy, Roland E. "A Consideration of the Classification 'Wisdom Psalms'," *VTSup* 9 (1962) 156-167. Reprinted in Crenshaw, *Studies*, 456-467.
_____. "Form Criticism and Wisdom Literature," *CBQ* 31 (1969) 475-483.
_____. "The Interpretation of Old Testament Wisdom Literature," *Int* 23 (1969) 289-301.
_____. "Wisdom--Theses and Hypotheses," in Gammie, *Israelite Wisdom*, 35-42.
_____. *The Forms of the Old Testament Literature, Volume 13: Wisdom Literature*. Grand Rapids: Eerdmans, 1981.
Mußner, Franz. *Der Jakobusbrief*. HTKNT 13.1. Freiburg, Basel, Wien: Herder, 1975[3].

Nauck, W. "Das οὖν-paraeneticum," *ZNW* 49 (1958) 134-135.
Neirynck, Frans. "Recent Developments in the Study of Q," *Logia: Les Paroles de Jésus-- The Sayings of Jesus. Mémorial Joseph Coppens*. ed. Joël Delobel. BETL 59. Leuven: Leuven University Press, 1982. 56-69.
_____. "Paul and the Sayings of Jesus," in Vanhoye, *L'Apôtre Paul*, 265-321.
Nel, Philip J. *The Structure and Ethos of Wisdom Admonitions in Proverbs*. BZAW 158. Berlin, New York: de Gruyter, 1982.
Neumann, Gerhard, ed. *Der Aphorismus: Zur Geschichte, zu den Formen und Möglichkeiten einer literarischen Gattung*. WF 356. Darmstadt: Wissenschaftliche Buchgesellschaft, 1976.
Neusner, Jacob. "Types and Forms of Ancient Jewish Literature: Some Comparisons," *HR* (1971-72) 354-390.
Neustadt, Ernst. "Der Zeushymnos des Kleanthes," *Hermes* 66 (1931) 387-401.
Niebuhr, Karl-Wilhelm. *Gesetz und Paränese: Katechismusartige Weisungsreihen in der frühjüdischen Literatur*. WUNT 2.28. Tübingen: Mohr-Siebeck, 1987.
Niederwimmer, Kurt. *Die Didache*. Kommentar zu den Apostolischen Vätern 1. Göttingen: Vandenhoeck & Ruprecht, 1989.
Nielen, Josef M. "Die paulinische Auffassung der λογικὴ λατρεία (rationabile obsequium; Röm 12.1) in ihrer Beziehung zum kultischen Gottesdienst," *TGl* 18 (1926) 693-701.
_____. *Gebet und Gottesdienst im Neuen Testament: Eine Studie zur biblischen Liturgie und Ethik*. Freiburg: Herder, 1963[2].
Norden, Eduard. *Agnostos Theos: Untersuchungen zur Formengeschichte religiöser Rede*. Leipzig, Berlin: Teubner, 1913. Reprint, Darmstadt: Wissenschaftliche Buchgesellschaft, 1956.
Norrick, Neal R. *How Proverbs Mean: Semantic Studies in English Proverbs*. Trends in Linguistics, Studies and Monographs 27. Berlin, New York, Amsterdam: Mouton, 1985.
North, Helen. *Sophrosyne: Self-Knowledge and Self-Restraint in Greek Literature*. Cornell Studies in Classical Philology 35. Ithaca: Cornell University Press, 1966.
Noth, Martin, and D. Winton Thomas, eds. *Wisdom in Israel and in the Ancient Near East: Presented to Professor Harold Henry Rowley*. VTSup 3. Leiden: Brill, 1955.
Nygren, Anders. *Agape and Eros*. trans. Philip S. Watson. Philadelphia: Westminster, 1953[2].

Oltramare, André. *Les Origines de la Diatribe Romaine*. Lausanne, Geneva, Neuchâtel: Payot, 1920.
Ong, Walter J. *Orality and Literacy: The Technologizing of the Word*. New Accents.

London, New York: Methuen, 1982.
Opelt, Ilona. "Epitome," *RAC* 5 (1962) 944-973.
Ortkemper, Franz-Josef. *Leben aus dem Glauben: Christliche Grundhaltungen nach Römer 12-13*. NTAbh 14. Münster: Aschendorff, 1980.

Patte, Daniel, ed. *Semeia 29. Kingdom and Children: Aphorism, Chreia, Structure*. Chico, CA: Scholars Press, 1983.
Pearson, Birger A. "Hellenistic-Jewish Wisdom Speculation and Paul," in Wilcken, *Aspects of Wisdom*, 43-66.
Peel, Malcolm L., and Jan Zandee. "The Teachings of Silvanus from the Library of Nag Hammadi," *NovT* 14 (1972) 294-311.
Perdue, Leo G. *Wisdom and Cult: A Critical Analysis of the Views of Cult in the Wisdom Literature of Israel and the Ancient Near East*. SBLDS 30. Missoula: Scholars Press, 1977.
_____. "Paraenesis and the Epistle of James," *ZNW* 72 (1981) 242-256.
_____. "The Wisdom Sayings of Jesus," *Forum* 2 (1986) 1-34.
Perdue, Leo G., and John G. Gammie, eds. *Semeia 50. Paraenesis: Act and Form*. Atlanta: Scholars Press, 1990.
Peretti, Aurelio. *Teognide nella tradizione gnomolica*. Classici e Orientali 4. Pisa: Libreria goliardiea, 1953.
_____. "Calchi gnomici nella silloge teognidea," *Maia* 8 (1956) 197-217.
Peter, Hermann W. G. *Der Brief in der römischen Literatur: Literargeschichtliche Untersuchungen und Zusammenfassungen*. Abhandlungen der philologisch-historischen Classe der königl. sächsischen Gesellschaft der Wissenschaften 20.3. Leipzig: Teubner, 1901.
Peters, Norbert. *Das Buch Jesus Sirach oder Ecclesiasticus*. EHAT 25. Münster i.W.: Aschendorff, 1913.
Piper, John. *"Love Your Enemies:" Jesus' Love Command in the Synoptic Gospels and in the Early Christian Paraenesis*. SNTSMS 38. Cambridge: Cambridge University Press, 1979.
_____. "Hope as the Motivation of Love: 1 Peter 3.9-11," *NTS* 26 (1979-80) 212-231.
Piper, Ronald A. *Wisdom in the Q-Tradition: The Aphoristic Teaching of Jesus*. SNTSMS 61. Cambridge: Cambridge University Press, 1989.
Plöger, Otto. *Sprüche Salomos (Proverbia)*. BKAT 17. 5 parts. Neukirchen-Vluyn: Neukirchener Verlag, 1984.
Pohlenz, Max. "Kleanthes' Zeushymnus," *Hermes* 75 (1940) 117-123.
Polag, Athanasius. *Fragmenta Q: Textheft zur Logienquelle*. Neukirchen-Vluyn: Neukirchener Verlag, 1979.
Powell, J. U., and E. A. Barber. *New Chapters in the History of Greek Literature*. Oxford: Clarendon, 1921.
Preuß, Horst D., Marianne Awerbuch, and Stefan Rehrl. "Demut," *TRE* 8 (1981) 459-468.

Radl, Walter. "Kult und Evangelium bei Paulus," *BZ* 31 (1987) 58-75.
Ramaroson, Léonard. "Charbons ardents: 'sur la tête' ou 'pour le feu' (Prov 25.22a--Rom 12.20b)," *Biblica* 51 (1970) 230-234.
Reese, James M. *Hellenistic Influence in the Book of Wisdom and its Consequences*. AnBib 41. Rome: Biblical Institute Press, 1970.
Reneham, Robert. "Classical Greek Quotations in the New Testament," *The Heritage of the Early Church: Essays in Honor of Georges V. Florovsky*. ed. David Neiman and

Margaret Schatkin. Orientalia Christiana Analecta 195. Rome: Institutum Studiorum Orientalium, 1973. 17-46.
Rengstorf, Karl H. "ἑπτά κτλ.," *TDNT* 2 (1964) 627-635.
Requadt, Paul. "Das Aphoristische Denken," in Neumann, *Der Aphorismus*, 331-377. Originally in idem. *Lichtenberg: zum Problem der deutschen Aphoristik.* Stuttgart: Kohlhammer, 1964[2]. 133-165.
Richard, Marcel. "Florilèges Grecs," *DSp* 5 (1964) 475-512.
Richardson, Peter, and John C. Hurd, eds. *From Jesus to Paul: Studies in Honour of Francis Wright Beare.* Waterloo, Ontario: Wilfred Laurier University, 1984.
Richter, Wolfgang. *Recht und Ethos: Versuch einer Ortung des weisheitlichen Mahnspruches.* SANT 15. Munchen: Kösel, 1966.
Rickenbacher, O. *Weisheitsperikopen bei Ben Sira.* OBO 1. Freiburg: Universitätsverlag; Göttingen: Vandenhoeck & Ruprecht, 1973.
Rigaux, Béda. *Saint Paul. Les Epîtres aux Thessaloniciens.* EBib. Paris: Gabalda; Gembloux: Duculot, 1956.
Ringgren, Helmer. *Sprüche.* ATD 16.1. Göttingen: Vandenhoeck & Ruprecht, 1981[3].
Robb, Kevin. "Preliterate Ages and the Linguistic Art of Heraclitus," in Robb, *Language and Thought,* 153-206.
Robb, Kevin, ed. *Language and Thought in Early Greek Philosophy.* La Salle, IL: Hegeler Institute, 1983.
Robertson, A. T. *A Grammar of the Greek New Testament in Light of Historical Research.* New York: Hodder and Stoughton, 1914.
Robinson, James M. "LOGOI SOPHON: On the Gattung of Q," *Trajectories through Early Christianty.* ed. idem and Helmut Koester. Philadelphia: Fortress, 1971. 71-113. Also in *The Future of Our Religious Past: Essays in Honor of Rudolf Bultmann.* ed. idem. New York, Evanston, San Francisco: Harper & Row, 1971. 84-130.
Rochaise, Henri-Marie. "Florilèges Latins," *DSp* 5 (1964) 435-460.
Röhrich, Lutz, and Wolfgang Mieder. *Sprichwort.* Realien zur Literatur. Stuttgart: Metzler, 1977.
Rordorf, Willy. "Le problème de la transmission textuelle de Didachè 1.3b-2.1," *Überlieferungsgeschichtliche Untersuchungen.* ed. Franz Paschke. TU 125. Berlin: Akademie Verlag, 1981. 499-513.
Rosenkranz, Bernhard. "Die Struktur der Ps-Isokrateischen Demonicea," *Emerita* 34 (1966) 95-129.
Roth, W. M. W. *Numerical Sayings in the Old Testament: A Form-Critical Study.* VTSup 13. Leiden: Brill, 1965.
Roth, Wolfgang. "On the Gnomic-Discursive Wisdom of Jesus Ben-Sirach," *Semeia* 17 (1980) 59-79.
Rupprecht, Karl. "Παροιμία," *PW* 36.3 (1949) 1707-1735.
──── . "Paroimiographoi," *PW* 36.3 (1949) 1735-1778.
Russell, D. A. "Letters to Lucilius," *Seneca.* ed. C. D. N. Costa. Greek and Latin Studies, Classical Literature and its Influence. London, Boston: Routledge & Kegan Paul, 1974. 70-95.
Russo, Joseph. "The Poetics of the Ancient Greek Proverb," *Journal of Folklore Research* 20 (1983) 121-130.
Rzach, Alois. "Hesiodos," *PW* 8.1 (1912) 1167-1250.

Safrai, Shmuel, ed. *The Literature of the Sages, First Part: Oral Tora, Halakha, Mishna, Tosefta, Talmud, External Tractates.* CRINT 2.3.1. Assen, Maastricht: Van Gorcum; Philadelphia: Fortress, 1987.

Saldarini, Anthony J. *The Fathers According to Rabbi Nathan (Abot de Rabbi Nathan): Version B*. SJLA 11. Leiden: Brill, 1975.
_____. *Scholastic Rabbinism: A Literary Study of the Fathers According to Rabbi Nathan*. BJS 14. Chico, CA: Scholars Press, 1982.
Saller, Richard P. *Personal Patronage under the Early Empire*. Cambridge, New York: Cambridge University Press, 1982.
Salom, A. P. "The Imperatival Use of the Participle in the New Testament," *AusBR* 11 (1963) 41-49.
Sanders, Jack T. *Ben Sira and Demotic Wisdom*. SBLMS 28. Chico, CA: Scholars Press, 1983.
Sato, Migaku. *Q und Prophetie: Studien zur Gattungs- und Traditionsgeschichte der Quelle Q*. WUNT 2.29. Tübingen: Mohr-Siebeck, 1988.
Sauer, Georg. *Jesus Sirach*. JSHRZ 3.5. Gütersloh: Mohn, 1981.
Sauer, Jürgen. "Traditionsgeschichtliche Erwägungen zu den synoptischen und paulinischen Aussagen über Feindesliebe und Wiedervergeltungsverzicht," *ZNW* 76 (1985) 1-28.
Schelkle, Karl H. *Die Petrusbriefe. Der Judasbrief*. HTKNT 13.2. Freiburg: Herder, 1961.
Schenk, Wolfgang. *Der Segen im Neuen Testament: Eine begriffsanalytische Studie*. Theologische Arbeiten 25. Berlin: Evangelische Verlagsanstalt, 1967.
_____. *Synopse zur Redenquelle der Evangelien: Q Synopse und Rekonstruktion in deutscher Übersetzung mit kurzen Erläuterungen*. Düsseldorf: Patmos, 1981.
Schilling, Othmar. *Das Buch Jesus Sirach*. HB 7.2. Freiburg: Herder, 1956.
Schlier, Heinrich. "Vom Wesen der apostolischen Ermahnung nach Römerbrief 12.1-2," *Die Zeit der Kirche*. Freiburg: Herder, 1972[5]. 74-89.
_____. *Der Römerbrief*. HTKNT 6. Freiburg, Basel, Vienna: Herder, 1977.
Schmeller, Thomas. *Paulus und die Diatribe: Eine vergleichende Stilinterpretation*. NTAbh 19. Münster: Aschendorff, 1987.
Schmid, Hans H. *Wesen und Geschichte der Weisheit: Eine Untersuchung zur altorientalischen und israelitischen Weisheitsliteratur*. BZAW 101. Berlin: Töpelmann, 1966.
Schmid, Josef. *Matthäus und Lukas: Eine Untersuchung des Verhältnisses ihrer Evangelien*. BibS (F) 23.2-4. Freiburg: Herder, 1930.
Schmithals, Walter. *Paul and the Gnostics*. Nashville: Abingdon, 1972.
_____. *Der Römerbrief als historisches Problem*. SNT 9. Gütersloh: Mohn, 1975.
_____. *Der Römerbrief: Ein Kommentar*. Gütersloh: Mohn, 1988.
Schnabel, Eckhard J. *Law and Wisdom from Ben Sira to Paul: A Tradition Historical Enquiry into the Relation of Law, Wisdom, and Ethics*. WUNT 2.16. Tübingen: Mohr-Siebeck, 1985.
Schnackenburg, Rudolf. "Die Seligpreisung der Friedensstifter (Mt 5,9) im mattäischen Kontext," *BZ* 26 (1982) 161-178.
Schneider, Carl, and Andreas Rumpf. "Eros," *RAC* 6 (1966) 306-342.
Schneider, H. *Die Sprüche Salomos*. HB 7.1. Freiburg: Herder, 1962.
Schneider, Norbert. *Die rhetorische Eigenart der paulinischen Antithese*. HUT 11. Tübingen: Mohr-Siebeck, 1970.
Schnider, Franz, and Werner Stenger. *Studien zum neutestamentlichen Briefformular*. NTTS 11. Leiden: Brill, 1987.
Schoedel, William R. "Jewish Wisdom and the Formation of the Christian Ascetic," in Wilken, *Aspects of Wisdom*, 169-199.
Schottroff, Willy. *Der altisraelitische Fluchspruch*. WMANT 30. Neukirchen-Vluyn: Neukirchener Verlag, 1969.
Schrage, Wolfgang. *Die konkreten Einzelgebote in der paulinischen Paränese: Ein Beitrag zur neutestamentlichen Ethik*. Gütersloh: Mohn, 1961.

_____. *The Ethics of the New Testament.* trans. David E. Green. Philadelphia: Fortress, 1982.
Schrey, Heinz-Horst. "Freundschaft," *TRE* 11 (1983) 590-599.
Schulz, Siegfried. *Q: Die Spruchquelle der Evangelisten.* Zürich: Theologischer Verlag, 1972.
Schürmann, Heinz. *Das Lukasevangelium.* HTKNT 3.1. Freiburg: Herder, 1969.
Schweinfurth-Walla, Sigrid. *Studien zu den rhetorischen Überzeugungsmitteln bei Cicero und Aristoteles.* Mannheimer Beiträge zur Sprach- und Literaturwissenschaft 9. Tübingen: Gunter Narr, 1986.
Scott, R. B. Y. "Solomon and the Beginnings of Wisdom in Israel," in Noth and Thomas, *Wisdom in Israel,* 262-279. Reprinted in Crenshaw, *Studies,* 84-101.
_____. "Wisdom in Creation: The *AMON* of Proverbs 8.30," *VT* 10 (1960) 213-220.
_____. "Folk Proverbs of the Ancient Near East," *Transactions of the Royal Society of Canada* 55 (1961) 47-56. Reprinted in Crenshaw, *Studies,* 417-426.
_____. *Proverbs. Ecclesiastes.* AB 18. Garden City, New York: Doubleday, 1965.
_____. *The Way of Wisdom in the Old Testament.* New York: Macmillan, 1971.
Segert, Stanislav. "Semitic Poetic Structures in the New Testament," *ANRW* II.25.2 (1984) 1433-1462.
Seidensticker, Philipp. *Lebendiges Opfer (Röm 12.1): Ein Beitrag zur Theologie des Apostels Paulus.* Münster: Aschendorff, 1954.
Seitel, Peter. "Proverbs: A Social Use of Metaphor," in Dundes and Mieder, *The Wisdom of Many,* 122-139. Originally in *Genre* 2 (1969) 143-161.
Sheppard, Gerald T. *Wisdom as a Hermeneutical Construct.* BZAW 151. Berlin, New York: de Gruyter, 1980.
Skehan, Patrick W. *Studies in Israelite Wisdom and Poetry.* CBQMS 1. Washington D.C.: Catholic Biblical Association, 1971.
_____. "Structures in Poems on Wisdom: Proverbs 8 and Sirach 24," *CBQ* 41 (1979) 365-379.
Skehan, Patrick W., and Alexander A. DiLella. *The Wisdom of Ben Sira: A New Translation with Notes.* AB 39. Garden City, New York: Doubleday, 1987.
Skladny, Udo. *Die ältesten Spruchsammlungen in Israel.* Göttingen: Vandenhoeck & Ruprecht, 1962.
Skutsch, Otto. "Dicta Catonis," *PW* 5.1 (1903) 358-370.
Smallwood, E. Mary. *The Jews under Roman Rule from Pompey to Diocletian: A Study in Political Relations.* SJLA 20. Leiden: Brill, 1981[2].
Smend, Rudolf. *Die Weisheit des Jesus Sirach erklärt.* Berlin: Reimer, 1906.
Snaith, John G. *Ecclesiasticus, or the Wisdom of Jesus, Son of Sirach.* Cambridge Biblical Commentary. Cambridge: Cambridge University Press, 1974.
Speyer, Wolfgang. "Fluch," *RAC* 7 (1969) 1160-1288.
Spicq, Ceslaus. *Agapè dans le Nouveau Testament: Analyse des Textes.* EBib. 2 vols. Paris: Librairie Lecoffre, 1958-59.
_____. *Notes de lexicographie neó-testamentaire.* OBO 22. 3 vols. Fribourg: Editions Universitaires; Göttingen: Vandenhoeck & Ruprecht, 1978-1982.
_____. *Connaissance et morale dans la Bible.* Etudes d'éthique chrétienne 13. Fribourg: Editions Universitaires; Paris: Cert, 1985.
Spicq, R. P. C. "L'Ecclésiastique," *La Sainte Bible.* ed. Louis Pirot and Albert Clamer. Paris: Letouzey et Ané, 1951[2]. 6.529-841.
Spoerri, W. "Gnome," *KP* 2 (1967) 822-829.
Staehle, Karl. *Die Zahlenmystik bei Philon von Alexandreia.* Leipzig, Berlin: Teubner, 1931.
Stanley, David M. "Pauline Allusions to the Sayings of Jesus," *CBQ* 23 (1961) 26-39.

Stecher, R. "Die persönliche Weisheit in den Proverbien Kap. 8," *ZKT* 75 (1953) 41-51.
Stendahl, Krister. "Hate, Non-Retaliation, and Love: 1QS 10.17-20 and Romans 12.19-21," *HTR* 55 (1962) 343-355.
Stern, Joseph P. *Lichtenberg: A Doctrine of Scattered Occasions*. Bloomington, IN: Indiana University Press, 1959.
Stewart, Zeph. "Democritus and the Cynics," *Harvard Studies in Classical Philology* 63 (1958) 179-191.
Stone, Michael E., ed. *Jewish Writings of the Second Temple Period: Apocrypha, Pseudepigrapha, Qumran Sectarian Writings, Philo, Josephus*. CRINT 2.2. Assen, Maastricht: Van Gorcum; Philadelphia: Fortress, 1984.
Stowers, Stanley K. *The Diatribe and Paul's Letter to the Romans*. SBLDS 57. Chico, CA: Scholars Press, 1981.
_____. *Letter-Writing in Greco-Roman Antiquity*. LEC 5. Philadelphia: Westminster, 1986.
Strobel, Friedrich A. "Die Friedenshaltung Jesu im Zeugnis der Evangelien," *ZEE* 17 (1973) 97-106.
Stuhlmacher, Peter. "Jesustradition im Römerbrief? Eine Skizze," *TBei* 14 (1983) 240-250.
_____. "Der Abfassungszweck des Römerbriefs," *ZNW* 77 (1986) 180-193.
_____. "The Theme of Romans," *AusBR* 36 (1988) 31-44.
Sussman, Lewis A. *The Elder Seneca*. Mnemosyne Sup 51. Leiden: Brill, 1978.
Sykes, D. A. "The *Poemata Arcana* of St. Gregory Nazianzen: Some Literary Questions," *Byzantinische Zeitschrift* 72 (1979) 6-15.
_____. "Gregory Nazianzen as Didactic Poet," *Studia Patristica* 16 (1985) 433-437.

Talbert, Charles H. "Tradition and Redaction in Romans 12.9-21," *NTS* 16 (1969-1970) 83-93.
Tannehill, Robert C. "Types and Functions of Apophthegms in the Synoptic Gospels," *ANRW* II.25.2 (1984) 1792-1829.
Taylor, Archer. *The Proverb and an Index to the Proverb*. Hatboro, PA: Folklore Associates; Copenhagen: Rosenkilde and Bagger, 1962².
Thackeray, H. J. "The Poetry of the Greek Book of Proverbs," *JTS* 13 (1911-12) 46-66.
Therrien, Gérard. *Le Discernement dans les Ecrits Pauliniens*. EBib. Paris: Gabalda, 1973.
Thieme, Karl. "Die ταπεινοφροσύνη Philipper 2 und Römer 12," *ZNW* 8 (1907) 9-33.
Thissen, Heinz-Josef. "Lehre des Anch-Scheschonqi," *LÄ* 3 (1980) 974-975.
Thom, Johan C. *The Golden Verses of Pythagoras: A Critical Investigation of its Literary Composition and Religio-historical Significance*. Ph.D. Dissertation, University of Chicago, 1989.
Thompson, John Mark. *The Form and Function of Proverbs in Ancient Israel*. The Hague: Mouton, 1974.
Tov, Emanuel. "Jewish Greek Scriptures," in Kraft and Nickelsburg, *Early Judaism*, 221-237.
_____. "The Septuagint," in Mulder, *Mikra*, 159-188.
Toy, Crawford H. *The Book of Proverbs*. ICC. New York: Scribner's Sons, 1899.
Treu, Kurt. "Freundschaft," *RAC* 8 (1972) 418-434.
Trilling, Wolfgang. "Die beiden Briefe des Apostels Paulus an die Thessalonicher: Eine Forschungsübersicht," *ANRW* II.25.4 (1987) 3365-3403.
Trillitzsch, Winfried. *Senecas Beweisführung*. Berlin: Akademie Verlag, 1962.
Tuckett, Christopher M. "1 Corinthians and Q," *JBL* 102 (1983) 607-619.
_____. "Paul and the Synoptic Mission Discourse?" *ETL* 60 (1984) 376-381.
_____. "Synoptic Tradition in the Didache," *The New Testament in Early Christianity: La Réception des Ecrits Néotestamentaires dans le Christianisme Primitif*. ed. Jean-Marie

Sevrin. BETL 86. Leuven: Leuven University Press, 1989.
Turner, Nigel. *Grammatical Insights into the New Testament.* Edinburgh: T. & T. Clark, 1965.

van der Horst, P. C. *Les Vers D'Or Pythagoriciens: Etudes avec une introduction et un commentaire.* Leiden: Brill, 1932.
van der Horst, Pieter W. "Pseudo-Phocylides Revisited," *JSP* 3 (1988) 3-30.
van der Ploeg, J. P. M. "Le Psaume 119 et la Sagesse," in Gilbert, *La Sagesse*, 82-87.
Vanhoye, Albert, ed. *L'Apôtre Paul: Personnalité, Style et Conception du Ministère.* BETL 73. Leuven: Leuven University Press, 1986.
van Leeuwen, Raymond C. *Context and Meaning in Proverbs 25-27.* SBLDS 96. Atlanta: Scholars Press, 1988.
van Straaten, F. T. "Gifts for the Gods," *Faith, Hope and Worship: Aspects of Religious Mentality in the Ancient World.* ed. H. S. Versnel. Studies in Greek and Roman Religion 2. Leiden: Brill, 1981. 65-151.
van Unnik, Willem C. "Die Rücksicht auf die Reaktion der Nicht-Christen als Motiv in der altchristlichen Paränese," *Judentum, Urchristentum, Kirche: Festschrift für Joachim Jeremias.* ed. Walther Eltester. Berlin: Töpelmann, 1960. 498-522. Reprinted in *Sparsa Collecta: The Collected Essays of Willem C. van Unnik.* NovTSup 29-31. 3 vols. Leiden: Brill, 1973, 1980, 1983. 2.307-322.
Vetschera, Rudolf. *Zur griechischen Paränese.* Programm des Staatsgymnasiums zu Smichow. Smichow: Rohlicek & Sievers, 1912. Reprinted 1988.
Via, Dan O., Jr. *Self-Deception and Wholeness in Paul and Matthew.* Minneapolis: Fortress, 1990.
von Gersau, Hans. "Hybris," *KP* 2 (1967) 1257-1258.
von Lips, Hermann. *Weisheitliche Traditionen im Neuen Testament.* WMANT 64. Neukirchen-Vluyn: Neukirchener Verlag, 1990.
von Nordheim, Eckhard. *Die Lehre der Alten: Vol. 1, Das Testament als Literaturgattung im Judentum der Hellenistisch-Römischen Zeit.* ALGHJ 13. Leiden: Brill, 1980.
von Rad, Gerhard. "Christliche Weisheit?" *EvT* 31 (1971) 150-155.
_____. *Wisdom in Israel.* trans. James D. Martin. London: SCM, 1972.
von Rad, Gerhard, and Werner Foerster. "εἰρήνη κτλ.," *TDNT* 2 (1964) 400-420.

Wachsmuth, Kurt. *Studien zu den griechischen Florilegien.* Berlin: Weidmann, 1882.
Walter, Nikolaus (with Ernst Vogt). *Poetische Schriften.* JSHRZ 4.3. Gütersloh: Mohn, 1983.
_____. "Paulus und die urchristlichen Tradition," *NTS* 31 (1985) 498-522.
Warnach, Victor. *Agape: Die Liebe als Grundmotiv der neutestamentlichen Theologie.* Düsseldorf: Patmos, 1951.
Wedderburn, A. J. M. *The Reasons for Romans.* SNTW. Edinburgh: T. and T. Clark, 1989.
Wefelmeier, Carl. *Die Sentenzensammlung der Demonicea.* Athens: Rossolatos, 1962.
Wehmeier, Gerhard. *Der Segen im Alten Testament: Eine semasiologische Untersuchung der Wurzel brk.* Theologische Dissertationen 6. Basel: Reinhardt, 1970.
Weiser, Artur. *The Psalms: A Commentary.* OTL. Philadelphia: Westminster, 1962.
Weiss, Johannes. "Beiträge zur Paulinischen Rhetorik," *Theologische Studien: Herrn Professor D. Bernhard Weiss zu seinem 70. Geburtstag dargebracht.* ed. C. R. Gregory et al. Göttingen: Vandenhoeck & Ruprecht, 1897. 165-247.
Wendland, Paul. *Anaximenes von Lampsakos: Studien zur ältesten Geschichte der Rhetorik.*

Berlin: Weidmann, 1905.
Wengst, Klaus. *Humility, Solidarity of the Humiliated: The Transformation of an Attitude.* trans. John Bowden. Philadelphia: Fortress, 1989.
Wenham, David. "Paul's Use of the Jesus Tradition: Three Samples," *The Jesus Tradition Outside the Gospels: Gospel Perspectives 5.* ed. idem. Sheffield: JSOT, 1985. 7-37.
West, Martin L. *Studies in Greek Elegy and Iambus.* Berlin, New York: de Gruyter, 1974.
_____. *Greek Metre.* Oxford, New York: Clarendon, 1983.
Westermann, Claus. "Weisheit im Sprichwort," *Schalom: Studien zu Glaube und Geschichte Israels, Festschrift Alfred Jepsen zum 70. Geburtstag.* ed. Karl-Heinz Bernhardt. Arbeiten zur Theologie 1.46. Stuttgart: Calwer, 1971. 73-85.
_____. *Blessing in the Bible and the Life of the Church.* trans. Keith Crim. Fortress: Philadelphia, 1978.
Whiting, Bartlett J. "The Nature of the Proverb," *Harvard Studies and Notes in Philology and Literature* 14 (1930) 273-307.
Whybray, R. N. "Proverbs 8.22-31 and its Supposed Prototypes," *VT* 15 (1965) 504-514. Reprinted in Crenshaw, *Studies*, 390-400.
_____. "Some Literary Problems in Proverbs 1-9," *VT* 16 (1966) 482-496.
_____. *Wisdom in Proverbs: The Concept of Wisdom in Proverbs 1-9.* SBT 45. Naperville: Allenson; London: SCM, 1967².
Wilken, Robert L. "Wisdom and Philosophy in Early Christianity," in Wilken, *Aspects of Wisdom*, 143-168.
Wilken, Robert L., ed. *Aspects of Wisdom in Judaism and Early Christianity.* University of Notre Dame Center for the Study of Judaism and Christianity in Antiquity 1. Notre Dame, London: University of Notre Dame Press, 1975.
Wilckens, Ulrich. *Weisheit und Torheit: Eine exegetisch-religionsgeschichtliche Untersuchung zu 1 Kor. 1 und 2.* BHT 26. Tübingen: Mohr-Siebeck, 1959.
_____. "ὑποκρίνομαι κτλ.," *TDNT* 8 (1972) 559-571.
_____. "Über Abfassungszweck und Aufbau des Römerbriefs," *Rechtfertigung als Freiheit: Paulusstudien.* Neukirchen: Neukirchener Verlag, 1974. 110-179.
_____. *Der Brief an die Römer.* EKKNT 6. 3 vols. Zürich, Einsiedeln, Cologne: Benziger Verlag; Neukirchen-Vluyn: Neukirchener Verlag, 1978, 1980, 1982.
Wilckens, Ulrich, with Alois Kehl and Karl Hoheisel. "Heuchelei," *RAC* 14 (1988) 1206-1231.
Williams, James G. "The Power of Form: A Study of Biblical Proverbs," *Semeia* 17 (1980) 48-52.
_____. *Those Who Ponder Proverbs: Aphoristic Thinking and Biblical Literature.* BLS 2. Sheffield: Almond, 1981.
Wimbush, Vincent L. "Sophrosyne: Greco-Roman Origins of a Type of Ascetic Behavior," in Goehring, *Gnosticism and the Early Christian World*, 89-102.
Winston, David. *The Wisdom of Solomon.* AB 43. Garden City, New York: Doubleday, 1979.
Winton, Alan P. *The Proverbs of Jesus: Issues of History and Rhetoric.* JSNTSup 35. Sheffield: JSOT/Almond, 1989.
Wischmeyer, Oda. "Das Adjectiv ΑΓΑΠΗΤΟΣ in den paulinischen Briefen: Eine traditionsgeschichtliche Miszelle," *NTS* 32 (1986) 476-480.
Wolf, Ernst. "Gewissen," *RGG* 2 (1958) 1550-1557.
Wolter, Michael. "Gewissen II," *TRE* (1984) 214-217.
Wolters, Al. "Proverbs XXXI.10-31 as Heroic Hymn: A Form-Critical Analysis," *VT* 38 (1988) 446-457.
Wyß, B. "Gregor II (Gregor von Nazianz)," *RAC* 12 (1983) 793-863.

Zandee, Jan. "The Teachings of Silvanus (NHC VII,4) and Jewish Christianity," *Studies in Gnosticism and Hellenistic Religions Presented to Gilles Quispel on the Occasion of his 65th Birthday*. ed. R. van den Broek and M. J. Vermaseren. EPRO 91. Leiden: Brill, 1981. 498-584.

Zauzich, Karl-Theodor. "Pap. Dem. Insinger," *LÄ* 4 (1982) 898-899.

Zeller, Dieter. *Juden und Heiden in der Mission des Paulus: Studien zum Römerbrief*. FB 8. Stuttgart: KBW, 1976[2].

_____. *Die weisheitlichen Mahnsprüche bei Synoptikern*. FB 17. Würzburg: Echter Verlag, 1983[2].

_____. *Der Brief an die Römer*. RNT. Regensburg: Pustet, 1985.

Zimmerli, Walther. "Concerning the Structure of Old Testament Wisdom," in Crenshaw, *Studies*, 175-207. Originally "Zur Struktur der alttestamentlichen Weisheit," *ZAW* 51 (1933) 177-204.

Zuntz, Günther. "Zum Kleanthes-Hymnus," *HSCP* 63 (1958) 289-308.

Index of Passages

Old Testament

Deuteronomy		36.27-28a	154	3.17	191
		36.27	154	3.21-35	143
32.35	146, 194	48	59	3.21	111, 143, 154
		91.7-9	61		
		111	59	3.22-25	144
Job		111.8	61	3.23	146, 191
		127	59	3.26	145
3.26	191			3.27-35	145, 174
5.11	182			3.27-28	146, 164, 190
5.23-24	191	*Proverbs*			
11.18	191			3.29-31	188
15.21	191	1-9	96	3.29-30	146
16.13	191	1.1-7	138	3.33-34	146
30.25	178	1.7	138	3.33	126, 170
34.3	139	1.22	182	3.34	146, 181, 182, 183, 184
		1.29-33	104		
		2.1-15	138		
Psalms		2.9	138	3.35	145, 197
		2.20-22	104	4.1ff.	96
1	59	2.20	116, 138	4.2	138
1.5	61	3.1-10	96	4.10	111
2.9	124	3.2	191	4.18-19	104
31	59	3.4	146, 157, 188	4.27	191
33	59, 174			5.1	138
33.13-15	154	3.5	181, 184	5.22-23	104
33.14	154, 191	3.7	146, 147, 182-183, 186	5.23	110
33.15	160, 191			6.6	164
33.18	182			6.9	164
33.16-22	61	3.11-35	96-105	6.11-12	138
36	59, 60, 149, 174, 203	3.11-12	136, 164	6.17	182
		3.11	109	7.18	152
		3.13	110	7.24-27	104
36.1-9	60	3.13-20	141	8	58-59, 101
36.11	191	3.13-18	140		
36.22	170	3.14-18	141, 144, 164	8.5	110
36.26	164			8.10	139

8.13	181, 182	16.32	188	22.17-24.22	69
8.21	138	17.1	137, 191	22.22	164
8.32-36	104	17.3	139	22.24	188
9.10a	138	17.5	163	22.27	116
10.1-22.16	69	17.9	188	23.1	116
10-15	74	17.11	188	23.4-5	181
10.1	35	17.13	187	23.18	116
10.10	191	17.14	188	24.5	32
10.29	184	17.16	181, 184	24.7	110
11.2	181, 182, 184	17.18	181	24.14	116
		17.19	188	24.16	164
11.12-13	181	17.21	110	24.17-22	188
11.24	164	17.24	181	24.21-22	184
11.26	164	18.1	163	24.22d	116
11.31	116	18.9	27	24.23-34	69
12.15-17	181	18.12	181, 184	24.29	188
12.16	188	18.14	188	25.1-29.27	69
12.20	191	18.18	188	25.3	29
13.9-10	181	18.19	164	25.6-7	181
13.10	182	19.7	164, 188	25.9-10	188
13.11-12	164	19.10	181, 182	25.14	181
13.13	181	19.11	164	25.15	164
14.3	181, 182	19.17	164	25.21-22	146, 164, 170, 195, 196
14.10	181, 182	19.18	181, 182		
14.12	181	19.19	188	26.1	33, 163
14.13	178	19.21	184	26.2	36
14.16	181	19.23	184	26.5	181
14.17	164	19.26-27	163	26.12	181
14.21	36, 164	20.3	188	26.13-16	164
14.29	188	20.4	164	26.16	181
14.30	181	20.9	181, 184	26.21	188
14.31	164	20.9c	193	26.27	188
15.1	188	20.13	164	27.1-2	181
15.8	137	20.20	163	27.3-4	188
15.12	110	20.22	164	27.3	28
15.14	110	20.24	184	27.5	153
15.18	188	21.2	181, 184	27.10	163
15.22-23	163	21.3	137	27.10b	32
15.25	182, 184	21.4	181, 184	27.13	182
15.27b	137	21.8	181, 184	27.18	163
15.28a	170	21.13	164	27.20-21	181
15.33	184	21.14	188	27.20	110
16.2	181, 184	21.24	181	27.21	139
16.5	181, 184, 191	21.25	164	27.22	116
		21.26	164	28.3	164
16.6	137	21.27	137	28.11	181
16.18-19	181	21.30-31	184	28.13	181, 184
16.18	182, 184	22.1	163	28.21	163
16.19	182	22.9-10	163	28.26	181
16.23	139	22.9	164	28.27	164
16.25	181	22.13	164		

Index of Passages

29.2	163	*Qohelet*		*Isaiah*	
29.8	188				
29.20	116	4.10-12	116	5.21-30	184
29.22	188	5.1-7	137	29.16	124
29.23	181, 185	5.6-6.9	175	41.25	124
29.26	184	6.6	116	45.9	124
30.1-33	69	7.8-9	181	64.8	124
30.7	163	7.9	184		
30.8	181	7.16	181		
30.10	170	7.20	181	*Jeremiah*	
30.15-31	28	7.23-24	181		
30.16	152	7.29	181	2.2	152
31.1-31	69	8.10-11	181	18.1-11	124
31.27	164	10.1-20	42		
		10.4	116	*Amos*	
		10.3-6	42		
				5.14-15	154

Old Testament Apocrypha

Baruch		4.7	163	7.10	164
		4.17-19	164	7.14	164
3.9-4.4	57	4.20	65	7.16-17	181, 184, 185-186
		4.21	37		
		4.31	164	7.32-35	178
Ben Sira		5.1-8	181	7.32-33	164
		5.1-3	185	7.34	178
1.11-30	184	5.7	185	8.1-19	163
1.18	191	5.12	116	8.1-7	181
1.27-39	184	6.6	191	8.1	30
1.28-30	181	6.7	116	8.3	29
2.1ff.	164	6.18-37	105-112, 115, 146, 175	8.4	110
2.1-18	184			8.11	182
2.1-6	49			9.12	184
2.1	116	6.18-19	136	10.3	110
2.5	139	6.23-37	143	10.6-18	181, 184
2.14	164	6.23	143, 154	10.6	182
2.17	181, 184	6.24-27	144, 164	10.8	182
3.1-16	163	6.28-31	144	10.12-18	174, 183
3.17-24	181, 184	6.32-37	104	10.14-18	57-58
3.20	182	6.32-33	145	10.15	182
3.30-4.6	164	6.37	125, 197	10.26-29	181
3.30	137	7.1-14.19	106, 142	10.28	163
4.7-10	178	7.4-6	181	11.1-7	184

Index of Passages

11.1-6	181	26.5-6	32	44.6	191
11.2-3	44-45	26.28	31-32	44.14	191
11.9	181	27.5	139	45.24	191
11.14-26	184	27.16-21	85-86,	47.13	191
11.25-28	65		175	47.16	191
12.1	116	27.22-28.26	188	50.6-10	164
12.6	184	27.22-28.11	175	50.23	191
12.8	37	27.28	184	51.8	164
13.18	191	28.1	193		
13.20	181	28.9	191		
14.3-19	164	28.12-16	49	*Tobit*	
15.11-20	49	28.13	191		
16.1-4	49	29.8-13	164	1.3	164
16.5-16	184	31.4	34	2.10	164
16.11	116	32.13	164	3.2	164
16.13	164	32.18	182	4.3-20	90
17.24	164	33.12	170	4.7-11	164
18.15-18	164	33.13	124	4.10-11	137
18.20-21	181, 186	34.10	139	4.13	181
18.21	184	34.21-35.13	137	4.19	184
18.30-19.3	49	34.26	139	12.8-9	164
19.18	152	34.29	164	13.14	178
19.22	32	34.31	164	14.9-11	164
20.1	65	35.3-4	164		
20.19	110	35.14-26	174, 184		
20.24	110	35.21	164	*Wisdom of Solomon*	
20.25	32	37.11	164		
21.1-10	49	37.15	164	1.3	139
21.1	164	38.8	191	2.19	139, 182
21.4	181, 182,	38.9	164	3.3	191
	184	38.27	164	3.6	139
21.5	164	39.1-11	138	3.9	152
21.26-27	170	39.1-3	80	4.18	182
22.1-2	164	39.4	139	5.8ff.	184
22.3	110	39.26	164	5.18	152
22.6	65	39.33-34	139	6.18	152
22.18	164	39.34	139	8.7	141
22.26	116	40.18-27	164	11.10	139
23.16-21	49	40.19a	32	14.22	191
23.16-18	32	40.20	31, 32,	15.7-13	124
24.7	65		152	16.22	164
24.12	139	41.1	191	17.5	164
24.19-22	104	41.2	164	18.9	137
25.7-8	32	41.14	191	18.16	152
26.1-4	49	42.8	139		
26.2	191	44-50	89		

Index of Passages

New Testament

Matthew

5.3	179
5.4	178
5.7	178
5.9a	191
5.39-41	188
5.41	198
5.44-47	188
5.44	167-171
6.24	180
7.1-5	188
10.24-25	44
11.29	182
25.26	164

Mark

9.50c	191

Luke

1.52	182
6.27-28	167-171
6.29-36	164
6.29	198
6.36-45	184
6.40	44
14.11	181
16.13	180
18.14	181

Q (Synoptic Sayings Source)

6.20b-49	90
6.27-28	167-171
6.46-49	104
9.57-62	90
10.2-11	90
10.16	49, 90
11.2-4	90
11.9-13	90
12.2-7	90
12.11-12	90
12.22-31	90
12.33-34	90
12.34	49
13.24	90
14.26	90
14.27	90
17.33	90

John

13.16	44
15.20	44

Romans

1-2	181
1.7	192
1.8-15	126
1.16-17	128
1.18-23	183
1.22	4, 181
1.26	188
1.28	139, 188
2.7	188
2.10	188
2.11	4
2.17-24	183
2.18	138, 139
3.4a	4
3.8b	4
3.21ff	128
5.3-4	4, 158, 164
5.5	154
5.8	154
6.4-6	128
6.12-13	128
6.19	128
7.6	128
8.2-6	128
8.11-13	128
8.24-27	164
8.35	154
8.39	154
9-11	206
9.20-23	124
11.20	158, 181
11.20b-21	184
11.25-32	183
11.25	158, 183
11.28	192
11.33-36	206
12.1-21	126-147
12.1-2	128-130, 136-139
12.2	154
12.3	4, 140-141, 163, 181
12.3-8	130, 139-142
12.6-8	144, 162
12.8	164
12.9-21	130-131, 142-147, 149ff.
12.9	138, 150-155
12.10-13	143-145, 156-165, 175
12.14-21	145, 172-177
12.14	165-171
12.15	177-179
12.16	163, 179-186
12.16a-b	156-165
12.17-19	186-195
12.17-19a	156-165
12.17	157
12.17a	160
12.17b	157, 188
12.19-20	169
12.20-21	195-198
12.21	138
13-15	128-129, 205, 209, 210
13.1-7	205
13.3-4	138
13.7	4, 163, 205

13.8	4, 205	14.38	4, 197	5.26	181
13.10	154	15.32-33	4	6.1	154
14.7	4, 55, 205	15.33	55	6.1b	158
14.10	171	16.3	139	6.3-4	181
14.15	154	16.13-14	4	6.4	139
14.18-19	191			6.9-10	65
14.18	163, 188			6.10	172, 188, 190
14.19	191, 205	*2 Corinthians*			
14.22b	4, 139, 181, 205			6.11-18	210
15.1	181	5.13-14	141		
15.5	158, 179	6.6	152	*Ephesians*	
15.22-29	126	6.14b	4		
15.30	154	7.6	182	5.10	139
16.1-19	126	7.11-12	164	5.17	139
16.5	192	8.1-23	48		
16.8	192	8.7-8	164		
16.9	192	8.8	139	*Philippians*	
16.12	192	8.10-12	48		
16.17-20	205	8.12	4	1.9-10	139
16.18	163	8.13-15	190	2.1-4	151
		8.16	164	2.1-3	4
		8.21	4, 157-158, 188	2.1-2	150
1 Corinthians		8.22	139	2.2	179
		8.24	158	2.3-4	163
1-3	181	9.6	4	2.4	4
1.18-3.23	4, 183	9.7	4	2.14	4
1.25	4, 181	10-13	181	2.17-18	178
1.29	4, 181	10.1	182	3.1	164
2.12-15	154	10.4-6	183	3.16	4, 177
3.13	139	10.14b	4	4.2	179
3.18	4, 181	10.18	4, 139, 181	4.5	4, 188
3.19	4, 181			4.8	4, 188
4.10	181	11.19	183		
4.12	167, 170, 172	11.28	181	*Colossians*	
		11.29	178		
5.6	55	11.31	181	4.5	188
7.10-11	166, 171	12.9b	4		
7.30	178	12.10	181		
8.1	4, 150	13.5	4, 139	*1 Thessalonians*	
8.2	4, 181	13.11	179, 191		
9.14	166, 171			1.9	163
11.23ff.	166			3.12	172, 188
11.28	139, 181	*Galatians*		4.12	188
12-13	131			5	154
12.10	154	4.12	4	5.12-22	158-160
12.26	178	4.18a	4	5.13b-22	4, 208
13	151, 207	5.9	4	5.13b	191
13.13	4, 150	5.13-24	210	5.15	160, 172, 187, 188, 189
14.21	158	5.25-6.10	4, 55, 208, 210		
14.37	166				

Index of Passages

5.21-22	139, 154-155	13.2a	164	4.10	182, 184
				4.11	42
				5.7-11	164
		James		5.7	42
1 Timothy				5.12-18	164
		1.2	42	5.12	42
1.5	152	1.3-4	164	5.19	42
5.8	188	1.9-10	184		
6.17	184	1.9	182		
		1.10	182	*1 Peter*	
		1.12	164		
2 Timothy		1.16	42	1.22	152
		1.19	42	2.12	188
1.5	152	1.22-24	45	2.15	188
2.22	191	2.1	42	3.8-12	158-160
		2.5	42	3.8	182, 184
		2.14	42	3.9	160, 187
Titus		3.1	42	3.11	160, 191
		3.9-10	170	5.5	182, 184
3.2	188	3.10	42	5.6	182
		3.12	42		
		3.13-4.10	116		
Hebrews		3.13	181	*2 Peter*	
		3.17-18	191		
3.9	139	3.17	152	1.4	164
10.30	158, 195	3.18	191		
12.14	191	4.6	182, 184		

Old Testament Pseudepigrapha

4 Maccabees		*Epistula Aristeas*		*Pseudo-Menander*	
1.18	141	225	189	408-409	180
		227	188		
		232	189		
Ahiqar		234	137	*Pseudo-Phocylides*	
123-124	188	*Joseph and Aseneth*		9-21	76-77, 175
		23.9	188	32-34	188
Apocalypse of Sedrach		28.4	187	42-47	48-49
		28.10	188	53-54	181
1.1-4	152	28.14	188	61	152
		29.3	188	62	182
				63-64	188
				67	152

70-96	112-119	228-230	137	*Naphtali*	
71-75	125				
74-75	188			2.2-3.5	119-126
76-96	143, 145	*Testaments of the*		2.6-8	140, 141
76-77	178	*Twelve Patriarchs*		2.8	140
76	140, 143			2.8b	141, 165
77-78	146	*Benjamin*		2.8c	144
77	188, 193			2.9-3.5	143
79-96	144, 145, 175	4.2-3	196-197	2.9-3.4	192
		5.1	191	2.9	143
79	145			3.1-5	145
80	146	*Gad*		3.1b	139, 145
82	65			3.5	147
95-96	197	6-7	152, 188		
118	181	6.1	154	*Simeon*	
121	65, 163				
122	181	*Issachar*		3.3	30
142-143	188			5.2-3	189
151	188	7.5	178		
160-161	116			*Zebulon*	
162-174	45	*Joseph*			
193	152			6.5	178
194	152	17.7	178	7.3-4	178
214	152				

Dead Sea Scrolls, Josephus, and Philo

Dead Sea Scrolls

1QS

10.17-20	172
10.17-18	197

Josephus

Antiquitates Judaicae

19.58	179

Bellum Judaicum

2.160	179

Philo

De Ebrietate

84	188

De Josepho

94	178

De Plantatione

30	137

De Specialibus Legibus

2.201	165

De Virtutibus

196	47

Heres

254	164

Rabbinic Literature

Derek Eres Rabbah		3.2	181	2.5	181
		3.5	181	2.9	181
2.1	181, 188	3.8	189	2.15	164
2.8	181	3.11	181	2.16	181
2.9	181	4.4	181	3.1	181
2.13	188	4.5	178	3.13	189
2.14	181	8.3	188	4.4	181
2.17	191	8.10	181	4.7	181
2.22	181	9.2-3	152	4.9	181
2.24	191	9.11	181, 184	4.12	181
7.7	178	9.12	191	4.18	181
				4.20	163
				4.28	181
Derek Eres Zuta		Pirke 'Abot		5.1-9	164
				5.19	152
1.7	188	1.12	191	5.22	181
2.6	181	1.13	181	6.1	181
2.8-10	163	2.1	189	6.5	181

Patristic Literature and Nag Hammadi Tractates

2 Clement		3.9b	181	Sextus	
17.3	179			Sententiae	
		Epistle of Barnabas			
				13	141
Clement of Alexandria		18-20	90	15	164
				16	189
Paedagogus				23	137
		Gregory of Nazianzus		38	189
1.107	20			42	30
		Carmina Moralia		43	197
		(PG 37)		46b	137
Dialogue of the Saviour				47	137, 164
		521-968	66	51	189
53	44	768	154	52	164
		908-910	67	64	181
		910-945	66	80	27, 164
				88	164
Didache				89	188
1-6	90			90	35
1.3b	167-171			96	188
3.7-10	181			102	137

250

Index of Passages

103	137	284	181	394	36
105	188	285	110	399	141
119	164	286	181	412	141
122	164	293	164	414-425	74-75
124	164	301	164	414	178
125	164	320	181	422	178
138	181	324	188	425	139
141	152	325	181	432	181
160	65	327	188		
163	65	330	164		
165b	197	333	181	*Teachings of Silvanus*	
183-184	188	339-342	164		
188	181	342	116, 181	87	181
199	34, 181	343	188	88	185
203	181	370	188	90	181
210-213	188	371	137	91	181
213	164	372	164	95	181
216	164	374	164	104	137, 185
217	164	375	164	108	185
235	141	378	164	110-112	185
260	189	381	190	110-111	181
266	164	386	188	114	185
273	141	389b	181	118	185
277	164	393	197		

Greco-Roman Sources

Aesop		6.302	63	Aristotle	
		7.67	63		
Proverbia		7.452	63	*Rhetorica*	
		7.472	63		
38	164	7.648	63	1.2	43
65	164	7.660	63	1.3.3-5	52
142	37	7.665	63	2.21	18
171	139	7.726	63	2.21.2-7	43
		7.731	63	2.21.2	44
Fabulae		7.736	63	2.21.5	190
		8	67	2.21.7	43
222.5	188	9.54	180, 190	2.21.9	47
		9.99	63	2.21.14	196
		9.335	63	2.21.15	52
Anthologia Graeca		9.379	196	2.21.16	52
		10.38	180	3.8	146
5.112	65	10.75	180	3.17.9	46
5.256	180	11.50.1-2	31		

Index of Passages

Babrius

Mythiamboi

5	66
6	66
13	66
14	66
18	66
20	66
21	66
22	66
24	66
29	66
31	66
33	66
37	66
44	66
47	66
50	66
52	66
56	66
58	66
59	66
64-67	66
69	66
71	66
79	66
81-85	66
87	66
92	66
94	66
96	65, 66
98	66
103	66
111	66
112	66
116	66
119	66
127	66

Carmen Aureum

1-8	163
6-8a	189-190
9-11	188
17-18	188

Cleitarchus

Chreiai

24	181
25	152
61	141
109	181
110	188
115	181
132	181
138	141

Cicero

De Officiis

3.5	20

Comparatio Menandri et Philistionis

1.63	139
1.85-86	164
1.169	139
1.199	139
1.250	182
1.256-257	141
1.295	180
2.1-10	67-68, 87

Cynic Epistles

Pseudo-Anacharsis

1.24-26	139

Pseudo-Crates

4.3	34
5.6-7	44

Pseudo-Diogenes

22.19-20	140, 180
28.5	36
40.22-23	180
49.1-10	180

Pseudo-Socrates

34.7-8	140

Demetrius

De Elocutione

2.106-110	197

Dicta Catonis

Prologue	74
1.31	189
1.36	188
2.1	164
2.7	189
2.29	189
4.34	188

Dionysius of Halicarnassus

De Compositione Verborum

25	146

Epicharmus

(c) 1-9	78

Epictetus

Dissertationes

1.2.1-2	45-46
1.4.1-12	50
2.5.23	178
2.6.25	182
4.5.24	191

Encheiridion

25.1	178
30	20

Index of Passages

Gnomica Homoeomata

10a	110
22	110
27	110
29	110
29a	110
32	65
39	110
42	110
45	110
47	29, 180
59	65
61	110
63	180
67	110
73	65
74b	65
97	180
109c	110
123	65
134	65
170a	180
173	110
182	110, 180

Appendix

19	178
21	153

Gnomologium Democrateum

52	180
67	141
71	65
84	180
86	180
88	180
94	65
95	141
97	153
102	190
107	37
111	182
114	34, 180
125	197
236	65

Gnomologium Epictetum

3	180
4	141
7	163, 189
10	141
10a	28
15	180
16	180
19	180
21	188
25	180, 188
27	188
29	197
43	164
45	180
49	36
54	139
67	189

Gnomologium Vaticanum

1	188
15	164
28	139, 164
34	31
39a	32
54	180
59	196
62	188
64	164, 180
70	189

Heraclitus

3-5	180
4	141, 196
22	180
28-29	180
29	141, 196
32	141
36-37	180
104	182

Hermogenes

Progymnasmata

4	43, 44, 46, 52

Hesiod

Opera et Dies

213-285	182
225	164
265-266	188
265	38
327	164, 188
353	179

Isocrates

Ad Nicoclem

2.3	61
20	137
43-44	61
50-53	189
50-52	139

Nicocles

7	139
41	31
44	139
52	155
54	31
57	31
61	31

Julian

Oration 6

199D-200A 62

Index of Passages

Menander

Sententiae

1	140
5	188
19	188
46	188
99	188
100 (app.)	182
134	34
138	180
208	164
238	116
245	116
246	116, 141
269	188
336	141
350	141
358	163, 180
410	182
431	180
448	179
510	180
520	180
542-545	164
545	141
554	164
581	141, 180
604	188
606	141
674	180
675	188, 193
762	180
778	180
792	182
794	180
795	182
807	163, 180
814	180
825	164, 190
827-828	164
850	182

Appendix

2.5	182

Fragment

7.9	192

Moschion

Hypothekai

10	30
17	180

Plato

Cratylus

422d	190
435c	190

Leges

757a	30

Republic

460a	190
466d	190

Symposium

207d	190

Timaeus

46c	190

Plutarch

Moralia

20c-22a	73
384c-438e	23

Polyaenus

Strategemata

5.12	197

Porphyry

Ad Marcellam

11-12	92

Pseudo-Aristotle

Rhetorica ad Alexandrum

28^{a}16-24	46
30^{a}23-39	43
30^{b}1-7	43
31^{a}35-40	43
38^{b}29-39^{a}38	44, 46
39^{a}8-39^{b}2	197
42^{b}34-43^{a}6	46

Pseudo-Cicero

Rhetorica ad Herennium

4.17.24-25	43
4.17.25	52
4.44.56-58	44
4.44.56-57	43

Pseudo-Isocrates

Ad Demonicum

2	46
12-17	92
16-17	189
16	163
19	44
25	139, 164
29	32
31	179
41	65
42	32
44	190

Index of Passages

Pseudo-Libanius

Epistolimaioi Charakteres

52	55
78	33, 55
83	55
84	55

Publilius Syrus

Sententiae

50	197
87-88	188
99	189
102	164
110	188
111	164
142-143	178, 188
142	170
220	164
241	188
290	188
293	164
311	188
344-345	188
390	164
443	164
450	164
504	164
512	164
548	188
550	188
599	188
628	188
643	188
680	188
702	188

Quintilian

Institutio Oratoria

1.9.3-5	18
1.9.3-4	77
5.14	43
6.3.96-98	196

8.5.1-35	18
8.5.4	43
8.5.6-7	42
8.5.8	47
8.5.9-10	43
8.5.10-13	49
8.5.13-14	49-50

Sayings of Secundus

11	151

Sayings of the Seven Sages

Bias

5	33

Chilon

1	23, 27, 180
5	37
20	182

Cleobulus

1	27, 151
20	180

Periander

2-4	151
2	27

Pittacus

1	65
8	28
11	151
12	180

Solon

1	26, 151, 196
10	38, 197

13	27, 180
20	35

Thales

11-13	151
20	180

Seneca

Epistulae Morales

94	20
94.1-15	47
94.10-11	43
94.27-28	20, 23
94.27	43
95	18, 20, 21
95.61-64	43
108.9-10	65

Sextus Empiricus

Adversus Mathematicos

1.271	79
1.279-281	43

Stobaeus

Anthologium

3.1.66	63
3.5	141
3.22	180
4.14	191

Theognis

31b-32	33
39-52	180
40	182
83-86	64, 180
115	117
151	182
153-154	180

Index of Passages

153	182	555-556	164	1051-1054	188
213-218	189	585	32	1071-1074	189
279-282	188	603	182	1103	182
291	182	627-628	178	1123-1128	164
301-302	189	657-658	164	1133-1134	188
307	182	731-752	64	1135-1150	64
309-312	189	732	182	1174	182
313-314	178, 189	817-818	164	1191-1194	64
325-328	188	833-836	180, 188	1217-1218	178
365-366	188	835	182	1219-1220	153
379	182	885	191	1223-1224	188
401-402	65	1029-1036	164		
541	182	1029-1030	188		

Near-Eastern Instructional Texts

Amenemope

4.10-5.19	188
4.10-17	194
10.16-17	189
22.1-23.11	188
25.1-15	181
30	87

Ankhsheshonqy

6.8	188
8.13-25	92
12.16	188
12.17	178
17.2	189
17.26	189
26.10	188

Any

5.6-7	188
6.11-15	181
6.15-7.4	188
7.11-12	188, 193
8.11-12	181
8.12	188

8.14-16	188, 193-194

Counsels of Wisdom

31-65	83-84, 174
41-44	170

P. Insinger

3.10-19	181
3.20	188
3.23	188
4.13-23	181
5.13	181
11.9	178
16.11-14	137
19.22	188
23.6	170, 188
27.7	188
27.9	170, 188
27.22-29.11	164
29.12ff.	188
33.7ff.	188
33.8-13	194
33.13	181
33.22	181

Ptahhotep

1-4	181
2-4	188
6	188
9-10	181
14	189
19	188
22	163
25	181
35	189
52	181

Index of Modern Authors

Abrahams, R. D. 19
Ahlert, P. 61
Ahrens, E. 61
Albright, W. F. 58
Allison, D. C. 165, 166, 169, 171, 191
Alster, B. 69, 83
Alt, A. 22
Alter, R. 16
Aly, W. 61
Appel, W. 64
Armstrong, A. H. 152
Asemisson, H. U. 24, 38
Asmis, E. 65
Attridge, H. 70
Audet, J.-P. 169
Auvray, P. 106
Awerbuch, M. 182

Baasland, E. 2
Barber, E. A. 62, 64, 65, 66
Barclay, J. M. G. 208, 211
Barley, N. 13, 19, 73
Barnes, J. 71, 72, 73, 77, 78, 79
Barnes, Jonathan 18, 73
Barr, J. 151, 152
Barrett, C. K. 156, 180, 193
Barth, M. 139
Barucq, A. 96
Bauckmann, E.G. 84, 105, 196
Baumert, N. 130
Baumgartner, W. 57, 106

Beardslee, W. A. 2, 24
Beare, F. W. 160
Becker, J. 119
Begrich, J. 59, 61
Behm, J. 137
Bennett, A. W. 44
Benoît, A. 182
Berger, K. 1, 14, 15, 18, 21, 38, 53, 56, 88, 101, 197
Bertram, G. 182
Betz, H. D. 4, 48, 54, 55, 80, 93, 101, 126, 127, 128, 129, 134, 137, 139, 158, 161, 167, 172, 173, 175, 180, 189, 190, 208, 210, 211
Beyer, H. W. 173
Bielohlawek, K. 18, 61
Bischoff, H. 61
Bjerkelund, C. J. 128
Black, D. A. 143, 145
Blank, J. 138
Blenkinsopp, J. 21, 139
Bornkamm, G. 153
Bosch, J. S. 130
Bowie, E. L. 62
Braak, I. 16
Brichto, H. C. 173
Brinsmead, B. H. 208
Brockhaus, U. 130
Brox, N. 160
Brueggeman, W. 22
Brun, L. 173
Brunner, H. 81, 82, 84, 87

Bryce, G. E. 22
Bultmann, R. 1, 4, 54, 151, 162
Burgess, T. 53, 54

Callaway, P. R. 21
Cameron, R. 2
Cancik, H. 20, 44, 53, 55, 93
Capelle, W. 54
Carlston, C. E. 1
Carmichael, C. M. 21
Carrington, P. 160
Chadwick, H. 67, 68, 71, 72, 77, 79, 211
Charlesworth, J. H. 57
Clarke, D. L. 44
Clarke, M. L. 18, 49
Coleman, R. 20
Collins, J. J. 18, 20, 22, 119, 138
Collins, R. F. 208
Connors, R. J. 17
Conybeare, F. C. 83
Conzelmann, H. 4, 151, 207
Corriveau, R. 129
Cosby, M. R. 165
Courcelle, P. 180
Cousin, J. 18
Cranfield, C. E. B. 5, 143, 153, 163, 172, 180, 188, 192, 195
Crenshaw, J. L. 12, 15, 19, 23, 24, 25, 57, 58, 59, 196

Index of Modern Authors

Crossan, J. D. 1, 2, 13, 14, 15, 17, 18, 24
Crüsemann, F. 57
Crusius, O. 70
Cullmann, O. 138

Daube, D. 156, 157, 162, 163, 178, 179
Davids, P. H. 2, 54
Davies, S. L. 2
Davies, W. D. 156, 157, 165, 191
Davis, J. A. 4
de Jonge, M. 119, 139, 152, 197
Delhaye, P. 68
Delling, G. 191
Derron, P. 113
Deselaers, P. 90
Dibelius, M. 2, 29, 45, 53, 54, 164, 170
Dihle, A. 20, 182
Dijkman, J. H. L. 157
DiLella, A. A. 49, 58, 74, 84, 85, 89, 105, 108, 111, 112, 137, 142, 178, 188, 192, 196
Dinkler, E. 191
Dinkler-von Schubert, E. 191
Doll, P. 102
Dörrie, H. 22, 62, 64
Doty, W. G. 55
Dover, K. J. 19
Draper, J. 168
Dudley, D. R. 61, 62, 63, 64, 79
Duesberg, H. 106
Dundes, A. 11, 25ff.
Dungan, D. L. 165
Dunn, J. D. G. 5, 126, 127, 130, 131, 134, 136, 137, 138, 143, 144, 150, 157, 162, 164, 169, 172, 175, 184, 189, 195, 206

Dupont, J. 168
Düring, I. 54

Ebeling, G. 208
Eberharter, A. 105
Eckstein, H.-J. 211
Eißfeldt, O. 12, 13
Ellis, E. E. 189
Elter, A. 29, 71, 79
Eltester, W. 119
Evans, C. 129, 138, 139

Fallon, F. T. 2
Ferguson, E. 137
Fichtner, J. 137
Figueira, T. J. 61
Finkelstein, L. 72
Fiore, B. 16, 45, 54, 55, 56, 78, 88
Fiorenza, E. S. 58
Fischel, H. A. 72
Fishbane, M. 23
Fisher, N. R. E. 182
Fitzmyer, J. A. 168
Fjärstedt, B. 165, 169
Foerster, W. 191
Fontaine, C. R. 12, 13, 14, 15, 20, 25, 38, 41, 142
Forbes, C. 181
Fredericks, D. C. 175
Friedländer, P. 61
Frohn-Villeneuve, W. 18
Frontenrose, J. 23
Furnish, V. P. 127, 141, 151, 156, 157, 165, 169, 172, 193, 195, 204

Gaiser, K. 53
Gammie, J. G. 53, 70
Gärtner, H. 22
Gemser, B. 23, 69, 88, 96
Gensichen, H.-W. 191

Gerhard, G. A. 56, 62, 63, 64, 66, 67, 68
Gerleman, G. 70
Gerstenberger, E. 21, 59
Gese, H. 57
Gilbert, M. 58, 59, 106, 113
Gladigow, B. 102
Glover, R. 168
Gnilka, J. 151, 177
Goldstein, H. 160
Goppelt, L. 160
Gorden, E. I. 69
Görler, W. 61, 71
Gow, A. S. F. 17, 63, 65
Greenstone, J. H. 96, 102
Grenzmann, W. 24, 38, 80
Griswold, C. L. 141
Grumach-Shirun, I. 82
Grundmann, W. 139, 182
Guglielmi, W. 69
Guillemin, A. M. 55
Gunkel, H. 59, 61
Gutas, D. 71, 77, 79, 80

Hainz, J. 130, 164
Hamp, V. 105
Hanslik, R. 152
Harris, J. R. 83
Hasluck, F. W. 21
Haspecker, J. 184
Hauck, F. 165
Hellwig, A. 18, 52
Hense, O. 63
Hermisson, H.-J. 12, 18, 24, 58, 69, 102
Hock, R. F. 15
Hoffmann, P. 168
Hoheisel, K. 153
Holbeck, B. 16
Hollander, H. W. 119, 139, 152, 197
Holtz, T. 208

Holzman, C. 64
Hoppe, R. 2
Horna, K. 11, 15, 18, 43, 46, 56, 61, 71, 72, 74, 77, 78, 79
Horsley, R. A. 4
Horst, F. 173
Huber, W. 191
Hultgård, A. 119

Jacob, E. 106
Jacobsen, T. 69
Jacobson, A. D. 19
Jansen, H. L. 57, 59
Jason, H. 19
Jefford, C. N. 169
Jellicoe, S. 70
Jeremias, J. 176
Johanson, B. C. 208
Johnson, E. E. 4, 183, 193, 206
Johnson, L. T. 116
Jolles, A. 12, 17, 18, 22
Joly, R. 152
Jones, E. 96
Jordan, M. D. 54, 94

Kahn, C. H. 16, 73
Kanjuparambil, P. 156
Karathanasis, D. K. 18
Käsemann, E. 5, 143, 150, 157, 162, 163, 172, 179, 183, 189
Kayatz, C. 58, 59, 81, 82, 96, 101, 102
Kee, H. C. 119
Kehl, A. 153
Kennedy, G. A. 52, 146
Kertelge, K. 130
Kettunen, M. 127
Keydell, R. 63, 66
Kidd, I. G. 20, 21
Kindstrand, J. F. 79
Kirk, J. A. 2
Kirshenblatt-Gimblett, B. 20

Kitchen, K. A. 81, 82
Klassen, W. 195
Klein, G. 208
Kloppenborg, J. S. 1, 15, 18, 21, 22, 23, 49, 66, 71, 72, 74, 77, 78, 80, 81, 82, 87, 88, 90, 93, 104, 142, 151, 166, 168, 170, 194
Knox, A. D. 62, 64, 66
Koch, K. 15
Koester, H. 173
Köhler, W.-D. 168
Krappe, A. H. 13
Kraus, W. 78
Krikmann, A. 20, 73
Kroll, W. 61
Krüger, H. 9
Kuntz, J. K. 57
Kutsch, E. 182
Küchler, M. 1, 18, 21, 22, 24, 66, 69, 71, 72, 73, 74, 79, 83, 88, 90, 113, 119

Labarbe, J. 17
Lambert, W. G. 69
Lampe, P. 173
Lang, B. 81, 96, 102
Laporte, J. 47
Larcher, C. 58, 86, 152
Lausberg, H. 14, 15, 18, 19, 42, 43, 45, 46, 49, 52
Layton, B. 169
Lee, T. R. 89
Leeman, A. D. 20
Légasse, S. 192
Leivestad, R. 182
Lerner, M. B. 72, 73, 83
Lewis, A. S. 83
Lewis, P. E. 22, 24, 73, 80
Lichtheim, M. 69, 82, 84, 86, 88, 164, 175, 192, 196

Lietzmann, H. 5
Lindenberger, J. M. 83
Lindström, V. 152
Lohse, E. 160
Long, A. A. 64
Luck, U. 2, 141
Lührmann, D. 59, 168
Luther, M. 150
Luyten, J. 59

Mack, B. L. 58, 89
Malgarini, A. B. 71
Malherbe, A. J. 18, 53, 54, 55, 56, 77
Maloney, G. 18
Marböck, J. 58, 105, 139
Margolius, H. 18, 22
Marrou, H.-I. 54, 77
Marshall, P. 181
Martin, J. 43, 46, 49
Martin, R. P. 2, 170
Mauer, C. 210
Mautner, F. H. 22
McDonald, J. I. H. 53
McKane, W. 17, 19, 69, 70, 81, 82, 83, 84, 86-87, 88, 96, 102, 142, 180, 184, 194, 195, 196
Meecham, H. G. 156
Meerwaldt, J. D. 64
Mehl, R. 182
Meijer, P. A. 64
Meinhold, A. 96, 102
Mensching, G. 182
Meunier, M. 66
Meyer, W. 68
Michel, O. 5, 138, 143, 144, 150, 160, 163, 172, 178, 180, 191, 197
Middendorp, Th. 106
Mieder, W. 9, 19, 22, 26, 38
Milobenski, E. 116
Mitchell, C. W. 173

Index of Modern Authors

Moore, C. A. 57
Morenz, S. F. 173
Moule, C. F. D. 156
Moulton, J. H. 156
Mouraviev, S. 11
Mowinckel, S. 59
Munch, P. A. 59
Munro, D. B. 178
Munro, W. 157
Murphy, R. E. 13, 15, 59, 69, 96
Mußner, F. 2

Nagy, G. 61, 64
Nauck, W. 128
Neirynck, F. 140, 165, 166, 168, 170, 171, 187, 198
Nel, P. J. 15, 21, 22, 24, 101, 102
Neumann, G. 9
Neusner, J. 72
Neustadt, E. 64
Niebuhr, K.-W. 53, 81, 88, 113, 139
Niederwimmer, K. 169, 181
Nielen, J. M. 137
Norden, E. 57
Norrick, N. R. 16, 17, 18, 25, 26, 38
North, H. 141
Nygren, A. 152

Oltramare, A. 54
O'Neil, E. N. 15
Ong, W. J. 17
Opelt, I. 80
Ortkemper, F.-J. 5, 127, 129, 138, 144, 156, 157, 158, 163, 164, 170, 180, 194, 195

Page, D. L. 17, 63, 65
Patte, D. 15
Patzer, H. 153

Pearson, B. A. 4
Peel, M. L. 84
Perdue, L. G. 2, 53, 81, 137
Peretti, A. 61
Perry, B. E. 66, 151
Peter, H. W. G. 55
Peters, N. 105
Piper, J. 146, 151, 157, 158, 160, 170, 172, 187, 188, 191, 195
Piper, R. A. 2, 90, 93, 180
Plöger, O. 96, 102
Pohlenz, M. 64
Polag, A. 168
Potter, P. 18
Powell, J. U. 62, 64, 65, 66
Preuß, H. D. 182
Pritchard, J. B. 69

Radl, W. 129, 138
Ramaroson, L. 195
Reese, J. M. 54, 58
Rehrl, S. 182
Reneham, R. 146
Rengstorf, K. H. 141
Requadt, P. 23, 24, 73
Richard, M. 68
Richardson, P. 166
Richter, W. 21
Rickenbacher, O. 105
Rigaux, B. 208
Ringgren, H. 96
Robb, K. 17, 86
Robertson, A. T. 156, 178
Robinson, J. M. 1
Rochaise, H.-M. 68
Röhrich, L. 9, 19, 22, 26, 38
Rordorf, W. 168
Rosenkranz, B. 88
Roth, W. 82, 106
Roth, W. M. W. 164

Rumpf, A. 152
Rupprecht, K. 12
Russell, D. A. 20
Rzach, A. 61

Saldarini, A. J. 72
Saller, R. P. 128
Salom, A. P. 156
Sanders, J. T. 84
Sato, M. 168
Sauer, G. 105
Sauer, J. 158, 166, 168, 187, 198
Schelkle, K. H. 160
Schenk, W. 168, 173
Schilling, O. 106
Schlier, H. 5, 129, 150, 163, 180, 183, 197
Schmeller, T. 54, 55
Schmid, J. 168
Schmid, H. H. 81, 82, 191
Schmidt, E. G. 64, 65
Schmithals, W. 5, 163, 172, 173, 175, 191, 195, 205
Schnabel, E. J. 4, 106, 139
Schnackenburg, R. 191
Schneider, C. 152
Schneider, H. 96
Schneider, N. 4
Schnider, F. 55
Schoedel, W. R. 54, 57, 84
Schottroff, W. 173
Schrage, W. 128, 129, 142, 172, 193, 209
Schrey, H.-H. 152
Schulz, S. 168
Schürmann, H. 168
Schweinfurth-Walla, S. 43
Scott, R. B. Y. 13, 22, 28, 28, 59, 96, 102
Segert, S. 105

Seidensticker, P. 138
Seitel, P. 20
Selwyn, E. G. 156, 160
Sheppard, G. T. 24, 80
Skehan, P. W. 49, 57, 58, 59, 74, 84, 85, 89, 105, 108, 111, 112, 137, 142, 178, 188, 196
Skladny, U. 69
Skutsch, F. 74
Smallwood, E. M. 173
Smend, R. 105
Snaith, J. G. 105
Speyer, W. 173
Spicq, C. 116, 141, 151, 152, 153, 164, 172, 182, 191, 195, 210, 211
Spicq, R. P. C. 105
Spoerri, W. 43, 49, 71, 72, 79
Staehle, K. 165
Stanley, D. M. 165, 166
Stecher, R. 59
Stendahl, K. 172, 195
Stenger, W. 55
Stern, J. P. 9, 24
Stewart, Z. 79
Stowers, S. K. 53, 54, 55, 181
Strobel, F. A. 191
Stuhlmacher, P. 126, 127, 165, 166
Sussman, L. A. 18
Sykes, D. A. 67

Talbert, C. H. 143, 144, 150, 156, 157, 158
Tannehill, R. C. 15
Taylor, A. 9, 13, 16, 22
Thackeray, H. J. 70, 105, 146
Therrien, G. 139, 210
Thieme, K. 182
Thießen, W. 191

Thissen, H.-J. 84
Thom, J. C. 66
Thompson, J. M. 14, 15, 17, 18, 21
Tov, E. 70
Toy, C. H. 96, 102
Treu, K. 152
Trilling, W. 208
Trillitzsch, W. 20
Tuckett, C. M. 165, 169
Turner, N. 156, 161

van der Horst, P. C. 66
van der Horst, P. W. 49, 72, 76, 88, 113, 114, 116, 117, 118, 152, 193, 196
van der Ploeg, J. P. M. 59
van Unnik, W. C. 189
van Leeuwan, R. C. 25, 73, 80
van Straaten, F. T. 137
Vetschera, R. 53, 54, 67
Via, D. O. 181
Vogt, E. 113
von Fritz, K. 15, 79
von Gersau, H. 182
von Lips, H. 1, 2, 4, 21, 53, 70, 90, 128, 137, 161, 163, 164, 178, 192, 193
von Nordheim, E. 119
von Rad, G. 14, 15, 16-17, 18, 19, 23, 24, 57, 59, 61, 65, 69, 101, 106, 137, 138, 142, 180, 184, 188, 191, 211

Wachsmuth, K. 68
Walter, N. 113, 166
Warnach, V. 151, 152
Wedderburn, A. J. M. 126, 127, 128, 130, 141, 175
Wefelmeier, C. 88
Wehmeier, G. 173

Weiser, A. 60
Weiss, J. 4
Wendland, P. 53, 88
Wengst, K. 169, 182
Wenham, D. 166, 169
Werner, J. 70
West, M. L. 61, 64, 146, 179, 182
Westermann, C. 12, 14, 173
Whiting, B. J. 13
Whybray, R. N. 59, 69, 96, 102, 138
Wilckens, U. 4, 5, 139, 152, 153, 157, 163, 172, 180
Wilken, R. L. 1, 74, 79
Williams, J. G. 13-14, 15, 16, 17, 20, 22, 24, 80, 138, 192
Wimbush, V. L. 141
Winston, D. 152
Winton, A. P. 2, 24, 25, 49
Wischmeyer, O. 192
Wolf, E. 210
Wolters, A. 57, 211
Wyß, B. 67

Zandee, J. 84
Zauzich, K.-T. 82
Zeller, D. 1, 5, 24, 72, 83, 90, 127, 140, 157, 162, 168, 170, 175, 188, 194, 195, 196
Zimmerli, W. 15, 22, 24
Zucchelli, B. 153
Zuntz, G. 64

Index of Subjects

advice 48, 53
aphorism 18-19

beatitude 31, 59, 101-102
blessing / cursing 104, 126, 170, 172-173
body of Christ 129, 130, 141-142

catchword 74, 75, 85, 102, 103, 116, 118, 158, 162
central statement 94-95, 103, 111, 118, 125, 143, 144, 145
charity 146, 164
chreia 15-16, 61
clusters 49, 51, 74, 162, 176, 179, 186-187
concatenation 29, 164
cultic sacrifice, critique of 137-138
Cynicism 61-64, 78-80

decreta 21
descriptive section 93-94, 101-102, 110, 116, 124-125, 139-142
diatribe 45-46, 50, 54-55, 65, 79, 180-181
dualism 124-126

enthymeme 43, 72
enumeration 31-32, 144, 164-165
envy 113, 115-116
epigram 17-18, 65
epilogue 43-44
epistolography 55-56
epitome 70
eschatology 184, 192-193, 195, 210
examples / illustrations 44-46, 54, 72, 94-95, 116-117, 124-126, 139-140, 147
exhortation 53-56

fables 66

fear of God 138, 173-175, 182-186, 192-195
florilegia 68-69

gnomic poetry 56-68, 88-90
gnomic saying:
  - contexts 41-51
  - description 11-24
  - definition 11-12
  - structure 24-39
gnomologia 68-81, 88-90

humility / pride 146, 163, 173-175, 180-186
hybrid genres 88-90, 112-113
hymns 56-60, 64, 84, 89, 93, 96, 101-102, 174
hypocrisy / deceit 152-155, 180-186

imperatival infinitives 157, 177-178
imperatival participles 156-163
inclusio 74, 75, 76, 85, 95, 103-104, 112, 118, 125, 144, 158

legal sayings 21-22
love 150-155, 172-174, 198-199, 202-204, 207, 209-212

meter / rhythm 70, 86, 105, 112, 146

non-violence / non-retaliation 146, 173-175, 187-188, 191-195

oracle 23-24
orational style 86
order / counter-order 14-15, 21-24, 81, 124-126, 140-142

paraenesis 53-54
paroemiographia 23, 70, 105
patience 164

peace 191
persecution 167-173
personal / familiar address 41-43, 96, 101, 103, 109, 110, 125, 136, 192
prayer 164
precept 20-21
prescriptive section 94-95, 102-105, 110-112, 125-126, 142-147
programmatic statement 93, 101, 109-110, 115-116, 124, 136-139
protreptic literature 53
protreptic maxim 94, 103, 110, 117, 125, 143
proverb vs. maxim 12-15

reason / rational ability 20-24, 73, 80-81, 86-87, 180-186, 189-191, 210-212
reputation 188-189

rhetoric 51-53
ring-composition 74, 76-77, 85-86, 95, 112, 118-119, 144, 145, 175-177
Romans, reasons for its composition 126-129, 205-207

sapiential discourse 92-93
sapiential vs. non-sapiential genres 51
solidarity / empathy 173-175, 178-180, 195-197
Stoicism 64-65, 78-80
strangers 164
synoptic tradition 90, 165-171, 191, 198

wisdom instruction 81-90
wisdom psalms 59-61, 149, 174
wisdom sentence vs. wisdom admonition 24-25

Index of Greek Words

ἀγαθός 136, 138, 154, 196-197
ἀγάπη 101, 129-131, 142, 144, 145, 150-155, 173-174, 178, 198-199, 202-204, 207, 209-212
ἀγαπητός 192
ἀνυπόκριτος 152-154
ἀποστυγέω 154

γνῶθι σαυτόν 23, 27, 180
γνώμη 11-12

δοκιμάζω 154-155
δυνατός 189-190

εἰρήνη 154, 160, 191
ἐπιφώνημα 49-50, 197-198
ἔρως 152-153
εὐλογέω 167, 170, 172, 178

καιρός 65, 118, 163

παιδεία 101-102, 109-111
παροιμία 12

πονηρός 154-155
προαίρεσις 52

σοφία 101-102, 110-111, 141
συνείδησις 210
σωφροσύνη 117-119, 140-141, 143

τάξις 124-126
ταπεινός 181, 182
τέλειος 136, 138, 165, 172

ὕβρις 182-186
ὑπόκριτος 152-153
ὑπομονή 164
ὑψηλός 184

φιλία 152-153
φιλοξενία 164

χάρισμα 130-131, 141-142
χρεία 15-16, 61

Wissenschaftliche Untersuchungen zum Neuen Testament

*Alphabetical index
of the first and the second series*

APPOLD, MARK L.: The Oneness Motif in the Fourth Gospel. 1976. *Volume II/1.*
BACHMANN, MICHAEL: Sünder oder Übertreter.1991.*Volume 59.*
BAMMEL, ERNST: Judaica. 1986. *Volume 37.*
BAUERNFEIND, OTTO: Kommentar und Studien zur Apostelgeschichte. 1980. *Volume 22.*
BAYER, HANS FRIEDRICH: Jesus' Predictions of Vindication and Resurrection. 1986. *Volume II/20.*
BETZ, OTTO: Jesus, der Messias Israels. 1987. *Volume 42.*
– Jesus, der Herr der Kirche. 1990. *Volume 52.*
BEYSCHLAG, KARLMANN: Simon Magnus und die christliche Gnosis. 1974. *Volume 16.*
BITTNER, WOLFGANG J.: Jesu Zeichen im Johannesevangelium. 1987. *Volume II/26.*
BJERKELUND, CARL J.: Tauta Egeneto. 1987. *Volume 40.*
BLACKBURN, BARRY LEE: 'Theios Anēr' and the Markan Miracle Traditions. 1991. *Volume II/40.*
BOCKMUEHL, MARKUS N. A.: Revelation and Mystery in Ancient Judaism and Pauline Christianity. 1990. *Volume II/36.*
BÖHLIG, ALEXANDER: Gnosis und Synkretismus. Part 1. 1989. *Volume 47* – Part 2. 1989. *Volume 48.*
BÜCHLI, JÖRG: Der Poimandres – ein paganisiertes Evangelium. 1987. *Volume II/27.*
BÜHNER, JAN A.: Der Gesandte und sein Weg im 4. Evangelium. 1977. *Volume II/2.*
BURCHARD, CHRISTOPH: Untersuchungen zu Joseph und Aseneth. 1965. *Volume 8.*
CANCIK, HUBERT (Ed.): Markus-Philologie. 1984. *Volume 33.*
CARAGOUNIS, CHRYS C.: The Son of Man. 1986. *Volume 38.*
DOBBELER, AXEL VON: Glaube als Teilhabe. 1987. *Volume II/22.*
EBERTZ, MICHAEL N.: Das Charisma des Gekreuzigten. 1987. *Volume 45.*
ECKSTEIN, HANS-JOACHIM: Der Begriff der Syneidesis bei Paulus. 1983. *Volume II/10.*
EGO, BEATE: Im Himmel wie auf Erden. 1989. *Volume II/34.*
ELLIS, E. EARLE: Prophecy and Hermeneutic in Early Christianity. 1978. *Volume 18.*
– The Old Testament in Early Christianity. 1991. *Volume 54.*
FELDMEIER, REINHARD: Die Krisis des Gottessohnes. 1987. *Volume II/21.*
FOSSUM, JARL E.: The Name of God and the Angel of the Lord. 1985. *Volume 36.*
GARLINGTON, DON B.: The Obedience of Faith. 1991. *Volume II/38.*
GARNET, PAUL: Salvation and Atonement in the Qumran Scrolls. 1977. *Volume II/3.*
GRÄSSER, ERICH: Der Alte Bund im Neuen. 1985. *Volume 35.*
GREEN, JOEL B.: The Death of Jesus. 1988. *Volume II/33.*
GUNDRY VOLF, JUDITH M.: Paul and Perseverance. 1990. *Volume II/37.*
HAFEMANN, SCOTT J.: Suffering and the Spirit. 1986. *Volume II/19.*
HECKEL, ULRICH: see HENGEL.
HEILIGENTHAL, ROMAN: Werke als Zeichen. 1983. *Volume II/9.*
HEMER, COLIN J.: The Book of Acts in the Setting of Hellenistic History. 1989. *Volume 49.*
HENGEL, MARTIN: Judentum und Hellenismus. 1969, [3]1988. *Volume 10.*
HENGEL, MARTIN and ULRICH HECKEL (Ed.:) Paulus und das antike Judentum. 1991.*Volume 58.*
HENGEL, MARTIN and ANNA MARIA SCHWEMER (Ed.): Königsherrschaft Gottes und himmlischer Kult. 1991. *Volume 55.*
HERRENBRÜCK, FRITZ: Jesus und die Zöllner. 1990. *Volume II/41.*
HOFIUS, OTFRIED: Katapausis. 1970. *Volume 11.*
– Der Vorhang vor dem Thron Gottes. 1972. *Volume 14.*
– Der Christushymnus Philipper 2,6 – 11. 1976, [2]1991. *Volume 17.*
– Paulusstudien. 1989. *Volume 51.*
HOLTZ, TRAUGOTT: Geschichte und Theologie des Urchristentums. Ed. by Eckart Reinmuth and Christian Wolff. 1991. *Volume 57.*
HOMMEL, HILDEBRECHT: Sebasmata. Volume 1. 1983. *Volume 31.* – Volume 2. 1984. *Volume 32.*
KAMLAH, EHRHARD: Die Form der katalogischen Paränese im Neuen Testament. 1964. *Volume 7.*
KIM, SEYOON: The Origin of Paul's Gospel. 1981, [2]1984. *Volume II/4.*
– »The ›Son of Man‹« as the Son of God. 1983. *Volume 30.*
KLEINKNECHT, KARL TH.: Der leidende Gerechtfertigte. 1984, [2]1988. *Volume II/13.*
KLINGHARDT, MATTHIAS: Gesetz und Volk Gottes. 1988. *Volume II/32.*

Wissenschaftliche Untersuchungen zum Neuen Testament

KÖHLER, WOLF-DIETRICH: Rezeption des Matthäusevangeliums in der Zeit vor Irenäus. 1987. *Volume II/24.*
KUHN, KARL G.: Achtzehngebet und Vaterunser und der Reim. 1950. *Volume 1.*
LAMPE, PETER: Die stadtrömischen Christen in den ersten beiden Jahrhunderten. 1987, [2]1989. *Volume II/18.*
MAIER, GERHARD: Mensch und freier Wille. 1971. *Volume 12.*
– Die Johannesoffenbarung und die Kirche. 1981. *Volume 25.*
MARSHALL, PETER: Enmity in Corinth: Social Conventions in Paul's Relations with the Corinthians. 1987. *Volume II/23.*
MEADE, DAVID G.: Pseudonymity and Canon. 1986. *Volume 39.*
MENGEL, BERTHOLD: Studien zum Philipperbrief. 1982. *Volume II/8.*
MERKEL, HELMUT: Die Widersprüche zwischen den Evangelien. 1971. *Volume 13.*
MERKLEIN, HELMUT: Studien zu Jesus und Paulus. 1987. *Volume 43.*
METZLER, KARIN: Der griechische Begriff des Verzeihens. 1991. *Volume II/44.*
NIEBUHR, KARL-WILHELM: Gesetz und Paränese. 1987. *Volume II/28.*
NISSEN, ANDREAS: Gott und der Nächste im antiken Judentum. 1974. *Volume 15.*
OKURE, TERESA: The Johannine Approach to Mission. 1988. *Volume II/31.*
PILHOFER, PETER: Presbyteron Kreitton. 1990. *Volume II/39.*
PROBST, HERMANN: Paulus und der Brief. 1991. *Volume II/45.*
RÄISÄNEN, HEIKKI: Paul and the Law. 1983, [2]1987. *Volume 29.*
REHKOPF, FRIEDRICH: Die lukanische Sonderquelle. 1959. *Volume 5.*
REINMUTH, ECKHARDT: see HOLTZ.
REISER, MARIUS: Syntax und Stil des Markusevangeliums. 1984. *Volume II/11.*
RICHARDS, E. RANDOLPH: The Secretary in the Letters of Paul. 1991. *Volume II/42.*
RIESNER, RAINER: Jesus als Lehrer. 1981, [3]1988. *Volume II/7.*
RISSI, MATHIAS: Die Theologie des Hebräerbriefs. 1987. *Volume 41.*
RÖHSER, GÜNTER: Metaphorik und Personifikation der Sünde. 1987. *Volume II/25.*
RÜGER, HANS PETER: Die Weisheitsschrift aus der Kairoer Geniza. 1991. *Volume 53.*
SÄNGER, DIETER: Antikes Judentum und die Mysterien. 1980. *Volume II/5.*
SANDNES, KARL OLAV: Paul – One of the Prophets? 1991. *Volume II/43.*
SATO, MIGAKU: Q und Prophetie. 1988. *Volume II/29.*
SCHIMANOWSKI, GOTTFRIED: Weisheit und Messias. 1985. *Volume II/17.*
SCHLICHTING, GÜNTER: Ein jüdisches Leben Jesu. 1982. *Volume 24.*
SCHNABEL, ECKHARD J.: Law and Wisdom from Ben Sira to Paul. 1985. *Volume II/16.*
SCHUTTER, WILLIAM L.: Hermeneutic and Composition in I Peter. 1989. *Volume II/30.*
SCHWEMER, A. M. – see HENGEL.
SIEGERT, FOLKER: Drei hellenistisch-jüdische Predigten. Part 1. 1980. *Volume 20.* – Part 2. 1991.
– Nag-Hammadi-Register. 1982. *Volume 26.*
– Argumentation bei Paulus. 1985. *Volume 34.*
– Philon von Alexandrien. 1988. *Volume 46.*
SIMON, MARCEL: Le christianisme antique et son contexte religieux I/II. 1981. *Volume 23.*
SNODGRASS, KLYNE: The Parable of the Wicked Tenants. 1983. *Volume 27.*
SPEYER, WOLFGANG: Frühes Christentum im antiken Strahlungsfeld. 1989. *Volume 50.*
STADELMANN, HELGE: Ben Sira als Schriftgelehrter. 1980. *Volume II/6.*
STROBEL, AUGUST: Die Studie der Wahrheit. 1980. *Volume 21.*
STUHLMACHER, PETER (Ed.): Das Evangelium und die Evangelien. 1983. *Volume 28.*
TAJRA, HARRY W.: The Trial of St. Paul. 1989. *Volume II/35.*
THEISSEN, GERD: Studien zur Soziologie des Urchristentums. 1979, [3]1989. *Volume 19.*
THORNTON, CLAUS-JÜRGEN: Der Zeuge des Zeugen. 1991. *Volume 56.*
WEDDERBURN, A. J. M.: Baptism and Resurrection. 1987. *Volume 44.*
WEGNER, UWE: Der Hauptmann von Kafarnaum. 1985. *Volume II/14.*
WILSON, WALTER T.: Love without Pretense. 1991. *Volume II/46.*
WOLFF, CHRISTIAN: see HOLTZ.
ZIMMERMANN, ALFRED E.: Die urchristlichen Lehrer. 1984, [2]1988. *Volume II/12.*

For a complete catalogue please write to
J. C. B. Mohr (Paul Siebeck), P. O. Box 2040, D-7400 Tübingen